Barcelona

Damien Simonis

LONELY PLANET PUBLICATIONS
Melbourne • Oakland • London • Paris

Barcelona
2nd edition – April 2001
First published – April 1999

Published by
Lonely Planet Publications Pty Ltd ABN 36 005 607 983
90 Maribyrnong St, Footscray, Victoria 3011, Australia

Lonely Planet Offices
Australia Locked Bag 1, Footscray, Victoria 3011
USA 150 Linden St, Oakland, CA 94607
UK 10a Spring Place, London NW5 3BH
France 1 rue du Dahomey, 75011 Paris

Photographs
All of the images in this guide are available for licensing from
Lonely Planet Images.
email: lpi@lonelyplanet.com.au

Front cover photograph
Chimneys of Gaudí's Casa Milà, Barcelona (Jenny Jones)

ISBN 1 86450 143 X

text & maps © Lonely Planet 2001
photos © photographers as indicated 2001

Printed by Colorcraft Ltd, Hong Kong

Contents

1

PLACES TO STAY   145

PLACES TO EAT   153

ENTERTAINMENT   166

SHOPPING   181

EXCURSIONS   187

LANGUAGE   207

GLOSSARY   216

INDEX   229

MAP SECTION   239

MAP LEGEND   back page

METRIC CONVERSION   inside back cover

The Author

Damien Simonis

With a degree in languages and several years reporting and sub-editing on Australian newspapers (including *The Australian* and *The Age*), Sydney-born Damien left Australia in 1989. He has since lived, worked and travelled extensively throughout Europe, the Middle East and North Africa. Since 1992, Lonely Planet has kept him busy writing for *Jordan*, *Syria*, *Egypt & the Sudan*, *Morocco*, *North Africa*, *Italy*, *Spain* and *Canary Islands*. More recently he has rattled off titles including *Madrid*, *Tuscany*, *Florence* and *Venice*, all of which have left him feeling a little dizzy. Still, he was back on the road again scribbling *Catalunya & the Costa Brava* as this book lay with the editors. Damien has also written and snapped photos for other publications in Australia, the UK and North America. When not on the road, he goes to ground in splendid Stoke Newington, deep in the heart of north London.

From Damien

Barcelona has become something of a second home. I owe a great deal to Michael van Laake and Susan Kempster. Susan especially gave me temporary refuge while I sorted out alternative lodgings at a key point in the project and managed to save me from my own stupidity on a couple of occasions. Michael, among many kindnesses, took up baby-sitting duties of Gnomo the invincible Renault while I was away from town.

The rest of the gang at Carrer de Sant Pere més alt (Paloma, Ferran and Montse) always had the welcome mat out, while Silvia Folch gave me shelter in the early days of the project before scarpering off to India and a better life.

Gràcies also to other friends for good times had and those to come: Loreta, Rocio Vázquez, Annabel Rodríguez, Caroline Diaz et al. Everyone contributed ideas here and there. Thanks to Adrian Walton for some very handy tips on the city's club scene. Late in the day I had the able and willing help of Geoff Leaver-Heaton, David & Jane Ellis and Max & Mel in the never-ending search for yet another place to drink and jive. Cheers for the fun and the headaches.

On the country estate in Solsona thanks to Mike 'Butterfly' and the gang for those memorably bucolic, gin-filled evenings.

Thanks to LP's Jen Loy (USA), Leonie Mugavin (Australia) and Didier Buroc (France) for help with air fare information.

This Book

Damien Simonis wrote the first edition of Lonely Planet's guide to *Barcelona* and updated this second edition.

From the Publisher

This edition of *Barcelona* was produced in Lonely Planet's London office. Michala Green was the coordinating editor and Angie Watts was responsible for mapping, design and layout. Thanks are due to Gadi Farfour who prepared the map database. Imogen Franks assisted with editing and the book was proofed by Abigail Hole and Michala. Paul Edmunds drew the climate chart, Adam McCrow designed the cover and Jim Miller drew the back-cover map. Lonely Planet Images provided photographs and illustrations were drawn by Mick Weldon and Jane Smith. Many thanks to Quentin Frayne for applying his linguistic expertise to the language chapter, and to Damien for working so hard on the book despite his other travelling commitments!

Thanks

Many thanks to the travellers who used the last edition and contacted us with helpful hints, advice and interesting anecdotes:

Vicky Anderson, James Barrett, Alain Bassoul, S Bishop, Jim & Helen Braden, Elizabeth Braun, Leon de Caluwe, H Cawood, Lesley Cornforth, Katherine Coventry, Leanne Currie-McGhee, Kerry Daly, Celia Davey, E DePalma, Brigitte Depiere, Shannon Dixon, Rachel Eisner, Laurence Elijah, Audre Engleman, Stephen Esrati, M Fairmont, Esther Feretto, Tony Fernando, David Forshaw, Jordi Garcia, Nick Garland, Jason Gedmin, Bruce Gibson, Alistair J Grant, Kevin Grisell, Iker Guimaraes, Anais Haas, M Hammond, Mairi Herbert, Erin Hodkinson, Tessa Hyams, Philipp Kinkelin, Dawn de Kock, Kathleen Korosi, Chris Leighton, Steve Levine, Yue Ling, Jez Lugg, Jose M Malagarriga, Campbell Mars, Susan Mitra, Sebastian Mock, Karli Nabours Palermo, Carol Nelson, Francisca Nijkamp, Jenny Peat, Jessica Perkins, Allan Petrie, D Quintano, Hans Reedijk, Jens Reimer, Christophe Renard, Margot Rosanes-Csuka, Nick Salt, Francesca Sarandrea, Crystal Sauve, L Schubert, Sue Sedwell, Boy Eng Seng, Budh Singh, Mark Stallings, Barbara Stevenson, Andy Stokes, Jordan Susselman, Paul Tomlinson, Dirk Wellens, Brian Williams, Cheryl Wisniewski, Cindy Wolfsen, Katie Zuzeck.

Foreword

ABOUT LONELY PLANET GUIDEBOOKS

The story begins with a classic travel adventure: Tony and Maureen Wheeler's 1972 journey across Europe and Asia to Australia. Useful information about the overland trail did not exist at that time, so Tony and Maureen published the first Lonely Planet guidebook to meet a growing need.

From a kitchen table, then from a tiny office in Melbourne (Australia), Lonely Planet has become the largest independent travel publisher in the world, an international company with offices in Melbourne, Oakland (USA), London (UK) and Paris (France).

Today Lonely Planet guidebooks cover the globe. There is an ever-growing list of books and there's information in a variety of forms and media. Some things haven't changed. The main aim is still to help make it possible for adventurous travellers to get out there – to explore and better understand the world.

At Lonely Planet we believe travellers can make a positive contribution to the countries they visit – if they respect their host communities and spend their money wisely. Since 1986 a percentage of the income from each book has been donated to aid projects and human rights campaigns.

Updates Lonely Planet thoroughly updates each guidebook as often as possible. This usually means there are around two years between editions, although for more unusual or more stable destinations the gap can be longer. Check the imprint page (following the colour map at the beginning of the book) for publication dates.

Between editions up-to-date information is available in two free newsletters – the paper *Planet Talk* and email *Comet* (to subscribe, contact any Lonely Planet office) – and on our Web site at www.lonelyplanet.com. The *Upgrades* section of the Web site covers a number of important and volatile destinations and is regularly updated by Lonely Planet authors. *Scoop* covers news and current affairs relevant to travellers. And, lastly, the *Thorn Tree* bulletin board and *Postcards* section of the site carry unverified, but fascinating, reports from travellers.

Correspondence The process of creating new editions begins with the letters, postcards and emails received from travellers. This correspondence often includes suggestions, criticisms and comments about the current editions. Interesting excerpts are immediately passed on via newsletters and the Web site, and everything goes to our authors to be verified when they're researching on the road. We're keen to get more feedback from organisations or individuals who represent communities visited by travellers.

Lonely Planet gathers information for everyone who's curious about the planet – and especially for those who explore it first-hand. Through guidebooks, phrasebooks, activity guides, maps, literature, newsletters, image library, TV series and Web site we act as an information exchange for a worldwide community of travellers.

5

Research Authors aim to gather sufficient practical information to enable travellers to make informed choices and to make the mechanics of a journey run smoothly. They also research historical and cultural background to help enrich the travel experience and allow travellers to understand and respond appropriately to cultural and environmental issues.

Authors don't stay in every hotel because that would mean spending a couple of months in each medium-sized city and, no, they don't eat at every restaurant because that would mean stretching belts beyond capacity. They do visit hotels and restaurants to check standards and prices, but feedback based on readers' direct experiences can be very helpful.

Many of our authors work undercover, others aren't so secretive. None of them accept freebies in exchange for positive write-ups. And none of our guidebooks contain any advertising.

Production Authors submit their raw manuscripts and maps to offices in Australia, USA, UK or France. Editors and cartographers – all experienced travellers themselves – then begin the process of assembling the pieces. When the book finally hits the shops, some things are already out of date, we start getting feedback from readers and the process begins again ...

WARNING & REQUEST

Things change – prices go up, schedules change, good places go bad and bad places go bankrupt – nothing stays the same. So, if you find things better or worse, recently opened or long since closed, please tell us and help make the next edition even more accurate and useful. We genuinely value all the feedback we receive. A well-travelled team reads and acknowledges every letter, postcard and email and ensures that every morsel of information finds its way to the appropriate authors, editors and cartographers for verification.

Everyone who writes to us will find their name in the next edition of the appropriate guidebook. They will also receive the latest issue of *Planet Talk*, our quarterly printed newsletter, or *Comet*, our monthly email newsletter. Subscriptions to both newsletters are free. The very best contributions will be rewarded with a free guidebook.

Excerpts from your correspondence may appear in new editions of Lonely Planet guidebooks, the Lonely Planet Web site, *Planet Talk* or *Comet*, so please let us know if you *don't* want your letter published or your name acknowledged.

Send all correspondence to the Lonely Planet office closest to you:

Australia: Locked Bag 1, Footscray, Victoria 3011
USA: 150 Linden St, Oakland, CA 94607
UK: 10A Spring Place, London NW5 3BH
France: 1 rue du Dahomey, 75011 Paris

Or email us at: talk2us@lonelyplanet.com.au

For news, views and updates see our Web site: www.lonelyplanet.com

HOW TO USE A LONELY PLANET GUIDEBOOK

The best way to use a Lonely Planet guidebook is any way you choose. At Lonely Planet we believe the most memorable travel experiences are often those that are unexpected, and the finest discoveries are those you make yourself. Guidebooks are not intended to be used as if they provide a detailed set of infallible instructions!

Contents All Lonely Planet guidebooks follow roughly the same format. The Facts about the Destination chapters or sections give background information ranging from history to weather. Facts for the Visitor gives practical information on issues like visas and health. Getting There & Away gives a brief starting point for researching travel to and from the destination. Getting Around gives an overview of the transport options when you arrive.

The peculiar demands of each destination determine how subsequent chapters are broken up, but some things remain constant. We always start with background, then proceed to sights, places to stay, places to eat, entertainment, getting there and away, and getting around information – in that order.

Heading Hierarchy Lonely Planet headings are used in a strict hierarchical structure that can be visualised as a set of Russian dolls. Each heading (and its following text) is encompassed by any preceding heading that is higher on the hierarchical ladder.

Entry Points We do not assume guidebooks will be read from beginning to end, but that people will dip into them. The traditional entry points are the list of contents and the index. In addition, however, some books have a complete list of maps and an index map illustrating map coverage.

There may also be a colour map that shows highlights. These highlights are dealt with in greater detail in the Facts for the Visitor chapter, along with planning questions and suggested itineraries. Each chapter covering a geographical region usually begins with a locator map and another list of highlights. Once you find something of interest in a list of highlights, turn to the index.

Maps Maps play a crucial role in Lonely Planet guidebooks and include a huge amount of information. A legend is printed on the back page. We seek to have complete consistency between maps and text, and to have every important place in the text captured on a map. Map key numbers usually start in the top left corner.

Although inclusion in a guidebook usually implies a recommendation we cannot list every good place. Exclusion does not necessarily imply criticism. In fact there are a number of reasons why we might exclude a place – sometimes it is simply inappropriate to encourage an influx of travellers.

Introduction

Location, location, location. If Barcelona were up for sale, it would pull in a fortune for position alone. You are never more than a few hours' drive from: southern France; the Pyrenees (skiing in winter, hiking in summer); the seaside lunacy of Sitges (the gay capital of the costas); Romanesque and Gothic monasteries and churches; the Penedès wine country; and the rugged splendours of the northern Costa Brava. Old rivals like medieval Girona (north) and Roman Tarragona (south) are easily accessible.

Barcelona is one of the most exciting cities on the western Mediterranean seaboard – sedulously promoting itself as a European metropolis, a link between the sub-Pyrenean peninsula and the heartland of Western Europe. At its worst over the centuries, it has been a parochial and smugly self-satisfied bourgeois town. At its best, it has a zest for life, artistic genius and sense of style few cities can rival.

Barcelona is and isn't Spain. The second city after Madrid, it is capital of the autonomous region of Catalunya, only fully incorporated into the state after defeat in battle in 1714. The Catalans speak their own language, and not just literally. Viewed with suspicion and envy by some from more southern parts, the *Polacos* ('Pollacks') are to Spain what the Scots are to Britain.

The Romans didn't much like Barcino, the city's Roman predecessor, but they should have stuck around. Medieval grandeur left it with one of the most impressive and varied Gothic legacies in all of Europe.

True, the city's fortunes slid as its Mediterranean empire crumbled and Madrid enforced tighter central rule, and artistically the city stagnated. But then came the Modernistas. Led by Antoni Gaudí, they cast across Barcelona an Art Nouveau splash unparalleled anywhere else. Some of the greatest artists of this century put in time here – Picasso and Miró make an impressive duo, and Dalí was born and lived much of his life just up the coast.

Barcelona is not just monuments and paintings. The city that shot into the limelight with the 1992 Olympic Games provides all sorts of entertainments, starting with the palate. Catalan cuisine is among Spain's best, so you're in for a treat. The wine you drink will probably come from the Penedès area, barely a half-hour's drive south-west of Barcelona and home to *cava*, the prized local bubbly.

If you thought it was time to head for bed after a meal that might not have begun before 10 pm, think again. You've barely begun. The city centre and several *barris* farther out heave to the joyous rhythms of the bar-hoppers. Barcelona doesn't quite match Madrid, but it leaves much of the rest of Europe for dead for the sheer concentration of bars, cafes and clubs.

In summer especially, various parts of the city seem to lose their sanity, giving themselves over to week-long *festes*. These outdoor parties feature bands, competitions and traditional parades of giants, dwarfs and demons *(gegants, capgrossos* and *dimonis)*. Not to mention the madness of fire-running *(correfoc)* through the narrow lanes of the old city with fire-breathing dragons during the late September *Festes de la Mercè*.

Right now, Barcelona is flavour of the month across Europe. New bars, cafes and restaurants are springing up all over town as the city council keeps up a cracking pace in its campaign to clean up its most rundown quarters. Fortunately Barcelona retains some of its rough diamond flavour, but a grunge-chic inner city set that would be at home in the East Village or emerging London haunts like Shoreditch appears here to stay.

If the country's prime minister, José María Aznar, was right in claiming *'España va bien'* ('Spain's doing well'), it is all the more true of 'Barna'.

Facts about Barcelona

HISTORY

The history of the second city of Spain, although far longer than that of its brasher Castilian rival Madrid, could be dismissed as that of an also-ran, a wannabe that at various moments was clearly on the brink of greatness but whose hopes and pretensions were all too often dashed by events.

For centuries Barcelona shrank in the shadow of greater cities and powers. When finally it emerged from the Dark Ages as the successful headquarters of a burgeoning mercantile empire across the Mediterranean, Barcelona still failed – just – to attain the grandeur of some of its major competitors.

Absorption into unified Spain at the close of the Middle Ages meant Barcelona not only was relegated to second place behind Madrid, the newly established centre of the Spanish empire, but frequently languished well behind other urban areas of greater imperial weight, such as Seville in the south.

Civil conflicts, revolts against Madrid and the disaster of 1714 contributed little to the city's happiness, but a tenacious optimism helped to fuel repeated sparks of growth and activity. By the end of the 19th century, Barcelona was probably *the* leading economic light in an otherwise vexed and gloomy country, shackled by poverty, inept government and incessant infighting.

Another Republican defeat in the Spanish Civil War again meant relegation. General Franco's rigid distaste for the devolutionist desires of the Catalans was most eloquently expressed by the official suppression of their language. Unsurprisingly, little love was lost between the diminutive dictator and the bulk of Barcelonins (as residents of Barcelona are called) – his demise in 1975 was greeted with palpable relief. Since the devolution process began in 1978 Barcelona has sparkled back to life.

Early Barcelona

The area around present-day Barcelona was certainly inhabited prior to the arrival of the Romans in Spain in 218 BC. By whom, and whether or not there was an urban nucleus, is open to debate.

Pre-Roman coins found in the area suggest the Iberian Laietani tribe may have settled here. As far back as 35,000 BC the tribe's Stone Age predecessors had roamed the Pyrenees and begun to descend into the lowlands to the south. In 1991 the remains of 25 corpses were found in Carrer de Sant Pau in El Raval – they had been buried some 4000 years BC. It has been speculated that in those days much of El Raval was a bay and that the hillock that is Plaça de Sant Jaume may have been home to a Neolithic settlement.

Other evidence hints at a settlement established around 230 BC by the Carthaginian conqueror (and father of Hannibal), Hamilcar Barca. It is tempting to see in his name the roots of the city's own name. Archaeologists believe that any pre-Roman town must have been built on the hill of Montjuïc.

Right in the centre of old Barcelona is Carrer d'Hèrcules (Hercules Street). Among the many feats attributed to this figure from Greek mythology is the founding of Barcelona – a claim not taken terribly seriously by anyone.

The Romans

The heart of the Roman settlement of Barcelona lay within what would later become the medieval city – now known as the Barri Gòtic. Its core was a low rise known as Mont Taber, where the temple was raised. Remains of city walls, temple pillars and graves all attest to what would eventually become a busy and lively town. Barcino (as the Romans knew it) was not a major centre, however. Tarraco (Tarragona) to the south and the one-time Greek trading centre of Empúries to the north were both more important. Tarraco became capital of the Roman province of Hispania Citerior.

It took the Romans some two centuries to fully subjugate the peninsula but the area around Barcelona enjoyed a mostly peaceful occupation, and in 15 BC Caesar Augustus was magnanimous enough to grant the town the title of Colonia Julia Augusta Faventia Pia. Evidence from sources such as the Latin poet Ausonius suggests a picture of contented prosperity – Roman Barcelona lived well off the agricultural produce in its hinterland and from fishing. Oysters, in particular, seem to have appeared regularly on the menu in ancient times.

Barbarian Invasions

All good things come to an end and, as the Roman Empire began to wobble, Hispania (as the Iberian Peninsula was known to the Romans) felt the effects. It is no coincidence that the bulk of the Roman walls, vestiges of which remain today, went up in the 4th century AD. Marauding Franks had visited a little death and destruction on the city in a prelude to what was to come – several waves of invaders flooded across the country like great Atlantic rollers. By 415 the comparatively Romanised Visigoths had arrived and, under their leader Athaulf, made a temporary capital in Barcelona before moving on to Toletum (Toledo). In all Hispania there were probably never more than a few hundred thousand Visigoths but they remained the ruling class – much aided by Hispano-Roman nobility and the emerging Christian clergy.

Islamic Blitzkrieg

In 711, the Muslim general Tariq landed an expeditionary force in present-day Gibraltar (Arabic for Tariq's Mountain). After the death in 632 of the prophet Mohammed in distant Arabia, Muslims had swept across Asia Minor and all of North Africa, conquering and converting as they went in an unprecedented spate of divinely inspired ad-hoc empire building.

In Spain Tariq found the Visigothic 'state' so rotten and divided that he had no trouble sweeping across the peninsula all the way into France, where he and his army were only brought to a halt in 732 by the Franks at Poitiers.

Barcelona fell under Muslim sway but this situation was short-lived. Little is known about the period. The town is mentioned in Arabic chronicles but it seems the Muslims resigned themselves early on to setting up a defensive line along the Riu Ebro to the south. Whatever the thinking at the time, Barcelona was taken by Louis the Pious, the future Frankish ruler, in 801.

The counts (*comtes*) who were installed here as Louis' lieutenants hailed from local tribes roaming on the periphery of the Frankish empire. Barcelona was a frontier town in what was known as the Frankish or Spanish March – a rough-and-ready buffer zone south of the Pyrenees designed to keep the Muslims and other undesirables at arm's length, and to be used as a springboard for later offensives.

A Hairy Beginning

The history of Barcelona, in a sense, only truly began at this point. The plains and mountains to the north-west and north of Barcelona were populated by the people who by then could be identified as 'Catalans' (although surviving documentary references to the term only date from the 12th century). Catalan, the language (and its many dialects) of these people, was closely related to the *langue d'oc*, the post-Latin lingua franca of southern France (of which Provençal is about the only barely surviving reminder). It is not, therefore, a dialect of Castilian Spanish.

The March was under nominal Frankish control but the real power lay with local potentates (themselves often of Frankish origin however) who ranged across the territory. One of these rulers went by the curious name of Guifré el Pelós, or Wilfred the Hairy. This was not a reference to uneven shaving habits. According to legend, old Guifré had hair in parts most people do not (exactly which parts was never specified!).

Through Holy Roman imperial decree and a dash of intrigue, Guifré, son of Sunifred d'Urgell, and his brothers managed to gain control of most of the Catalan counties. These included Barcelona (something of a glorified country town at the time).

FACTS ABOUT BARCELONA

This task was completed by 878 and Guifré entered the folk mythology of Catalunya. A great funder of religious foundations in Barcelona (none of which survive) and across Catalunya (some of which do), he astutely won for himself the benevolence of the only people who could write in those days – the clergy. They began a tradition of eulogy that has never really died since. If Catalunya can be called a nation, then its 'father' was the hirsute Guifré.

Guifré and his immediate successors continued, at least in name, to be vassals of the Franks. In reality, his position as 'Comte de Barcelona' (Count of Barcelona; even today many refer to Barcelona as the *ciutat comtal*, or city of counts) was assured in his own right.

The Comtes de Barcelona

By the late 10th century the Casal de Barcelona (House of Barcelona) was the senior of several counties (whose leaders were all related by family ties) that would soon be a single, independent principality covering most of modern Catalunya except the south, plus Roussillon (which today lies across the border in France).

This was the only Christian 'state' on the Iberian Peninsula not to fall under the sway of Sancho III of Navarra in the early 11th century. One last Muslim assault came when Al-Mansur raided Barcelona in 985. The city was torched and many of those citizens who were not slaughtered were marched off into slavery in Córdoba.

Calls for Frankish aid to repulse Al-Mansur had gone unheeded so from this

---

Born in Blood

Guifré el Pelós founded the Casal de Barcelona (House of Barcelona) more or less with the consent of his Frankish overlords. But what's a new political entity without a flag of some sort? Scribblers of history and other tall tales soon hit upon a particularly gratifying account for the existence of Catalunya's national colours (the following story and several different versions began to circulate sometime around the 16th century).

Called upon to join the holy fight against the wicked Muslims with an army of Frankish good guys, the gutsy Guifré fell wounded in hair-raising style on the field of battle. The Frankish emperor, Charles the Bald (this is not a joke), was so touched by his vassal's loyalty that he wanted to reward him in some way. No, not with an all-expenses paid holiday to Rome or a gold-plated letter-opener. Upon seeing Guifré's bright golden shield embarrassingly bereft of a coat of arms, old Charles dipped his fingers in a pool of Guifré's fresh warm blood and drew four finger stripes, *les quatre barres*, down the shield.

So much for the story-telling. From this tale came the Catalan coat of arms, concrete evidence of which first appears in 1150 in a seal of Count Ramon Berenguer IV. The same heraldic sign (said to be the fourth oldest in all Europe) can also be made out on the coffin of Ramon Berenguer II (in the cathedral in Girona), who died in 1082. Its origins remain a mystery. The coat of arms went on later to become that of the so-called Crown of Aragon, the state formed in 1137 of a coalition comprising the principality of Catalunya, Aragón, Valencia, the Balearic Islands and Roussillon (in present-day France).

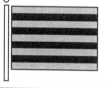

The Catalan flag (in which the stripes become horizontal) is first documented in the 13th century and became the official symbol of the modern, autonomous region of Catalunya in 1979. A similar symbol to the coat of arms, but oval in shape, was concocted in 1932 and now represents the Generalitat, or regional government. The same colour combination also appears in the heraldry of the former members of the Crown of Aragón.

time on the counts implicitly refused to acknowledge Frankish suzerainty. The Franks never contested the new status quo and so a new entity – Catalunya – acquired tacit recognition across Europe.

Throughout Spain, a confusion of counties, principalities and kingdoms vied, jockeyed and fought for local or peninsula domination. It was as common for Muslim warlords to team up with Christian rulers in local spats as for Christians and Muslims to challenge one another. These were, to say the least, interesting times. Particularly so for the counts of Barcelona, who managed to pick up a lot of booty by judicious meddling in Muslim squabbles to the south.

This booty was put to good use. Count Ramon Berenguer I was able to buy the counties of Carcassonne and Béziers, north of Roussillon, with Muslim bullion. Barcelona would maintain ambitions in France for two more centuries – at one point it held territory as far east as Provence. Under Ramon Berenguer III (1082–1131) sea trade developed and Catalunya launched its own fleet. This was the era of great Catalan Romanesque art, with its masterly church frescoes. See Arts later is this chapter.

Marriage of Convenience?

In 1137 Ramon Berenguer IV clinched what must have seemed an unbeatable deal. He was betrothed to Petronilla, heiress to the throne of Catalunya's western neighbour Aragón, thus creating a joint state that set the scene for Catalunya's golden age. This state, known as the Corona de Aragón (the Crown of Aragón), was ruled by *comtes-reis* (in Catalan parlance) or count-kings. The title enshrined the continued separateness of the two states, and both retained many (but not all) of their own laws. The arrangement was to have unexpected consequences as it tied Catalunya to the destiny of the rest of the peninsula in a way that ultimately would not appeal to many Catalans.

In the meantime, however, Don Ramon wasn't content to lie about with Petronilla. In the course of the 1140s he wrested control of southern Catalunya from the Muslims. This southwards expansion heralded a major shift in policy, which until then had been concerned with the north.

Don Ramon's son Alfons I styled himself as king of Aragón, as would his successors, but already trouble had begun to brew as Catalan rulers tended to clash with Aragonese nobles. The latter felt considerable sympathy for the Castilian rulers and their campaign of wresting back the Iberian Peninsula from the Muslims (the Reconquista, or reconquest). The Catalans viewed this enthusiasm for the Castilians with some suspicion.

More pressing problems lay around the corner however. Pere I died in the Battle of Muret in 1213 and France pounced on virtually all Catalan possessions north of the Pyrenees.

Mediterranean Empire

The French blow induced some serious thinking in Barcelona on how to proceed. Not content to leave all the glory of the Reconquista to the Castilians, Jaume I (1213–76) embarked on his own spectacular missions.

Although Barcelona's shallow, silty harbour was hardly ideal, the city's importance by now should have made it a logical launchpad for Mediterranean sea trade, at this time largely the preserve of Italian city states such as Genoa, Pisa and Venice, and their North African counterparts. Indeed, when prevailing winds were favourable, sailing vessels zipped across from Barcelona to the Balearic Islands. There was just one problem. These islands were occupied by Muslim North Africans who were making a nice living by using them as a customs staging post and as a base for piracy.

Jaume I took a while to convince the Aragonese nobility of the attractions of seizing the islands and thus opening the doors to expanded commerce, but eventually the nobles came around. In 1229 Jaume, with a kind of divine fervour, set off on an expedition that involved fleets from Tarragona, Barcelona, Marseilles and other ports. His object was Mallorca, which he won. Six years later he had Ibiza and Formentera in hand. Things were going so well that, prodded by the Aragonese, for good measure he took control of Valencia (on the mainland) too. This was no easy task and was only completed in 1248 after 16 years of grinding conquest. All this activity helped fuel a boom in Barcelona and Jaume raised new walls that increased the size of the enclosed city ten-fold.

Mallorca, in particular, became a commercial centre of great importance and was quickly Catalanised. This didn't stop it from wangling a large degree of independence from Barcelona in 1276, a situation only reversed in 1343.

The empire-building program shifted into top gear in the 1280s. Jaume I's son Pere II (1240–85) took Sicily in 1282. Pere was married to the daughter of the last of the island's Hohenstaufen rulers, who opposed the claims of Charles d'Anjou (who had papal backing) to mastery of the island. Charles was dislodged in the night of the Sicilian Vespers and Pere moved in with his troops in a largely bloodless conquest.

The easternmost part of the Balearics, Menorca, was not so lucky, falling to Alfons II in 1287 in a bloodbath. Most of its people were killed or enslaved and the island remained largely deserted throughout its occupation. Malta, Gozo and Athens were also taken, but not held for long. A half-hearted attempt was made on Corsica but the most determined and ultimately fruitless assault began on Sardinia in 1324. The island became the Corona de Aragón's Vietnam. As late as 1423 Naples also came under the influence of the Catalo-Aragonese.

In spite of the carnage and the expense of war, this was Barcelona's golden age. The grandest city in the Catalo-Aragonese coalition, Barcelona was the base for what was now a thriving mercantile empire. The western Mediterranean had been turned into a Catalan lake and trade proceeded apace, not only among the occupied territories but also with North Africa (through which Barcelona dominated the African gold trade) and to a lesser extent in the Levant.

The Rise of Parliament

The rulers of the Casal de Barcelona and then the count-kings of the Corona de Aragón had a habit of regularly absenting themselves from Barcelona. Initially, local city administration was in the hands of a viscount but in the course of the 12th century local power began to shift.

Citizens of senior rank already had some say in the running of city affairs and, in 1249, Jaume I authorised the election of a committee of top citizens to advise his officials. The idea developed and by 1274 the Consell dels Cent Jurats (Council of the Hundred Sworn-In) formed a kind of electoral college from which an executive body of five *consellers* (councillors) was nominated to run city affairs.

In 1283, the Corts Catalanes met for the first time. This legislative council for Catalunya (equivalent bodies sat in Aragón and Valencia) was made up of representatives of the nobility, clergy and high-class merchants to form a counterweight to regal power. The Corts Catalanes met at first annually, then every three years, but had a permanent secretariat known as the Diputació del General or Generalitat. Its home was, and remains, the Palau de la Generalitat in Plaça de Sant Jaume.

The Court and Council increased their leverage as trade grew and their respective roles in raising taxes and distributing wealth became more important. As the count-kings required money to organise wars and other enterprises they came increasingly to rely on Barcelonin and Catalan impresarios who were best represented through these two oligarchic bodies.

Those citizens not considered of high enough quality to break into these clubs, but who increasingly contributed a good amount of wealth to the city and state, became restless. Occasional uprisings and riots were fomented in the streets of Barcelona and the city was roughly divided into two factions: the dominant Biga and the opposition Busca (who at times appeared to get a nudge and a wink from regal sources, just to keep a little pressure on the institutions). Barcelona was as violent as any other average medieval city but the trouble was always contained. The count-kings had an interest in stirring things up

Fanfare for the Common Man

Under the House of Barcelona a system of feudal government and law evolved that had little to do with the more centralised and absolutist models that would emerge in subsequent centuries in the Castile reconquered from the Muslims. In language and politics, the Catalans tended to look northwards to France and shared the destiny of the remainder of post-Carolingian Europe.

A hodgepodge of Roman-Visigothic laws combined with emerging feudal practice found its way into the written bill of rights called the '*Usatges de Barcelona*' from around 1060.

Feudalism was by and large no picnic for the lower classes. Knights, more preoccupied with their own chivalry (and frequently less noble pursuits), and the ruling class of counts, dukes and lords above them spent a good deal of time extracting high taxes from overworked peasants with few rights. The Usatges, at least, encouraged what one writer has dubbed 'responsible feudalism'.

The Usatges were put together by legal experts immersed in the study of Roman law as well as the customs of the land. Although they no doubt introduced greater security for the lower classes (vassals), the aim behind these laws was a little less noble. The Count of Barcelona was in some respects no more than one among many counts across Catalan territory. Establishing a universal law code of which the Count of Barcelona should be the supreme arbiter was one means of placing the nobles in check.

Some articles of the code could not spell out more clearly the intention of the Counts of Barcelona to enforce their rule over all Catalan nobility: '…let none of the magnates hereafter presume in any way to either punish criminals…or to build a new castle against the prince (Count)…' (article 73). The same article reserves the right to judge criminal cases 'only to the rulers'.

Justice in those days may seem a little rough for modern tastes: '…let them (the rulers) render justice as it seems fit to them: by cutting off hands and feet, putting out eyes, keeping men in prison for a long time and, ultimately, in hanging their bodies if necessary.' Was there an element of misogyny in the Usatges? 'In regard to women, let the rulers render justice by cutting off their noses, lips, ears and breasts, and by burning them at the stake if necessary…'

In many cases, absence of proof meant that those sitting in judgement had to rely on oaths and violence. A series of articles weighed the value of individuals' oaths in monetary terms and according to status. For instance, 'the oaths of peasants who possess a homestead and work it with a yoke of oxen shall be believed, up to the amount of seven silver sous'. A knight's oath was valued in gold coins – owing to the dubious assumption that his rank accorded him greater nobility and probity.

Where all this was considered insufficient, the only options left in many cases were 'judicial battle' or trial by ordeal. The former involved duelling (oneself or by proxy) while the latter involved what was tantamount to torture with boiling and freezing water.

Accusations of adultery (which only men could make) were generally resolved by judicial battle (by proxy) or ordeal of boiling water (in the case of peasants). 'If the wife is victorious, let her husband honourably keep her and make compensation to her…'! One can only wonder what would compensate for a prolonged bath in boiling water.

The Usatges did improve the legal lot of the lower classes (it's not hard to improve on abject misery), but they hardly made it perfect: 'When a peasant suffers injury to the body or damage to his property or fief, let him in no way dare take vengeance…but as soon as he suffers the wrong, then let him make an end to this matter in accordance with his lord's command' (article 95). Serfs, of course, barely got a look in.

The Usatges de Barcelona gained widespread acceptance in territories subsequently occupied by the Catalans, and under the Crown of Aragón the Usatges remained a pillar of law-making. By the 16th century they formed the historical basis of what came to be known as the Constitucions de Catalunya. Defeat by Bourbon King Felipe in 1714 brought this situation to an end, although today the Usatges form part of the region's legal heritage.

every now and then, but not in precipitating unbridled power struggles that might have slipped out of control.

The Court and Council lasted until all local rights were abrogated by the Bourbon king, Felipe V, in 1714.

Meanwhile, Barcelona's trading wealth paid for the great Gothic buildings that still bejewel the city. The cathedral, the Capella Reial de Santa Àgata and the churches of Santa Maria del Pi and Santa Maria del Mar were all built in the late 13th or early 14th century. King Pere III (1336–87) created the breathtaking Reials Drassanes (royal shipyards) and extended the city walls again, this time to include the El Raval area west of La Rambla.

Decline & Castilian Domination

Empire began to exhaust Catalunya. Sea wars with Genoa, resistance in Sardinia, the rise of the Ottoman Empire and the loss of the gold trade all drained the coffers. Commerce collapsed. The Black Death and famines killed about half Catalunya's population in the 14th century. Barcelona's Jewish population suffered a pogrom in 1391.

After the last of Guifré el Pelós' dynasty, Martí I, died heirless in 1410, a special council elected Fernando (Ferran to the Catalans) de Antequera, a Castilian prince of the Trastámara house, to the Aragonese throne. This, the so-called Compromiso de Caspe (Caspe Agreement) of 1412 was engineered by the nobility in Aragón, who saw a chance to reduce Catalan influence over their affairs. Fernando and his successors were soon at daggers drawn with their Catalan subjects, who felt they were being exploited for Castilian interests. A rebellion that began in 1462 against King Joan II ended in a siege in 1473 that devastated Barcelona.

Joan II's son, Fernando, succeeded to the Aragonese throne in 1479 and his marriage to Isabel, queen of Castile, united Spain's two most powerful monarchies. Just as Catalunya had been hitched to Aragón, now the combine was hitched to Castile, and Ramon Berenguer IV's clever marriage in 1137 in retrospect must have seemed like a nasty trap.

Catalunya effectively became part of the Castilian state, although it jealously guarded its own institutions and system of law. Juridically, Catalunya had never ceased to be a distinct entity within the Catalo-Aragonese arrangement. Rather than attack the problem head on, Fernando and Isabel side-stepped it, introducing the hated Inquisition to Barcelona. The local citizenry implored them not to do so as what was left of business life in the city lay largely in the hands of *conversos* (Jews at least nominally converted to Christianity) who were a particular target of Inquisitorial attention. The pleas were ignored and the conversos packed their bags and shipped out their money. Barcelona was reduced to penury.

To make matters worse, the Catholic Monarchs banned the Catalans from trading directly with the newly established American colonies. Everything had to go through the recently enriched Castilian ports of Seville and Cádiz. As Spain hit a high point under Carlos I (or Karl V of the Habsburg empire) and his successor Felipe II, Catalunya, now brought further to heel under a viceroy from Madrid, continued to sink.

Impoverished and disaffected by growing financial demands from the crown, Catalunya revolted again in the 17th century and declared itself an independent 'republic', under French protection, in the Guerra dels Segadors (Reapers War; 1640–52). Countryside and towns were devastated, and Barcelona was finally besieged into submission. The French protection was less than convincing (and in the end largely resented) however, and seven years later, when France and Spain concluded hostilities, Louis XIV and Felipe IV signed a peace that cost Spain chunks of Catalan territory – in particular Roussillon and parts of Cerdanya.

War of the Spanish Succession

By now Spain itself was on the skids, and Catalunya was going down with it. When the last of the Habsburgs, Carlos II, died in 1700, he left no obvious successor. France imposed the investiture of a Bourbon, Felipe V. Although the Catalans preferred the

Austrian candidate, Archduke Carlos, they did not at first actively oppose Felipe's enthronement. Schooled in French-style absolutism and centralism, Felipe soon proved vexatious to the Catalans, who threw in their lot with England, Holland, some German states, Portugal and the House of Savoy in their decision to bat for Austria. In 1702 the War of the Spanish Succession broke out. Catalans thought they were onto a winner. They were wrong, however, and in 1713 the Treaty of Utrecht left Felipe V in charge in Madrid.

Felipe had already taken control of Valencia and Aragón anyway. Barcelona had little to hope for from Felipe V and decided to resist. The siege began in March 1713 and ended on 11 September 1714.

There were no half measures. Felipe V abolished the Generalitat, built a huge fort (the Ciutadella) to watch over Barcelona, and banned writing and teaching in Catalan. What was left of Catalunya's possessions were farmed out to the great powers: Menorca had gone to the British in 1713, Naples and Sardinia went to Austria, and Sicily to the House of Savoy.

A New Boom

After the initial shock, Barcelona found the Bourbon rulers to be comparatively lighthanded in their treatment of the city. Indeed, its prosperity and productivity was in the country's interest. Throughout the 18th century the Barcelonins concentrated on what they do best – industry and commerce.

The big break came in 1778 when the ban on American trade was lifted. Some enterprising traders had already sent vessels across the Atlantic to deal directly in the Americas – still technically forbidden. Their early ventures were a commercial success and the lifting of the ban stimulated business. In Barcelona itself, growth was modest but sustained. Small-scale manufacturing provided employment and profit. Wages were rising and city fathers even had a stab at town planning, creating the grid-based workers' district of La Barceloneta.

Before the industrial revolution, based initially on the cotton trade with America,

could really get underway, Barcelona and the rest of Spain had to go through a little more pain. A French revolutionary army was launched Spain's way (1793–5) with limited success, but when Napoleon turned his attentions to the country in 1808 it was another story. Barcelona and Catalunya suffered along with the rest of the country until the French were expelled in 1814 (Barcelona was the last city in the hands of the French, who left in September).

By the 1830s Barcelona was beginning to ride on a feel-good factor that would last for most of the century. Wine, cork and iron industries developed. Steamships were launched off the slipways from the mid-1830s onwards. In 1848, Spain's first railway line was opened between Barcelona and Mataró.

Well, not everyone was feeling so good. Creeping industrialisation and prosperity for the business class did not translate so well down the line. Wages were higher than in Madrid, but working-class families lived in increasingly putrid and cramped conditions. Poor nutrition, bad sanitation and disease were the norm in workers' districts, and riots, predictably, resulted. As a rule they were put down with little ceremony – the 1842 rising was bombarded into submission. Some relief came in 1854 with the knocking down of the medieval walls but the pressure remained acute. The population was increasing by up to 28% per annum.

In 1869, a revolutionary plan to expand the city was begun. Ildefons Cerdà designed l'Eixample (The Enlargement) as a grid, broken up with gardens and parks and grafted on to the old town, beginning at Plaça de Catalunya.

It became (and to a large extent remains) the most sought-after chunk of real estate in Barcelona – but the parks were sacrificed to an insatiable demand for housing. The flourishing bourgeoisie paid for lavish, ostentatious buildings, many of them in the unique, Modernista (Catalan Art Nouveau) style.

There seemed to be no stopping this town. In 1888 it hosted a Universal Exhibition. It did so in spite of going almost broke in the process, partly due to lack of funding from Madrid. Little more than a year before, work on the exhibition buildings and grounds had not even begun but they were all completed, and only 10 days late. Although the Exhibition attracted more than two million curious visitors, it did not get the international attention some had hoped for.

Nevertheless, Barcelona had become something of a world centre. Changing the cityscape had by now become habitual. La Rambla de Catalunya and Avinguda del Paral.lel were both slammed through in 1888. The rather odd Monument a Colom and Arc de Triomf also saw the light of day that year. Columbus had passed through Barcelona but his Atlantic exploits had precious little to do with that city and, however triumphant the town denizens were feeling at this stage, arches were probably not the most appropriate expression of their mood.

Renaixença

Barcelona was comparatively peaceful for most of the second half of the 19th century. This is not to say that the city was politically inert. The relative calm and growing wealth that came with commercial success helped revive interest in all things Catalan.

The so-called Renaixença (Renaissance) reflected the feeling in Barcelona of renewed self-confidence. The mood was both backward- and forward-looking. Politicians and academics increasingly studied and demanded the return of former Catalan institutions and legal systems. The Catalan language was readopted by the middle and upper classes and a new Catalan literature emerged.

In 1892, the Unió Catalanista (Catalanist Union) was formed and demanded the re-establishment of the Court in a document known as the Bases de Manresa. In 1906 the suppression of Catalan news-sheets was greeted by the formation of Solidaritat Catalana (Catalan Solidarity, a nationalist movement). Led by Enric Prat de la Riba, it attracted a broad band of Catalans, not all of them nationalists.

Perhaps the most dynamic expression of the Catalan Renaissance occurred in the world of art. Barcelona was the home of Modernisme, the Catalan version of Art Nouveau. While the rest of Spain largely stagnated, Barcelona was a hotbed of artistic activity. It was an avant-garde base with close links to Paris. The young Picasso spread his artistic wings here and drank in the artists' hang-out, Els Quatre Gats.

1898

This was a very bad year. While textiles and mills formed the backbone of local industry in Barcelona, a good chunk of the wealth was generated in Spain's remaining possessions abroad, Cuba and Puerto Rico in particular. A push for home rule in Cuba became a militant independence movement and proved fatal to what remained of Spain's 'empire'.

Rather than meet the claims halfway, Madrid chose the heavy (and ham-fisted) approach. The USA had had its eye on these territories for some time and it was not too hard for it to pose as guardian angel to independence movements. Trouble had also been brewing in the Philippines. Everyone but the Spanish government seemed to realise that Spain could not hope to win a naval tussle with this nascent superpower. To cut a long story short, virtually the entire ill-equipped Spanish navy was sunk in two ignominious battles in Cuba and the Philippines, and the colonies were lost to the USA.

For Barcelona, the news was disastrous. Many families with considerable business interests in the overseas possessions lost everything. The ragtag Spanish army was slowly transported home and, at the turn of the century, the most common sight on Barcelona's once bustling docks was near-starving and disease-ridden returned conscripts. They had nothing to do and nowhere to go. Storm clouds once again gathered on the horizon.

Mayhem

Barcelona's proletariat was growing fast. The total population grew from 115,000 in 1800 to over 500,000 by 1900 and over one million by 1930 – boosted, in the early 19th century, by poor immigrants from rural

Catalunya and later from other regions of Spain. All this made Barcelona ripe for unrest.

The city became a swirling vortex of anarchists, Republicans, bourgeois regionalists, gangsters, police terrorists and hired gunmen *(pistoleros)*. Madrid could not resist introducing a meddling hand into this dangerous cocktail. (Read Gerald Brenan's *The Spanish Labyrinth* or Eduardo Mendoza's novel *City of Marvels* for a taste of some of the unbelievable things that went on: in one episode related by Brenan, gangsters in police pay planted 2000 bombs at or near the bourgeoisie's factories to provide the police with an excuse for arresting anarchists.) One genuine anarchist bomb at the Liceu opera house on La Rambla in the 1890s killed 20 people. Anarchists were also reckoned to be behind the Setmana Tràgica (tragic week) in 1909 when, following a military call-up for Spanish campaigns in Morocco, mobs wrecked 70 religious buildings and workers were shot on the streets in reprisal.

The political front was also active. In 1914, Solidaritat Catalana launched the Mancomunitat de Catalunya, a kind of shadow parliament that demanded a Catalan state within a Spanish federation.

In the post-WWI slump, unionism took hold. This movement was led by the anarchist Confederación Nacional del Trabajo (CNT), or National Confederation of Work, which embraced as many as 80% of the city's workers. During a wave of strikes in 1919 and 1920, employers hired assassins to eliminate union leaders. The 1920s dictator General Miguel Primo de Rivera opposed both bourgeois-Catalan nationalism and working-class radicalism, banning the CNT and Mancomunitat and even closing Barcelona football club, a potent symbol of Catalanism. But he did support the staging of a second world fair in Barcelona, the Montjuïc World Exhibition of 1929.

A Taste of Nationhood

Rivera's repression only succeeded in uniting, after his fall in 1930, the pent-up fervour of Catalunya's radical elements. Within

days of the formation of Spain's Second Republic in 1931, leftist Catalan nationalists – ERC (Esquerra Republicana de Catalunya) – led by Francesc Macià and Lluís Companys, proclaimed Catalunya a republic within an imaginary 'Iberian Federation'. Madrid quickly pressured them into accepting unitary Spanish statehood, but in 1932 Catalunya got a new regional government, with the old title of Generalitat.

Francesc Macià, its first president, died in 1933 and was succeeded by Lluís Companys who, in 1934, tried again to achieve near-independence, proclaiming the 'Catalan State of the Spanish Federal Republic'. The Madrid government responded with an army bombardment of the Generalitat offices and Barcelona's city hall. The Generalitat was closed and its members given 35-year jail terms. They were released and the Generalitat restored when the leftist Popular Front won the Spanish general election in February 1936. Now, briefly, Catalunya gained genuine autonomy. Companys, its president, carried out land reforms and planned an alternative Barcelona Olympics to the official 1936 games in Nazi Berlin.

But things were racing out of control. The left and the right across Spain were shaping up for a showdown. Anarchists (and their trade union, the CNT) and socialists (embodied in the Unión General de Trabajadores; General Workers' Union) lined up on the left, the former of the two the most vocal advocate of revolt.

Ranged against them were disgruntled sectors of the armed forces (among whom General Francisco Franco was a key figure), a mixed bag of royalists and conservatives routed in the 1936 polls, and the Falange movement of José Antonio Primo de Rivera (the ex-dictator's dapper son), all of whom were moving closer to forming a single front.

The Civil War

On 17 July 1936, the day before the Barcelona games were due to start, an army uprising in Morocco kick-started the Spanish Civil War. Barcelona's army garrison attempted to take the city for Franco but was defeated by armed anarchists and police loyal to the government.

Franco's forces quickly took hold of most of southern and western Spain. Galicia and Navarra in the north were also his. Most of the east and industrialised north stood with Madrid and the Republic. Initial rapid advances on Madrid were stifled and the two sides settled in for almost three years of misery.

Most, but not all, of the army backed the coup. Franco's forces soon had the upper hand economically, occupying much of the grain and grazing country. By the end of 1936, Hitler's Germany and Mussolini's Italy had recognised Franco and were supplying arms, troops, airforce units and cash.

The Republican side had most of the airforce and navy (the latter proved unbelievably ineffectual), and much of the country's industry. Although France was sympathetic, the West decided to keep out and even blocked military supplies in the interests of 'neutrality'. The only help came from Stalin's Soviet Union – in the form of military advisers and hardware. But this assistance was never enough and was bought at the price of the nation's entire gold reserves. The rather romantic International Brigades contributed in particular to the defence of Madrid, but were illustrative of the Republic's biggest handicap – splintering.

Language wasn't the main problem. Ideology was ultimately what killed the Republicans' chances. While radical anarchists wanted to pursue social revolution at all costs, the increasingly tough and militant communists ostensibly set winning the war as their primary goal, all the while devoting considerable energy to suppressing anarchists and even moderate socialists – their own allies! Their infighting was one of Franco's greatest allies.

The War in Barcelona

The civil war broke the Catalan class alliance. For nearly a year Barcelona was run by anarchists and the POUM (Partido Obrero de Unificación Marxista; the Marxist Unification Workers' Party) Trotskyist militia, with Companys as president only in name. Factory owners and rightists fled the city. Unions took over factories and public services, hotels and mansions became hospitals and schools, everyone wore workers' clothes, bars and cafes were collectivised, trams and taxis were painted red and black (the colours of the anarchists), private cars vanished from the streets, and even one-way streets were ignored as they were considered part of the old system.

The anarchists were a disparate lot ranging from gentle idealists to hardliners who drew up death lists, held kangaroo courts, shot priests, monks and nuns (over 1200 of whom were killed in Barcelona province during the civil war), and burnt and wrecked churches – which is why so many Barcelona churches are today oddly plain inside.

The revolutionary atmosphere waned as anarchists began to join the Catalan and Spanish Republican governments and, under Soviet influence, the PSUC (Partit Socialista Unificat de Catalunya; Catalan communist party) grew more powerful. In May 1937 Companys ordered police to take over the anarchist-held telephone exchange on Plaça de Catalunya. After three days of street fighting, chiefly between anarchists and the PSUC, in which at least 1500 died, the anarchists asked for a cease-fire. They and the POUM were soon disarmed.

Barcelona became the Republicans' national capital in autumn 1937. The city was first bombed from the air in March 1938. In the first three days 670 people were killed; after that, the figures were kept secret. In the end, after the Republicans' defeat in the Battle of the Ebro around Tortosa in southern Catalunya in summer 1938 – the last big set-piece clash of the war – Barcelona was left undefended. Combatants and the Catalan and Spanish Republican governments joined the civilians who were fleeing to France – around 500,000 in all – and the city fell to the Nationalists on 25 January 1939.

Up to 35,000 people were shot in the ensuing purge, and the executions continued into the 1950s. Lluís Companys was arrested in France by the Gestapo in August 1940, handed over to Franco, and shot in secret on

15 October on Montjuïc. He is reputed to have died with the words '*Visca Catalunya!*' ('Long live Catalunya!') on his lips.

The Franco Era

Franco didn't hang about waiting for the war to end before he abolished the Generalitat yet again. This symbolic act was carried out in 1938. Companys was succeeded as the head of the Catalan government-in-exile by Josep Irla, a former ERC MP who remained in charge until May 1954. Irla was succeeded by the charismatic Josep Tarradellas after the parliament-in-exile met in Mexico. Tarradellas remained at the head of the government-in-exile until after the death of Franco.

Franco, meanwhile, embarked on a program of Castilianisation in Catalunya. He banned public use of Catalan and had all town, village and street names rendered in Spanish. Book publishing in Catalan was allowed from the mid-1940s, but education, radio, TV and the daily press remained in Spanish.

In response the occasional anarchist bombing or shooting took place in the 1940s, but by the 1950s opposition had turned to peaceful mass protests and strikes. In 1960 an audience at the city's Palau de la Música Catalana concert hall sang a banned Catalan anthem in front of Franco. The ringleaders included a young Catholic banker, Jordi Pujol, who spent two years in jail as a result. Pujol was to become Catalunya's president in the post-Franco era.

The big social change under Franco was a flood of immigrants from poorer parts of Spain, chiefly Andalucía, attracted by economic growth in Catalunya. Some 750,000 came to Barcelona in the 1950s and '60s, and almost as many to the rest of Catalunya. Many lived in appalling conditions. While some made the effort to learn Catalan and integrate as fully as possible into local society, the majority came to form great Spanish-speaking pockets in the poorer working-class districts of the city. In the earlier days many lived in shanty towns or even caves, worked extraordinary hours for very low pay and generally struggled along.

Spain as a whole suffered in the postwar years, but when economic take-off began in the 1960s many of Barcelona's newcomers reaped at least some of the benefits.

After Franco

Two years after Franco's death in 1975, Josep Tarradellas was invited to Madrid by the newly elected Adolfo Suárez to hammer out the Catalan part of a regional autonomy policy. Shortly afterwards, Barcelonins celebrated the Diada, which marks the 1714 defeat, on 11 September, with a huge pro-autonomy march across the city – some say as many as a million people marched.

Eighteen days later, King Juan Carlos I decreed the re-establishment of the Generalitat and recognised Josep Tarradellas as its president. When Tarradellas finally returned to Barcelona he announced simply: '*Ja soc aquí*' ('I am finally here').

The new Spanish constitution promulgated in 1978 included a policy of autonomy not only for Catalunya but for all the regions. Catalan and Basque claims for some form of devolution were historically the strongest, but the constitution's architects wanted to leave nothing to chance. Rather than risk upsetting some regions that would inevitably claim they were getting the short end of the stick, it was decided to embark on a staggered program of devolution for the whole country.

In Catalunya, a commission of experts had already cobbled together an autonomy statute in 1977. This got the royal seal of approval in 1979. The Catalan nationalist, Jordi Pujol, was elected Tarradellas' successor in April 1980 and he has remained at the helm of the Generalitat ever since.

Catalan Regeneration

Pujol has waged a constant war of attrition with Madrid, eking out ever more powers. Catalunya has made considerable advances on this front, controlling a range of areas including local police, education, trade, tourism, agriculture, hospitals, social security, culture and so on. In 1996 Catalunya and other regions won the right to collect one-third of national income tax.

Pujol's nationalists lost leverage on Madrid when José María Aznar's centre-right Partido Popular won an absolute majority at the March 2000 elections.

Politics aside, the big event in post-Franco Barcelona was the successful 1992 Olympics, which spurred a burst of public works and brought new life to areas such as Montjuïc, where the major events were held. The once-shabby waterfront has been transformed with promenades, beaches, marinas, restaurants, leisure attractions and new housing.

The games may be receding from the public mind but the impetus created has hardly slowed. Enormous projects to 'rehabilitate' vast tracts of run-down central Barcelona continue and the city's profile continues to rise. One recent study placed it behind only New York, Paris and Amsterdam as UK holiday-makers' favourite city-break destination; in 2000 British Airways reported that it had overtaken Paris as its top European city destination. It may disappoint Jordi Pujol that not too many people outside Spain have ever heard of Catalunya – but Barcelona needs no introduction.

GEOGRAPHY

Barcelona spreads south-west to north-east along the Catalan coast in what is known as the Pla de Barcelona (Barcelona Plain), roughly midway between the French border and the regional frontier with Valencia. The plain averages about 4m above sea level. Mont Taber, the little elevation upon which the Romans built their town, is 15m above sea level. To the south-west, Montjuïc is 173m high.

Urban sprawl tends to be channelled along the coast in either direction, as the landward side is effectively blocked off by the Serralada Litoral mountain chain, which between the Riu Besòs and Riu Llobregat is known as the Serra de Collserola. Tibidabo is the highest point of this chain at 512m, with commanding views across the whole city. As is typical for any large and growing European metropolis, surrounding villages have tended to be swallowed up in the expanding conurbation.

Badalona to the north-east and l'Hospitalet to the south-west mark the municipal boundaries of the city – although, as you drive through them, you'd never know where any began and ended. The Llobregat, which rises in the Pyrenees, empties into the Mediterranean just south of l'Hospitalet. Just over the southern side of the river is El Prat de Llobregat and Barcelona's airport. To the north, the Besòs in part marks the northern limits of the city.

CLIMATE

Barcelona enjoys a Mediterranean climate, with cool winters and hot summers. July is the most torrid month, with August just behind. Highs can reach 37°C. The seaside location promotes humidity, but sea breezes can bring relief (especially if you happen to be sitting in a seaward apartment room a few floors up). A hotel room with a fan or air-conditioning can make all the difference to a good night's sleep.

In the depths of winter (especially in February) it gets cold enough (average lows of 6.7°C) for you to wish you had heating in your room but by March, with a little luck, things begin to thaw out. Oddly enough, you can get lucky with the weather in January, which has a tendency to be quite sunny if not terribly warm.

As a rule rainfall is highest in autumn and winter. In September and into October Barcelona often gets a washdown in cracking, late-summer thunderstorms.

As Barcelona is downwind from the Pyrenees, cold snaps are always on the cards and the April–May period is changeable. At its best, May can be the most pleasant month of the year – clear and fresh.

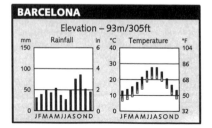

ECOLOGY & ENVIRONMENT

Problems of air pollution are typical of a crowded Mediterranean conurbation such as Barcelona. Although some restrictions apply to parking and driving through the centre of town, the city is generally full to bursting. Cars jostle and the air is none too clean. Sea breezes occasionally manage to shift the smog around a bit.

The water along the beaches is not the most inviting you will see on the Catalan coast but, compared with the way the beaches once were, it is remarkably clean and perfectly OK to swim in.

The disposal of garbage remains a fairly unecological affair. True, large brightly coloured containers have been scattered about the city for the separated collection of paper, glass and cans, but use of them depends entirely on the citizens. Discouragingly, it is not unusual to see mounds of rubbish piling up around these and other general refuse containers – the stuff is eventually hauled off, but it is hard to escape the feeling that it is not a big priority. You will also no doubt notice that many Barcelonins have a love affair with canines. This is never clearer than in the narrow lanes of the Barri Gòtic, where poochy waste products can make unpleasant close encounters with your shoes.

Barcelona, as so many Spanish cities, is justly acclaimed for its nightlife. Those long summer nights are perfect for sitting at open-air cafes and bars *(terrasses/terrazas)*, sipping away into the wee hours. To the general hubbub are added the dubious pleasures of impromptu street entertainment and busking. Fantastic. But spare a thought for the poor sods who live on the squares and streets where all the fun is going on. Noise pollution is a big problem throughout the city. Rowdy traffic, late-night garbage collection, lusty use of sirens by the emergency services and trigger-happiness with car horns all help to keep nerves well jangled.

GOVERNMENT & POLITICS

The Generalitat de Catalunya, the regional parliament of Catalunya, was resurrected by royal decree in 1977. Its power as an autonomous government is enshrined in the statutes of the national Spanish constitution of 1978, and by the Estatut d'Autonomia (devolution statute), which got the royal green light in 1979. The Govern, as the government is also known, is housed in the Palau de la Generalitat on Plaça de Sant Jaume in central Barcelona.

The Generalitat has wide powers over matters such as education, health, trade, industry, tourism and agriculture. Education is now nearly all in Catalan which, at the time of Franco's death, had been in some danger, not only because of the immigration of Castilian-speakers but also because many Catalans, although they spoke Catalan, could no longer read or write it.

Since the first post-Franco regional elections in March 1980, Jordi Pujol's nationalist, right-of-centre Convergència i Unió (CiU) coalition has been at the controls in the Palau de la Generalitat. CiU does not want full independence from Spain but constantly seeks to strengthen Catalan autonomy. Indeed, only a few Catalans seriously contemplate the idea of independence. The pro-independence party Esquerra Republicana de Catalunya (ERC; Republican Left of Catalonia) has won only 8% to 10% of the vote in recent elections. ERC is avowedly nonviolent and there's no Catalan equivalent of the Basque ETA.

In spite of the popular Spanish image of the Catalan populace as a kind of rude, Catalan-babbling separatist movement, the *Ajuntament* (town hall) is proof that there is more to this than meets the eye. The Ajuntament stands opposite the Palau de la Generalitat and has traditionally been a Socialist haven. The Partit Socialista de Catalunya (PSC) is as pro-devolution as anyone else in Catalunya but moderate in its approach. The CiU gets a lot of its support from the Catalan provinces. Barcelona, the one-time haven of anarchist revolution, is unsurprisingly less tolerant of nationalist rigidity of any kind. The PSC, aligned with the main Spanish socialist party, the Partido Socialista Obrero Español (PSOE), has a younger leadership than the CiU, which probably also helps to explain its appeal to Barcelonin voters.

Until 1997, the highly popular Pascual Maragall was *alcalde* (mayor) at the head of the Ajuntament. Much of the go-ahead feeling of Barcelona today is attributed to his forward-looking vision. He was succeeded by Joan Clos who, although less charismatic, seems equally set on maintaining the momentum. Pujol is finding it increasingly difficult to get his own way. In the October 1999 regional elections, he and the CiU came the closest yet to losing power. Maragall just failed to dislodge Pujol from the presidential post.

Things got worse in March 2000, when the right-wing centrist Partido Popular (PP) won a record absolute majority in national elections, making José María Aznar prime minister, and eliminating the leverage Pujol had previously enjoyed in the national parliament. Indeed, for the first time in a century a national (or *españolista*) right-of-centre party (the PP) came close to dislodging the Catalan nationalist right (in the form of the CiU) as the biggest party in Catalunya itself.

Elections to both the Ajuntament and Generalitat take place every four years. They are free and by direct universal suffrage. The members of each house thus elected then vote to appoint the president of the Generalitat and the mayor.

For administrative purposes Barcelona is divided into 10 *districtes*, each with its own *ajuntament* (local council).

Oh What a Tangled Web

A curious angle on the expression of nationalist sentiment in Catalunya has emerged in the Internet era. During Spain's national elections in March 2000, the *El País* newspaper noticed that most nationalist parties (in Catalunya and other autonomous regions such as the Basque Country and Galicia) refused to use the '.es' (for España) suffix on their Web site and email addresses. Most prefer to be '.com' or '.org'. One of Convergència i Unió's candidates, Xavier Trias, even included in his political program the creation of a '.ct' domain suffix for Catalunya.

ECONOMY

Barcelona has a reputation for being a hard-working industrial and mercantile city. The roots of its trading culture lie in the days of Mediterranean empire-building, but industry first stirred to life in the small-scale textiles factories that emerged in the 18th century.

Industry took off in the mid-19th century and metallurgy and engineering became sources of pride to prosperous Barcelona. Steamships were launched here and Spain's first trains were 'made in Barcelona'.

But business relied on heavy protection, meaning that with the loss of the last American possessions in 1898, Barcelona had to rely almost exclusively on selling inside Spain. With few raw materials of its own, Barcelona played second fiddle to Bilbao (País Vasco) and Oviedo (Asturias) in mining and secondary industry, especially iron and other metals.

In the 1950s and '60s, hundreds of thousands of immigrants in search of work converged on Barcelona from the rest of a largely impoverished Spain. The conditions they encountered were often miserable, but most were absorbed eventually into the local industrial workforce.

With all its ups and downs, Barcelona is today an economic powerhouse. An estimated 24.4% of all Spanish exports came from Catalunya in 1999 and three-quarters of the region's industry is in or near the capital. Textiles remain big business, alongside leather goods, chemicals, pharmaceuticals and cosmetics. The heart of the city's metal and other heavy industries was La Barceloneta and then Poble Nou, but in the past couple of decades it has shifted farther from the city centre.

It was just outside Barcelona (in Martorell) that the national car manufacturing company, Seat, came into being. The company is still turning out cars, although it is now part-owned by the German company Volkswagen, which actually considered pulling the plug in the mid-1990s. Since that blip things seem to be going better and Seat cars are sold with increasing success in markets as far away as Australia.

Across Catalunya about 60% of the population is employed in the service sector, 36% in industry and 4% in agriculture. Tourism represents 14% of the city's GDP. Some 3.3 million visitors were registered in the city's hotels in 1999. Of these, the split between tourists and business people is roughly even. And business just gets better, with the number of visitors rising constantly in the past few years.

Not all the news is good, however. Wages rise 2% on average each year but rent and house prices in the city rocketed up 17.5% and 11%, respectively, in 1999 alone.

By European standards, Catalunya is not doing too badly in the employment stakes. According to statistics, 15.01% of the entire Spanish population is out of work, but in Catalunya the figure is 9.71%. Governments in Spain prefer to use a different measure – the number of people officially registered as unemployed. On that basis, 9.1% is the national rate, while in Catalunya 6.1% of the active population is out of a job. Unemployment has been falling steadily throughout the country since halfway through the 1990s, and the Catalan figure is the lowest since the 1970s. Inflation is a bigger problem in Catalunya (3.5%) than across the nation (2.9%).

All up the optimists are glowing. Although there are some concerns about losing ground to Madrid on some scores, Catalan economists claim that Barcelona is fifth on the ladder of industrial capitals in Europe.

POPULATION & PEOPLE

The city of Barcelona is home to 1.5 million, although the greater Barcelona area, which takes in villages that will sooner or later be swallowed up in the city administration, counts 2.8 million people. The population for the entire region of Catalunya is 6.09 million (Spain's is 39.8 million). The average age in Catalunya is 39½ – almost two years above that for the rest of Spain. If it weren't for a continued trickle of inwards migration, population growth would stand at zero.

Most of the growth in Barcelona came this century, particularly in the decades following the civil war when poverty in other parts of Spain spurred up to 750,000 people to migrate to Barcelona and its surrounding areas in search of work. It is estimated that at the height of this exodus in the late 1960s, a quarter of those flocking to the city were from rural Catalunya. Roughly 30% came from Andalucía, 11% from the two Castiles, 7% from Extremadura and about 6% each from Galicia and Aragón. In all, it is estimated that from 1950 to 1975, 1.4 million migrants from the rest of Spain moved to Catalunya. For this reason alone you are just as likely to hear Castilian as Catalan spoken in Barcelona.

Officially, some 43,000 foreigners are registered as residents in Barcelona, although the floating population is likely to be considerably higher. People from Latin America (especially Peru, the Dominican Republic and Argentina) make up 36% of the figure. Residents of 'European origin' (mostly Brits, Germans, French and Italians) come second at 34%. Asians (mostly Filipinos) make up 18.6%, followed by the equally broad category of Africans (11.4%), most of whom are Moroccans. It is thought 2.4% of the population of Catalunya is made up of foreigners.

Interestingly, a recent study found that this migrant population contributed a net annual benefit of 73 billion pesetas to the regional economy, a statistic that flatly contradicts fears that foreigners would take local jobs and drain the coffers.

EDUCATION

Each region in Spain administers its own education system, although overall guidelines are similar throughout the country. In Catalunya about 1.3 million people are enrolled in some kind of educational institute, from pre-school to university.

The Generalitat's drive to foment the use of Catalan has meant that it is increasingly the standard language of education in schools. Some fear Castilian is being pushed into the back seat.

University education is in some respects a more complex issue. Some classes are still held in Castilian, but ideally the Generalitat would like to change that too. Making the speaking of Catalan a prerequisite for lecturing would exclude the rest of the country's academics from teaching in Catalunya, something that ultimately might do more harm than good.

Illiteracy is still an issue in Catalunya, as it is in the rest of Spain – and, contrary to popular belief, in many Western countries. Some 3.3% of the Catalan population is illiterate (the national average is 3.9%). Since the bulk of these people are in older age groups, it is to be supposed that the problem will gradually diminish.

ARTS
Painting & Sculpture
Medieval Painting A great many anonymous artists left their work behind in medieval Catalunya, mostly in the form of frescoes, altarpieces and the like in Romanesque and Gothic churches. But a few leading lights managed to get some credit. Ferrer Bassá (c1290–1348) is considered one of the region's first masters. Influenced by the Siennese school, his few surviving works include murals with a slight touch of caricature in the Monestir de Pedralbes. The style of which he is commonly considered to be the originator is also known as Italo-Gothic.

The style soon displayed a more international flavour, best expressed in the work of Bernat Martorell (1400–52), a master of chiaroscuro who was active in the mid-15th century. As the Flemish school gained influence, painters such as Jaume Huguet (1415–92) adopted its sombre realism and lightened it with Hispanic splashes of gold, as can be seen in Huguet's *Sant Jordi* in the Museu Nacional d'Art de Catalunya. Another of his paintings hangs in the Museu Frederic Marès. See the Things to See & Do chapter for details.

While in that museum you will be overwhelmed by the collection of medieval wood sculpture. Mostly anonymous sculptors were busy throughout Catalunya, from at least the 12th century, carving religious images for the growing number of churches. Although

saints and other characters sometimes figured, by far the most common subjects were Christ crucified and the Virgin Mary with the Christ child sitting on her lap. Romanesque churches were largely bereft of stone sculptural decoration, although this gradually changed as the style gave way to Gothic. Some of the most exquisite sculpture is to be found in sarcophagi of important persons.

There are a few clues to enable you to distinguish between the Romanesque and the Gothic. Firstly, much Romanesque work was done al fresco on church walls and the like; by the Gothic period, such mural painting had largely ceased in Catalunya. Gothic figures are more lifelike than the intentionally two-dimensional didactic representations of the Romanesque period. The latter served to convey the otherworldliness of their subject, far removed from the grubby earthly reality in which their admirers toiled. That distinction was maintained in Gothic paintings and sculpture but artists began to inject *feeling* into their portraits.

Decline & the 19th Century It is fair to say that little of greatness was achieved in the field of Catalan painting or sculpture from the end of the Middle Ages to the 19th century. Barcelona neither produced nor attracted any El Grecos, Velázquezs, Zurbaráns, Murillos or Goyas.

By the mid-19th century, Realisme was the modish medium on the canvas, reaching something of a zenith with the work of Marià Fortuny (1838–74). You can see some of his stuff, and that of his contemporaries, in the Museu Nacional d'Art Modern de Catalunya. The best known (and largest) of his paintings is the 'official' version of the *Batalla de Tetuán* (1863), when Spanish arms managed a rousing victory over a ragtag Moroccan enemy in North Africa.

Modernisme As the years progressed, painters developed a greater eye for intimate detail and less for epic themes and this led painters into Anecdotisme, out of which would emerge a fresher generation of artists – the Modernistas of the turn of the century.

Influenced by their French counterparts (Paris was seen as Europe's artistic capital), the Modernistas allowed themselves greater freedom in interpretation than the Realists. They sought not so much to portray observed 'reality' as to interpret it subjectively and infuse it with flights of their own fantasy. But neither Barcelona nor any other place in Spain was exactly at the forefront of innovation. Ramón Casas (1866–1932) and Santiago Rusiñol (1861–1931) were easily the most important exponents of the new forms in Barcelona. The former was a wealthy dilettante of some talent, the latter perhaps a more earnest soul who ran a close second. Although both were the toast of the bohemian set in turn-of-the-century Barcelona, neither was destined for greatness.

Noucentisme From about 1910, as Modernisme was fizzling out, the more conservative cultural movement Noucentisme sought, in general, to advance Catalunya. In the next 20 years, illiteracy was attacked with force, generalised education spread rapidly and telecommunications were extended across the region. Artistically speaking, Noucentisme claimed to be looking back to more classical models. A return to clarity and 'Mediterranean light' were favoured over what by some were seen as the obscure symbolism of the Modernistas.

From about 1917 a second wave of Noucentistas challenged such notions, which had began to feel like an artistic straitjacket. Some of their work was clearly influenced by the likes of Cézanne. Joaquim Sunyer (1874–1956) and Isidre Nonell (1876–1911) are among the better known of a gaggle of Noucentista painters who, just as had happened to their Modernista predecessors, were soon largely forgotten and overshadowed by true genius.

Picasso Born in Málaga (Andalucía), Pablo Ruiz Picasso (1881–1973) was already sketching by the age of nine. After a stint in La Coruña (Galicia), he landed in Barcelona in 1895. His father had obtained a post teaching art at the Escola de Belles Artes de la Llotja (the stock exchange building) and had his son enrolled there too. It was in Barcelona and Catalunya that Picasso developed his style, spending the next 10 years there ceaselessly drawing and painting.

Although schooled in an academic style, his paintings soon showed a diversity of style and an unusual verve of brushstroke movement. His father sent him to the Escuela de Bellas Artes de San Fernando in Madrid for a year in 1897, but the precocious Picasso was bored with school and took himself to the Prado to learn from the masters and to the streets to depict life as he saw it.

Back in Catalunya he spent six months with his friend Manuel Pallarès in bucolic Horta de Sant Joan – he would later claim that it was here he learned everything he knew. In Barcelona Picasso lived and worked in the Barri Gòtic and got an introduction to the underside of life in the Barri Xinès. By 1900 he was a young regular of Els Quatre Gats, the Modernistas' tavern and lair of the avant-garde in Barcelona. He exhibited here and in the same year made his first trip to Paris.

MICK WELDON

Picasso's precocious artistic talent drew him into Barcelona's progressive intellectual circle.

By the time Picasso moved to France in 1904, he had already explored his first personal style. In this so-called Blue Period, many of his canvases have a melancholy feel heightened by the dominance of dark blues. This was followed by the Pink Period; the subjects became merrier and the colouring leaned towards light pinks and greys.

Picasso was a turbulent character and gifted not only as a painter but as a sculptor, graphic designer and ceramicist, and his work encompassed many different style changes. With *Les Demoiselles d'Avignon* (1907), Picasso broke with all forms of traditional representation, introducing a deformed perspective that would later spill over into cubism. By the mid-1920s he was dabbling with surrealism. His best-known work is *Guernica*, a complex painting portraying the horror of war inspired by the German aerial bombing of the Basque town, Gernika, in 1937.

Picasso was prolific during and after WWII and he was still cranking out paintings, sculptures, ceramics and etchings until the day he died in 1973.

Joan Miró By the time the 13-year-old Picasso arrived in Barcelona, his near contemporary, Joan Miró (1893–1983), was cutting his teeth on rusk biscuits in the Barri Gòtic, where he was born and would spend all his younger years. Indeed, he passed a third of his life in his home town. Later in life he divided his time between France, the Tarragona countryside and Mallorca, where he ended his days.

Like Picasso, Miró attended the Escola de Belles Artes de la Llotja. He was a shy man and initially less certain about his artistic vocation – in fact he studied commerce. Nevertheless, from 1915 he produced a series of panoramas that betrayed the influence of Cézanne and portraits reminiscent of the naivety of Romanesque frescos.

His first trip to Paris came in 1920 but he was still deeply drawn to the Catalan countryside and coast. From 1919 to the early 1930s Miró wintered in Paris and spent the summers at his family's farmhouse at Montroig on the southern Catalan coast. In Paris he mixed with Picasso, Hemingway, Joyce and friends, and made his own mark, after several years of struggle, with an exhibition in 1925. The masterpiece from this, his so-called realist period, was *La Masia* (The Farmhouse).

In the early 1930s Miró went through an artistic crisis, temporarily rejecting painting in favour of collage and other techniques: 'Painting must be murdered' was his cry. The civil-war years provoked strong reactions from the painter, particularly with a series of lithographs entitled *Barcelona*.

But it was during WWII, while living in seclusion in Normandy, that his definitive leitmotivs finally emerged. Among Miró's most important images are women, birds (the link between earth and the heavens), stars (the unattainable heavenly world, source of imagination), and a sort of net entrapping all these levels of the cosmos. The Miró that most people are acquainted with emerged from this time – arrangements of lines and symbolic figures in primary colours, with shapes reduced to their essence.

MICK WELDON

Miró's work is recognisable from his use of primary colours and just the essence of shapes.

In the 1960s and '70s Miró devoted more time to sculpture and textiles. From 1956 he lived in Mallorca, home of his wife Pilar Juncosa, until his death in 1983.

Dalí Salvador Dalí i Domènech (1904–89) spent precious little of his time in Barcelona, and nothing much of his can be seen there. But it would be churlish to leave him out of the picture altogether. He was born and died in Figueres, where he left his single greatest artistic legacy, the Teatre-Museu Dalí.

Prolific painter, showman, shameless self-promoter or just plain weirdo, Dalí was nothing if not a character – probably a little too much for the conservative small-town folk of Figueres.

From the age of 13 he was taking drawing lessons and by 1922 his name had appeared in Barcelona's press as an up-and-coming artist. His move to Madrid that year to study at the Escuela de Bellas Artes de San Fernando was important, not for what he studied (he no more liked the school than Picasso) but for his meetings with the poet Federico García Lorca and future film director Luis Buñuel.

Every now and then a key moment arrives that can change the course of one's life. Dalí's came in 1929 when the French poet Paul Eluard visited Cadaqués with his Russian wife Gala. The rest, as they say, is histrionics. Dalí shot off to Paris to be with Gala and plunged into the world of surrealism. He was prolific – perhaps one of the best-known works of this time was *El Gran Masturbador* (1929), now in Madrid's Centro de Arte Reina Sofía.

In the 1930s, Salvador and Gala returned to live at Port Lligat on the north Catalan coast, where they played host to a long list of fashionable and art-world guests until the war years – the parties were by all accounts memorable. From the outbreak of war until his return to Port Lligat in 1948, Dalí spent time in France and the USA. Excluded by now from the surrealist movement, his painting style underwent something of an about-face, reaching back to classical roots – but it remained unmistakably Dalian. Hallucination seems always to have been its hallmark.

MICK WELDON

Salvador Dalí – prolific surrealist painter, showman and shameless self-promoter

Besides painting, Dalí collaborated in the theatre and cinema, mostly working on sets, and dabbled in writing. All he did seemed calculated to increase his prestige and income, and André Breton, poet and leading light of the surrealist movement, dubbed him Avida Dollars (an anagram of his name).

Back in Port Lligat, the international guest list again grew, as did the scope of the partying. The stories of sexual romps and Gala's appetite for young local boys are legendary. The 1960s saw Dalí painting pictures on a grand scale, including his 1962 reinterpretation of Marià Fortuny's *Batalla de Tetuán*. From 1979 things began to go rapidly downhill. Gala died and Dalí became a recluse, nearly dying in a fire at his property at Púbol. On his death in 1989 he was buried (according to his own wish) in the Teatre-Museu he had created in the old theatre in central Figueres, which now houses the single greatest collection of Dalí's work (see the Excursions chapter).

Contemporary After such a trio, all other artists and their work seem a little dull by comparison. But Antoni Tàpies (born 1923)

is one important contemporary artist who has often been overlooked in all the commotion over the big three. Much of his work can now be seen in the Fundació Antoni Tàpies (see the Things to See & Do chapter). Early on in his career (from the mid-1940s onwards) he seemed very keen on self-portraits, but also experimented with collage using all sorts of materials from wood to rice. This use of a broad range of material to achieve texture and depth in his works has remained a feature to this day. In his 1994 *Duat* he even attached window shutters to his 'canvas'. He is still producing prolifically and is considered one of country's leading artists.

To get an idea of what is happening in Catalan art today, you should make for the MACBA art gallery (see the Things to See & Do chapter). There is no shortage of Barcelona-born artists beavering away at all sorts of things. Among them are Susana Solano (born 1946), Xavier Grau (born 1951), Sergi Aguilar (born 1946), Joan Hernàndez Pijuan (born 1931), Ignasi Aballí (born 1958), Jordi Colomer (born 1962), José Luis Pastor Calle (born 1971), Cristina Fontsaré Herraiz (born 1969), Laia Solé Coromina (born 1976) and Mercè Roura i Molas (born 1977).

Avant-Garde in the Streets Barcelona hosts quite an array of street sculpture, from Miró's *Dona i Ocell*, which stands in the park dedicated to the artist, to the *Peix* by contemporary architect Frank Gehry, on the Vila Olímpica waterfront.

Others you may want to keep an eye out for are *Barcelona's Head* by Roy Lichtenstein (Map 6; on Moll de la Fusta, the waterfront area by Maremàgnum) and Fernando Botero's characteristically tumescent *El Gat* at Carrer del Portal de Santa Madrona, behind the Drassanes (Map 6).

Perhaps the weirdest monument is what looks like a pile of square containers with windows leaning precariously, like so many dice, on La Barceloneta beach. Made in 1992 by Rebecca Horn, it is called *Homenatge a la Barceloneta* (Homage to La Barceloneta).

Architecture

When most people think of architecture and Barcelona, it is Gaudí's name that usually springs to mind. But the genius of that architect was in a sense the fruit of all that went before. The Romans built a modest town here and medieval Barcelona was at first full of Romanesque monuments. But if you were to sum up the city in a word, it would be Gothic. Barcelona is one of Europe's great Gothic treasure houses and it was largely on the legacy of this artistic dish that the Modernistas of the late 19th and early 20th centuries supped so keenly, adapting the old to fit their new ways of seeing and building.

Early Barcelona What Caesar Augustus and friends called Barcino was a fairly standard Roman rectangular job. The forum lay more or less where Plaça de Sant Jaume is today and the whole place covered little more than 10 hectares.

Today there remain some impressive leftovers of the 4th-century walls that once comprised 70 towers. In the basement of the Museu d'Història de la Ciutat you can inspect parts of a tower and the wall, as well as other Roman remains. Elsewhere in the immediate vicinity stand temple columns and, a little farther north, a modest burial ground (in Plaça de la Vila de Madrid).

Romanesque Unfortunately, little remains of Barcelona's Romanesque past – it was torn down to make way for what were considered greater Gothic spectacles as the city moved into its golden age. If you have the opportunity, a tour through the northern reaches of Catalunya should tell more than satisfy your curiosity as to what form the Catalan version of this first great wave of Christian European architecture took.

It was Lombard artisans from northern Italy who first introduced this style of monumental building to Catalunya. It is characterised by a pleasing simplicity. The exterior of most early Romanesque edifices that have not been tampered with is virtually bereft of decoration. Churches tend to be austere, angular constructions, with tall, square-based bell towers. There were a few notable concessions to the curve – almost always semicircular or semicylindrical. These included the barrel vaulting inside the churches, the apse (or apses – as the style was developed up to five might be tacked on to the 'stern' of a church) and arches atop all the openings.

The main portal and windows are invariably topped with straightforward arches. When builders got a little saucy, they might adorn the main entrance with several arches within one another. From the late 11th century, stonemasons began to fill the arches with statuary.

One of the more charming examples of simple Catalan Romanesque is the Església de Sant Climent in Taüll, in north-western Catalunya. But it is by no means the only one – northern (or Old) Catalunya is peppered with as many as 2000 such churches. The most magnificent structure is the Església de Sant Vicenç in the castle complex dominating Cardona (less than an hour by car north-west of Barcelona). As for Romanesque decoration, the main doorway to 12th-century Santa Maria de Ripoll, north of Barcelona, is the most extravagant display you will see in Catalunya.

In Barcelona itself you can espy only a few Romanesque remnants. In the Catedral the 13th-century Capella de Santa Llúcia survives, along with part of the cloister doors. The 12th-century former Benedictine Monestir de Sant Pau del Camp is also a good example, especially the cloisters. There are a few other scattered reminders, but if Romanesque is your thing and you want to see a little more without really leaving Barcelona, catch the FGC train north to Sant Cugat del Vallès. Although much was incorporated into a later Gothic construction, the 12th-century cloister is fine and the Lombard bell tower is Romanesque.

The counterpoint to Romanesque architecture was the art used to decorate so many of the churches and monasteries built in the style. In this respect Barcelona is *the* place to be, as the best of Romanesque art from around Catalunya has been concentrated in the Museu Nacional d'Art de Catalunya.

Gothic This soaring form of architecture took off in France in the 13th century and spread across Europe. In Barcelona, its emergence coincided with Jaume I's march into Valencia and annexation of Mallorca and Ibiza, accompanied by the rise and rise of a trading class and a burgeoning mercantile empire. The enormous cost of the grand new monuments could thus be covered by the steady increase in the city's wealth.

Gothic buildings did not simply pop up like mushrooms from one day to the next. The style of architecture reflected the development of building techniques. The introduction of buttresses, flying buttresses and ribbed vaulting in ceilings allowed engineers to raise edifices that were loftier and seemingly lighter than ever before. The pointed arch became a standard characteristic and the great rose windows were the source of light inside these enormous spaces. Think about the little hovels that most of the labourers on such enormous projects lived in, the precariousness of wooden scaffolding and the primitive nature of building materials available and you get some idea of the degree of awe the great cathedrals, once completed, must have inspired.

Catalan Gothic, however, did not follow exactly the same course. Decoration tends to be more sparing than in northern Europe and the most obvious defining characteristic is the triumph of breadth over height. While some northern European cathedrals reach for the sky, Catalan Gothic has a tendency rather to push to the sides, stretching vaulting design to the limit.

The Saló del Tinell, with a parade of 15m arches (among the largest ever built without reinforcement) holding up the roof, is a perfect example of Catalan Gothic. Another is the Drassanes, Barcelona's enormous medieval shipyards (and home today to the Museu Marítim).

In their churches, too, the Catalans opted for a more robust shape and lateral space – step into Santa Maria del Mar or Santa Maria del Pi and you'll soon get the idea. It seems that the long, narrow and high naves of many northern European Gothic churches

JANE SMITH

Església de Santa Maria del Mar – Barcelona's finest example of Catalan Gothic

spread, Barcelona's coffers had been filled but, by the mid-14th century, when Pere III was in command, the city had been pushed to the ropes by a series of disasters: famine, repeated plagues, and pogroms.

Maybe the king didn't notice. He built, or began to build, much of the Catedral, the Drassanes shipyards, the Llotja stock exchange, the Saló del Tinell, the Casa de la Ciutat (which houses the Ajuntament) and numerous lesser buildings, not to mention part of the city walls. Along with the Catedral, the churches of Santa Maria del Pi and Santa Maria del Mar were completed by the end of the century. The last of these is considered by many to be the finest of Barcelona's great Gothic monuments.

Gothic had a longer use-by date in Barcelona than in many other European centres. It seemed that with this style the city had found the expression of its soul. Even several centuries later, architects still felt subject to it. By the early 15th century the Generalitat still didn't have a home worthy of the name and the architect Marc Safont set to work on the present building on Plaça de Sant Jaume. Even renovations carried out a century later were largely in the Gothic tradition, although some Renaissance elements eventually snuck in – the facade on Plaça de Sant Jaume is a rather disappointing result.

Carrer de Montcada, in La Ribera, was the result of a late medieval act of town planning – a street laid out by design rather than simply 'evolving'. Eventually, mansions belonging to the moneyed classes of 15th- and 16th-century Barcelona were erected along it. Many now house museums and art galleries. Although these former mansions appear austere and forbidding on the outside, their interiors often reveal another world altogether, of pleasing courtyards and decorated staircases.

The great bulk of Barcelona's Gothic heritage lies, predictably enough, within the boundaries of the Ciutat Vella, but a few examples can be found beyond it, notably the Monestir de Pedralbes in the *barri* (district) of Sarrià, which until 1921 was a separate village.

inspired more claustrophobia than admiration in the Catalans. While on the subject of churches, a peculiarly Spanish touch that can be seen here and throughout the peninsula is the presence of a *coro*, or enclosed choir stall, smack in the middle of the main nave – the one in the Catedral is a good specimen.

Another notable departure from what you might have come to expect of Gothic beyond the Pyrenees is the lack of spires and pinnacles. Bell towers tend to terminate in a flat or nearly flat roof. Occasional exceptions prove the rule – the main facade of Barcelona's Catedral, with its three gnarled and knobbly spires, does vaguely resemble the outline that confronts you in Chartres or Cologne.

Perhaps the single greatest building spurt came under Pere III. Odd in a sense because, as Dickens might have observed, it was not only the best of times, but also the worst. As the Mediterranean empire had

The Modernistas

DAMIEN SIMONIS

Say Barcelona and most people respond with 'Gaudí' (often pronouncing it 'gaudy', in some cases an expression of artistic judgement).

Antoni Gaudí (1852–1926; pronounced gow-**di**, with the emphasis on the i) was born in Reus and initially trained in metalwork. He obtained his architecture degree in 1878. He personifies, and in large measure transcends, a movement in architecture that brought a thunderclap of innovative greatness to an otherwise middle-ranking (artistically speaking) European city. This startling wave of creativity subsided just as quickly – the bulk of the Modernistas' work was done from the 1880s to about 1910.

What the Catalans call Modernisme emerged as a trend in all the arts in Barcelona in the 1880s. The avowed aims (especially in litera-ture) of its followers were perhaps outlandish and pretentious, but the

OLIVER STREWE

Title page: Gaudí's unfinished Sagrada Família (photograph by Manfred Gottschalk)

Top: Flamboyant Modernista tiling

Left: The soaring spires of the Sagrada Família, decorated with messages for the angels

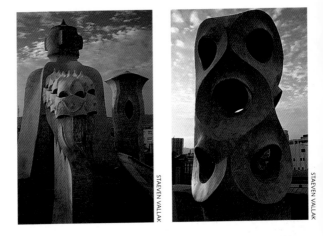

STAEVEN VALLAK

STAEVEN VALLAK

urge to seek innovation in expression coincided with a period of gen-eralised optimism in Barcelona and throughout much of Western Europe. In spite of the loss of Cuba and the Philippines in 1898 and the spread of violence in the city in the first decade of the 20th century, Barcelona experienced a *belle époque* to equal those that occurred elsewhere.

Modernisme did not appear in isolation in Barcelona. To the British and French the style was Art Nouveau; to the Italians it was *lo stile Liberty*; the Germans called it *Jugendstil* (Youth Style) and their Aus-trian confreres *Sezession* (Secession).

There is something misleading about the name Modernisme. It sug-gests the adoption of new means of construction and/or decoration and the rejection of the old. In a sense, nothing could be further from the truth. From Gaudí down, Modernista architects looked to the past for inspiration. Gothic, Islamic and Renaissance all had something to offer. At its most playful, Modernisme was able to intelligently flout the rulebooks on all these styles and create new and exciting cocktails. Even many of the materials used by the Modernistas were traditional – the innovation came in their application.

The search for a source or spirit was complemented by a desire to renew and transform those sources into a new expression, or re-expression, of timeless values in a contemporary universe. Those roots and their transformation are of course more readily observed in some Modernista constructions than in others.

As many as 2000 buildings in Barcelona and throughout Catalunya display at least some Modernista traces and Gaudí also undertook a handful of projects beyond Catalunya. It is one thing to have at hand an architect of genius. It is still more remarkable that several others of considerable talent should have been working at the same time. But

Top left & right:
The bizarre chimneys of Gaudí's organic Casa Milà

the proliferation of their work was due, above all, to the availability of hard cash – as with most great artists down the centuries, genius required both a muse *and* a patron. Gaudí and friends had no shortage of orders. By happy coincidence Modernisme picked up pace at the same time as Barcelona's urban expansion project, the area known as l'Eixample, was gathering steam. The money for building was available and so was the space.

Modernisme also emerged within the context of the Catalan Renaixença, a rebirth or rediscovery of Catalan heritage by a certain intellectual elite. This rebirth expressed itself in many ways, from the founding of avowedly Catalan nationalist political pressure groups that sought the re-establishment of autonomous rights for the region through to the (self-) conscious resurrection of Catalan as an active literary language. The good and the great of Barcelona felt too that their town was emerging on the world stage. After all it had been the first city in Spain to stage a Universal Exhibition (all the rage in Europe at that time), in 1888.

Three Geniuses

Gaudí, although a Catalan nationalist, does not appear to have been particularly vocal on the subject. The two architects who most closely followed him in talent, Lluís Domènech i Montaner (1850–1923) and Josep Puig i Cadafalch (1867–1957), were prominent nationalists. Puig i Cadafalch, in fact, was an important politician and president of the Catalan Mancomunitat (see Mayhem under History in the Facts about Barcelona chapter) from 1916 to 1923.

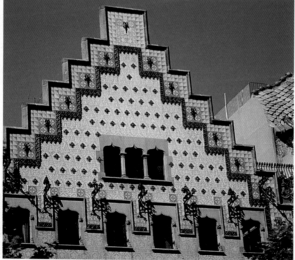

BETHUNE CARMICHAEL

Left: The straight lines of Puig i Cadafalch's Casa Amatller contrast starkly with neighbouring Casa Batlló.

A quick comparison of some of the work by these three architects is enough to illustrate the difficulty in defining closely what is Modernisme. As Gaudí became more adventurous he increasingly appeared as a lone wolf. With age he became almost exclusively motivated by stark religious conviction and devoted much of the latter part of his life to what remains Barcelona's call sign – the unfinished Sagrada Família church. His inspiration in the first instance here is clearly Gothic. But you don't have to take too close a look at the parts built in his lifetime to see that he is right out there by himself. Gaudí sought the perfection of harmony and perspective he observed in nature. Straight lines were out. Man was hard-pressed to emulate the works of nature, but he could try. Gaudí found his inspiration in the forms of plants and stones and used complex string models weighted with plumb drops to

BETHUNE CARMICHAEL

Right: The glittering facade and undulating roof of Casa Batlló – said to represent St George and the dragon

make his calculations (you can see an example in the upstairs mini-museum in La Pedrera). The architect's work is at once a sublime reaching out to the heavens and yet an earthy appeal to the sinewy movement – even in stillness – of nature's own constructs.

Other key works by Gaudí show a similar preoccupation with the forms of nature, such as the Casa Milà (La Pedrera) and Casa Batlló (see the Things to See & Do chapter for more detail), where not a single straight line appears anywhere.

For real contrast, just look from Casa Batlló to Puig i Cadafalch's Casa Amatller next door, where the straight line is all too much in evidence. This architect has also looked to the past and to foreign influence (the gables are borrowed from the Dutch), and still managed to create a house of startling beauty and invention. Domènech i Montaner, too, clearly looked into the Gothic past but never simply copied, as evidenced by the Castell dels Tres Dragons (built as a cafe-restaurant for the Universal Exhibition in 1888 and now home to the Museu de Zoologia) or the Hospital de la Santa Creu i de Sant Pau. In these buildings, Domènech i Montaner put his own spin on the past, in both decoration and in structure. In the case of the Castell dels Tres Dragons, the main windows are more of a neo-classical borrowing, and Islamic touches can be made out in the detail. Domènech i Montaner seems to come closest to Gaudí's ideas in the Palau de la Música Catalana. The structure may be largely linear, the decor is anything but.

The curve implies movement, and hence vitality, and this idea informed a great deal of Art Nouveau thinking across Europe, in part inspired by long-standing tenets of Japanese art.

DALE BUCKTON

Left: Domènech i Montaner's Palau de la Música Catalana – a crescendo of Modernista styles

Materials & Decoration

All three of the 'greats', and a whole gaggle of lesser-known figures of the Modernista style, relied heavily on artisanal skills which, by now, had been all but relegated to history. There were no concrete pours for these guys. Unclad brick, exposed iron and steel frames, copious use of glass and tiles in decoration were all features of the new style – and indeed it is often in the decor that Modernisme is at its most flamboyant and identifiable.

The kinds of craftsmen required to execute these tasks were the heirs of the guild masters, and had absorbed centuries of know-how about just what could and could not be done with these materials. Forged iron and steel were newcomers, but the approach in learning how they could be used was not dissimilar to that adopted for more traditional materials. Gaudí, in particular, relied on these old skills and even ran schools in the Sagrada Família workshops to keep them alive.

Iron came into its own in this period. Nowhere is this more evident than in Barcelona's great covered markets: Mercat de la Boqueria, Mercat del Born (now empty and destined for conversion into a library) and Mercat de Sant Antoni, just to name the main ones. Their grand metallic vaults not only provided shade over the produce for sale but were also a proclamation both of Barcelona's dynamism and the success of 'ignoble' materials in grand building.

The Rome-trained sculptor Eusebi Arnau (1864–1934) was one of the most constant figures called up to decorate Barcelona's great Modernista buildings, both inside and out. The appearance of the Hospital de la Santa Creu i de Sant Pau is one of his legacies and he was heavily involved in the design and embellishment of monuments in the Parc de la Ciutadella. He also had a hand in the Palau de la Música Catalana, the Fonda Espanya restaurant in El Raval, and Casa Amatller among others.

Top & right: Tilework on the Hospital de la Santa Creu i de Sant Pau – designed to cheer patients up!

CHRISTOPHER GROENHOUT

Decorators of several less-grand establishments were quick to jump onto the Modernista bandwagon. Casa Quadros on La Rambla, with its Chinese dragon and impossible cladding of umbrellas, remains a dreamy example of daring shopfront design. Less obvious but just as clearly Modernista on a closer look are the many surviving shop fronts of, above all, pharmacies (for example, Carrer de València 256 and Carrer de Mallorca 312) and bakeries (for example, Antiga Casa Figueras, La Rambla 83).

Where to Look

Barcelona is full of Modernista traces. A separate guidebook would be needed to detail all of them. In the Walking Tours chapter there is a selective tour of the main Modernista sights (largely concentrated in l'Eixample or nearby, although there are some important exceptions). A number of lesser sights are also mentioned in passing. The main ones are discussed in more detail in the Things to See & Do chapter.

Tourist offices can also provide pamphlets and other material with detailed maps covering a greater range of Modernista sights. Remember that many of these Modernista buildings are still private houses and/or offices so it is often difficult to see inside them.

DAMIEN SIMONIS

Top & bottom:
Advertising, Modernista style – the Casa Quadros used to sell umbrellas.

Renaissance & Baroque The strong Barcelonin affection for Gothic, coupled with a decline in the city's fortunes that led to a decrease in urban development, seems to have largely closed Barcelona to the extravagances that elsewhere in Europe accompanied the Renaissance and baroque periods. Such modest examples of baroque as can be found in Barcelona are generally decorative rather than structural, and are usually additions to pre-existing Gothic structures.

Among the more important but restrained baroque constructions in Barcelona are the Església de la Mercè, home to the medieval sculpture of Mare del Déu de la Mercè (Our Lady of Mercy; Barcelona's co-patron with Sant Eulàlia), the Església de Sant Felip Neri and the Jesuits' Església de Betlem (largely destroyed in the civil war and since rebuilt). Also worth a look is the courtyard of the Palau Dalmases, in Carrer de Montcada, reworked from the original Gothic structure.

Modernisme For this remarkable, if brief, flurry of fantasy-filled design and architecture in Barcelona, which took off in the 1880s and was already sputtering to a close by 1910, see the colour special section 'The Modernistas' on pages 33–40.

After Modernisme Even before Gaudí died in 1926, Modernisme had been swept aside. In the aftermath of WWI especially, it seemed already stale, decadent and somehow unwholesome.

While other movements replaced it in fine arts and literature, architecture took a bit of a nose dive from here on. Between the two world wars a host of neo-classical and neo-baroque edifices went up in the cities. In the aftermath of the Civil War there was little money, time or willingness for architectural fancy work. Apartment blocks and offices, designed with a realism and utilitarianism that to most mortals seems deadly dull, were now erected.

Barcelona Today The title of Llàtzer Moix's study of architecture and design in modern Barcelona, *La Ciudad de los Arquitectos* (The City of Architects), could just as well serve as an epithet for the city.

In the run-up to the 1992 Olympics, more than 150 architects were beavering away on almost 300 building and design projects! The Port Olímpic area (Map 1), dominated by the Hotel Arts and Mapfre towers, is a strange result – an improvement on the ramshackle state of affairs that preceded it but somehow oddly characterless too.

Things have slackened off a little since then, but that doesn't mean Barcelona has lost its taste for building.

Ricard Bofill's team designed the Teatre Nacional de Catalunya – a mix of neoclassicism and the modern. Across the road, Rafael Moneo's L'Auditori has become one of the city's top venues for classical music. Moneo is now busy causing a storm in Madrid with his project to expand the Prado.

The World Trade Centre, now largely completed and already operating, is touted as the biggest commercial centre in any European port and a building of the 'latest generation'.

As these projects wind up, Barcelona looks further ahead to the next big event – the World Cultural Forum in 2004. Exactly what this will be remains a little hazy, but in the meantime it provides an excuse to further spruce up the city. The area from Port Olímpic to the Riu Besós is set to be revamped as a new waterfront residential haven, and the so-called Front Marítim along the shore has been earmarked for gardens, a marine zoo, hotels, fair grounds, new housing and a marina. The Avinguda Diagonal will finally stretch uninterrupted from Pedralbes to the sea just short of the Riu Besós.

Shopping centres are always popular and right on Plaça de Catalunya a new one, El Triangle, threw open its doors in 1999. It contains some of the city's most expensive office and retail space.

And not only is the airport due for a third runway, the nearby Riu Llobregat will be diverted too in what is claimed will be an environmentally friendly redevelopment of the whole area.

Literature

Beginnings The earliest surviving documents written in Catalan date from the 12th century. Most of them are legal, economic, historical and religious texts. The oldest of them is a portion of the Visigothic law code, the *Liber Iudicorum*, rendered in the vernacular. The oldest original texts in Catalan are the *Homilies d'Organyà*, a religious work.

The first great Catalunyan writer was Ramon Llull (1235–1315), who eschewed the use of either Latin or Provençal in literature. His two best-known works are perhaps *El Llibre de les Bèsties* and *El Llibre d'Amic i Amat*, the former an allegorical attack on feudal corruption and the latter a series of short pieces aimed at daily meditation – both inspired in part by Islamic works.

The count-king Jaume I was a bit of a scribbler himself and penned a rare autobiographical work, the *Llibre dels Feyts* (Book of Deeds), in the late 13th century. Ramon Muntaner (1265–1336), more of a propagandist than anything else, spent a good deal of his life eulogising various Catalan leaders and their deeds in his *Crónica*.

Segle d'Or Everyone seems to have a 'golden century', and for Catalan writers it was the 15th. Ausiàs March (1400–59), actually from Valencia, announced he had abandoned the style of the troubadours and went ahead to forge a Catalan poetic tradition. His style is tormented and highly personal, and continues to inspire Catalan poets to this day.

Most European peoples seem to feel it necessary to claim to have produced the first European novel. The Catalans claim it was Joanot Martorell's *Tirant lo Blanc*. Cervantes himself thought it the best book in the world. Martorell (c1405–65) was also a busy fighting knight and his writing tells of bloody battles, war, politics and sex. Some things don't change. More obscure names of the epoch include Bernat Metge (who saw out the 14th century), Roís de Corella and Jaume Roig.

Renaixença Catalan literature declined rapidly after the 15th century and suffered a seemingly mortal blow when the Bourbon king Felipe V banned the language after his victory in 1714.

As Catalunya began to enjoy a burgeoning economy in the 19th century, there was sufficient leisure time for intellectuals, writers and artists to take a renewed interest in all things Catalan. The revival of Catalan literature is commonly dated to 1833 when the rather saccharine poem *A la Pàtria* was written in Madrid by Carles Aribau (1798–1862).

From 1859, when Catalan intellectuals reintroduced Catalan language poetry competitions, Jocs Florals, a steady stream of material that was generally fit to be ignored started to dribble out of the tap. True quality in poetry came only with the appearance in 1877 of a country pastor, Jacint Verdaguer (1845–1902), whose *L'Atlantida* is an epic that defies easy description. To the writer's contemporaries, however, the poem confirmed Catalan's arrival as a 'great' language. Verdaguer inspired others, above all the novelist Narcís Oller (1846–1930) and playwright Àngel Guimerà (1845–1924). The former's *La Febre d'Or* (1893) describes the shaky world of speculative finance that dominated much of boomtime Barcelona.

Modernisme & Noucentisme Modernisme's main literary voice of worth was the poet Joan Maragall (1860–1911). Also noteworthy is the work of Víctor Català (1873–1966), a pseudonym of Caterina Albert – why did women have to pretend to be men in order to get anywhere? Her principal work is *Solitud*, a mysterious novel charting the awakening of a young woman whose husband has taken her to live in the Pyrenees.

Eugeni d'Ors (1881–1954), more of a journalist, critic and social commentator than writer, was one of the leading figures of Noucentisme, which aimed in part to rid the cultural scene of Modernisme. Carles Riba (1893–1959), was the period's most outstanding poet, although that is not saying an awful lot.

Borges Bags Barcelona

As you wander around the bustling streets of modern Barcelona, you might find it hard to fathom how someone could hate the place.

The writer and sophisticate from Buenos Aires, Jorge Luis Borges, travelled with his family to Spain in 1920 and seems not have been overly impressed with what he found. If his letters reveal disdain for Spain ('so rough…so sad'), they display a venomous dislike for Barcelona, where he ended up for a time in May. In one epistle he wrote: 'Barcelona is an unpleasant city. I'm tempted to add that it's the worst city in the peninsula: ugly, vulgar and strident.'

Modernista architecture reminded Borges of the kind of taste one might expect in brothels, and he was no less dismissive of Catalan intellectuals. He reserved particular dislike for writer Eugeni d'Ors: 'It may well be,' he wrote, 'that a ridiculous gentleman is best placed to explain the essence of something as artificial and absurd as neo-classical Catalanism…'

To the Present Mercé Rodoreda (1909–83) was one of the major writers in Catalan of the 20th century. Her first successful novel was *Paloma* (1938), which tells the story of a young girl seduced by her brother-in-law. After the civil war Rodoreda went into exile and in 1962 published one of her best-known works, *Plaça del Diamant*, which recounts life in Barcelona seen through the eyes of a working-class woman. The book has been translated into English and several other languages.

Josep Pla (1897–1981) was a prolific writer who, after the victory of Franco in 1939, spent many years abroad. He wrote in Catalan and Castilian and his work ranged from travel writing to histories and fiction. His complete works total 46 volumes.

Since the demise of Franco, the amount of literature being produced in Catalan has increased greatly, but some of the region's more noteworthy scribblers write in Spanish too, and in some cases prefer to do so.

Juan Goytisolo (born 1931) started off in the neo-realist camp but his more recent works, such as *Señas de Identidad* and *Juan sin Tierra*, are decidedly more experimental. Goytisolo lives in Marrakesh. Goytisolo's pal, Jaime Gil de Biedma (1929–90), was one of the 20th century's most influential poets in Catalunya and indeed across Spain.

A highly accessible writer is Barcelona-born José Luis Sampedro (born 1917). A professor of structural economics (!) and one-time senator, his novels are wide-ranging and thought-provoking. He considers *Octubre, Octubre* his life testament. In his latest adventure, *El Amante Lesbiano*, he makes a frontal assault on what may for some be social givens.

Jorge Semprún (born 1923), who lost his home and family in the civil war, ended up in a Nazi concentration camp for his activities with the French Resistance in WWII. He writes mostly in French. His first novel, *Le Grand Voyage*, is one of his best.

Eduardo Mendoza (born 1943) is a fine Barcelonin writer, whose *La Ciudad de los Prodigios* (also published in English as The City of Marvels) is an absorbing novel set in the city in the period between the Universal Exhibition of 1888 and the World Exhibition in 1929. It was filmed, with disappointing results, in 1999. Together with his sister, Cristina, Mendoza has also written *Barcelona Modernista*.

Terenci Moix (born 1942) is a successful columnist and writer who tends to write in Castilian (although not exclusively). His books are fairly lightweight, but highly popular, literature exploring Spanish society and often involving a lot of self-discovery. A big hit was *Lleonard o el Sexo de los Ángeles*; he has also written a couple of historical novels.

Momentos Decisivos, the third novel by Félix de Azúa (born 1944), is set in the Barcelona (his home town) of the 1960s, the years before the transition from Francoist dictatorship to democracy. For Azúa, the attitudes that would awaken Spain from its torpor were formed in those 'opaque' years.

Enrique Vila-Matas (born 1948) has won fans well beyond his native Barcelona. His novels have been translated into a dozen languages. In his latest effort, *Bartleby y Compañía*, a writer convinced that modern works are vapid enters a crisis, strongly attracted to nothingness.

Montserrat Roig (1946–91) crammed a lot of writing (largely in Catalan), journalistic and fiction, into her short life. Her novels include *Ramon Adéu*, *El Temps de les Cireres* and *L'Hora Violeta*.

Manuel Vázquez Montalbán (born 1939) is one of the city's more prolific writers, best known for his Pepe Carvalho detective novel series.

Ana María Moix (born 1947) gained considerable acclaim in 1970 with her prize-winning *Julia*, but then fell silent until 1985 when she resurfaced with a collection of short stories, *Las Virtudes Peligrosas,* that take a caustic look at society.

Quim Monzó (born 1952) is a prolific writer of short stories, columns and essays (in Catalan). His wide-ranging work is marked by a mordant wit and an abiding interest in pornography. He revised the best of his stories and published them in one volume, *Vuitanta-sis Contes*, in 1999.

A promising talent is Carlos Castañer (born 1960). In his *Museo de la Soledad*, characters and stories come to melancholy life in this, the strangest of museums.

Theatre

Barcelona is possibly the most dynamic centre of theatre in Spain, although *madrileños* (citizens of Madrid) might contest this. Purely Catalan theatre was revived, amid the rhetoric of the Renaixença, in the late 19th century, with playwright and all-round Catalan nationalist Àngel Guimerà as its principal driving force.

Possibly one of the wackiest theatre companies is La Fura dels Baus. These guys turn theatre spaces (often warehouses) into a kind of participatory apocalypse – 60 minutes of at times spine-chilling performance. The audience becomes an integral part of the 'act', prodded and cajoled to contribute its own two cents' worth. The company grew

out of Barcelona's street-theatre culture in the late 1970s and, although it has grown in technical prowess, it has not abandoned the rough-and-ready edge of the street.

Tricicle is another big Barcelona name. It's a three-man mime team easily enjoyed by anyone – no need to understand Catalan. Els Comediants and La Cubana are two highly successful groups that also owe a lot to the impromptu world of street theatre.

A big name in Catalan theatre is – or was – Josep Maria Flotats who, after a long career in Paris, took control of the Teatre Nacional de Catalunya. Flotats fell out with the Generalitat in 1997 and bowed out of the Teatre Nacional. He moved to Madrid, where he declared in early 2000 that he now felt himself to be a *madrileño*.

A rising star of Barcelona theatre is director Roger Bernat (born 1968), an *enfant terrible* whose company General Elèctrica plays the main theatres but leaves the establishment perplexed with such coups as including a live sex scene in one work.

Music

Traditional It is hard to know into what category to put the medieval troubadours. In many respects the verses they sang (largely the plaintive cries of courtly love inspired by French traditions) represent some of the earliest medieval literature in Mediterranean Europe. Provençal and not Catalan, however, remained the universal language for a long time.

The strongest musical tradition to have survived to some degree in popular form in Catalunya is that of the *havaneres*, nostalgic songs and sea shanties brought back from Cuba by Catalans who lived, sailed and traded there. Even after Spain lost Cuba in 1898, the *havanera* tradition continued, especially in Barcelona and along the Catalan coast, as a melancholy memory of good times past (although they had not always been so great for the Cubans). Today the havaneres are enjoying something of a revival, and in some coastal towns you can turn up to listen to an evening's *cantada de havaneres*. Calella on the Costa Brava is particularly well known for this.

Baroque The Catalan Jordi Savall (born 1941) has assumed the task of rediscovering a Europe-wide heritage in music that predates the era of the classical greats. Born in Igualada, Savall studied at the conservatorium in Barcelona. He and his wife, the soprano Montserrat Figueras, have been largely responsible, along with musicians from other countries, for resuscitating the beauties of medieval, Renaissance and, above all, baroque music. In 1987 Savall founded La Capella Reial de Catalunya and two years later he formed the baroque orchestra, Le Concert des Nations.

Classical Spain's contribution to the world of classical music has been comparatively marginal, but Catalunya did produce a few exceptional composers.

Perhaps best known is Camprodon-born Isaac Albéniz (1860–1909), a gifted pianist who later turned his hand to composition. Among his best remembered works is the *Iberia* cycle.

Lleida's Enric Granados i Campina (1867–1916) came on to the scene in the early 20th century. Another fine pianist, he established Barcelona's conservatorium in 1901 and composed a great many pieces for piano, including *Danzas Españolas, Cantos de la Juventud* and *Goyescas.*

Other Catalan composers/musicians of some note include Eduard Toldrà and Frederic Mompou.

Opera Monsterrat Caballé is Barcelona's most successful voice. Born in Gràcia in 1933, the soprano made her debut in 1956 in Basel (Switzerland). Her home-town launch came four years later in the Gran Teatre del Liceu. In 1965 she performed at New York's Carnegie Hall to wild acclaim. She hasn't looked back and remains one of the world's top sopranos. Catalunya's other world-class opera star is the renowned tenor Josep (José) Carreras (born 1946).

Contemporary A good deal of Spain's most representative modern music has grown out of the lively Barcelona *movida*, that post-Franco outburst of activity and nightlife that filled the streets of Spain in the early 1980s.

For years a big rock drawcard was El Último de la Fila, a fine Barcelona duo that finally decided to pack it in in 1997. Milder and poppier are Los Fresones Rebeldes, a fresh-faced sextet and a light-hearted departure from the trend towards indie groups and techno blare.

Mojinos Escozíos tout themselves as 'fat, ugly and heavy to the death'. Although three of the five members are from Seville, the other two are Catalans and all live near Barcelona. They are the latest flavour in heavy rock, a genre that gets quite a following throughout Spain.

Rock Catalá (Catalan rock) is not essentially different from rock anywhere else, except that it is sung in Catalan by local bands that appeal to local tastes. Among the most popular bands are: Els Pets (one of the region's top acts), The Mad Makers, Ja T'ho Diré, Sopa de Cabra, Lax'n'Busto, Whiskyn's, Les Pellofes Radioactives, Fes-te Fotre, Glaucs, No Nem Bé, Dr Calypso, In Extremis (from Lleida), Obrint Pas, Baked Beans, Gore's Romance, Zea Mays and Antónia Font.

Lluís Llach is one of an older generation of singer-songwriters and probably the best-known name in Catalan pop. Gossos is a four-man band that specialises in folk-rock much along the lines of Crosby, Stills & Nash. Since August 1998 the annual Senglar Rock concert has been *the* date for Catalan rock music. It was held in Montblanc at the end of June in 2000, but dates and location can change, so keep your eyes peeled from about June on.

Dance
Contemporary Barcelona is the capital of contemporary dance in Spain. This is not necessarily saying much, as dance does not thrive here as in other European cities such as Paris, Brussels and even London.

Ramon Oller is one of the city's leading choreographers, working with one of the country's most solidly established companies, Metros. Its dance is rooted in comparatively formal technique. Four other

A Slow Number

The Catalan dance, par excellence, is the *sardana*; its roots lie in the far northern Empordà region of Catalunya. Compared with flamenco it is a sober sight indeed but is not unlike a lot of folk dances seen in various parts of the Mediterranean.

The dancers hold hands in a circle and wait for the 10 or so musicians to begin. The performance starts with the piping of the *flabiol*, a little wooden flute. When the other musicians join in, the dancers begin – a series of steps to the right, one back and then the same to the left. As the music 'heats up' the steps become more complex, the leaps are higher and the dancers lift their arms. Then they return to the initial steps and continue. If newcomers wish to join in, space is made for them as the dance continues and the whole thing proceeds in a more or less seamless fashion.

In Barcelona the best chance you have of seeing people dancing the sardana is at noon on Sunday in front of the Catedral. Other possibilities are at 6.30 pm on Saturday and 7 pm on Wednesday. In summer these times tend to change and, in August, about your only chance will be during one of the local festes (such as la Festa Major de Gràcia).

prominent companies worth keeping an eye out for are: Cesc Gelabert (run by the choreographer of the same name), Mudanzas (Àngels Margarit), Lanonima Imperial (Juan Carlos García) and Mal Pelo (Maria Muñoz and Pep Ramis). All four tend to work from a base of 'release technique', which favours 'natural' movement, working from the skeleton, over reliance on muscular power.

Cinema

In December 1896, the Cinématographe Lumière was installed in the Salón Fotográfico Napoleón and the first brief movies were shown to an appreciative audience. The French brothers Lumière were roundly congratulated in the Barcelona press for their success – the Catalan city was present at the earliest stages in the life of the 'seventh art'. Two years later, the first film theatre was opened on La Rambla.

In 1932, Francesc Macià, president of the Generalitat, opened Spain's first studios for making 'talkies' and a year later Metro Goldwyn Mayer had a dubbing studio in Barcelona. Prior to the civil war, *El Fava d'en Ramonet* was about the only cinematic hit in Catalan to make it to the screen.

In the wake of Franco's victory, pretty much all cinematic production happened in Madrid and was, in any case, a mix of propaganda and schmaltz. In 1952 a small group of Catalans made a film called *El Judes*, in Catalan, but it was banned.

In 1956, the so-called Escola de Barcelona began to produce experimental stuff, some of which did see the light of the day. Film-makers such as Vicente Aranda (born 1926) cut their teeth here. Aranda later gained fame for *Amantes* (1991), set in the Madrid of the 1950s and based on the real story of a love triangle that ends particularly badly. He followed it three years later with the steamy *La Pasión Turca*.

All in all, it has been slow going in the Catalan film world. Since Franco's death restrictions on theme or use of Catalan have disappeared, but the centre of Spanish cinema remains Madrid. Since even the European cinema heavyweights – such as Britain, France and Italy – have trouble keeping national cinema afloat in the face of Hollywood, it is hardly surprising that the Catalan industry has even greater problems, despite subsidies from the Generalitat.

Possibly the biggest name in Catalan film directing, at least for his abiding interest in the erotic, is José Juan Bigas Luna (born 1946). His *Angoixa* (Anxiety) was a worldwide success. He also directed the popular comedy *Jamón, Jamón* in 1992, his best effort in more than a decade.

Ventura Pons (born 1945) is a veteran of Catalan theatre and film-making. His *Morir (o No)*, made in 2000, follows seven stories that end in someone's death and then dovetails them into one tale in which none of the characters dies. He has churned out a feature film almost every year since he really got moving in 1989.

Pedro Almodóvar's Golden Globe award winning hit of 1999, *Todo Sobre Mi Madre* (All About My Mother) was partly shot in Barcelona (including around the Palau de la Música Catalana).

Daniel Calparsoro (born 1968) has tended to see the dark side in his flicks. His fourth and latest, *Asfalto*, looks at some less savoury aspects of life in the mean streets of Madrid. His other films have been equally violent and somewhat uneven, but there is promise. Actress Laura Mañá (born 1968) turned to directing and writing with her quirky 2000 debut, *Sexo por Compasión*, in which a well-intentioned woman sets about getting her husband back by sleeping with all the neighbours.

An up-and-coming actor is Sergi López (born 1965), whose latest success was a French movie, *Une Relation Pornographique* (2000), in which two people get together for sex and actually find lurve.

In 2000 Barcelona hosted the Goya awards, Spain's version of the Oscars, for the first time ever.

SOCIETY & CONDUCT

Catalans have a bit of a reputation for being reserved. That may or may not be true, but as a rule Barcelonins are tolerant and courteous.

No-one really expects you to speak Catalan, but if you can stumble along good-humouredly in Castilian in shops and other situations you'll generally meet with a friendly response.

Codes of good manners differ the world over, and what can sometimes seem brusque treatment to Anglos is not intended as anything of the sort. While the latter may be obsessed with 'please' and 'thank you', you'll find your average Barcelonins not overly fussed. Profusions of *'por favors'* (please) are not part of the local mindset. In bars and the like you are likely to hear the most respectable people simply say 'give me...' whatever it might be. But Catalans stand on ceremony in other ways. It is common to wish all and sundry *'bon dia/buenos días'* when entering a shop or bar and to say *'adéu/adiós'* on the way out. Not mandatory, but common.

Spaniards, in general, are individualistic and Catalans are not much of an exception to that rule. That is not to say they are lone wolves. Although not as party conscious as some of their more southern neighbours, Barcelonins love to hang out in bars and open-air cafes. Invitations to people's homes are more of an exception than the rule.

Dos & Don'ts

The standard form of greeting between men and women (even when meeting for the first time) and between women is a kiss on each cheek, right then left. Now, we're not talking about big sloppy ones – a light brushing of cheeks is perfectly sufficient. Men seem to be able to take or leave handshakes on informal occasions, but they are pretty much standard in a business context.

In some older bars it is quite the norm to chuck your rubbish – paper, toothpicks, cigarette butts and so on – on to the floor. At the end of the day it will all be swept up. This does not apply everywhere so don't start indulging your deeply buried urges to be a litterbug unless you are quite sure you are in a sufficiently grungy bar. A quick inspection of the floor and of other customers' behaviour should clue you in.

These days, on the beaches and in the swimming pools, you'll see just as many women with bikini tops off as on. It basically isn't a problem in Barcelona.

Treatment of Animals

Although bullfighting does not have the same appeal in Barcelona as elsewhere in Spain, it is still a popular sport. There is little doubting its cruelty and the subject can generate animated debate.

For the aficionados (enthusiasts) it is an art, a virtuoso display of courage that generally ends in the honourable death of the bull – a better fate than the abattoir they will tell you. Its opponents are simply sickened by the spectacle.

You can contact the organisations listed below for further information about bullfighting and suggested action:

People for the Ethical Treatment of Animals
UK (☎ 020-7388 4922, fax 7388 4925)
PO Box 3169, London NW1 2JF
USA (☎ 757-622-PETA, fax 622 1078)
501 Front St, Norfolk, VA 23510

World Society for the Protection of Animals
UK (☎ 020-7793 0540, fax 7793 0208)
2 Langley Lane, London SW8 1TJ
USA (☎ 617-522 7000, fax 522 7077)
PO Box 190 Boston, MA 02130
Canada (☎ 416-369 0044, fax 369 0147)
44 Victoria St, suite 1310, Toronto, M5C 1Y2

For more information about the bullfight, see Spectator Sports in the Entertainment chapter.

RELIGION

Barcelona, like the rest of Spain, is largely Catholic, at least in name. But a strong anarchist and socialist tradition, which historically has almost always meant anti-clericalism, has left an indelible mark here and many Barcelonins pay little more than lip service to their faith.

From the end of the 19th century through to the end of the Civil War, church-burning was a popular pastime. The two worst waves came in 1909 during the Setmana Tràgica and at the outbreak of the Civil War in 1936. Under Franco, Catholicism was again made a state religion and the Church played a preponderant role in society, although less markedly so in Barcelona where vast sections of the populace remained essentially 'red'.

Many Spanish theologians, much as their counterparts elsewhere in Europe and the USA has, have criticised the Church for its conservatism on issues such as sex, abortion and divorce, warning that it will lose even further ground with Spaniards if it does not 'modernise'.

LANGUAGE

Catalan and Spanish (the latter is more appropriately known as *castellano*, or Castilian) have equal legal status in Barcelona. Given the city's history of immigration from other parts of Spain, you'll probably hear the latter spoken as much as, if not more than, the former. This may change in the coming years but generally the foreigner will be well enough received just for trying their luck in Spanish. English is not as widely spoken as you might expect in such a city and French even less so, although among younger people you are likely to have more luck with the former. In some hotels and restaurants (even at budget level) you may also be able to make yourself understood. An effort on your part to come to grips with some of the basics of Catalan or Spanish will be a useful investment. To get you started, turn to the Language chapter.

Facts for the Visitor

WHEN TO GO

Spring and early summer is the best time to be in Barcelona. The weather is usually pleasantly warm, the number of other tourists manageable and the city humming. High summer (particularly mid-July to late August) is asphyxiating – locals get the hell out of the sticky summer heat and leave it to the *guiris* (foreigners).

September is not a bad month, when the city recovers its normal rhythms, the heat eases off and tourist numbers drop, but the weather can be dodgy. For *real* rain, hang about in October.

Winter is not especially distressing. Things are more subdued, but at least you can get around the place in peace. It can get quite nippy (you will want a room with heating), so come prepared.

ORIENTATION

Barcelona's coastline runs roughly from north-east to south-west and many streets are parallel or perpendicular to this.

Major arteries include: Gran Via de les Corts Catalanes, running parallel to the coast right across the city; Avinguda Meridiana, which cuts a (nearly) straight path north out of the city; Avinguda del Paral.lel (according to tradition, the road was built along parallel 41°, 44') and its continuation under other names, which would run perpendicular to the Meridiana if the two actually met; and Avinguda Diagonal, which cuts a swathe across the city from Pedralbes towards the coast.

The city is divided into 10 municipalities, which themselves are subdivided (by tradition if not officially) into *barris/barrios* (districts). The areas of most interest to visitors can be broken down thus:

La Rambla & Plaça de Catalunya

The focal axis of the city is La Rambla, a 1.25km boulevard running north-west and slightly uphill from Port Vell (the old harbour) to Plaça de Catalunya. The latter marks the boundary between the Ciutat Vella (old city) and the more recent parts farther inland.

Montjuïc & Tibidabo

Two good pointers to indicate which way you're facing are the hills of Montjuïc and Tibidabo. Montjuïc, the lower of the two, begins about 700m south-west of La Rambla. Tibidabo, is 6km north-west of the top of La Rambla. It's the high point of the range of wooded hills forming a backdrop to the whole city.

Ciutat Vella

The Ciutat Vella, a warren of narrow streets, centuries-old buildings and a lot of bottom-end and mid-range accommodation, spreads either side of La Rambla. Its heart is the lower half of the section east of La Rambla called the Barri Gòtic (Gothic quarter), which is where the medieval core of the city grew on the site of the old Roman settlement. West of La Rambla is the at times seedy El Raval, while north-east of the Barri Gòtic, across Via Laietana, is La Ribera.

Waterfront

Port Vell has an excellent modern aquarium and two marinas. At its north-eastern end is La Barceloneta, the old sailors' and fishermen's quarter, from where beaches and a pedestrian promenade stretch 1km north-east to the Port Olímpic, a harbour built for the 1992 Olympic Games.

L'Eixample

Plaça de Catalunya at the top of La Rambla marks the beginning of l'Eixample (el Ensanche in Spanish), the grid of straight streets into which Barcelona spread in the 19th century. This is where you'll find most of Barcelona's *Modernista* architecture – including La Sagrada Família – as well as its glossiest shops and many expensive hotels. The main avenues are Passeig de Gràcia and Rambla de Catalunya, running parallel to the north-west from Plaça de Catalunya. The part to the west of Passeig de Gràcia is known as L'Esquerra (the Left) de l'Eixample, while to the east it's La Dreta (the Right) de l'Eixample.

Gràcia

Beyond l'Eixample you're in the suburbs – some of which have plenty of character as they began life as villages outside the city. Gràcia, beyond the wide Avinguda Diagonal on the northern edge of central l'Eixample, is a net of narrow streets and small squares with a varied population. It can be a lively place to spend a Friday or Saturday night. Just north of Gràcia is Gaudí's Parc Güell.

Main Transport Terminals

The airport is 14km south-west of the centre at El Prat de Llobregat. The main train station is Estació Sants (Map 4), 2.5km west of La Rambla, on the western fringe of l'Eixample. The main bus station, Estació del Nord (Map 1), is 1.5km north-east of La Rambla (metro Arc de Triomf). See the Getting There & Away chapter also.

MAPS

Tourist offices hand out free city and transport maps that are OK, but better is Lonely Planet's *Barcelona City Map* (1:24,000 with a complete index of all streets and sights). If you can't find it, try the Michelin No 40 *Barcelona* map (950 ptas). You can buy it with a comprehensive street index (Michelin No 41), bringing the price to 1200 ptas. Plenty of stalls on La Rambla sell maps – but prices vary considerably.

If you intend to hang about for a while and want a handy map book, Editorial Pamias' *Guía Urbana Barcelona* (around 2000 ptas) is a compact and complete guide to city streets and is packed with information. Otherwise, the ringbound *Guía Urbana de Barcelona* published by GeoPlaneta is good and costs 1700 ptas.

TOURIST OFFICES
Local Tourist Offices

The Oficina d'Informació de Turisme de Barcelona (Map 6; ☎ 906 30 12 82 from within the country, ☎ 93 304 34 21 from abroad) at Plaça de Catalunya 17-S (underground) concentrates on city information and can help book accommodation. It opens 9 am to 9 pm daily.

In the *Ajuntament* (town hall; Map 6) on Plaça de Sant Jaume there is another information office. It opens 10 am to 8 pm Monday to Saturday, and until 2 pm on Sunday and holidays.

The regional tourist office (Map 2; ☎ 93 238 40 00) is located in the late-19th-century neo-classical Palau Robert, Passeig de Gràcia 107. It opens 10 am to 7 pm Monday to Saturday, 10 am to 2.30 pm Sunday. They have a host of material, audiovisual stuff, a bookshop and a branch of Turisme Juvenil de Catalunya (where you can get Euro<26 cards – see Student, Teacher & Youth Cards later in this chapter). By the way, if you are feeling hot and bothered, you can retire out the back to the lovely gardens.

Turisme de Barcelona in Estació Sants (Map 4) covers Barcelona only. It opens 8 am to 8 pm daily (it closes at 2 pm on weekends and holidays from October to May).

There's also a tourist office (☎ 93 478 05 65) in the airport's EU arrivals hall, open 9.30 am to 8 pm Monday to Saturday, 9.30 am to 3 pm Sunday (about a half-hour later in summer). They have information on all Catalunya. The office at the international arrivals hall (☎ 93 478 47 04) opens the same hours.

Another useful office for information on events (and tickets) is the Palau de la Virreina arts information office at La Rambla de Sant Josep 99 (Map 6; ☎ 93 301 77 75).

You can find out about accommodation on ☎ 93 304 32 32 or at www.deinfo.es/barcelona-on-line.

A couple of general information lines worth bearing in mind are ☎ 010 and ☎ 012. The first is for Barcelona and the second for all Catalunya (run by the Generalitat). You sometimes strike English speakers although for the most part operators are Catalan/Castilian bilingual. They can often answer quite obscure questions.

Finally there is a nationwide tourist information line in several languages, which might come in handy if you are calling from elsewhere in Spain. Call ☎ 901 30 06 00, 9 am to 6 pm daily, for basic information in Spanish, English and French.

Tourist Offices Abroad

Information on Barcelona is available from the following branches of the Oficina Española de Turismo abroad:

Belgium
(☎ 02-280 1926, fax 230 2147,
e bruselas@tourspain.es) Avenue des Arts 21, B-1040 Brussels
Web site: www.tourspain.be
Canada
(☎ 416-961 3131, fax 961 1992,
e toronto@tourspain.es) 2 Bloor St West, 34th floor, Toronto M4W 3E2
Web site: www.tourspain.toronto.on.ca
Denmark
(☎ 33 15 11 65, fax 33 15 83 65,
e copenhague@tourspain.es) NY Østergade 34, 1, DK-1101 Copenhagen
Web site: www spanien-turist.dk
France
(☎ 01 45 03 82 57, fax 01 45 03 82 51,
e paris@tourspain.es) 43, rue Decamps, 75784 Paris, Cedex 16
Web site: www.espagne.infotourisme.com
Germany
(☎ 030-882 6036, fax 882 6661,
e berlin@tourspain.es) Kurfürstendamm 180, D-10707 Berlin (also branches in Düsseldorf, Frankfurt am Main and Munich)
Italy
(☎ 06 678 31 06, fax 06 679 82 72,
e roma@tourspain.es) Via del Mortaro 19, interno 5, 00187 Rome
Japan
(☎ 03-34 32 61 41, e tokio@tourspain.es)
Daini Toranomon Denki Bldg 4f, 3-1-10 Toranomon, Minato-Ku
Netherlands
(☎ 070-346 5900, fax 364 9859,
e infolahaya@tourspain.es) Laan Van Meerdervoort 8a, 2517 The Hague
Web site: www.spaansverkeersburo.nl
Portugal
(☎ 21-357 1992, e lisboa@tourspain.es)
Avenida Sidónio Pais 28-3° Dto, 1050 Lisbon
UK
(☎ 09063-640630, brochure request ☎ 09001-669920 at 60p a minute, fax 7486 8034,

e londres@tourspain.es) 22–23 Manchester Square, London W1M 5AP
Web site: www.tourspain.co.uk
USA
(☎ 212-265 8822, fax 265 8864,
e oetny@tourspain.es) 666 Fifth Ave, 35th floor, New York, NY 10103 (also branches in Chicago, Los Angeles and Miami)
Web site: www okspain.org

TRAVEL AGENCIES

Barcelona is hardly one of Europe's discount flight capitals. That said, you can still find reasonable deals to main Western European destinations, and occasionally to the USA. You could start with the following agents, but there is no substitute for shopping around.

usit Unlimited (Map 5; ☎ 93 412 01 04), at Ronda de l'Universitat 16, sells youth and student air, train and bus tickets. It has a branch in the Turisme Juvenil de Catalunya office at Carrer de Rocafort 116–122 (Map 4; metro Rocafort). Another member of the growing usit group is Viatgi (Map 4; ☎ 93 317 50 98) at Ronda de l'Universitat 1.

Viajes Wasteels at Catalunya metro station (Map 5) has similar youth and student fares.

Halcón Viatges is a reliable chain of travel agents that sometimes has good deals. Its branch at Carrer de Pau Claris 108 (Map 2) is one of 28 around town. Their national phone reservation number is ☎ 902 30 06 00.

The Generalitat also operates a handful of tourist offices abroad, dedicated exclusively to Catalunya:

Belgium
(☎ 02-732 1260) Avenue des Cerisiers 15, Brussels
Sweden
(☎ 08-411 01 06) Kungsgatan 27, 4 TR, 11156 Stockholm
UK
(☎ 020-7583 8855) 3rd Floor, 17 Fleet St, London EC4Y 1AA

DOCUMENTS
Visas

Spain is one of 15 countries that have signed the Schengen Convention, an agreement whereby all EU member countries (except the UK and Ireland) plus Iceland

FACTS FOR THE VISITOR

and Norway have agreed to abolish checks at internal borders by the end of 2000.

The other EU countries are Austria, Belgium, Denmark, Finland, France, Germany, Greece, Italy, Luxembourg, the Netherlands, Portugal and Sweden. Legal residents of one Schengen country do not require a visa for another Schengen country. In addition, nationals of a number of other countries, including the UK, Canada, Ireland, Japan, New Zealand and Switzerland, do not require visas for tourist visits of up to 90 days to any Schengen country.

Various other nationals not covered by the Schengen exemption can also spend up to 90 days in Spain without a visa. These include Australian, Israeli and US citizens. However, all non-EU nationals entering Spain for any reason other than tourism (such as study or work) should contact a Spanish consulate as they may need a specific visa. If you are a citizen of a country not mentioned in this section, you should check with a Spanish consulate whether you need a visa.

The standard tourist visa issued by Spanish consulates is the Schengen visa, valid for up to 90 days. A Schengen visa issued by one Schengen country is generally valid for travel in all other Schengen countries. However, individual Schengen countries may impose additional restrictions on certain nationalities. Check before travelling.

Those needing a visa must apply *in person* at the consulate. Postal applications are not accepted. In the UK you will be required to produce a UK residence permit, proof of sufficient funds, an itinerary, return tickets and a letter of recommendation. Finally, the visa does *not* guarantee entry.

You can apply for no more than two visas in any 12-month period and they are not renewable once you are in Spain. Options include 30-day and 90-day single-entry visas (in London these cost UK£17.75 and UK£21.30, respectively), 90-day multiple-entry visas (UK£24.85), and various transit visas. Schengen visas are free for spouses and children of EU nationals.

Although we do not recommend it, you *could* avoid the visa if you are willing to gamble. Travelling from the UK by boat or train there is a chance your passport will not be checked on entering France or Belgium. From there you could travel overland with some hope (but no certainty) of not having your passport checked. Travelling by air you have no chance.

Visa Extensions & Residence Schengen visas cannot be extended. Nationals of EU countries, Norway and Iceland can virtually enter and leave Spain at will. Those wanting to stay in Spain longer than 90 days are supposed to apply during their first month for a resident's card *(tarjeta de residencia)*. This is a lengthy procedure.

People of other nationalities who want to stay in Spain longer than 90 days are also supposed to get a resident's card, and for them it's a truly nightmarish process, starting with a residence visa issued by a Spanish consulate in your country of residence. Start the process a long time in advance.

Travel Insurance

Medical costs might already be covered through reciprocal healthcare agreements (see Health later in this chapter) but you'll still need cover for theft or loss and for unexpected changes in travel plans (ticket cancellation etc). Check what's already covered by your local insurance policies and credit card: you might not need separate travel insurance. In most cases, however, this secondary type of cover is limited and its small print is laced with loopholes. For peace of mind, nothing beats straight travel insurance at the highest level you can afford.

Driving Licence & Permits

All EU member states' driving licences are recognised throughout the Union. If you have a licence from another country you should in theory obtain an International Driving Permit from your automobile association before leaving home. In practice your national licence will often suffice.

For information on other vehicle paperwork and insurance, see the Car & Motorcycle section in the Getting There & Away chapter.

Hostel Cards

A valid HI (Hostelling International) card or youth hostel card from your home country is required at most HI youth hostels in Spain, including those in Barcelona. If you don't have one, you can get an HI Card, valid until 31 December of the year you buy it, at most HI hostels in Spain. You pay in instalments of 300 ptas for each night you spend in a hostel, up to 1800 ptas. (People legally resident in Spain for at least a year can get a Spanish hostel card for 1000 ptas.)

The cards are also available from the Xarxa d'Albergs de Catalunya (☎ 93 483 83 63, fax 93 483 83 50), which is in the Turisme Juvenil de Catalunya office at Carrer de Rocafort 116–122 (Map 4; metro Rocafort).

Student, Teacher & Youth Cards

These cards can get you worthwhile discounts on travel and reduced prices at some museums, sights and entertainments.

The International Student Identity Card (ISIC), for full-time students, and the International Teacher Identity Card (ITIC), for full-time teachers and academics, are issued by more than 5000 organisations around the world. They include STA Travel, usit Campus, Council Travel and other well-known student travel agency chains. For more on some of these see the Getting There & Away chapter.

Anyone under 26 can get a GO25 card or a Euro<26 card. Both give similar discounts to the ISIC and are issued by most of the same organisations. The Euro<26 is known as the Under 26 Card in England and Wales and the Carnet Joven Europeo in Spain (or Carnet Jove in Catalunya). For information you can contact usit Campus (☎ 0870 240 1010), 52 Grosvenor Gardens, SW1W 0AG, or visit its Web site at www.usitcampus .co.uk. In Spain, the Euro<26 is issued by various youth organisations, including Barcelona's Turisme Juvenil de Catalunya office (see Hostel Cards above).

Copies

All important documents (passport data page and visa page, credit cards, travel insurance policy, air/bus/train tickets, driving licence etc) should be photocopied before you leave home. Leave one copy with someone at home and keep another with you, separate from the originals.

There is another option for storing details of your vital travel documents before you leave – Lonely Planet's on-line Travel Vault. Storing details of your important documents in the vault is safer than carrying photocopies. It's the best option if you travel in a country with easy Internet access. Your password-protected travel vault is accessible on-line at anytime. You can create your own travel vault for free at www.ekno .lonelyplanet.com.

EMBASSIES & CONSULATES

It's important to realise what your own embassy – the embassy of the country of which you are a citizen – can and can't do to help you if you get into trouble. Generally speaking, it won't be much help in emergencies if the trouble you're in is remotely your own fault.

Remember that you are bound by the laws of the country you are visiting. Your embassy will not be sympathetic if you end up in jail after committing a crime locally, even if such actions are legal in your own country.

In genuine emergencies you might get some assistance, but only if other channels have been exhausted. For example, if you need to get home urgently, a free ticket home is exceedingly unlikely – the embassy would expect you to have insurance. If you have all your money and documents stolen, it might assist with getting a new passport, but a loan for onward travel is out of the question.

Some embassies used to keep letters for travellers or have a small reading room with home newspapers, but these days the mail holding service has usually been stopped and even newspapers tend to be out of date.

Spanish Embassies & Consulates

Here is a list of Spanish embassies in a selection of countries throughout the world:

FACTS FOR THE VISITOR

Andorra (☎ 82 00 13) Carrer Prat de la Creu 34, Andorra la Vella

Australia (☎ 02-6273 3555, ⓔ embespau@ mail.mae.es) 15 Arkana St, Yarralumla, Canberra, ACT 2600
  Consulates: Brisbane (☎ 07-3221 8571)
  Melbourne (☎ 03-9347 1966)
  Perth (☎ 09-9322 4522)
  Sydney (☎ 02-9261 2433)

Canada (☎ 613-747 2252, ⓔ spain@ docuweb.ca) 74 Stanley Avenue, Ottawa, Ontario K1M 1P4
  Consulates: Toronto (☎ 416-977 1661)
  Montreal (☎ 514-935 5235)

France (☎ 01 44 43 18 00, ⓔ ambespfr@ mail.mae.es) 22, avenue Marceau, 75008 Paris, Cedex 08

Germany (☎ 030-261 60 81, ⓔ embesde@ mail.mae.es) Lichtensteinallee 1, 10787 Berlin
  Consulates: Düsseldorf (☎ 0211-43 90 80)
  Frankfurt am Main (☎ 069-959 16 60)
  Munich (☎ 089-98 50 27)

Ireland (☎ 01-269 1640) 17A Merlyn Park, Balls Bridge, Dublin 4

Japan (☎ 03-35 83 85 33, ⓔ embesjpj@ mail.mae.es) 1-3-29 Roppongi Minato-ku, Tokyo 106

Morocco (☎ 07-26 80 00, ⓔ embesjpj@ mail.mae.es) 3 Zankat Madnine, Rabat
  Consulates: Rabat (☎ 07-70 41 47)
  Casablanca (☎ 02-22 07 52)
  Tangier (☎ 09-93 70 00)

Netherlands (☎ 070-364 38 14, ⓔ embespnl@ mail.mae.es) Lange Voorhout 50, 2514 EG The Hague

New Zealand
  See Australia

Portugal (☎ 21-347 2381, ⓔ embesppt@ mail.mae.es) Rua do Salitre 1, 1250 Lisbon

UK (☎ 020-7235 5555, ⓔ espemblon@ espemblon.freeserve.co.uk) 39 Chesham Place, London SW1X 8SB
  Consulates: London (☎ 020-7589 8989)
  Manchester (☎ 0161-236 1233)
  Edinburgh (☎ 0131-220 18 43)

USA (☎ 202-452 0100) 2375 Pennsylvania Ave NW, Washington, DC 20037
  Consulates: Boston (☎ 617-536 2506)
  Chicago (☎ 312-782 4588)
  Houston (☎ 713-783 6200)
  Los Angeles (☎ 213-938 0158)
  Miami (☎ 305-446 5511)
  New Orleans (☎ 504-525 4951)
  New York (☎ 212-355 4080)
  San Francisco (☎ 415-922 2995)

Consulates in Barcelona

Most countries have diplomatic representation in Spain, but all the embassies are in the capital, Madrid. Consulates in Barcelona, including the following, are generally open 9 or 10 am to 1 or 2 pm, Monday to Friday. You can find them listed in the phone book under Consulat/Consulado.

Australia (Map 3; ☎ 93 330 94 96) 9th floor, Gran Via de Carles III 98

Belgium (Map 2; ☎ 93 467 70 80) Carrer de la Diputació 303

Canada (Map 2; ☎ 93 215 07 04) Passeig de Gràcia 77

Denmark (Map 4; ☎ 93 488 02 22) Rambla de Catalunya 33

France (Map 5; ☎ 93 270 30 00) Ronda de l'Universitat 22B 4rt

Germany (Map 2; ☎ 93 292 10 00) Passeig de Gràcia 111

Italy (Map 2; ☎ 93 487 00 02) Carrer de Mallorca 270

Japan (Map 3; ☎ 93 280 34 33) Avinguda Diagonal 662–664

Netherlands (Map 3; ☎ 93 410 62 10) Avinguda Diagonal 601

Sweden (Map 2; ☎ 93 488 25 01) Carrer de Mallorca 279

Switzerland (Map 3; ☎ 93 330 92 11) Gran Via de Carles III 94

UK (Map 3; ☎ 93 419 90 44) Avinguda Diagonal 477

USA (Map 1; ☎ 93 280 02 95) Passeig de la Reina Elisenda de Montcada 23–25

Embassies in Madrid

Embassies (*embajadas* in the phone book) in Madrid include:

Australia (☎ 91 441 93 00) Plaza del Descubridor Diego de Ordás 3–2, Edificio Santa Engrácia 120

Canada (☎ 91 431 45 56) Calle de Núñez de Balboa 35

France (☎ 91 310 11 12) Calle del Marquès Ensenada 10

Germany (☎ 91 557 90 00) Calle de Fortuny 8

Ireland (☎ 91 436 40 95) Paseo de la Castellana 46

Morocco (☎ 91 563 79 28) Calle de Serrano 179
  Consulate: (☎ 91 561 21 45) Calle de Leizaran 31

Netherlands (☎ 91 350 32 36) Avenida del Comandante Franco 32

New Zealand (☎ 91 523 02 26 or ☎ 91 531 09 97) Plaza de la Lealtad 2

Portugal (☎ 91 561 78 00) Calle del Pinar 1
  Consulate: (☎ 91 577 35 38) Calle Lagasca 88

Tunisia (☎ 91 447 35 16) Plaza de Alonso Martínez 3

UK (☎ 91 308 06 18) Calle de Fernando el Santo 16
  Consulate: (☎ 91 308 53 00) Calle del Marquès Ensenada 16

USA (☎ 91 577 40 00) Calle de Serrano 75

CUSTOMS

People entering Spain from outside the EU are allowed to bring in duty-free one bottle of spirits, one bottle of wine, 50ml of perfume and 200 cigarettes.

Duty-free allowances for travel between EU countries were abolished in 1999. For *duty-paid* items bought at normal shops in one EU country and taken into another, the allowances are 90L of wine, 10L of spirits, unlimited quantities of perfume and 800 cigarettes. VAT-free shopping *is* available in the duty-free shops at airports for people travelling between EU countries.

MONEY

A combination of travellers cheques and credit or cash cards is the best way to carry your money.

Introducing the Euro

On 1 January 1999 a new currency, the euro (€), was introduced in Europe. Along with national border controls, the currencies of various EU members are being phased out. Not all EU members have adopted the euro. Denmark, Sweden and the UK all rejected or postponed participation. The 12 countries participating from the start are: Austria, Belgium, Finland, France, Germany, Greece, Ireland, Italy, Luxembourg, the Netherlands, Portugal and Spain.

In January 1999 exchange rates of the participating countries were fixed to the euro (€1 equals 166.386 ptas). On 1 January 2002 euro banknotes and coins will be introduced. They will circulate alongside the local currency for two months, after which local currencies in the 12 countries will be withdrawn. Only euro notes and coins will remain in circulation as legal tender.

There will be seven euro notes. They come in denominations of €500, €200, €100, €50, €20, €10 and €5, in different colours and sizes. The eight euro coins will be in denominations of €2 and €1, then 50, 20, 10, five, two and one cents.

On the reverse side of the coins each participating state will be able to decorate the coins with their own designs, but all euro coins can be used anywhere that accepts euros.

Once euro cash is in circulation, travellers should check bills carefully to make sure that the correct conversion rate from local currency is applied. The most confusing period will probably be between January 2002 and March 2002 when there will be two sets of notes and coins.

The euro should eventually make things easier for the traveller. Prices in the countries of what has been dubbed Euroland will be directly comparable, avoiding all those tedious calculations. And once euro notes and coins are issued, you won't need to change money at all when travelling within Euroland.

Currency

Until the euro notes and coins are in circulation, Spain's currency will remain the peseta (pta). It comes in coins of one (increasingly rare), five, 10, 25, 50, 100, 200 and 500 ptas, and notes of 1000, 2000, 5000 and 10,000 ptas.

A five ptas coin is widely known as a *duro* and it's fairly common for small sums to be quoted in duros: *dos duros* for 10 ptas, *cinco duros* for 25 ptas, even *veinte duros* for 100 ptas.

Exchange Rates

country	unit		pesetas/euros
Australia	A$1	=	102 ptas/€0.61
Canada	C$1	=	122 ptas/€0.74
France	1FF	=	25 ptas/€0.15
Germany	DM1	=	85 ptas/€0.51
Italy	L1000	=	86 ptas/€0.52
Japan	¥100	=	170 ptas/€1.02
New Zealand	NZ$1	=	79 ptas/€0.47
UK	UK£1	=	273 ptas/€1.64
USA	US$1	=	189 ptas/€1.14

euro currency converter €1 = 166 ptas

FACTS FOR THE VISITOR

Exchanging Money

You can change cash or travellers cheques at virtually any bank or exchange office, at bus and railway stations and at the airport. The main-road border crossings also usually have exchange facilities. Banks tend to offer the best rates, with minor differences between them. Many banks have ATMs (automated teller machines), known as *caixers/cajeros* in Catalan/Spanish.

Barcelona is crawling with banks, including several around Plaça de Catalunya and more on La Rambla.

Exchange offices (you'll see many along La Rambla and elsewhere in central Barcelona), usually indicated by the word *canvi/cambio* (exchange), generally offer longer opening hours and quicker service than banks, but often offer poorer exchange rates. American Express can be reliable, but in any case you should always shop around.

Travellers cheques usually get a better exchange rate than cash but often attract higher commissions than cash exchange.

Wherever you change money, ask about commissions first and confirm that the exchange rates are as posted.

Commissions vary from bank to bank, may be different for travellers cheques and cash, and may depend on how many cheques, or how much in total, you're cashing. A typical commission is 3%, with a minimum of 300 ptas to 500 ptas, but there are places with a minimum commission of 1000 ptas or even 2000 ptas. Places that advertise 'no commission' may offer poor exchange rates.

Remember that there should be no commission payable on exchange between currencies that have signed up for the euro, or for changing euro travellers cheques into cash pesetas. You can be sure of this being the case if you change at the Banco de España, Plaça de Catalunya 17–18 (Map 6), where you can change up to €2000 (about 332,000 ptas) per person per day.

American Express (Map 2; ☎ 93 415 23 71 or ☎ 93 217 00 70) at Passeig de Gràcia 101 (the entrance is on Carrer del Rosselló) has a machine giving cash on American Express cards. The office opens 9.30 am to 6 pm Monday to Friday, 10 am to noon on Saturday. There is another branch on La Rambla dels Caputxins 74 (Map 6), which opens 9 am to midnight daily April to September. The rest of the year it opens 9 am to 8.30 pm Monday to Friday, 10 am to 7 pm on Saturday (closed 2 to 3 pm for lunch).

Cash Don't bring wads of cash from home (travellers cheques and plastic are safer). If you wander around with pounds and dollars in your pockets you are inviting light fingers to make you instantly poor. It is, however, an idea to keep an emergency stash separate from other valuables in case you should lose travellers cheques and credit cards.

You will, of course, need pesetas in cash for many day-to-day transactions (many small pensiones, eateries and shops take cash only). Try not to carry around more than you need at any one time.

Travellers Cheques These protect your money because they can be replaced if they are lost or stolen. They can be cashed at most banks and exchange offices. American Express and Thomas Cook are widely accepted brands. For American Express travellers cheque refunds you can call ☎ 900 99 44 26 from anywhere in Spain.

It doesn't really matter whether your cheques are denominated in pesetas or in the currency of the country you buy them in: Spanish exchange outlets will change most non-obscure currencies. Get most of your cheques in fairly large denominations (the equivalent of 10,000 ptas or more) to save on any per-cheque commission charges.

It's vital to keep your initial receipt and a record of your cheque numbers and the ones you have used, separate from the cheques themselves.

Take along your passport when you go to cash travellers cheques.

Credit/Debit Cards You can use plastic to pay for many purchases (including meals and rooms at many establishments, especially from the middle price range up, and long-distance trains), and you can use it to withdraw cash pesetas from banks and ATMs. Among the most widely usable cards are Visa, MasterCard, Eurocard, American Express, Cirrus, Plus, Diners Club and JCB.

On the exchange rate front you also generally get a better deal than with cash and cheques, even taking into account any charges levied on foreign transactions and cash advances (usually around 1.5%, but sometimes minimum charges per withdrawal apply).

A high proportion of Spanish banks, even in small towns and villages, have an ATM that will dispense cash pesetas at any time (and no queues!) if you have the right piece of plastic to slot into it. Some stop accepting foreign cards at midnight.

Check with your card's issuer before leaving home on: how widely usable your card will be, how to report and replace a lost card, your withdrawal/spending limits, and whether your personal identification number (PIN) will be acceptable (some European ATMs don't accept PINs of more than four digits).

American Express are among the easiest cards to replace – you can call ☎ 902 37 56 37 or ☎ 91 572 03 03 (in Madrid) at any time. Always report a lost card straight away: for Visa cards call ☎ 900 97 44 45, for MasterCard/EuroCard ☎ 900 97 12 31, for Diners Club ☎ 91 547 40 00 (Madrid).

TravelMoney Visa TravelMoney comes in the form of a prepaid disposable credit card you can buy from selected banks or travel agencies for amounts from UK£100 to UK£5000. It works for ATM withdrawals wherever the Visa sign is displayed. Inquire at Thomas Cook (☎ 01733-318900 in the UK) or call Visa before you travel.

International Transfers To have money transferred from another country, you need to organise someone to send it to you (through a bank there or a money-transfer service such as Western Union or Money-Gram) and a bank (or Western Union or MoneyGram office) in Barcelona at which

to collect it. If there's money in your bank account back at home, you may be able to instruct the bank yourself.

For information on Western Union services and branches, call ☎ 900 63 36 33 free from anywhere in Spain. For MoneyGram call ☎ 900 20 10 10.

A bank-to-bank telegraphic transfer typically costs the equivalent of about 3000 ptas or 4000 ptas and should take about a week. Western Union and MoneyGram can supposedly hand money over to the recipient within 10 minutes of it being sent. The sender pays a fee in proportion to the amount sent.

It's also possible to have money sent through American Express.

Security
Keep only a limited amount of cash and the bulk of your money in more easily replaceable forms such as travellers cheques or plastic. If your accommodation has a safe, use it. If you have to leave money in your room, divide it into several stashes and hide them in different places.

For carrying money on the street the safest thing is a shoulder wallet or under-the-clothes money belt. An external money belt attracts rather than deflects attention from your valuables.

Barcelona has been ranked Europe's worst city for credit card theft (the writer is one of the unhappy victims!) so pay attention!

Costs
As Spain's second city, Barcelona is expensive by local standards, but northern Europeans generally find it quite reasonable. Travellers from beyond the EU (such as the USA and Australia) tend to find anywhere in Europe pricey. Costs of accommodation, eating out and transport are lower than in Britain or France. If you are frugal, it's just about possible to scrape by on 4000 ptas to 5000 ptas per day. This would involve staying in the cheapest possible accommodation, not eating in restaurants or going to museums or bars, and not moving around too much.

euro currency converter €1 = 166 ptas

A more comfortable budget would be 7000 ptas per day. This could allow you around 2500 ptas for accommodation; 700 ptas for breakfast (coffee, juice and a pastry); 1000 ptas to 1400 ptas for a set lunch; 300 ptas for public transport (two metro or bus rides); 1000 ptas for museums; and 1000 ptas for a simple dinner, with maybe a bit over for a drink or two.

With 25,000 ptas per day or more you can stay in excellent accommodation, splurge in Barcelona's better restaurants and even hire a car for a few days' touring outside town.

Ways to Save Two people can travel more cheaply (per person) than one by sharing rooms. You'll also save money by avoiding the peak tourist seasons (Christmas, Easter, summer), when room prices can go up. A student or youth card, or a document such as a passport proving you're at least over 60, brings worthwhile savings on some travel costs and admission to some museums and sights (see Documents earlier in this chapter). Museums and sights have free days now and then.

Prolific letter-writers can save a few pesetas on long-distance mail by sending aerograms instead of standard letters or postcards (this does not apply to letters under 20g posted to European countries).

Tipping & Bargaining

In restaurants, the law requires that menu prices include service charges, and tipping is a matter of personal choice – most people leave some small change if they're satisfied and 5% is usually plenty. It's common to leave small change at bar and cafe tables. Hotel porters will generally be happy with 200 ptas and most won't turn their noses up at 100 ptas.

In some pensiones and hotels it is worth asking about discounts for prolonged stays.

Taxes & Refunds

Value-added tax (VAT) is known as IVA ('**ee**-ba', *impuesto sobre el valor añadido*). On accommodation and restaurant prices, IVA is 7% and is sometimes included in quoted prices. On retail goods IVA is 16%. On vehicle hire it seems to fluctuate between 7% and 16%. To check whether a price includes IVA, you can ask: '*¿Está incluido el IVA?*' ('Is IVA included?')

Visitors are entitled to a refund of the 16% IVA on purchases costing more than 15,000 ptas, from any shop, if they take the goods out of the EU within three months. Ask the shop for a Cashback refund form showing the price and IVA paid for each item and identifying the vendor and purchaser. Then present the form to the customs booth for IVA refunds when you leave Spain (or elsewhere from the EU). You will need your passport and boarding card that shows you are leaving the EU. The officer will stamp the invoice and you hand it in at a bank at the departure point for the reimbursement. At Barcelona airport, look for the La Caixa bank in Terminal B, which hosts the Cashback refund desk. Otherwise you can use the envelope provided to have the tax paid back to your credit card or by cheque.

POST & COMMUNICATIONS
Post

Stamps are sold at most *estancs/estancos* (tobacconist shops with 'Tabacs/Tabacos' in yellow letters on a maroon background), as well as at *Correus i Telègrafs/Correos y Telégrafos* (post offices).

The main post office (Map 6; ☎ 902 19 71 97) is on Plaça d'Antoni López opposite the north-eastern end of Port Vell. It opens for stamp sales, poste restante (windows No 7 and 8) and information 8 am to 9.30 pm Monday to Saturday.

The post office also has a public fax service, as do many shops and offices around the city.

Another useful post office is at Carrer d'Aragó 282 (Map 2), just off Passeig de Gràcia, open 8.30 am to 8.30 pm Monday to Friday, 9.30 am to 1 pm Saturday. Other district offices tend to open 8 am to 2 pm Monday to Friday only.

Rates A postcard or letter weighing up to 20g costs 70 ptas to other European countries, 115 ptas to North America and

Getting Addressed

Just because you have an address in your hot sweaty palm doesn't mean you will have no trouble finding what you are after. If the pension you are looking for is at C/ de Montcada 23, 3°D Int, just off Av Marqués, you could be forgiven for scratching your head a little. Abbreviations contain a lot of information, and in Barcelona things are made worse by the fact that some people may give you the Catalan version of an address while others may give you the Castilian version. Here are some common abbreviations:

Av or Avda	Avinguda/Avenida
Bda	Baixada/Bajada
C/	Carrer/Calle
Cí or C°	Camí/Camino
Ctra, Ca or Cª	Carretera
Cró/Cjón	Carreró/Callejón
Gta	Glorieta (major roundabout)
Pg or P°	Passeig/Paseo
Ptge/Pje	Passatge/Pasaje
Plc/Plz	Placeta/Plazuela
Pl, Pza or Pª	Plaça/Plaza
Pt or Pte	Pont/Puente
Rbla	Rambla
Rda	Ronda
s/n	sense numeració/ sin número (without number)
Tr or Trav	Travessera
Trv	Travessia/Travesía
Urb	Urbanització/Urbanización

MICK WELDON

The following are used where there are several flats, *hostales*, offices etc in one building. They're often used in conjunction, eg 2°C or 3°I Int:

Ent	Entresuelo (ground floor)
Pr	Principal (what Brits & Co would consider the 1st floor)
1°	1st floor (2nd floor to Brits & Co)
2°	2nd floor (3rd floor to Brits & Co)
C	centre/centro (middle)
D	dreta/derecha (right-hand side)
Esq, I or Izq	esquerra/izquierda (left-hand side)
Int	interior (a flat or office too far inside the building to look onto any street – usually has windows onto an interior patio or shaft – the opposite is Ext, exterior)

If someone's address is Apartado de Correos 206 (which can be shortened to Apdo de Correos 206 or even Apdo 206), don't bother tramping the streets in search of it – it is a post office box.

Street names often get short shrift too. Carrer de Madrid (literally 'Street of Madrid') will often appear simply as Carrer Madrid. In spoken exchanges the word Carrer is often dropped. Thus Carrer del Comte d'Urgell will be referred to simply as Comte d'Urgell.

185 ptas to Australasia or Asia. Three A4 sheets in an air-mail envelope weigh between 15g and 20g. An aerogram costs 85 ptas to anywhere in the world.

Certificado (registered mail) costs an extra 175 ptas for international mail. *Urgente* service, which means your letter may arrive two or three days quicker, costs an extra 230 ptas for international mail. You can send mail both urgente and certificado (which costs 240 ptas when added to urgente).

A day or two quicker than urgente service – but a lot more expensive – is Postal Exprés, sometimes called Express Mail Service (EMS). This uses courier companies for international deliveries. Packages weighing up to 1kg cost 4100 ptas to anywhere in Europe, 7000 ptas to North America and 8000 ptas to Australia or New Zealand.

Sending Mail It's quite safe to post your mail in the yellow street postboxes *(bústies/ buzones)* as well as at post offices. Ordinary mail to other Western European countries normally takes up to a week; to North America up to 10 days; to Australia or New Zealand up to two weeks.

Receiving Mail Delivery times are similar to those for outbound mail. Using the Spanish five-digit postcode (which goes *before* the name of the city) will help speed up the process.

Poste restante mail can be addressed to you at *lista de correos*. It will be delivered to the main post office unless another one is specified. Take your passport when you go to pick up mail. A letter addressed to poste restante in central Barcelona should look like this:

> Jenny JONES
> Lista de Correos
> 08080 Barcelona
> Spain

American Express card or travellers cheque holders can use the free client mail-holding service at its main office in Barcelona (see Money above).

Couriers Most international courier services have reps in Barcelona. United Parcel Service (UPS; ☎ 900 10 24 10), for instance, has an office on the corner of Avinguda Diagonal and Carrer de Fra Luis de Granada (Map 3). DHL (☎ 902 12 24 24) has an office out at Hospitalet de Llobregat.

Telephone

The ubiquitous blue payphones are easy to use for international and domestic calls. They accept coins, phonecards issued by the national phone company Telefónica *(tarjetas telefónicas)* and, in some cases, various credit cards. Tarjetas telefónicas come in 1000 ptas and 2000 ptas denominations (the latter usually have 2100 ptas worth of call time as an enticement) and, like postage stamps, are sold at post offices and *estancs/estancos*.

Public phones inside bars and cafes, and phones in hotel rooms, are nearly always a good deal more expensive than street pay phones.

There are telephone and fax offices at Estació Sants (open 8.30 am to 9.30 pm daily except Sunday) and the Estació del Nord bus station.

Costs As elsewhere in Europe, the cost of making a phonecall is slowly falling in Spain. Within Spain you can make three types of call: metropolitana (local), provincial (a call within the same province) and interprovincial (national). Note that calls from payphones cost about 35% more than from private phones.

The cost of a call depends on when you make it. Three cost bands operate. Punta is the dearest and runs from 8 am to 5 pm Monday to Friday and from 8 am to 2 pm on Saturday. Normal operates from 5 to 10 pm Monday to Friday. The rest of the time is Reducida rate, the cheapest band.

A three-minute pay-phone call costs around 25 ptas within your local area, 65 ptas to other places in the same province and 110 ptas to other Spanish provinces.

For international calls, two bands operate, Normal and Reducida – the latter is the same as for national calls. A three-minute

Mobile Phones

Spain uses GSM 900/1800, compatible with the rest of Europe and Australia but not with the North American GSM 1900 or the totally different system in Japan (although some North Americans have GSM 1900/900 phones that do work here). If you have a GSM phone, check with your service provider about using it in Spain, and beware of calls being routed internationally (very expensive for a 'local' call).

It is possible to rent phones in Spain, but hardly worth it. You can buy decent phones that operate with prepaid cards for about 10,000 ptas, with 4000 ptas (sometimes more) of calls thrown in.

pay-phone call at standard rate to Australia will cost 820 ptas per minute. To the USA you pay 280 ptas. Calls to the rest of Europe cost 230 ptas for about three minutes.

Calls to Spanish numbers starting ☎ 900 are free. Calls to numbers starting ☎ 902 cost around 75 ptas for three minutes. Calls to mobile phones – numbers starting with 6 – cost 230 ptas for three minutes.

Cut Rate Phonecards If you're arriving from the USA or the UK, you are probably already acquainted with the idea of buying cut-price phone cards. You buy the card, dial a toll-free number and then follow the instructions – they can bring savings on international calls if you are calling from a payphone. Compare rates (where possible before buying). Cheap call centres are also springing up across town, especially in areas of heavy migrant population like El Raval. Some are *not* a good deal, so check rates. The one on the corner of Carrer de la Riera Alta and Carrer de la Lluna is good (Map 6).

eKno Communication Service Lonely Planet's eKno global communication service provides low-cost international calls – for local calls you're usually better off with a local phonecard. eKno also offers free messaging services, email, travel information and an on-line travel vault, where you can securely store all your important documents. You can join on-line at www.ekno.lonelyplanet.com, where you will find the local access numbers for the 24-hour customer-service centre.

Once you have joined, always check the eKno Web site for the latest access numbers for each country and updates on new features.

Domestic Calls There are no area codes in Spain. All numbers have nine digits and you just dial that nine-digit number. Older signs still give the first two or three digits as an area code (the 93 with which all Barcelona numbers start was, until early 1998, a two-digit area code).

Dial ☎ 1009 to speak to a domestic operator, including for a domestic reverse-charge (collect) call *(una llamada por cobro revertido)*. For directory inquiries dial ☎ 1003; calls cost about 60 ptas from a payphone.

International Calls The access code for international calls is ☎ 00. To make an international call dial the access code, wait for a new dialling tone, then dial the country code, area code and number you want.

International collect calls are simple: dial ☎ 900 followed by a code for the country you're calling:

Australia	99 00 61
Belgium	99 00 32
Canada	99 00 15
Denmark	99 00 45
France	99 00 33
Germany	99 00 49
Ireland	99 03 53
Israel	99 09 72
Italy	99 03 91
Japan	98 09 81; 98 08 11; 98 08 12
Netherlands	99 00 31
New Zealand	99 00 64
Portugal	99 03 51
UK	99 00 44 for BT; 99 09 44 for Cable & Wireless
USA	99 00 11 for AT&T; 99 00 13 for Sprint; 99 00 14 for MCI; 99 00 17 for Worldcom

euro currency converter €1 = 166 ptas

FACTS FOR THE VISITOR

Codes for other countries are sometimes posted up in pay phones. You'll get straight through to an operator in the country you're calling. The same numbers can be used with direct-dial calling cards.

If for some reason the above information doesn't work for you, in most places you can get an English-speaking Spanish international operator on ☎ 1008 (for calls within Europe) or ☎ 1005 (rest of the world).

For international directory inquiries dial ☎ 025.

Calling Barcelona from Abroad Spain's country code is ☎ 34. Follow this with the full nine-digit number you are calling.

Fax

Most main post offices have a fax service: sending one page costs about 350 ptas within Spain, 1115 ptas to elsewhere in Europe and 2100 ptas to 2500 ptas to other countries. However, you'll often find cheaper rates at shops or offices with 'Fax Público' signs.

Email & Internet Access

Travelling with a portable computer is a great way to stay in touch with life back home, but unless you know what you're doing it's fraught with potential problems. If you plan to carry your notebook or palmtop computer invest in a universal AC adapter, which will enable you to plug in your computer anywhere without frying the innards. You'll also need a plug adapter for Spain – the standard European two round pin variety – this is easier to buy before you leave home.

Also, your PC-card modem may or may not work once you leave your home country – and you won't know for sure until you try. The safest option is to buy a reputable 'global' modem before you leave home, or buy a local PC-card modem if you're spending an extended time in Spain.

Spanish phone sockets have mostly been standardised to the US RJ-11 type. For more information on travelling with a portable computer, see www.teleadapt.com or www.warrior.com.

Major Internet service providers (ISPs) such as AOL (www.aol.com), CompuServe (www.compuserve.com) and AT&T Business Internet Services (www.attbusiness .net) have dial-in nodes throughout Europe, including in the major Spanish cities. It's best to download a list of the dial-in numbers before you leave home.

If you access your Internet email account at home through a smaller ISP or your office or school network, your best option is either to open an account with a global ISP, like those mentioned above, or to rely on cybercafes and other public access points to collect your mail.

If you do intend to rely on cybercafes, you'll need three pieces of information to access your Internet mail account: your incoming (POP or IMAP) mail server name, your account name and your password. Your ISP or network supervisor will be able to give you this information, which should enable you to access your Internet mail account from any net-connected machine in the world, provided it runs some kind of email software. It pays to become familiar with the process for doing this before you leave home. A final option to collect mail through cybercafes is to open a free Web-based email account such as HotMail (www.hotmail.com) or Yahoo! Mail (mail .yahoo.com). You can then access your mail from anywhere in the world from any net-connected machine running a standard Web browser.

You might consider opening a similar account with eKno, which provides free email and the ability to autoforward emails to other accounts. See eKno Communication Service under Telephone above.

Cybercafes Dozens of places, ranging from cafes to computer stores, offer Internet access in Barcelona (they all seem to close on Sundays). Some options include:

easyEverything
Ronda de l'Universitat 35 (Map 5). With 300 terminals and some ridiculous offers – such as six hours on-line for 200 ptas if you start between 6 am and 9 am (but more like 45 minutes

at most other times), this place is run by the Greek businessman who set up the UK-based budget airline easyJet. It opens 24 hours and you can fuel up on coffee and donuts.

Conéctate

(Map 2; ☎ 93 467 04 43) Carrer de Pau Claris. This is a similar place, also open 24 hours and providing net time at a flat rate of 200 ptas per hour.

El Café de Internet

(Map 2; ☎ 93 302 11 54, **e** cafe@cafeinternet .es) Gran Via de les Corts Catalanes 656 (see also Places to Eat – l'Eixample). You can go on-line for 600 ptas per half-hour (or 800 ptas an hour for students).

Cybermundo

(Map 5; ☎ 93 317 71 42) Carrer Bergara 3. It opens 9 am to midnight daily. You pay 790 ptas an hour, or 400 ptas before 4 pm.

Café Insòlit

(Map 5; ☎ 93 225 81 78, **e** bar.internet@insolit .es), located in the waterfront Maremàgnum shopping complex. They are open to midnight most nights, except Friday and Saturday, when they are still going at 5 am. Going on-line costs 1000 ptas an hour.

Café Interlight

(Map 2; ☎ 93 301 11 80) Carrer de Pau Claris 106. They charge 700 ptas an hour and 400 ptas per half-hour.

Pere Noguera Ciberclub Internet

(Map 5; ☎ 93 442 11 04) Carrer de Sant Pau 124.

Cyber Play

(Map 2; ☎ 93 454 02 31) Carrer de Mallorca 204.

Inet.center

(Map 6; ☎ 93 268 73 55) Plaça de Ramon Berenguer el Gran 2. It opens 10.30 am to 9 pm. They have a branch at Carrer de Sardenya 306 (Map 2).

INTERNET RESOURCES

The World Wide Web is a rich resource for travellers. You can research your trip, hunt down bargain air fares, book hotels, check on weather conditions or chat with locals and other travellers about the best places to visit (or avoid!).

There's no better place to start your Web explorations than the Lonely Planet Web site (www.lonelyplanet.com). Here you'll find succinct summaries on travelling to most places on earth, postcards from other travellers and the Thorn Tree bulletin board,

where you can ask questions before you go or dispense advice when you get back. You can also find travel news and updates to many of our most popular guidebooks, and the sub-WWWay section links you to the most useful travel resources elsewhere on the Web.

Many useful sites are multilingual (eg Catalan, Castilian, English and French). Some you might like to surf include:

All About Spain A varied site with information on everything from fiestas to hotels and a yellow pages guide to tour operators around the world that do trips in Spain.
www.red2000.com

Barcelona This general Web site is administered by the Ajuntament and offers a wide variety of information on the city's services and events.
www.bcn.es

Barcelona.de A German-language (also in Spanish and Catalan) information site on Barcelona, with a forum for message exchange.
http://barcelona.de

Barcelona Hoy This is one of the better sites (Spanish only). It is comprehensive and gives broad listings, general news, links to white and yellow pages sites and more.
www.barcelonahoy.com

Barcelona On Line This is the single most useful Web site on Barcelona, with numerous links to wider Catalan and Spanish topics and loads of busy pages covering restaurants, places to stay (including home stays), bars and discos, shops, tourist information, museums, weather information, Spanish and Catalan newspaper and magazine Web site links, transport information and so on. You can also plug into lots of chat forums.
www.deinfo.es/barcelona-on-line

Cities.Com Search for Barcelona on this site and it takes you to a list of other potentially interesting sites, some of which appear in this list.
www.cities.com

Generalitat de Catalunya The Generalitat's Web site contains some curious pages dealing with various aspects of Catalunya's history and culture.
www.gencat.es

Infobarn Turisme de Barcelona's official site, with information on sights, eateries and other aspects of Barcelona interest, along with up-to-date details on what's on in the city. You can email them on central@infobarna.com.
www.barcelonaturisme.com

Internet Cafe Guide At this site you can get a list of Internet cafes in Barcelona (and around

Spain). It's not as up-to-date as you might expect, but it is a start (see also Cybercafes above).
www.netcafeguide.com

RENFE Timetables, tickets and special offers on Spain's national rail network.
www.renfe.es

Spanien.Com Another German-language site, this time run by the big Spanish portal Jazztel. Click on the Barcelona 'cityguide' for general information and listings.
www.spanien.com

TMB For everything you wanted to know, and probably plenty you didn't, on Barcelona's public transport system.
www.tmb.net

Turespaña This is the Spanish tourist office's official site, with lots of general information about the country and some interesting links.
www.tourspain.es

Turisme Juvenil de Catalunya Information on official Xarxa d'Albergs de Catalunya, which covers most of the HI youth hostels in Barcelona and the region. This is also the place to look for other information on youth and student travel and issues in Catalunya.
www.gencat.es/tujuca/hometuju.htm

Viapolis.Com Pick a city (in this case Barcelona) on this Spanish site and you will end up in a busy listings site.
www.viapolis.com

BOOKS

Most books are published in different editions by different publishers in different countries. As a result, a book might be a hard-cover rarity in one country and readily available in paperback in another.

Fortunately, bookshops and libraries search by title or author, so your local bookshop or library is best placed to advise you on the availability of the listed recommendations.

In London several good bookshops specialise in travel. For guidebooks and maps, Stanfords bookshop (☎ 020-7836 2121), 12–14 Long Acre, London WC2E 9LP, is acknowledged as one of the better first ports of call. A well-stocked source of travel literature is Daunts Books for Travellers (☎ 020-7224 2295), 83 Marylebone High Street, London W1M 4AL.

For books in Spanish, one of the best options is Grant & Cutler (☎ 020-7734 2012),

55–57 Great Marlborough St, London W1V 2AY.

Books on Spain (☎ 020-8898 7789, fax 8898 8812, ℮ keithharris@books-on-spain.com), PO Box 207, Twickenham TW2 5BQ, UK, can send you mail-order catalogues of hundreds of old and new titles on Spain. Visit its Web site at www.books-on-spain.com.

In Australia, the Travel Bookshop (☎ 02-9261 8200), 3/175 Liverpool Street, Sydney, is worth a browse. In the USA, try Book Passage (☎ 415-927 0960), 51 Tamal Vista Boulevard, Corte Madera, California, and The Complete Traveler Bookstore (☎ 212-685 9007), 199 Madison Ave, New York. In France, L'Astrolabe Rive Gauche (☎ 01 46 33 80 06), 14 rue Serpente, Paris, is recommended.

Lonely Planet

If you're planning to travel extensively from Barcelona, check out Lonely Planet's companion titles, including *Spain*, *Walking in Spain*, *Andalucía*, *Madrid* and *France*. In addition, Lonely Planet's *Catalunya & the Costa Brava* will be published in autumn 2001. *World Food Spain* is a trip into Spain's culinary soul, while the *Spanish phrasebook* will enable you to fill some of the gaps between ¡hola! and adiós.

Guidebooks

An interesting walking guide to the city is *Dotze Passejades per la Història de Barcelona* (12 Strolls Through Barcelona's History), published by the Fundació de la Caixa. The only extant versions seem to be in Catalan but, given that two of its co-authors were Anglos, you might get lucky and strike an English-language version kicking around.

Another good one is George Semler's *Barcelona Walks*, which you can sometimes find in the Palau de la Virreina's bookshop (Llibreria de la Virreina, see the Shopping chapter).

A still more comprehensive street-by-street guide to the city is *50 Vegades Barcelona* (50 Times Barcelona), published by the Ajuntament.

Barcelona's festivals are a riot of colour and music. *Gegants* (giants) and *capgrossos* (big heads) parade through the city, whilst the *correfoc* (fire-running) is a pyromaniac's dream.

Hanging about on the beach

A game of dominoes takes the heat out of the afternoon.

Thanks to the Olympics-inspired redevelopment program, the coast is now teeming with life.

Catalunya's traditional dance, the *sardana*

Living statue on La Rambla

History & People

Homage to Barcelona by Colm Tóibín (1990) is an excellent personal introduction to the city's modern life and artistic and political history, by an Irish journalist who has lived there.

Homage to Catalonia, on the other hand, is George Orwell's account of the 1936–9 civil war in Catalunya, moving from the euphoria of the early days in Barcelona to disillusionment with the disastrous infighting on the Republican side. If you want a good general history of the war, get *The Spanish Civil War* by Hugh Thomas.

The Usatges of Barcelona, translated by Donald J Kagay, is the Catalan equivalent of the Magna Carta. The document, and Kagay's commentary, gives a fascinating insight into the historical backdrop for Catalunya's separateness from the rest of Spain.

A guidebook with a difference leads you on strolls around Barcelona while recounting the histories and stories of its women. Called *Guia de Dones de Barcelona*, it is by Isabel Segura and also available in Castilian. An unevenly translated but accessible history of the city is Joan Castellar-Gossol's *Barcelona – A History*.

Arts

It is no easy task to categorise Robert Hughes' *Barcelona*, a witty and passionate study of the art and architecture of the city through history. It is neither flouncy artistic criticism nor dry history, rather a distillation of the life of the city and people and an assessment of its expression.

Architecture

A useful building-by-building account of architecture in the city is *Passejant per Barcelona – Art i Espais Urbans* (Strolling Around Barcelona – Art and Urban Spaces), by Núria Casas and Lourdes Mateo. If your Spanish is good you shouldn't have too much trouble deciphering at least some of the Catalan.

If you prefer English, *Barcelona Architecture Guide*, by Antoni González Moreno-Navarro and Raquel Lacuesta Contreras,

adopts a more technical approach to the same subject, but only covers the years 1929 to 1996. The same authors have also put out the *Guía de Arquitectura Modernista de Cataluña*.

Xavier Güell's *Gaudí Guide* (available in several languages) is poor in text but rich in black and white photography. In the handy Thames & Hudson series on artistic movements, *Romanesque Art* by Meyer Schapiro covers the pre-Gothic era that so sharply marked early Catalan architecture.

Cuisine

Several books have been published locally on Catalan cuisine. If you really want to test yourself you could try *Cuina Catalana* by Pere Sans – in Catalan. If English is more your thing, take a look at *Catalan Cuisine* by Colman Andrews.

General

To put things in context, you may want to read a little more widely about Spain. The two best overall introductions to modern Spain are *The New Spaniards* by John Hooper, a former Madrid correspondent for the *Guardian*, and the more controversial and personal *Fire in the Blood* by Ian Gibson, based on a British TV series. Gibson has also written a weighty biography of Salvador Dalí.

If you can, grab a copy of Eduardo Mendoza's *La Ciudad de los Prodigios* (City of Marvels), a novel set in Barcelona between the Universal Exhibition of 1888 and the World Exhibition of 1929.

FILM

The city hasn't been the focus of foreign cinematic interest all that often. One relatively recent exception was Whit Stillman's *Barcelona* (1994), which follows the loves and trials of two American cousins in post-Franco Barcelona.

Back in 1978 the French director Jacques Deray set his *Un Papillon sur l'Epaule*, a mystery thriller, partly in Barcelona.

In early 2000 Judy Davis was in Barcelona for three months shooting in Susan Seidelman's *Tardes con Gaudí* (Afternoons with

Gaudí), in which Gaudí is present through his works alone. Davis plays the part of a translator living rather poorly in Barcelona and helping a friend to look for her husband, who left her and scarpered to BCN.

One of the best films to be set in Barcelona is Pedro Almodóvar's 1999 hit, *Todo Sobre Mi Madre* (All About My Mother).

NEWSPAPERS & MAGAZINES

You can easily find a wide selection of national daily newspapers from around Europe at newsstands all over central Barcelona and especially along La Rambla. The *International Herald Tribune*, *Time*, *The Economist*, *Le Monde*, *Der Spiegel* and a host of other international magazines are also available.

Spanish National Press

The main Spanish dailies can be identified along roughly political lines, with the old-fashioned paper *ABC* representing the conservative right, *El País* identified with the PSOE (Spain's centre-left socialist party) and *El Mundo,* a more radicalised left-wing paper that prides itself on breaking political scandals. For a good spread of national and international news, *El País* is the pick. One of the best-selling dailies is *Marca*, devoted exclusively to sport.

Local Press

El País includes a daily supplement devoted to Catalunya, but Barcelona is home to a lively home-grown press too. *La Vanguardia* and *El Periódico* are the main local Castilian-language dailies. The latter also publishes an award-winning Catalan version. The more Catalan-nationalist oriented daily is *Avui.*

Useful Publications

Barcelona's entertainment bible is the weekly Castilian-language magazine *Guía del Ocio* (125 ptas), which comes out on Thursday and lists almost everything that's on in the way of music, film, exhibitions, theatre and more. You can pick it up at most newsstands. An alternative is *La Agenda de Barcelona* (225 ptas).

The free monthly English-language *Barcelona Metropolitan* is a handy magazine with articles on the local scene and classifieds that will lead you to English-speaking doctors, dentists, baby-sitters and other useful information. It's aimed at long-term residents. You can pick it up at various bars (including Cafè de l'Òpera), restaurants and shops (such as the Come In bookshop). Once you have a copy, keep the page at the back, which has a list of places where you can find next month's magazine.

Business Barcelona (200 ptas), a monthly English-language business paper, is often full of insightful articles on the commercial life of the city, and more besides. It is on sale at the Come In bookshop.

RADIO & TV
Radio

You can pick up BBC World Service broadcasts on a variety of frequencies. Broadcasts are directed at Western Europe on, among others, 648, 9410 and 12,095 kHz (short wave).

Voice of America can be found on various short-wave frequencies, including on 9700, 9760 and 15,205 kHz depending on the time of day. The BBC and VOA broadcast around the clock, but the quality of reception varies considerably.

The Spanish national network Radio Nacional de España (RNE) has several stations: RNE 1 (738 AM; 88.3 FM in Barcelona) has general interest and current affairs programs; RNE 3 (98.7 FM) presents a decent range of pop and rock music; RNE 5 (576 AM) concentrates on sport and entertainment. Among the most listened to rock and pop stations are 40 Principales (93.9 FM), Onda Cero (89.1 FM) and Cadena 100 (100 FM).

Those wanting to get into Catalan can tune into Catalunya Ràdio (102.8 FM) or Ràdio Espanya Catalunya (94.9 FM). There is also a host of small local radio stations.

You can hear the American InRadio program on 107.6 FM on Monday, Tuesday, Wednesday and Friday from 9 to 10 pm.

TV

Most TVs receive seven channels – two from Spain's state-run Televisión Española (TVE1 and La 2), three independent (Antena 3, Tele 5 and Canal Plus), the Catalunya regional government station (TV-3) and another Catalan station (Canal 33). Most TV sets will also get the local city station, Barcelona TV.

News programs are generally decent and you can occasionally catch an interesting documentary or film (look out for the occasional English-language classic late at night on La 2). Otherwise, the main fare is a rather nauseating diet of soaps (many from Latin America), endless talk shows and almost vaudevillian variety shows (with plenty of glitz and tits). Canal Plus is a pay channel dedicated mainly to movies: you need a decoder and subscription to see the movies, but anyone can watch the other programs.

Many private homes and better hotels have satellite TV, serving up the usual diet of CNN, Eurosport and the like.

VIDEO SYSTEMS

If you want to record or buy video tapes to play back home, you won't get a picture if the image registration systems are different. Spanish TVs, and nearly all pre-recorded videos on sale in Spain, use the PAL (phase alternation line) system common to most of Western Europe and Australia.

France uses the incompatible SECAM system and North America and Japan use the incompatible NTSC system. PAL videos can't be played back on a machine that lacks PAL compatibility.

PHOTOGRAPHY & VIDEO
Film & Equipment

Most main brands of film are widely available and processing is fast and generally efficient. A roll of print film (36 exposures, ISO 100) costs around 600 ptas and can be processed for around 1250 ptas (dearer for same day service), although there are often better deals if you have two or three rolls developed together. The equivalent in slide *(diapositiva)* film is around 750 ptas plus 800 ptas for processing.

There are plenty of places to have films developed. Panorama Foto, which has seven branches around town, including Passeig de Gràcia 2 (Map 5), will develop most photos, including slides, in an hour. They also sell standard blank video cassettes.

Technical Tips

For handy hints on improving your snaps, try Lonely Planet's *Travel Photography: A Guide to Taking Better Pictures*, written by internationally renowned travel photographer, Richard I'Anson. It's full colour throughout and designed to take on the road.

Airport Security

Your camera and film will be passed routinely through airport X-ray machines. These shouldn't damage film but you can ask for inspection by hand if you're worried. Lead pouches for film, available in some specialised camera stores, are another solution.

TIME

Spain (and hence Barcelona) is on GMT/UTC plus one hour during winter, and GMT/UTC plus two hours during the daylight-saving period from the last Sunday in March to the last Sunday in October. Most other Western European countries have the same time as Spain year round, the major exceptions being Britain, Ireland and Portugal, which are an hour behind.

When it's noon in Barcelona, it's 11 am in London, 6 am in New York and Toronto, 3 am in San Francisco, 9 pm in Sydney and 11 pm in Auckland. Note that the changeover to/from daylight usually differs from the European setup by a couple of weeks in North America and Australasia.

ELECTRICITY

The electric current in Barcelona is 220V, 50Hz, as in the rest of continental Europe. Several countries outside Europe (such as the USA and Canada) have 60Hz, which means that appliances with electric motors (such as some CD and tape players) from those countries may perform poorly. It is always safest to use a transformer.

FACTS FOR THE VISITOR

Plugs have two round pins, again as in the rest of continental Europe.

WEIGHTS & MEASURES

The metric system is used in Spain. Like other continental Europeans, the Spanish indicate decimals with commas and thousands with points. You will sometimes see years written thus: 1.998. See also the conversion charts at the end of this book.

LAUNDRY

Self-service laundries are a rarity indeed. One is Lavomatic at Carrer del Consolat de Mar 43–45 (Map 6). A 7kg load of washing costs 600 ptas and drying costs 110 ptas for five minutes. They have another branch at Plaça de Joaquim Xirau 1 (Map 6).

Wash'N Dry, on the corner of Carrer de Torrent de l'Olla and Carrer Ros de Olano in Gràcia (Map 2), charges 700 ptas for an 8kg load and 100 ptas for six minutes drying time. It opens 7 am to 10 pm.

Lavandería Tigre at Carrer d'En Rauric 20 (Map 6) in the Barri Gòtic will wash, dry and fold 3kg in a couple of hours for 890 ptas (7kg for 1370 ptas). The laundry opens 8 am to 7 pm daily except Sunday.

TOILETS

Public toilets are not particularly common in Spain but it's OK to wander into most bars and cafes to use their toilet, even if you're not a customer (although this writer prefers to do them the courtesy of having a quick coffee). It's worth carrying some loo paper with you, though, as many toilets don't have it.

LEFT LUGGAGE

Left luggage facilities can be found at the airport, Estació Sants, Estació de França and the main bus station. Turn to the Getting There & Away and Getting Around chapters for more details.

HEALTH

You should encounter no particular health problems in Barcelona. Your main risks are likely to be sunburn, dehydration or mild gut problems at first if you're not used to a lot of olive oil.

Medical Kit Check List

Following is a list of items you should consider including in your medical kit – consult your pharmacist for brands available in your country.

- ☐ **Aspirin** or **paracetamol** (acetaminophen in the USA) – for pain or fever
- ☐ **Antihistamine** – for allergies, eg, hay fever; to ease the itch from insect bites or stings; and to prevent motion sickness
- ☐ **Cold** and **flu tablets**, **throat lozenges** and **nasal decongestant**
- ☐ **Multivitamins** – consider for long trips, when dietary vitamin intake may be inadequate
- ☐ **Antibiotics** – consider including these if you're travelling well off the beaten track; see your doctor, as they must be prescribed, and carry the prescription with you
- ☐ **Loperamide** or **diphenoxylate** –'blockers' for diarrhoea
- ☐ **Prochlorperazine** or **metaclopramide** – for nausea and vomiting
- ☐ **Rehydration mixture** – to prevent dehydration, which may occur, for example, during bouts of diarrhoea; particularly important when travelling with children
- ☐ **Insect repellent**, **sunscreen**, **lip balm** and **eye drops**
- ☐ **Calamine lotion**, **sting relief spray** or **aloe vera** – to ease irritation from sunburn and insect bites or stings
- ☐ **Antifungal cream** or **powder** – for fungal skin infections and thrush
- ☐ **Antiseptic** (such as povidone-iodine) – for cuts and grazes
- ☐ **Bandages**, **elastic plasters** and other wound dressings
- ☐ **Water purification tablets** or **iodine**
- ☐ **Scissors**, **tweezers** and a **thermometer** – note that mercury thermometers are prohibited by airlines

Spain has reciprocal health agreements with other EU countries. Citizens of those countries need to get hold of an E111 form from their national health bodies (in the case of the UK and Ireland, get one at the local post office). If you should require medical help you will need to present this, plus photocopies and your national health card. This is only valid for Spanish public healthcare.

Travel insurance is still a good idea, however. You should really get it to cover you for theft, loss and unexpected travel cancellations anyway, so you will be covered for the cost of private healthcare as well.

No vaccinations are required for Spain unless you are coming from an infected area (this generally relates to yellow fever – you may be asked for proof of vaccination), but it is recommended that everyone keeps up-to-date with vaccinations such as tetanus, polio and diphtheria.

For minor health problems you can head to your local *farmàcia* where pharmaceuticals tend to be sold more freely without prescription than in places like the USA, Australia or UK.

Medical Services & Emergency

Hospitals with emergency service include the Hospital Creu Roja (Map 1; ☎ 93 300 20 20), Carrer del Dos de Maig 301, and Hospital de la Santa Creu i de Sant Pau (Map 1; ☎ 93 291 90 00), Carrer de Sant Antoni Maria Claret 167.

For an ambulance, call ☎ 061, ☎ 93 329 97 01 or ☎ 93 300 20 20; for emergency dental help try ☎ 93 277 47 47.

There are 24-hour pharmacies at La Rambla 98 (Map 6), Carrer d'Aribau 62 (Map 4) and another at Passeig de Gràcia 26 (Map 2). A fourth, Farmàcia Saltó (Map 1; ☎ 93 339 63 32), is somewhat out of the centre at Avinguda de Madrid 222. Otherwise, for information on duty chemists call ☎ 010. Note that at some late-night pharmacies you have to knock at a small shutter for service; often they will only fill prescriptions or deal with urgent problems outside normal business hours – this is not the time to buy your shampoo.

AIDS & HIV

Although the spread of AIDS/HIV (SIDA/VIH in Castilian Spanish) has slowed in the past couple of years, it remains a big problem in Spain. Barcelona is no exception.

The Hospital del Mar (Map 5; ☎ 93 221 10 10) has a special AIDS-testing clinic, but it is entirely probable that you will be first asked to visit your local public GP, or CAP (Centre d'Assistència Primària) to fill in forms. As non-resident foreign visitors won't have a CAP, they may be obliged to go to a private clinic for a test (which in turn may well *not* be covered by insurance).

For AIDS-related information you can call the service run by the Generalitat on ☎ 93 339 87 56. It operates 9 am to 5.30 pm Monday to Friday. Other AIDS information lines include Stop Sida (☎ 900 60 16 01) and Associació Antisida (☎ 93 317 05 05).

STDs

Gonorrhoea, herpes and syphilis are among these diseases; sores, blisters or rashes around the genitals, discharges or pain when urinating are common symptoms. In some STDs, such as wart virus or chlamydia, symptoms may be less marked or not observed at all, especially in women. Syphilis symptoms eventually disappear completely but the disease continues and can cause severe problems in later years. While abstinence from sexual contact is the only 100% effective prevention, using condoms is also effective. The different STDs are treated with specific antibiotics. There is no cure for herpes or AIDS.

WOMEN TRAVELLERS

As visitors have flooded into Barcelona, the fascination of the local boys with foreign women has tended to diminish. In general terms, therefore, harassment is unlikely to be much more apparent here than in any other European metropole.

Since the death of Franco, women have surged into the workforce and become far more assertive, but the truisms that apply elsewhere in the world apply here too. More often than not women are paid less than their male counterparts. Household duties still tend to fall onto the shoulders of women (even among younger people) and in many cases working women find themselves doing most of the family raising too.

Organisations

The first stop for anyone seeking information on women's issues should be the Institut Català de la Dona (Map 6; ☎ 93 495 16 00), Carrer de Portaferrissa 1–3. They can point you in the right direction for: information on rape/assault counselling; marriage, divorce and related issues for long-termers; social activities, women's clubs and so on.

Ca la Dona (Map 2; ☎ 93 412 71 61), Carrer de Casp 38, is the nerve centre of Barcelona's feminist movement. It includes about 25 diverse women's groups and has been going since 1988.

The Centre Municipal d'Informació i Recursos per a les Dones (Map 1; ☎ 93 291 84 92), Carrer de la Llacuna 161, is a local government-run information service. Among other things it publishes the *Guia de Grups i Entitats de Dones de Barcelona*, which is a comprehensive guide to all associations and groups connected with women and women's issues in the city.

On the subject of assault, the nationwide Comisión de Investigación de Malos Tratos a Mujeres (Commission of Investigation into the Abuse of Women) has a free 24-hour national emergency line for victims of physical abuse: ☎ 900 10 00 09. English may be in short supply, however.

GAY & LESBIAN TRAVELLERS

Gay and lesbian sex are both legal in Spain and the age of consent is 16 years, the same as for heterosexuals. Catalunya went a step further in October 1998 by introducing a law recognising gay and lesbian couples. A similar law at national level has been stalled in the Cortes by the ruling conservative Partido Popular (PP). The Catalan law does not yet sanction marriage of such couples, nor the adoption of children by them.

Entiendes, a gay magazine, costs 500 ptas. *Mensual* (500 ptas) is a monthly gay guys' listings magazine with bars, hotels, saunas and so on listed for all Spain. It is available in gay bookshops. *Nosotras* is a bi-monthly lesbians' review.

An international gay guide worth tracking down is the *Spartacus Guide for Gay Men* (the Spartacus list also includes the comprehensive *Spartacus National Edition España*, in English and German), published by Bruno Gmünder Verlag, Mail Order, PO Box 61 01 04, D-10921 Berlin. It is not always terribly up to date, but it's a good start. Lesbians might try *Places for Women*, published by Ferrari Publications, Phoenix, AZ, USA.

There are a few Spanish queer sites on the Internet. The Barcelona-based Coordinadora Gai-Lesbiana has a good site with nationwide links at www.pangea.org/org/cgl. Here you can zero in on information ranging from bar, sauna and hotel listings through to contacts pages. Apart from Barcelona, you will find information on the rest of Catalunya and links to other parts of Spain. Another source of listings is Gay in Spain (www.gayinspain.com).

Organisations

Casal Lambda (Map 6; ☎ 93 412 72 72), Carrer Ample 5 in the Barri Gòtic, is a gay and lesbian social, cultural and information centre. Coordinadora Gai-Lesbiana (Map 1; ☎ 93 298 00 29, fax 93 298 06 18, [e] cogailes@ pangea.org), Carrer de Finlàndia 45, is the city's main coordinating body for gay and lesbian groups. Some of the latter, such as Grup de Lesbianes Feministes (☎ 93 412 77 01), are to be found at Ca la Dona (see Women Travellers above). There is a free gay helpline (which is also the number for Stop Sida, the AIDS helpline) on ☎ 900 60 16 01.

Sextienda, a gay sex shop at Carrer d'En Rauric 11 in the Barri Gòtic (Map 6), has a give-away map of gay Barcelona showing lesbian and gay bars, discos and restaurants.

DISABLED TRAVELLERS

Like most cities, Barcelona is a bit of an obstacle course for the disabled. Some museums and offices provide wheelchair access but many older buildings do not have lifts, so getting up to hostales and the like can be difficult. Some public transport (such as metro line 2, some buses and taxis) is equipped to cater to the needs of the disabled. For information on public transport facilities for the disabled call ☎ 93 486 07 52.

Some Spanish tourist offices in other countries can provide a basic information sheet with some useful addresses for disabled travellers and give details of accessible accommodation.

The UK-based Royal Association for Disability & Rehabilitation (RADAR) publishes a useful guide called *European Holidays & Travel Abroad: A Guide for Disabled People*, which provides an overview of facilities available to disabled travellers throughout Europe. Contact RADAR (☎ 020-7250 3222), Unit 12, City Forum, 250 City Rd, London EC1V 8AS, or visit their Web site at www.radar.org.uk.

Another organisation worth contacting is Holiday Care (☎ 01293-774535), 2nd Floor, Imperial Buildings, Victoria Rd, Horley, Surrey RH6 7PZ. They produce an information pack on Spain for disabled people and others with special needs. Tips range from hotels with disabled access through to where you can hire equipment and specialist tour operators.

Organisations

In Barcelona itself, ECOM (Map 4; ☎ 93 451 55 50, fax 93 451 69 04), Spain's federation of private organisations for the disabled, is at Gran Via de les Corts Catalanes 562, 08011 Barcelona. They can provide information on accommodation with disabled people's facilities, public and private transport options as well as leisure time and holiday possibilities in and around Barcelona.

For more city information you could also try the Institut Municipal de Persones amb Disminució (Map 1; ☎ 93 291 84 00, fax 93 423 26 49), Carrer de Llacuna 161.

SENIOR TRAVELLERS

There are reduced prices for people aged over 60, 63 or 65 (depending on the place) at some attractions and occasionally on transport. You usually need to provide ID proof of age. It is always worth asking. You should also seek information in your own country on travel packages and discounts for senior travellers, through senior citizens' organisations and travel agents.

BARCELONA FOR CHILDREN

You will generally have no problem taking your kids about with you in restaurants, hotels, cafes and the like, although few locals are inclined to take their *peques* (little ones) out for a night on the tiles.

Kids can open doors where adults alone never would. This is especially so where a language barrier impedes communication – cute kids doing the cute things that cute kids sometimes do can be a great ice-breaker.

Catalans have fewer qualms about keeping their children up late than people from more northerly climes. In summer especially, you'll see them at the local *festes* until the wee hours. Taking children to cafes or snack bars that have outdoor tables (preferably in pedestrian zones) is no problem at all. Of course your wee bairn's body clock may not quite be up to it.

What to Do with Anklebiters

Some of the museums appear to have been thought out for kids as much as for adults. The Museu Marítim and Museu d'Història de Catalunya fall into that category, the former with its audiovisual trek through time and the latter with its various hands-on gadgets.

The Parc d'Atraccions up on Tibidabo is perfect for the kids and few young ones will turn up their noses at the beach or outdoor pools in summer. If you've been cruel enough to subject them to the Museu d'Art Modern in the Parc de la Ciutadella, why not compensate with an ice-cream and a stroll through the park, a trip to the zoo and/or a bit of a row on the little artificial lake?

Still not satisfied? Try a ride in a Barcelona Globus balloon near the zoo or the Màgic BCN train ride nearby.

The high-level *funicular aereo* (cable car) between Montjuïc and La Barceloneta might be the go, as indeed could be a harbour excursion on one of the *golondrina* boats.

The watery tunnels of L'Aquàrium, Europe's biggest fish 'zoo', should be a winner and you could also try the nearby Imax cinema.

In the early evening, the Teatre Tantarantana sometimes puts on children's shows.

euro currency converter €1 = 166 ptas

Finally, even the most adventurous of children will at times feel nostalgia for toys back home. Bring a couple of favourites along to keep them occupied in dull moments, or when you're trying to take a rest yourself.

Before You Go

There are no particular health precautions you need to take, though kids tend to be more affected than adults by unaccustomed heat, changes in diet and sleeping patterns, and just being in a strange place. Nappies, creams, lotions, baby foods and so on are all easily available in Barcelona, but if there's some particular brand you swear by it's best to bring it with you.

Lonely Planet's *Travel with Children* has lots of practical advice on the subject and first-hand stories from many Lonely Planet authors, and others, who have done it.

USEFUL ORGANISATIONS

The Instituto Cervantes, with branches in over 30 cities around the world, exists to promote the Spanish language and cultures. It's mainly involved in Spanish teaching and library and information services. The library at the London branch (☎ 020-7235 0353), 102 Eaton Square, London SW1W 9AN, has a wide range of reference books, literature, books on history and the arts, periodicals, over 1000 videos including feature films, language-teaching material, electronic databases and music CDs.

In New York, the institute (☎ 212-689 4232) is at 122 East 42nd St, suite 807, New York, NY 10168. You can find further addresses on the institute's Web site at www.cervantes.es.

UNIVERSITIES

Barcelona has five universities spread about the city. Teaching is predominantly in Catalan, meaning that even Castilian speakers may have difficulties at first. European students in Barcelona are mostly on one-year programs as part of the Erasmus scheme. They do this as part of their undergraduate studies. You need to approach the Socrates and Erasmus council in your country for more information.

Of the universities, the oldest and biggest is the Universitat de Barcelona (☎ 93 402 11 00), with campuses at Gran Via de les Corts Catalanes 585 (Map 4) and the Zona Universitària (Map 1).

The remaining institutions are:

Universitat Politècnica de Catalunya (Map 1; ☎ 93 401 62 00), Avinguda del Doctor Marañón 42 (metro Zona Universitària). As the name suggests, it is a technical and engineering university.

Universitat Pompeu Fabra (Map 6; ☎ 93 542 22 28), Plaça de la Mercè 10–12. Based in the old city, this university concentrates on social sciences and has faculties dotted about central Barcelona (eg just off La Rambla on Plaça de Joaquim Xirau, Map 6).

Universitat Autònoma de Barcelona (☎ 93 581 10 00), Bellaterra. This place is outside the city near Sabadell and an unlikely choice for foreigners.

Universitat Ramon Llull (☎ 93 253 04 50), Carrer de Sant Joan de la Salle 8. A private institute for students with fat wallets. The faculty buildings are spread across town.

Foreign students in Barcelona can get help on a range of information from lodgings to language tuition, how to organise work experience in local companies, cultural activities and so on, at Punt d'Informació Juvenil (Map 4; ☎ 93 483 83 84), Carrer de Calàbria 147.

CULTURAL CENTRES

British Council (Map 3; ☎ 93 241 99 77), Carrer d'Amigó 83 (FGC Muntaner). English classes, library services, film seasons and other cultural events.

Institute for North American Studies (Map 3; ☎ 93 200 24 67), Via Augusta 123 (FGC Muntaner). Library material is also available here.

Institut Français de Barcelona (Map 2; ☎ 93 209 59 11), Carrer de Moià 8 (metro Diagonal). Puts on films, concerts and exhibitions.

Goethe Institut (Map 4; ☎ 93 292 60 06), Carrer de Manso 24–28. Apart from German classes and library services, the institute organises lectures, exhibits, film seasons and the like.

Istituto Italiano di Cultura (Map 2; ☎ 93 487 53 06), Passatge de Méndez Vigo 5 (metro Passeig de Gràcia). The institute's main aim is to teach Italian. It also has a library and puts on lectures and film seasons.

DANGERS & ANNOYANCES
Barcelona is a fairly secure city, although petty crime (in particular theft) is a problem and its victims are often newcomers in town.

Before You Leave Home
You can take a few precautions before you even arrive in Barcelona. Inscribe your name, address and telephone number *inside* your luggage and take photocopies of the important pages of your passport, travel tickets and other important documents. Keep the copies separate from the originals and ideally leave one set of copies at home. These steps will make things easier if you do suffer a loss or theft. Travel insurance against theft and loss is another very good idea.

Prevention
...is better than cure! Only walk around with the amount of cash you intend to spend that day or evening. Hidden money belts or pouches are a good idea. The popular 'bum bags' and external belt pouches people wear around their tummies are like shining beacons to hawks looking for targets. You may as well wear a neon sign saying: 'Pick me: I'm a tourist.'

Theft & Loss
You need to keep an eye out for pickpockets and bagsnatchers in the most heavily touristed parts of town, especially La Rambla and the Ciutat Vella. The Barri Xinès, the lower end of La Rambla and the area around Plaça Reial, although much cleaned up in recent years, remain dodgy.

Fifty Ways to Lose a Wallet

The tales of woe from unlucky travellers who have been stung in Barcelona are remarkable most of all for the degree of fantasy apparently employed by muggers and other crooks. If it's any consolation, this writer has been done too!

Try these for size. You're walking down a street and suddenly you feel a glob of what looks like bird shit on your shoulder. An obliging fellow with a tissue emerges from nowhere and helps you remove the mess. Then he removes himself and shortly thereafter you notice he has also removed the contents of your pockets – the 'shit' was a chocolate and milk mix.

Another fun one involves somebody bending over in front of you (say on an escalator to pick up something they have dropped). You are distracted and hey, presto, no more wallet. The variations on that theme are innumerable. 'Tourists' asking for directions are another common gag.

Pickpocketing happens on the streets, in the metro, at the bus stations...and even in clubs. Don't wear money belts and the like in clubs if you can help it (unless they are well hidden) as there have been cases of them being snipped.

Sadly, less inventive and more threatening incidents do occasionally take place. One reader reports having been grabbed in a headlock from behind while his trouser pockets were slashed and emptied. The reader was alone late at night in a dark street in the Barri Xinès – not a good idea at the best of times.

In the same part of town you'll still see some fairly tawdry looking damsels (some with remarkably deep voices) of the night lolling about. If you're male and particularly unlucky you may find one suddenly attaching their hand in vice-like fashion to your nether region and smiling gap-toothedly at you while suggesting some back alley frolics. While you engage in a delicate attempt to recover possession of your genitals and make your excuses, you can be fairly sure you are being relieved of your possessions.

Finally, if someone asks to see your passport, don't be too willing about whipping it into view. The only people with a right to see it are hoteliers and police.

Don't panic, just don't let your guard down!

Pick-pocketing is rife in busy spots such as the area in front of the Catedral. Indeed shopkeepers there have recently demanded greater policing there.

As a rule, dark, empty streets are to be avoided. Luckily, Barcelona's most lively nocturnal areas are generally busy with crowds having a good time – and there is definitely safety in numbers. Keep alert on the metro as well.

In summer, the beach (especially at La Barceloneta) is a particularly popular playground for thieves – always keep your belongings within reach and in view. The beach theft problem is bad enough for local police to mount a special anti-theft operation on the beach each summer.

Never leave anything visible in your car and preferably leave nothing at all. Temptation usually leads at least to smashed windows and loss – it happens in broad daylight too, so take this seriously. Foreign and hire cars are especially vulnerable. In hotels and hostels, use the safe if there is one. Try not to leave valuables in your room. If you must, then bury them deep in your luggage.

If anything does get lost or stolen, you need to report it to the police and get a written statement from them if you intend to claim on insurance. If your ID or passport disappears, you must also contact your nearest consulate, as soon as possible, to arrange for a replacement.

Lost & Found

The city's main lost-and-found *(objetos perdidos)* office is on ☎ 93 402 31 61. If you leave anything in a taxi, you can call ☎ 93 223 40 12 to see if it's been handed in. If you leave anything in the metro, you can try the Centre d'Atenció al Client (☎ 93 318 70 74) at the Universitat stop (Map 4). It acts as a lost-and-found office for the metro. If you lose anything at the airport try ☎ 93 298 33 49.

EMERGENCIES

The general EU standard emergency number is ☎ 112. You can reach all emergency services on this number and occasionally even get multi-lingual operators.

Barcelona abounds with different kinds of police. The Guàrdia Urbana (city police; ☎ 092) has a station at La Rambla 43, opposite Plaça Reial (Map 6). If you need to report theft or loss of passport and other belongings, head to the comisaría of the Policía Nacional (☎ 091) at Carrer Nou de la Rambla 80 (Map 5). There's usually an English speaker on duty.

The Mossos de Esquadra (☎ 93 300 91 91) is a Catalan force that is replacing the Spanish Guàrdia Civil (☎ 062) in some tasks (like highway patrol). The latter are a military-style police force involved in everything from security to highway patrol.

Asistencia al Turista (☎ 93 482 05 26) may also be able to help distressed visitors. If you have been a victim of a crime and are at a loss what to do next, you could try the Servei d'Atenció a la Víctima (Map 1; ☎ 900 12 18 84), Carrer de Roger de Flor 62–68.

For the fire brigade call ☎ 080.

LEGAL MATTERS

If you're arrested you will be allotted the free services of a duty solicitor *(abogado de oficio)*, who may speak only Catalan and/or Spanish. You're also entitled to make a phone call. If you phone your embassy or consulate, it will probably be able to do no more than refer you to a lawyer who speaks your language. If you end up in court, the authorities are obliged to provide a translator.

Drugs

Spain's liberal drug laws were severely tightened in 1992. The only legal drug is cannabis, and then only for personal use – which means very small amounts.

Public consumption of any drug is apparently illegal, yet you may still come across the occasional bar where people smoke joints openly. In short, be discreet if you use cannabis. There is a reasonable degree of tolerance when it comes to people having a smoke in their own home, but it would be unwise to do so in hotel rooms or guesthouses, and could be risky in even the coolest of public places.

BUSINESS HOURS

Generally, people work Monday to Friday from about 9 am to 2 pm and then again from 4.30 or 5 pm for another three hours. Shops and travel agencies are usually open these hours on Saturday too, although some may skip the evening session. Big supermarkets and department stores such as El Corte Inglés often stay open all day Monday to Saturday, from about 9 am to 9 pm. A handful of shops are open on Sunday. Many government offices don't bother with afternoon opening any day of the year.

See earlier sections of this chapter for bank and post office hours.

PUBLIC HOLIDAYS & SPECIAL EVENTS
Vacation Periods

The two main periods when Barcelonins go on holiday are Setmana Santa (the week leading up to Easter Sunday) and, more noticeably, the month of August. In Easter, incoming tourists make up in numbers for the leaving locals (accommodation is at a premium this week), but in August the city is like a ghost town, even though in recent years the tendency has been to stagger departures and returns in two-week chunks over July and August.

Public Holidays

In Barcelona, as in the rest of Spain, there are 14 official holidays a year – some observed nationwide, some locally. When a holiday falls close to a weekend, people like to make a *puente* (bridge) – meaning they take the intervening day off too. On the odd occasion when a couple of holidays fall close, they make an *acueducto* (aqueduct)! Offices, banks and many shops close on holidays. Restaurants, bars and the like soldier on, as do most museums and other sights and attractions.

The seven national holidays are:

Any Nou/Año Nuevo (New Year's Day)
1 January – plenty of parties in the discos and clubs on New Year's Eve (Cap d'Any/Noche Vieja) – expect to pay higher than usual prices. As the clock strikes midnight you are expected to eat a grape for each chime.

Divendres Sant/Viernes Santo (Good Friday)
March/April – although not, in general, celebrated with the verve it is accorded farther south in Spain, you get a taste of it with the procession from the Església de Sant Agustí in El Raval in the early afternoon of Good Friday.

Accompanying the huge image of the Virgin that is the centrepiece of the march (which then proceeds up La Rambla and on to Plaça de Catalunya) are solemn bands, members of various religious fraternities *(cofradías)* dressed in robes and *capilotes* (tall conical hoods).

Most striking perhaps are the barefoot women penitents dressed in black and dragging heavy crosses and chains around their ankles.

Dia del Treball/Fiesta del Trabajo (Labour Day)
1 May – in this one-time anarchist stronghold where nowadays the Socialists always win the municipal elections, Labour Day once attracted big demonstrations. That is all but a memory now – you'll probably hardly notice it's a holiday except for all the closed offices, banks and shops.

L'Assumpció/La Asunción (Feast of the Assumption)
15 August

Festa de la Hispanitat/Día de la Hispanidad (Spanish National Day)
12 October – the day off is appreciated, but no special celebrations mark this occasion.

La Immaculada Concepció/La Inmaculada Concepción (Feast of the Immaculate Conception)
8 December

Nadal/Navidad (Christmas)
25 December – this is a family time. Many celebrate with a big midday meal, although some prefer to eat on Christmas Eve *(nit de Nadal/nochebuena)*.

One of the oddest things about Christmas is the nativity scenes that families traditionally set up at home (a giant one goes up in Plaça de Sant Jaume too). The cribs themselves are common throughout the Catholic world, and particularly in the Mediterranean. What makes these ones different is the presence, along with the baby Jesus, Mary, Joseph and the Three Kings, of a chap who has dropped his pants and is doing number twos.

The Catalans proudly claim the *caganer* (the crapper) as their own but if, indeed, he is a Catalan invention, he has wide appeal – similar figures can be seen in the family cribs as far away as the Canary Islands.

In addition to these national holidays, the Generalitat and Ajuntament add the following holidays during the year:

FACTS FOR THE VISITOR

Epifanía (Epiphany) or El Dia dels Reis/Día de los Reyes Magos (Three Kings' Day)

6 January – when children traditionally receive presents (generally they get little or nothing at Christmas).

Dilluns de Pasqua Florida (Easter Monday)

April

Dilluns de Pasqua Granda

May/June – the day after Pentecost Sunday.

Dia de Sant Joan/Día de San Juan Bautista (Feast of St John the Baptist)

24 June – the night before the people of Barcelona hit the streets or hold parties at home to celebrate the *berbena de Sant Joan*, an evening of drinking, dancing and fireworks. The latter can be seen in districts all over town (and indeed across Catalunya), for which reason the evening is also known as La Nit del Foc, or Fire Night.

The traditional pastry to eat on this summer solstice is a kind of dense candied cake known as *coca de Sant Joan*.

Diada Nacional de Catalunya

11 September – Catalunya's national day commemorates Barcelona's surrender to the Spaniards at the conclusion of the War of the Spanish Succession in 1714. It is a relatively sober occasion, when small independence groups demand the predictable without anyone paying too much attention.

Festes de la Mercè

24 September – these four days of intense festivities begins shortly after the official close of summer and acts as a final burst of pre-winter madness all over Barcelona, although the bulk of the activities take place in the centre of town. Nostra Senyora de la Mercè (whose image lies in the church of the same name on Plaça de la Mercè) was elevated to co-patron of the city after she single-handedly beat off a plague of locusts in 1637.

In 1714, as Barcelona faced defeat in the War of the Spanish Succession, light-headed town elders at one point appointed Our Lady commander-in-chief of the city's defences (an eloquent expression of hopelessness if ever there was one).

This is the city's *festa major* or Big Party. There's a swimming race across the harbour, a fun run, an outstanding series of free concerts organised under the auspices of BAM (Barcelona Acció Musical; see Festivals below), and a bewildering program of cultural events all over town and in many of the museums and galleries. There's also all the predictable stuff that usually accompanies a major Catalan festa: *castellers* (human castle builders), *sardanes* (traditional

folk dancing), parades of *gegants* and *capgrossos* (giants and big heads) and a huge *correfoc* (fire race). The latter is a pyromaniac's dream. It's held on the last night (a Sunday), and crowds hurl themselves through the streets before fire-spurting demons (not to mention kids armed with high-calibre fire-crackers) who have been released from the Porta de l'Infern (Gate of Hell), located before the Catedral.

The fire race can be dangerous and you are advised to wear old cotton clothes (long sleeves and trousers) and a hood to cover up your head, earplugs and running shoes if you intend to participate in all the madness. The heat can be intense, but an old habit of tipping water from balconies above over participants has been banned – apparently mixing water with gun powder can have unpredictable consequences.

El Dia de Sant Esteve

26 December – the local equivalent of Boxing Day, it is a family occasion, much like Christmas Day, with festive lunches.

Festivals

Barcelona is perhaps not as addicted to partying as some more southerly Spanish cities, but it puts in a fair effort with some wild occasions dotting the calendar in between the official holidays. Several *barris* celebrate their own *festes majors*. See also Public Holidays above, as some of the official holidays are themselves cause for much merry-making.

Cavalcada dels Reis

5 January – the day preceding Epiphany (a public holiday) sees the Three Kings 'arrive' in Barcelona at Moll de la Fusta and then parade up into town (the route tends to change). As the Kings parade around with floats, they hurl sweets to the kids in the crowd.

Festes dels Tres Tombs

17 January – a key part of the district festival of Sant Antoni, the festa of the Three Circuits involves a parade of horsemen who march around Ronda de Sant Antoni to Plaça de Catalunya, down La Rambla and back up Carrer Nou de la Rambla. Sant Antoni Abat (St Anthony the Abbot) is apparently the patron saint of muleteers. It was once one of the more important of Barcelona's celebrations, but is fairly muted nowadays.

Festes de Santa Eulàlia

February – coinciding with Carnaval (see the next entry), this is the feast of Barcelona's first patron saint. The Ajuntament organises all sorts of cultural events, from concerts through to performances by castellers and the appearance of *mulasses* (dragons) in the main parade.

Carnestoltes/Carnaval

February/March – *(Carnival)* – Several days of fancy-dress parades and merrymaking, usually ending on the Tuesday 47 days before Easter Sunday. For about 10 days there are parades and dancing, and parties in the discos and clubs. It is not as riotous as the Canary Islands version of Carnaval, but busy enough to keep most punters happy. As it does elsewhere in Spain, the carnival culminates in the Enterrament de la Sardina (burial of the fish), often on Montjuïc. The whole affair is a dramatic celebration of the end of winter.

Dia de Sant Jordi

23 April – the day of Catalunya's patron saint and also the Day of the Book – men give women a rose, women give men a book; publishers launch new titles, La Rambla and Plaça de Sant Jaume are filled with book and flower stalls.

L'Ou com Balla

May/June – a curious tradition with several centuries of history, the 'Dancing Egg' is an empty shell that bobs on top of the flower-festooned fountain in the cloister of the Catedral. This spectacle is Barcelona's way of celebrating Corpus Christi (the Thursday after the eighth Sunday after Easter Sunday). Other dancing eggs can be seen on the same day in the courtyard of the Casa de l'Ardiaca and various other fountains in the Barri Gòtic.

Dia per l'Alliberament Lesbià i Gai

28 June – gay and lesbian festival and parade.

Festa Major de Gràcia

Around 15 August – apart from the Festes de la Mercè, this is one of the biggest local festivals in Barcelona. More than a dozen streets in Gràcia are decorated by their inhabitants according to a certain theme as part of a competition for the most imaginative street of the year. Locals set up tables and benches to enjoy local feasts, but people from all over the city pour in to participate. In squares (particularly Plaça del Sol) and intersections all over the *barri*, bands compete for attention. Snack stands abound and there are numerous bars open onto the streets to sell rivers of drink. Local residents who hope to get any sleep in this week tend to stay with friends or leave town!

Festa Major de Sants

Around August 24 – this barri launches its own version of decorated mayhem, hard on Gràcia's heels. Although the festival has neither the history nor the grandeur of the Gràcia festival, locals have in recent years injected an increasing amount of life into it and here you'll experience the true flavour of the barri.

Festa Major de la Barceloneta

September/October – Barcelona's partiers barely get a chance to relax before the next opportunity for merry-making comes along. Although on a small scale, La Barceloneta's gig still involves plenty of dancing and drinking (especially down on the beach).

Arts & Music Festivals

Barcelona plays host to several arts-oriented festivals in the course of the year. Among the more important are:

Sonar

June – Barcelona's celebration of electronic music. It is claimed to be Europe's biggest such event and you can get into the latest house, hip-hop, trip-hop, eurobeat and anything else they have come up with in the meantime.

Festival del Grec

Late June to August – many theatres shut down for the summer but into the breach steps this eclectic program of theatre, dance and music. Performances are held all over the city, not just at the amphitheatre on Montjuïc (Map 7) from which the festival takes its name. Programs and tickets are available from the Palau de la Virreina on La Rambla (see under Tourist Offices) and at a temporary booth set up on Avinguda del Portal del Àngel (just off Plaça de Catalunya).

BAM

Around 24 September – all the great free music put on for the Festes de la Mercè (see above) is organised as Barcelona Acció Musical. Most of the performances take place on squares in the centre of town and/or on the waterfront.

Festival Internacional de Jazz de Barcelona

Late October to late November – jazz and blues around the city.

DOING BUSINESS

The Barcelonins are often viewed by their counterparts in Madrid as rather dull workaholics and tightwads.

The image is not without foundation and, especially since manufacturing took off here in the 19th century, the city has had (and indeed cultivated) an image of industriousness which is viewed with a mix of envy and scorn by much of the rest of Spain.

This has been in Barcelona's favour as Spain has integrated into the EU and the global market in the past 20 years. The city is now viewed enthusiastically by both the foreign business community and tourists. A Europe-wide survey in 2000 put Barcelona in sixth place among the top 10 European cities for business, ahead of cities like Milan and Zürich.

Business Services

Business people who need to work in Barcelona temporarily or long term, and people hoping to set up new businesses here, should first contact the trade department of the Spanish embassy or consulate in their own country. The next port of call should be the Cambra Oficial de Comerç, Indústria i Navegació (Map 2; ☎ 902 44 84 48, fax 93 416 93 01), Avinguda Diagonal 452. It has a documentation centre and business-oriented bookshop, the Llibreria de la Cambra. It also has a services centre, or Centre de Relacions Empresarials (aka Business Center; ☎ 93 478 67 99, fax 93 478 67 05), at the airport on the first floor of Terminal B, with an information desk and several office spaces (with phone, basic office equipment and screens for presentations) to rent.

Barcelona Activa (Map 1; ☎ 93 401 97 77), Gran Via de les Corts Catalanes 890, aims to help with business start-ups. It is mainly aimed at locals, but could be a useful port of call if you want to start a business in Barcelona. Self-employed people (*autónomos*) may want to contact Autempresa (☎ 902 20 15 20) for information on bureaucracy and tax questions.

The Fira de Barcelona's information office (see Exhibitions & Conferences) offers business services (communications etc), meeting rooms and other facilities for people working at trade fairs.

Have you brought your portable computer along? It's malfunctioning? You can find several ads for English-speaking computer technicians in the free English-language magazine, *Barcelona Metropolitan* or *Business Barcelona* – see the Newspapers & Magazines section above.

Exhibitions & Conferences

With more than 70 trade fairs a year and a growing number of congresses of all types, Barcelona is becoming an important centre of international business in Europe. It claims to rank fifth worldwide for the organisation of congresses, in part due to the lower costs involved – the Fira de Barcelona, the city's trade fair, claims that organising congresses costs 20% less here than in other major European cities.

The nature of the fairs ranges from fashion to technology, from furniture to recycling, jewellery to books.

The main trade fair is located between the base of Montjuïc and Plaça d'Espanya, with 90,000 sq m of exhibition space (of a total area of 224,000 sq m). To cope with expansion in the past years, the Fira 2 (Fair No 2) south-west of Montjuïc, will have 40,000 sq m of exhibition space. This may be expanded again later on. The Palau de Congressos at Fira 1 can host up to 1650 people, and smaller conference halls abound. The Fira has an information centre (Map 7; ☎ 93 233 20 00) right on Plaça d'Espanya. It can provide limited communications facilities for business people and professionals involved in the fairs.

Another number you can try if you want advice on organising conventions in Barcelona is the Barcelona Convention Bureau (☎ 93 368 97 00, fax 93 368 97 01, e bcb@barcelonaturisme.com), Rambla de Catalunya 123.

A privately run Palau de Congressos (☎ 93 364 44 04, e comercialpalau@pcongresos.com), with a capacity of 2300, was opened in mid-2000 on the outskirts of town as part of the Hotel Rey Juan Carlos I complex, at Avinguda Diagonal 661–671. Down at Port Vell, work continues on the World Trade Centre, already partly up and running.

WORK

Although Catalunya has one of the lowest unemployment levels in Spain, this is hardly the ideal place to look for work. But there are a few ways of earning your keep (or almost) while you're here.

Bureaucracy

Nationals of EU countries, Norway and Iceland may work in Spain without a visa, but for stays of more than three months they are supposed to apply within the first month for a *tarjeta de residencia* (residence card). If you are offered a contract, your employer will usually steer you through the labyrinth.

Virtually everyone else is supposed to obtain, from a Spanish consulate in their country of residence, a work permit and, if they plan to stay more than 90 days, a residence visa. These procedures are well-nigh impossible unless you have a job contract lined up before you begin them. Quite a few people do work, discreetly, without bothering to tangle with the bureaucracy.

Language Teaching

This is the obvious option, for which language-teaching qualifications are a big help (often indispensable). Be warned. English teaching is not the gold mine it was a few decades ago. Every English-speaking bum and his dog tries to get work like this nowadays, so competition is fierce. English teachers are actually paid less today in Barcelona than prior to the Olympics in 1992. Classroom rates have settled around the 1600 ptas to 2200 ptas mark, depending on your experience and the school.

Predictably, Barcelona is loaded with 'cowboy outfits' that pay badly and often aren't overly concerned about quality. Still, the only way you'll find out is by hunting around. Schools are listed under Acadèmias de Idiomas' in the yellow pages.

Sources of information on possible teaching work – school or private – include foreign cultural centres (the British Council, Institut Français etc), foreign-language bookshops (such as Come In), universities and language schools. Many of these have notice boards where you may find work opportunities, or where you can advertise your own services.

Bar Work & Waiting

If your Spanish (and preferably Catalan as well) are in reasonable shape, you can sometimes swing jobs waiting tables or, more easily, in bars. For English speakers the city's pseudo-Irish bars are the first obvious port of call.

Buskers & Street Artists

La Rambla is one of the great busking stages of Europe, so you could try your luck here. It's no easy road though. Competition is fierce and the quality of some acts is surprisingly high, but if you have an original and well-rehearsed act to present, this could be the place to try it out.

Street artists may also find the going tough. The Ajuntament has applied a quota (a maximum of 50 artists can work La Rambla) and hopefuls must apply for a permit if they do not want to be moved along by the police.

FACTS FOR THE VISITOR

Getting There & Away

After Madrid, Barcelona is Spain's biggest international transport hub. It's easy to reach by air from anywhere in Europe and North America. Regular rail and bus links and a smooth super highway plug Barcelona into France and the rest of Europe and there are plenty of air and land connections to destinations all over Spain.

AIR

A phalanx of airlines fly direct to Barcelona from the rest of Europe. It pays to shop around and, for short stays, consider flight/hotel packages. From North America the cheaper flights may entail a stopover en route (either Madrid or another European centre). Travellers from more distant locales, like Asia and Australasia, have fewer choices. Increasingly travellers are turning to the Internet to look for flight deals and book tickets. Most airlines and many travel agents now operate interactive Web sites.

For more detailed information on airport facilities, see the Getting Around chapter.

Departure Tax

Airport taxes are factored into ticket prices, but fares are generally quoted without the taxes. They are in a continual state of flux but at the time of writing ranged from 3200 ptas for most European destinations to 10,700 ptas for the USA. The passport formalities are minimal.

Other Parts of Spain

Flying within Spain is generally not an economical affair. Iberia (☎ 902 40 05 00) and the small franchise subsidiaries Iberia Regional-Air Nostrum (☎ 93 379 74 11) and Binter Mediterráneo cover all destinations, with a range of fares. Ask about discounts and special rates. You get about 25% off flights departing after 11 pm (admittedly there are few of these). People aged under 22 or over 63 get 25% off *return* flights and another 20% off night flights. Its Web site is at www.iberia.com.

A standard one-way fare between Madrid and Barcelona ranges from 12,150 ptas to 16,200 ptas.

Competing with Iberia are Spanair (☎ 902 13 14 15, e spanair@spanair.es) and Air Europa (☎ 902 40 15 01). Air Europa is the bigger of the two, with regular flights from Barcelona to Madrid, Palma de Mallorca, Málaga and a host of mainland Spanish destinations.

Air Europa flights connect Madrid with Barcelona three to eight times daily. The cheapest one-way economy *(turista)* fare is 10,400 ptas. Fares for return trips range from 12,000 ptas to about 30,000 ptas. What you pay depends on when you fly and the conditions attached.

Canary Islands

From Barcelona, Iberia, Air Europa, Spanair and charters all fly to Tenerife and Las Palmas (Gran Canaria). Tourist-class return flights between Santa Cruz de Tenerife and Barcelona average around 28,000 ptas to 35,000 ptas, although return charter fares can be as low as 18,900 ptas.

The UK

Most British travel agents are registered with ABTA (Association of British Travel Agents) and all agents that sell flights in the UK must hold an Air Travel Organiser's Licence (ATOL). If you have paid for your flight with an ABTA-registered or ATOL agent who then goes bust, the Civil Aviation Authority will guarantee a refund or an alternative under the ATOL scheme. Unregistered travel agents are riskier but sometimes cheaper.

Travellers are increasingly using the Internet to search for good fares and some airlines, particular the budget ones, encourage you to book on-line.

One of the more reliable, but not necessarily cheapest, agencies is STA Travel (☎ 020-7361 6145 for European flights). STA has several offices in London, as well

Air Travel Glossary

Alliances Many of the world's leading airlines are now intimately involved with each other, sharing everything from reservations systems and check-in to aircraft and frequent flyer schemes. Opponents say that alliances restrict competition. Whatever the arguments, there is no doubt that big alliances are the way of the future.

Cancelling or Changing Tickets If you have to cancel or change a ticket, you need to contact the original travel agent who sold you the ticket. Airlines only issue refunds to the purchaser of a ticket – usually the travel agent who bought the ticket on your behalf. There are often heavy penalties involved; insurance can sometimes be taken out against these penalties.

Courier Fares Businesses often need to send urgent documents or freight securely and quickly. Courier companies hire people to accompany the package through customs and, in return, offer a discount ticket which is sometimes a bargain. However, you may have to surrender all your baggage allowance and take only carry-on luggage.

Fares Airlines traditionally offer 1st class (coded F), business class (coded J) and economy class (coded Y) tickets. These days there are so many promotional and discounted fares available that few passengers pay full fare.

Lost Tickets If you lose your airline ticket an airline will usually treat it like a travellers cheque and, after enquiries, issue you with another one. Legally, however, an airline is entitled to treat it like cash and if you lose it then it's gone forever. Take good care of your tickets.

Onward Tickets An entry requirement for many countries is that you have a ticket out of the country. If you're unsure of your next move, the easiest solution is to buy the cheapest onward ticket to a neighbouring country or a ticket from a reliable airline which can later be refunded if you do not use it.

Open-Jaw Tickets These are return tickets where you fly out to one place but return from another. If available, this can save you backtracking to your arrival point.

Overbooking Since every flight has some passengers who fail to show up, airlines often book more passengers than they have seats. Usually excess passengers make up for the no-shows, but occasionally somebody gets 'bumped' onto the next available flight. Guess who it is most likely to be? The passengers who check in late. If you do get 'bumped' you are normally offered some form of compensation.

Reconfirmation Some airlines require you to reconfirm your flight at least 72 hours prior to departure. Check your travel documents to see if this is the case.

Restrictions Discounted tickets often have various restrictions on them – such as needing to be paid for in advance and incurring a penalty to be altered or cancelled. Others are restrictions on the minimum and maximum period you must be away.

Round-the-World Tickets RTW tickets give you a limited period (usually a year) in which to circumnavigate the globe. You can go anywhere the carrying airlines go, as long as you don't backtrack. The number of stopovers or total number of separate flights is decided before you set off and they usually cost a bit more than a basic return flight.

Ticketless Travel Airlines are gradually waking up to the realisation that paper tickets are unnecessary encumbrances. On simple one-way or return trips, reservations details can be held on computer, and the passenger merely shows ID to claim his or her seat.

Transferred Tickets Airline tickets cannot be transferred from one person to another. Travellers sometimes try to sell the return half of their ticket, but officials can ask you to prove that you are the person named on the ticket. On an international flight tickets are always compared with passports.

as branches on many university campuses and in cities such as Bristol, Cambridge, Leeds, Manchester and Oxford. Visit its Web site at www.statravel.co.uk.

A similar place is Trailfinders (☎ 020-7937 1234, for European flights). Its short haul booking centre is at 215 Kensington High St, London W8 7RG They also have agencies in Bristol, Birmingham, Glasgow, Manchester and Newcastle. Its Web site is at www.trailfinder.com.

usit Campus (☎ 0870 240 1010), 52 Grosvenor Gardens, London SW1W 0AG, is in much the same league and has several other branches in London and around the country. Its Web site is www.usitcampus.co.uk.

The two flagship airlines linking the UK and Spain are British Airways (BA; ☎ 0845 773 3377), 156 Regent St, London W1R 5TA, and Spain's Iberia (☎ 020-7830 0011, in London, ☎ 0845 601 2854 rest of UK), Venture House, 27–29 Glasshouse St, London W1R 6JU. Of the two, BA is more likely to have special deals; its Web site is at www.british-airways.com. Cheaper alternatives abound however.

Air Europa (☎ 0870 240 1501) has a flight each day except Saturday to London via Madrid.

British Midland (☎ 0870 606 0360) began three direct flights daily to Barcelona from London Heathrow in November 2000, costing around £140 return in the low season. Check its Web site at www.iflybritish midland.co.uk. It also flies to Barcelona from Manchester, Edinburgh, Glasgow and Belfast via Heathrow.

easyJet (☎ 0870 600 0000) has tickets from London's Luton airport to Barcelona for as little as UK£49 each way, plus UK£10 tax. In slow periods (such as winter weekdays), prices one way have been known to drop as low as UK£19 plus tax! Once fares approach the UK£99 mark (one way) it is time to look elsewhere.

You can book tickets on its Web site at www.easyjet.com. In Spain contact the company on ☎ 902 29 99 92.

Providing direct competition is the BA-run Go (☎ 0845 605 4321). Departures are from London Stansted (a 40-minute train ride from Liverpool St train station). If you comply with certain restrictions (easily done if you are planning to spend a week or more in Spain) you are looking at around UK£50 to UK£60 one way plus taxes to Barcelona. At the time of writing it was offering cheap return flights from Barcelona at 17,500 ptas (including taxes). The number in Spain is ☎ 901 33 35 00. You can book on-line at www.go-fly.com.

Spanish Travel Services (☎ 020-7387 5337), 138 Eversholt St, London NW1 1BL, can get scheduled return flights with Iberia, BA, Air Europa and other airlines for as little as UK£90 in the low season and around UK£150 in the high season (including taxes).

The Charter Flight Centre (☎ 020-7565 6755), 15 Gillingham St, London SW1V 1HN, has return flights, valid for up to four weeks in the low season, for around UK£130 (including taxes). Remember that if you miss a charter flight, you have lost your money.

Several times a year, usually around Easter and again in autumn (any time from September to November), various charter companies put on four- and five-day long-weekend fares to Barcelona and/or other Spanish destinations for silly prices: UK£49 return is not unknown.

The budget airlines' fare structure makes it easy to plan open-jaw flights. You pay a one-way fare to one destination and leave from another. With other airlines it is also possible, if sometimes a little more complicated, to make such arrangements.

You needn't fly from London, as many good deals are easily available from other centres in the UK.

Continental Europe

Short hops can be expensive, but for longer journeys you can often find fares that beat overland alternatives on cost.

France Return flights from Paris to Barcelona with Iberia frequently cost under 2000FF. Otherwise charter and discount flights can come in as low as 1000FF to 1300FF.

From Barcelona in the high season you are looking at 39,800 ptas return if you book two weeks in advance.

Regional Airlines (☎ 91 401 21 36) links Barcelona (and Madrid) with Bordeaux in France, where you can get connecting flights to other French destinations. It is aimed mainly at business travellers. In France you can call them on ☎ 0 803 00 52 00. Air Littoral (☎ 0 803 83 48 34 in France) operates flights from Nice to Barcelona. Neither of these airlines is all that cheap.

Germany In Berlin you could try STA Travel (☎ 030-311 09 50), Goethestrasse 73. It also has offices in Frankfurt am Main, including Bockenheimer Landstrasse 133 (☎ 069-70 30 35), and in 16 other cities across the country. Its Web site is at www.statravel.de.

High season return flights from Frankfurt to Barcelona range from DM395 with Sabena to DM690 with Iberia. Taxes range from DM39 to DM53.50.

The Netherlands & Belgium Amsterdam is a popular departure point. The student travel agency NBBS (☎ 020-624 0989), Rokin 66, offers reliable and reasonably low fares. Compare them with the pickings in the bucket shops along Rokin before deciding. NBBS has several branches throughout the city as well as in Brussels, Belgium.

Brussels is the main hub for Virgin Express (☎ 02-752 0505). Up to seven flights daily connect Brussels with Barcelona (☎ 93 226.66 71). One-way fares can range from about f3800 to f5200 each way.

KLM's new budget subsidiary, Basiq Air, was due to start cheap flights from Amsterdam to Barcelona in December 2000.

Italy The best place to look for cheap fares is CTS (Centro Turistico Studentesco), with branches countrywide. In Rome it is at Via Genova 16 (☎ 06 46791).

Virgin Express (☎ 800 097097) has one flight daily from Rome to Barcelona. Fares range from L119,000 to L256,000 each way.

Portugal Flying between Barcelona and Lisbon is a costly business. Iberia, Air Europa and TAP do it for around 35,000$00 return in the high season.

The USA

Several airlines fly to Barcelona (usually with a stopover), including Iberia, BA and KLM-Royal Dutch Airlines.

Standard fares can be expensive. Discount and rock-bottom options from the USA include charter flights, stand-by and courier flights. One agent specialising in budget airfares is Discount Tickets in New York (☎ 212-391 2313).

Stand-by fares are often sold at 60% of the normal price for one-way tickets. Airhitch (☎ 212-864 2000, ☎ 800 326 2009 toll free), 2641 Broadway, 3rd floor, suite 100, New York, NY 10025, is a specialist. One-way travel from the USA to Europe costs from US$159 (east coast) to US$239 (west coast) plus taxes.

Airhitch has several other offices in the USA, including Los Angeles (☎ 310-726 5000 or ☎ 888-AIRHITCH). In Europe it operates a central office in France (☎ 01 47 00 16 30) at 5 rue de Crussol, 75001, Paris. Check out the Web site at www.airhitch.org. In summer it has a rep in Madrid on ☎ 91 366 79 27.

Otherwise, reliable travel agents include STA (☎ 800 781 4040) and Council Travel (☎ 800-2COUNCIL). Their Web sites are www.sta-travel.com and www.counciltravel.com, respectively, and both have offices in major cities.

Courier flights involve you accompanying a parcel to its destination. A New York–Barcelona return on a courier flight can cost under US$300 in the low season (more from the west coast). You may have to be a US resident and apply for an interview first. Most flights depart from New York.

Now Voyager (☎ 212-431 1616), suite 307, 74 Varrick St, New York, NY 10013, is a courier flight specialist. The Denver-based Air Courier Association (☎ 303-278 8810) also does this kind of thing.

Iberia flies nonstop between Barcelona and New York, but often you can get better

GETTING THERE & AWAY

deals with other airlines if you are prepared to fly via other European centres.

The best value, low season (November, December) fares from the east coast (New York) hover around US$550 return. From Los Angeles you are looking at around US$200 more. In the high season (June to August) you are looking at around US$700 to US$1200. Plenty of flights leave from other cities, usually connecting through New York. Fares from Chicago, for example, are comparable to those from Los Angeles. Flying from Barcelona you are looking at fares from 68,000 ptas (with Lufthansa Airlines, changing in Frankfurt) to 78,900 ptas (Air France via Paris), plus tax (10,700 ptas) for a round trip.

Air Europa (☎ 718-244 7055 or ☎ 888-2EUROPA in the USA) has flights to New York via Madrid. Occasionally they come up with good deals.

If you can't find a good deal, consider a cheap transatlantic hop to London and stalking the unbonded travel agencies or budget airlines there.

Canada
Scan the travel agents' ads in the *Globe & Mail*, *Toronto Star* and *Vancouver Sun*. Canada's main student travel organisation is Travel CUTS (www.travelcuts.com; known as Voyages Campus in Quebec):

Toronto
(☎ 416-977 0441) 74 Gerrard St East
Montreal
(☎ 514-398 0647) Université McGill, 3480 rue McTavish

For courier flights originating in Canada, contact FB On Board Courier Services (☎ 514-631 2077 in Toronto).

Iberia has direct flights to Barcelona from Toronto and Montreal. Other major European airlines offer competitive fares to Barcelona via other European capitals. Low season fares from Montreal start at around C$620, and C$830 from Vancouver. In the high season you are looking (usually) at C$1000/1200 respectively, although good deals crop up in Montreal.

Australia
STA Travel (Australia-wide fast fares on ☎ 1300 360 960) and Flight Centre (☎ 1310 362 665 Australia-wide) are major dealers in cheap airfares, although heavily discounted fares can often be found at your local travel agent. Their Web sites are at www.statravel.com.au and www.flightcentre.com.au, respectively. The Saturday editions of Melbourne's *The Age* and the *Sydney Morning Herald* have many advertisements offering cheap fares to Europe.

As a rule there are no direct flights from Australia to Spain. You will have to fly to Europe via Asia and change flights (and possibly airlines).

Low season return fares to Barcelona cost from around A$1370 to A$1590 on airlines such as Olympic Airways, Thai Airways International and Lauda Air.

On some flights between Australia and cities like London, Paris and Frankfurt, a return ticket between your destination and Barcelona is included. Such flights cost around A$1790 to A$2300 in the low season.

For courier flights try Jupiter (☎ 02-9317 2230), 3/55 Kent Rd, Mascot, Sydney 2020.

New Zealand
As with Australia, STA Travel and Flight Centre are popular agents. A round-the-world ticket may be cheaper than a normal return. Otherwise, you can fly from Auckland to pick up a connecting flight in Melbourne or Sydney. Low season return fares start from around NZ$2015 with Thai Airways International and Air New Zealand.

Airline Offices in Barcelona
You can find airlines listed under Línias Aèries/Líneas Aéreas in the phone book. They include:

Air Europa
(☎ 902 40 15 01) Airport
Alitalia
(Map 2; ☎ 902 10 03 23) Avinguda Diagonal 403
Delta Air Lines
(☎ 93 412 43 33) Airport
easyJet
(☎ 902 29 99 92) Airport

Iberia
(Map 2; ☎ 902 40 05 00 or ☎ 93 401 33 73)
Passeig de Gràcia 30
KLM-Royal Dutch Airlines
(☎ 93 379 54 58) Airport
Lufthansa Airlines
(Map 2; ☎ 93 487 03 52) Passeig de Gràcia 55–57
Spanair
(☎ 902 13 14 15) Airport
TWA
(Map 2; ☎ 93 215 84 86) Carrer del Consell de Cent 360
Virgin Express
(☎ 93 226 66 71) Airport

BUS

The bus is generally cheaper than the train, but less comfortable for the long haul.

The main intercity bus station is the modern Estació del Nord at Carrer d'Alí Bei 80 (Map 1). Its information desk (☎ 93 265 65 08) opens daily from 7 am to 9 pm. Left-luggage lockers are outside by the bus stands and cost 600 ptas for 24 hours.

A few long-distance services – most importantly some international buses and the few buses to Montserrat – use Estació d'Autobusos de Sants beside Estació Sants train station (Map 4).

The main international services are run by Eurolines/Julià Via (☎ 93 490 40 00) from Estació d'Autobusos de Sants, and by Eurolines/Linebús (both ☎ 93 265 07 00) from Estació del Nord.

Also note that a handful of regional services within Catalunya depart from other parts of town. If you are unsure, call the tourist office or Estació del Nord information line to find out about your destination.

Other Parts of Spain

You can ride buses to most large Spanish cities. A plethora of companies operate to different parts of the country, although many come under the umbrella of Enatcar. For schedule information call ☎ 93 245 88 56.

Departures from Estació del Nord include the following, with journey time and fare (where frequencies vary, the lowest figure is usually for Sunday):

to	buses daily	duration (hours)	cost
Almería	2	12¾ to 13½	7120 ptas
Burgos	2 to 4	7½	5000 ptas
Granada	3	13 to 14¼	7915 ptas
Madrid	11 to 18	7 to 8	3400 ptas
Salamanca	3	11½	6415 ptas
Seville	1 or 2	16	9135 ptas
Valencia	5 to 10	4½	2900 ptas
Vigo	1 or 2	15½	6835 ptas
Zaragoza	11	4½	1655 ptas

The UK

Eurolines (☎ 0870 514 3219), 52 Grosvenor Gardens, Victoria, London SW1 0AU (the terminal is a couple of blocks away), runs buses to Barcelona on Saturday, Monday (leaving at 11 am; connection to Alicante) and Wednesday (9.30 pm). The trip takes 24 to 26 hours. The one-way and return fares are UK£84 and UK£119, respectively, (UK£76 and UK£109 for under-26s and seniors). UK passengers may have to change buses in Paris. The standard adult one-way fare the other way is 14,075 ptas.

France

Eurolines has offices in several French cities, including the Paris bus station (☎ 01 49 72 51 51), 28 Ave du Générale de Gaulle. It has another more central office (☎ 01 43 54 11 99) at rue St-Jacques 55, off blvd St-Michel. From Paris you pay 405FF (under 26) or 520FF. The standard fare from Barcelona is 11,975 ptas.

Other International Services

Eurolines/Julià Via also has services at least three times weekly to Amsterdam, Brussels, Florence, Geneva, Milan, Montpellier, Nice, Perpignan, Rome, Toulouse, Venice and Zürich, and twice a week to Morocco.

TRAIN

The main international and domestic station is Estació Sants, on Plaça dels Països Catalans, 2.5km west of La Rambla (Map 4).

Only a handful of services, including one to Madrid, now use Estació de França, on Avinguda del Marquès de l'Argentera, 1km east of La Rambla (Map 5).

euro currency converter €1 = 166 ptas

Other useful stations for long-distance and regional trains are Catalunya on Plaça de Catalunya (metro Catalunya), and Passeig de Gràcia, on the corner of Passeig de Gràcia and Carrer d'Aragó, 10 minutes' walk north of Plaça de Catalunya (metro Passeig de Gràcia).

Note that the entrance for RENFE (Red Nacional de los Ferrocarriles Españoles) long-distance trains is at the northern end of Plaça de Catalunya and quite separate from the entrances to the metro and FGC lines. Similarly, the RENFE entrance at Passeig de Gràcia is three blocks north of the metro entrance. All this can be a little confusing for the harried traveller.

Information

It's advisable to book at least a day or two ahead for most long-distance trains, domestic or international. There's a RENFE information and booking office in Passeig de Gràcia station, open daily 7 am to 10 pm (9 pm on Sunday). You'll find some left-luggage lockers on Via (platform) 2.

At Estació Sants, the Informació Largo Recorrido windows give information on all except suburban trains. The station has a *consigna* (left-luggage lockers) open 5.30 am to 11 pm (400 ptas or 600 ptas for 24 hours), a tourist office, a telephone and fax office, a hotel reservations office, currency exchange booths open from 8 am to 9.30 pm daily, and ATMs.

Estació de França has a train information office and consigna (open 6 am to 11 pm).

For information on all RENFE train services call ☎ 902 24 02 02.

Train timetables are posted at the main stations. Impending arrivals *(arribades/llegadas)* and departures *(sortides/salidas)* appear on big electronic boards and TV screens. Timetables for specific lines are generally available free of charge.

Eurail, InterRail, Europass and Flexipass tickets are valid on the national rail network, RENFE, throughout Spain.

Types of Train in Spain

A host of different train types coast the wide-gauge lines of the Spanish network. A saving of a couple of hours on a faster train can mean a big hike in the fare.

For short hops, bigger cities have a local network known as *cercanías*. In Barcelona they are known as *rodalies*.

Most long-distance *(largo recorrido)* trains have 1st and 2nd class. The cheapest and slowest of these are the *regionales*, generally all-stops jobs between provinces within one region (although a few travel between regions). If your train is a *regional exprés* it will make fewer stops.

All trains that do journeys of more than 400km are denominated Grandes Líneas services – really just a fancy way of saying long distance. Among these are *diurnos* and *estrellas*, the standard inter-regional trains. The latter is the night-time version of the former.

Faster, more comfortable and expensive are the Talgos (Tren Articulado Ligero Goicoechea Oriol). They make only major stops and have extras such as TVs. The Talgo Pendular is a sleeker, faster version of the same thing that picks up speed by leaning into curves.

Some Talgos and other modern trains are used for limited-stop trips between major cities. These services are known as InterCity (and, when they're really good, InterCity Plus!).

A classier derivative is the Talgo 200, a Talgo Pendular using the standard-gauge, high-speed Tren de Alta Velocidad Española (AVE) line between Madrid and Seville on part of the journey to such southern destinations as Málaga, Cádiz and Algeciras.

The most expensive way to go is to take the high-speed AVE train itself along the Madrid–Seville line (another line between Madrid and Barcelona, which would link up with the French TGV, is planned).

Other new and fast services include the Barcelona–Valencia–Alicante Euromed and Arcos trains, and the Alaris service between Madrid and Castelló (via Albacete and Valencia).

Autoexpreso and Motoexpreso wagons are sometimes attached to long-distance services for the transport of cars and motorcycles, respectively.

euro currency converter 1000 ptas = €6.01

A *trenhotel* is an expensive sleeping-car train. There can be up to three classes on these trains, ranging from *turista* (for those sitting or in a couchette), *preferente* (sleeping car) and *gran clase* (sleeping in sheer bloody luxury).

Catalunya Services

Three types of local trains fan out from Barcelona across Catalunya. The slowest all-stops ones are called Regionals. Making fewer stops are the Deltas, while Catalunya Exprès trains are the fastest (and about 15% dearer than the others).

Long-distance main-line trains also stop at several Catalunya destinations, but fares are often more expensive still. Regional trains within Catalunya depart from Estació Sants; many also stop at Catalunya and/or Passeig de Gràcia.

Rodalies are a more reliable way to get to some destinations not too far out from Barcelona (such as Sitges). They run on a fixed-fare six-zone system. Line 1 connects the centre of town with the airport – with piped classical music in the background, this is a highly civilised introduction to Barcelona (see the Getting Around chapter)! These trains often stop at several stations with metro connections, including Estació Sants, Catalunya, Passeig de Gràcia, Arc de Triomf and Clot.

See individual destination sections in the Excursions chapter for how to get about Catalunya.

Other Parts of Spain

Trains run from Barcelona to most Spanish cities. There is a mind-boggling array of fare options. Most trains depart daily from Estació Sants (some also stopping at Passeig de Gràcia). Only a handful of trains use Estació de França, including one to Madrid, a couple to Zaragoza and one to Murcia.

The trip to Madrid can take 6½ to 9½ hours and a basic 2nd-class fare is 5100 ptas. The Talgo (which is quickest) costs 6600 ptas. If you buy a return ticket, you get 20% off the return run (25% for a same-day return). Other examples of 2nd-class travel in diurno/estrella trains include:

to	one-way fare	duration (hours)
Granada	6400 ptas	12½
Pamplona	4400 ptas	6½ to 10
San Sebastián	5000 ptas	8¼ to 10
Zaragoza	2900 ptas	3½ to 4½

Euromed & Arco A high-speed AVE train on standard Spanish track connects Barcelona with Valencia (three hours) five times daily, and thrice daily with Alicante (4¾ hours). The respective *turista/preferente* (2nd/1st class) fares are 5100/7400 ptas to Valencia and 6800/9900 ptas to Alicante. The service is known as Euromed.

In late 1999 a stylish new train known as Arco entered service between Portbou and Alicante. It takes only 20 minutes more than Euromed to reach Valencia, and 35 minutes more to Alicante. Turista/preferente fares are 4300/5600 ptas to Valencia (four times daily) and 5800/7600 ptas to Alicante (twice daily).

The UK

Your choices from London are limited by the options in Paris, where you have to change trains. Trains run from Charing Cross or Victoria station to Paris (via ferry from Dover to Calais or Folkestone to Boulogne), or from Waterloo (Eurostar). You arrive at Gare du Nord and must proceed to Gare d'Austerlitz (take the RER B to St Michel and change there for the RER C to Austerlitz), Gare de Montparnasse (Metro 4) or Gare de Lyon (RER B to Châtelet and then RER A for Gare de Lyon). See also the following section on France.

The one-way/return fares to Barcelona are UK£90/143 (more if you take the Eurostar), and tickets are valid for two months. Under-26s can get Wasteels or BIJ (Billet International de Jeunesse) tickets for UK£68/121.

Children qualify for discounts and those aged over 60 can get a Rail Europe Senior Railcard (valid only for trips that cross at least one border). You pay UK£5 for the card, but you must already have a Senior Railcard (UK£18), available to anyone who can prove that they are over 60 (you are not required to be a UK resident). The card entitles you to roughly 30% off standard fares.

For information on all international rail travel (including Eurostar services), call European Rail (☎ 020-7387 0444) or go to the Wasteels office opposite platform 2 at Victoria station in London. You can also get information on Eurostar and rail passes from the Rail Europe Travel Centre (☎ 0870 584 8848) at 179 Piccadilly, London, W1V 0BA. For Eurostar you can also make enquiries and buy tickets at Waterloo station, from where the trains depart.

France
The only truly direct train to Barcelona is the *trenhotel* sleeper-only job. It leaves Gare d'Austerlitz, Paris, at 8.47 pm daily and arrives at 8.53 am or 9 am (stopping at Dijon, Figueres, Girona and Barcelona Sants). The standard one-way fare in a couchette is 757FF. Going the other way, the trenhotel leaves Barcelona Sants at 8.05 pm and arrives at 8.14 am in Paris. The couchette costs 16,900 ptas. Reservations on this train can be made in Barcelona by calling ☎ 93 490 11 22.

Otherwise, the cheapest and most convenient option to Barcelona is the 9.47 pm from Gare d'Austerlitz, changing at Latour-de-Carol and arriving in Barcelona Sants at 11.27 am. A reclining seat costs 492FF one way, or the fare is 562FF in a 2nd-class couchette. There is an alternative train with a change at Portbou (on the coast). Under-26s get a 25% reduction. Note also that fares rise in July and August.

Up to three TGVs (Trains de Grande Vitesse – high-speed trains) also put you on the road to Barcelona (leaving from Paris Gare de Lyon), with a change of train at Montpellier or Narbonne. Prices and time-tables vary, so check the latest details.

A direct Talgo service also connects Montpellier with Barcelona (245FF or 6400 ptas in 2nd class, 4½ hours). A couple of other slower services (with a change of train at Portbou) also make this run. All stop in Perpignan.

When appropriate track is eventually laid, Barcelona will be linked to the French TGV network.

From Estació Sants, eight to 10 trains daily run to Cerbère (2½ hours) and four to five to Latour-de-Carol (3½ hours). From these stations you have several onwards connections to Montpellier and Toulouse, respectively.

Other International Services
Direct overnight trains from Estació Sants also run to Zürich (13 hours) and Milan (12¾ hours), from three to seven days per week, depending on the season. These trains meet connections for numerous other cities.

CAR & MOTORCYCLE
To give you an idea of how many clicks you'll put behind you if travelling with your own wheels, Barcelona is 1932km from Berlin, 1555km from London, 1146km from Paris, 1300km from Lisbon, 1199km from Milan, 780km from Geneva and 690km from Madrid – quite central in its own way!

Paperwork & Preparations
Vehicles must be roadworthy, registered and insured for third party at least. The Green Card, an internationally recognised proof of insurance, is compulsory.

A European breakdown assistance policy such as the AA Five Star Service or the RAC Eurocover Motoring Assistance is a good investment.

In the UK, further information can be obtained from the RAC (☎ 0870 572 2722) or the AA (☎ 0870 550 0600). Their Web sites are www.rac.co.uk and www.theaa.co.uk, respectively.

For details of driving conditions in Barcelona and renting or purchase, see Car & Motorcycle in the Getting Around chapter. See also Driving Licence & Permits in the Facts for the Visitor chapter.

Access Roads
The A-7 *autopista* is the main toll road from France (via Girona and Figueres). It skirts

inland around the city before proceeding south to Valencia and Alicante. About 40km south-west of Barcelona, the A-2, also a toll road, branches westwards off the A-7 towards Zaragoza. From there it links up with the N-II dual carriageway for Madrid (no tolls). Other tollways include: the A-19, which follows the coast northeast as far as the southern end of the Costa Brava; the A-18, which winds north to Manresa and peters out in the foothills of the Pyrenees at Sallent; and the A-16, which follows the coast south-west of Barcelona to Sitges and links up with the A-7 26km short of Tarragona.

As a rule alternative toll-free routes are busy (if not clogged). The N-II is the most important. From the French border it follows the A-7, branches off to the coast and then follows the A-19 into Barcelona, from where it heads west to Lleida. From there it follows the A-2 to Zaragoza and becomes the main highway to Madrid. It is interesting to note that drivers in Catalunya are the most heavily penalised – one-third of the entire country's tollways are in this region.

Coming from the UK you can put your car on a ferry from Portsmouth to Bilbao with P&O European Ferries (☎ 0870 242 4999) or from Plymouth or Portsmouth to Santander with Brittany Ferries (☎ 0870 901 2400). Their Web sites are www.poef.com and www.brittany-ferries.com, respectively. From either destination you still have a fair drive to Barcelona.

Alternatively, you can take a car ferry or the Channel Tunnel across to France. The Channel Tunnel runs around the clock, with up to four crossings (35 minutes) an hour in the high season. You pay for the vehicle only and fares vary according to the time of day and season. Low season economy return tickets cost UK£219, or UK£119 for motorcycles. Peak fares can rise as high as UK£180 each way. You can book in advance (☎ 0870 535 3535), but the service is designed to let you just roll up on the day.

Driving in Spain

Road Rules In general, standard European road rules apply. In built-up areas the speed limit is usually 50km/h, rising to 100km/h on major roads and 120km/h on *autopistas* and *autovías* (toll and toll-free motorways).

Motorcyclists must use headlights at all times. Crash helmets are obligatory on bikes of 125cc or more.

Vehicles already on roundabouts have right of way.

The blood-alcohol limit is 0.05%. Fines for many traffic offences range from around 50,000 ptas to 100,000 ptas. Nonresident foreigners can be fined up to 50,000 ptas on the spot. Pleading linguistic ignorance will not help – your traffic cop will produce a list of infringements and fines in as many languages as you like.

Petrol Prices vary (up to 4 ptas a litre) between service stations *(gasolineras)* and fluctuate with oil tariffs and tax policy. Super (due to be phased out in January 2002 in compliance with EU rules) costs 149.9 ptas/litre and diesel (or *gasóleo*) 113.9 ptas/litre. Lead-free (*sin plomo*; 95 octane) costs 139.9 ptas/litre and a 98 octane variant (also lead free) that goes by various names, up to 153.9 ptas/litre.

Road Assistance The Real Automóvil Club de España's head office (RACE; ☎ 900 20 00 93) is at Calle de José Abascal 10 in Madrid. For RACE's 24-hour, country-wide emergency breakdown assistance, you can try calling ☎ 900 11 22 22.

The Catalunya version of the RACE is the Reial Automòbil Club de Catalunya (RACC; ☎ 902 30 73 07) with headquarters at Avinguda Diagonal 687 (Map 1). Their assistance number is ☎ 902 10 61 06.

As a rule, holders of motoring insurance with foreign organisations such as the RAC, AA (UK) or AAA (USA) will be provided with an emergency assistance number to use while travelling in Spain, so in general you should not require the above numbers.

Whichever numbers you use, in Catalunya you may well be assisted by the RACC. If you plan on a long stay in Barcelona, you may want to take out local insurance with the RACC, which is quite possible for foreign registered cars.

BICYCLE

If you plan to bring your own bike, check with the airline about any hidden costs. It will have to be disassembled and packed for the journey. Bicycle (especially mountain bike) touring is growing in popularity in Catalunya. UK-based cyclists planning to do some of this during their time in Barcelona might want to contact the Cyclists' Touring Club (☎ 01483-417217), Cotterell House, 69 Meadrow, Godalming, Surrey GU7 3HS, UK. It can supply information to members on cycling conditions, itineraries and cheap insurance. Membership costs UK£25 per annum or UK£15 for those aged under 26.

HITCHING

Hitching is never entirely safe in any country in the world, and we don't recommend it. Travellers who decide to hitch should understand that they are taking a small but potentially serious risk. People who do choose to hitch will be safer if they travel in pairs and let someone know where they are planning to go.

To get out of Barcelona you need to start well out of the city centre. The chances of anyone stopping for you on autopistas are low – try the more congested national highways (such as the N-II described above).

BOAT

Balearic Islands

Passenger and vehicular ferries to the Balearic Islands, operated by the Trasmediterránea line, dock close to its office near the Moll de Barcelona wharf in Port Vell (Map 1). Information and tickets are available from Trasmediterránea (☎ 902 45 46 45) there, or from travel agents.

Scheduled services are: Barcelona–Palma (eight hours, seven to 21 services weekly); Barcelona–Maó (nine hours, two to eight services weekly); and Barcelona–Ibiza city (9½ hours or 14½ hours via Palma, three to six services weekly). The standard one-way fare to any of the islands is 6920 ptas for a 'Butaca Turista' (seat). You can also get sleeping berths and transport vehicles. In summer, Trasmediterránea also operates a 'Fast Ferry' service to Palma (8990 ptas, 4¼

hours, up to eight services a week), but you'll often find cheaper airfares for return-trip tickets.

Italy

After a 15-year absence, the so-called *canguro* (kangaroo) shipping run between Barcelona and Genoa was relaunched by the Italian group Grimaldi in 1998.

There are departures from Barcelona on Tuesday, Thursday (both 10 pm) and Sunday (2 am). Going the other way, departures are Monday (10 pm), Wednesday and Friday (9 pm). An airline-style seat costs from L113,000 one way in the low season to L167,000 in the high season. A car costs anywhere from L161,000 to L256,000 one way depending on the size of the vehicle and time of year. The trip lasts about 17 hours.

In Genoa, Grimaldi (☎ 010 58 93 31, fax 010 550 92 25) is at Via Fieschi 17/17a. The ferry terminal is at Via Milano (Ponte Assereto). You can book direct over the phone, through a travel agent, at the docks (if there is space) or (if the Web site is working) at www.grimaldi.it. In Barcelona, where you can book through any travel agent, the boat docks at Moll de San Beltran (Map 1).

ORGANISED TOURS

If you prefer to opt for a package trip to Barcelona, perhaps including some day trips to some of the destinations beyond the capital suggested in the Excursions chapter, you'll find a host of tour operators willing to separate you from your money. Approach your closest Spanish tourist office for a list of tour operators in your country. You can really do it all with comparatively little difficulty yourself, but a package can save you some hassle – at a price.

The UK

Cresta Holidays (☎ 0161-927 7000), Tabley Court, Victoria St, Altrincham, Cheshire WA14 1EZ, offers a range of city tours, fly-drive trips and other holidays to Spain.

Another Spain specialist is The Individual Travellers Spain (☎ 08700-773773, fax 780190, ⓔ holidays@indiv-travellers

.com), Manor Court Yard, Bignor, Pulborough RH20 1QD. City Escapades (☎ 020-8563 89 59, fax 8748 3731), 227 Shepherds Bush Rd, London W6 7AS, also does long weekend breaks. Kirker Travel Ltd (☎ 020-7231 3333, fax 7231 4771), 3 New Concordia Wharf, Mill St, London SE1 2BB, offers a range of more expensive quality city breaks. Wine buffs might approach Arblaster & Clarke Wine Tours (☎ 01730-893344, fax 892888), Clarke House, Farnham Rd, West Liss, Petersfield, Hants GU33 6JQ.

Cruises Barcelona has become a major port of call for cruise ships. Trips tend to take a couple of weeks and typically include a stop of a night or two in Barcelona. One company is Fred. Olsen Cruise Lines (☎ 01473-292222, fax 292345, e cruises@fredolsen .co.uk), Fred. Olsen House, White House Rd, Ipswich, Suffolk IP1 5LL. More expensive is the Holland America Line (☎ 020-7729 1929, fax 7739 7512), 77–79 Great Eastern St, London EC2A 3HU.

The USA
In the USA, Spanish Heritage Tours (☎ 800 221 2250), 47 Queens Blvd, Forest Hills, NY 11375, is a reliable operator that offers a range of tours. Saranjan Tours (☎ 800 858 9594), 12865 PO Box 292, Kirkland WA 98033, does city break packages.

Australia
You can organise trips through Ibertours Travel (☎ 03-9670 8388) 1st floor, 84 William St, Melbourne 3000, Victoria (www .ibertours.com.au) and Spanish Tourism Promotions (☎ 03-9650 7377, e sales@ spanishtravels.com.au) level 1, 178 Collins St, Melbourne 3000, Victoria.

Warning

The information in this chapter is particularly vulnerable to change: Prices for international travel are volatile, routes are introduced and cancelled, schedules change, special deals come and go, and rules and visa requirements are amended. Airlines and governments seem to take a perverse pleasure in making price structures and regulations as complicated as possible. You should check directly with the airline or a travel agent to make sure you understand how a fare (and ticket you may buy) works. In addition, the travel industry is highly competitive and there are many lurks and perks.

The upshot of this is that you should get opinions, quotes and advice from as many airlines and travel agents as possible before you part with your hard-earned cash. The details given in this chapter should be regarded as pointers and are not a substitute for your own careful, up-to-date research.

Getting Around

EL PRAT AIRPORT

Barcelona's airport lies 12km south-west of the city at El Prat de Llobregat. The airport building contains three terminals. Terminal A handles non-EU international arrivals and all arrivals/departures by non-Spanish airlines. Terminal B handles EU arrivals and international and domestic departures with Spanish airlines. Since early 2000 it has also taken on the over spill of about a dozen foreign airlines from an overloaded Terminal A. Terminal C is for the Pont Aeri (Puente Aereo), the Barcelona–Madrid shuttle.

The arrivals halls are all on the ground floor; departures are on the 1st floor. The main airport tourist office is on the ground floor of Terminal A. It opens 9.30 am to 8 pm Monday to Saturday, to 3 pm on Sunday (about a half-hour later in summer) and has information on all Catalunya. Another office on the ground floor of Terminal B opens 9.30 am to 3 pm Monday to Saturday.

ATMs are scattered about all three terminals and currency exchange facilities are available at Terminals A and B. You'll also find a *correus* (post office) at these two terminals. Newspaper stands and bookshops, a smattering of bars and restaurants and duty-free gift shops provide all the essentials for airport survival.

When you arrive inside the terminals, follow the *Recollida d'Equipatges/Recogida de Equipajes* (baggage claim) signs to passport control (there is usually no passport control for arrivals from Schengen countries (see Documents in the Facts for the Visitor chapter).

For flight information call ☎ 93 298 38 38 (it's an automated service, so you'll need to understand Spanish enough to choose English on the options menu).

Left Luggage

The left luggage *(consigna)* is on the ground floor at the end of Terminal B closest to Terminal C. It opens 24 hours and charges 635 ptas per item per 24-hour period or fraction thereof. See the Facts for the Visitor chapter for other left luggage options around town.

TO/FROM THE AIRPORT

Train

The airport is the terminus for *rodalies* (*cercanías* in Castilian) train line 1 (which heads for Mataró and beyond on the northeastern edge of Barcelona). You are in zone 4 here and the trip into the centre of town (zone 1) costs 355 ptas.

Main stops include Estació Sants, Plaça de Catalunya, Arc de Triomf and El Clot–Aragó. Trains run every 30 minutes from 6.13 am to 10.41 pm daily. It takes 16 minutes to Sants and 21 minutes to Catalunya. Departures from Sants to the airport are from 5.43 am to 10.13 pm; from Catalunya they're five minutes earlier.

The only drawback with the train is that it's a five-minute hike (eased by moving walkways when they work) to/from the terminal buildings – a bit of a pain if you're heavily loaded up. The station lies between terminals A and B. You get tickets either at the booth or from the automatic machines if you have coins; you then stamp them in the turnstile slot as you pass onto the platform.

Metro

In June 2000 a plan to build a new metro line (Línia 9) was approved. It will start at the airport and cross Barcelona to the planned high-speed train (AVE) station at Sagrera and beyond. Optimists predict it will be in operation by 2004.

Bus

The A1 Aerobús service runs from the airport to Plaça de Catalunya via Estació Sants every 15 minutes from 6 am to midnight Monday to Friday (from 6.30 am on weekends and holidays). Departures from Plaça de Catalunya are from 5.30 am to 11.15 pm Monday to Friday (6 am to 11.20 pm on weekends and holidays). The trip is about 40 minutes – depending on traffic – for 500 ptas.

Cheaper suburban buses (Buses EA and its night version, the EN) leave every one hour and 20 minutes for Plaça d'Espanya and cost 150 ptas. They take about an hour.

In both cases you pay on the bus (unless, on the suburban bus, you have some kind of multi-trip ticket or pass – see Public Transport below).

Taxi
A taxi to/from the centre – about a half-hour ride depending on traffic – costs about 2500 ptas. There is generally no shortage of them.

Parking
The short-term car parks in front of the main terminal buildings charge 225 ptas an hour for the first two hours, then 150 ptas an hour. If you leave the car for eight hours or more, the daily charge becomes 1475 ptas. From the sixth day on you pay 1050 ptas per day. You pay at the machines (coins or credit cards) before going to your car – once you have paid, you have 20 minutes to get your car out of there.

If you intend to leave your car for any lengthy period at the airport, you may wish to avail yourself of the Parking VIP service. You drive to the terminal and a driver takes your car to a covered parking area that offers permanent surveillance. When you return, you call ahead to have your car delivered to you at your arrival terminal. The daily parking fee is 1850 ptas (it goes down slightly from the sixth day on), the driver's fee is a one-off 975 ptas and you have to add 16% IVA. Since you are charged for a minimum of two days, the least you will pay is 5425 ptas for one or two days' parking. For information and to book ahead, call ☎ 93 478 66 71 or fax 93 478 14 85.

PUBLIC TRANSPORT
The metro is the easiest way of getting around and reaches most places you're likely to visit. It is supplemented by a few train lines run by Ferrocarrils de la Generalitat de Catalunya (FGC).

The main tourist office gives out the comprehensive *Guia d'Autobusos Urbans de Barcelona*, with a metro map and all bus routes. For public transport information you can call ☎ 010 or ☎ 93 412 00 00 (☎ 93 205 15 15 for FGC trains only). For information on disabled facilities call ☎ 93 486 07 52.

TMB, the public transit authority, runs four Centres d'Atenció al Client (customer service centres): in Estació Sants (the mainline RENFE station) and the metro stops of Universitat, Diagonal and Sagrada Família. The one at Estació Sants opens 7 am to 9 pm daily and the others 8 am to 8 pm Monday to Friday.

Targetas
Targetas are multiple-trip transport tickets and offer worthwhile savings. They are sold at most city-centre metro stations. Targeta T-1 (825 ptas) gives you 10 rides on the metro, buses and FGC trains. Each ride is valid for an hour and permits you to make changes between metro and FGC lines. The Targeta T-10x2 is similar but gives you 75 minutes for each ride and allows you to transfer between metro, FGC *and* bus (1325 ptas). Targeta T-DIA (625 ptas) gives unlimited metro, bus, FGC, RENFE and night bus travel in one day.

Many other options exist, including monthly passes for unlimited use of all public transport at 5550 ptas. For this you need to get a Targetren ID card, available at the Centres d'Atenció al Client. The Targeta T-50/30 (for 50 trips within 30 days; 3500 ptas) and discounted tickets/passes for pensioners and students are further possibilities.

If you plan to move around a lot over a short period, using buses, metro and FGC trains, the three and five-day Abonament tickets are good value at 1600/2400 ptas.

If you take the Aerobús from the airport, you can get an all-in ticket for the bus and unlimited use of Barcelona's buses and metro for three days (2000 ptas) or five days (2500 ptas).

euro currency converter €1 = 166 ptas

GETTING AROUND

Bus

Buses run along most city routes every few minutes from 5 or 6 am to 10 or 11 pm. On Friday, Saturday and the day before public holidays the service runs to 2 am. Many routes pass through Plaça de Catalunya and/or Plaça de la Universitat. After 11 pm (or 2 am), a reduced network of yellow *nitbusos* (night buses) run until 3 to 5 am. All night-bus routes pass through Plaça de Catalunya and most run every 30 to 45 minutes. A single fare on any bus is 150 ptas.

Bus Turístic

This bus service covers two circuits (24 stops) linking virtually all the major tourist sights. Tourist offices, TMB offices and many hotels have leaflets explaining the system. Tickets, available on the bus, cost 2000 ptas for one day's unlimited rides, or 2500 ptas for two consecutive days. Frequency of buses varies from 10 to 30 minutes, depending on the season, from 9 am to 7.45 pm.

Tickets entitle you to discounts of up to 300 ptas on admission fees to more than 20 attractions, the tramvia blau, funiculars and cable cars, as well as shopping discounts and a meal at Kentucky Fried Chicken and Pizza Hut (oh great!). The discounts don't have to be used on the day(s) you use the bus.

Tombbus

The T1 Tombbus route has been thought out for shoppers and runs regularly from Plaça de Catalunya up to Avinguda Diagonal, along which it proceeds west to Plaça de Pius XII, where it turns around. On the way you pass such landmarks as El Corte Inglés (several of them), Bulevard Rosa, FNAC and Marks & Spencer. Tickets cost 180 ptas.

Metro

The metro has five lines, numbered and colour-coded, and is efficient and easy to use. A single ride costs 150 ptas and tickets are easily available from machines and staffed booths at most stations. At interchange stations, you just need to work out which line and direction you want. The metro runs from 5 am to 11 pm Monday to Thursday, 5 am to 2 am on Friday, Saturday and the day before public holidays, 6 am to midnight on Sunday, 6 am to 11 pm on other holidays, and 6 am to 2 am on holidays immediately preceding another holiday. Line 2 has access for the disabled and a handful of stations on other lines have lifts. See the colour metro map at the back of the book.

FGC Suburban Trains

Suburban trains run by the FGC include a couple of useful city lines. One heads north from Plaça de Catalunya. A branch of it will get you to Tibidabo and another within spitting distance of the Monestir de Pedralbes. Some trains along this line continue beyond Barcelona to Sant Cugat, Sabadell and Terrassa.

The other FGC line heads to Manresa from Plaça d'Espanya and is less likely to be of use (except for the trip to Montserrat – see the Excursions chapter).

These trains run 5 am to 11 or 11.30 pm Sunday to Thursday, 5 am to 2 am on Friday and Saturday. Rides within the city cost 150 ptas.

Rodalies/Cercanías

These RENFE-run local trains serve towns around Barcelona, as well as the airport. For more details see the Getting There & Away chapter.

Fines

The fine for being caught without a ticket on public transport is 5000 ptas.

CAR & MOTORCYCLE

An effective one-way system makes traffic flow fairly smoothly, but you'll often find yourself flowing the wrong way – unless you happen to have an adept navigator and a map with a comprehensive street index showing the one-way streets (as do the more expensive map guides).

It's better to abandon your car while you're here and use Barcelona's public transport.

euro currency converter 1000 ptas = €6.01

Parking

As you will soon discover, parking is no easy task (except in August, when half the city departs on annual vacation). Parking in the Ciutat Vella is virtually impossible and frankly not worth trying for all the stress it will cause. The narrow streets of Gràcia are almost worse. The broad boulevards of l'Eixample offer a few possibilities, but you need to watch out for a lot of things. On some streets you may not park at all. In other cases you will see parts of streets marked in red – also no go. Blue markings mean you must stick money in the meter (a maximum of 510 ptas for two hours) and leave the ticket on the dash. Obviously you can't park in driveways and the like, and anything marked in yellow usually means you are permitted to stop for up to 30 minutes for loading and unloading *(càrrega)* and *(descàrrega)*. Many people opt to take their chances and leave cars in such zones for longer – eventually you'll get a ticket and towing is common.

MICK WELDON

As a rule the zones marked in yellow are only problematic from 8 am to 8 pm Monday to Saturday. This includes most of the handy, chopped-off angles *(chaflanes)* at intersections in l'Eixample. Meter parking is enforced during similar hours (with a break for a couple of hours around lunchtime).

There are streets in l'Eixample where – if you can find a space – you can park without worry. If the only road markings you see are white and there are no parking restriction signs, you should be OK.

The same rules apply elsewhere in the centre. Other tricks abound though. In some roads you can only park on one side, and this is swapped around every two weeks – this should be signposted (usually a round no-parking symbol with '1–15' or '16–31', meaning the first and second fortnight of the month). If you leave your car for any length of time and find it has been shifted days later, it's probable that some kind of road works had to be done and your car was moved.

Parking motorbikes and scooters is obviously easier. On occasion you'll see spaces marked out especially for bikes.

If you get towed, call the Dipòsit Municipal (car pound) on ☎ 93 428 45 95. You'll probably be sent to the one right on Plaça de les Glòries Catalanes (metro Glòries). You pay 15,175 ptas for the tow and 255 ptas per hour (maximum of 2550 ptas per day). Oh, the first four hours your car is held are free!

Car Rental

You obviously wouldn't want to rent a car to slope around Barcelona, but one could come in handy for touring the surrounding countryside. It won't pay if you only intend to make a few simple day trips however.

If you haven't organised a rental car from abroad, local firms such as Julià Car, Ronicar and Vanguard are generally cheaper than the big international names. From these a typical small car like a Ford Ka or Fiat Punto should cost from around 2800 ptas per day plus 25 ptas a km, plus IVA.

For unlimited kilometres, they're around 18,000 ptas for three days or 35,000 ptas a week, plus IVA. You pay insurance on top, which can come to around 1500 ptas per day. Special low weekend rates (from Friday lunchtime or afternoon to Monday morning) are worth looking into. Rental firms (several have branches scattered about town) include:

GETTING AROUND

Avis (Map 2; ☎ 902 13 55 31 or ☎ 93 237 56 80) Carrer de Còrsega 293–295, l'Eixample

Europcar (Map 2; ☎ 902 10 50 30) Gran Via de les Corts Catalanes 680

Hertz (Map 2; ☎ 902 40 24 05 or ☎ 93 270 03 30) Carrer d'Aragó 382–384, l'Eixample

Julià Car (Map 4; ☎ 93 402 69 00) Ronda de la Universitat 5, l'Eixample

National/Atesa (Map 4; ☎ 902 10 01 01 or ☎ 93 323 07 01) Carrer de Muntaner 45, l'Eixample

Ronicar (Map 3; ☎ 989 06 34 73) Carrer d'Europa 34–36, Les Corts

Vanguard (Map 3; ☎ 93 439 38 80) Carrer de Londres 31, l'Eixample

Avis, Europcar, Hertz and several other big companies have desks at the airport, Estació Sants train station and Estació del Nord bus terminus.

Vanguard also rents out motorcycles. If you want something decent for touring outside Barcelona, you'll be looking at around 12,000 ptas per day (plus 16% IVA).

Purchase

Only people legally resident in Spain may buy vehicles there. One way around this is to have a friend who is a resident put the ownership papers in their name.

Car-hunters need a reasonable knowledge of Spanish to get through paperwork and understand dealers' patter. Trawling around showrooms or looking through classifieds can turn up second-hand Seats (eg, Ibiza) and Renaults (4 or 5) in good condition costing from around 300,000 ptas. The annual cost of third-party insurance on such a car, with theft, fire cover and national breakdown assistance, comes in at between 40,000 ptas and 50,000 ptas (with annual reductions if you make no claims).

Vehicles of five years and older must be submitted for roadworthiness checks, known as Inspección Técnica de Vehículos (ITV). If you pass, you get a sticker for two years. You have to do it annually once the car is 10 years old. Check that this has been done when buying: the test costs about 4000 ptas.

You can get second-hand 50cc *motos* (mopeds) for anything from 40,000 ptas to 100,000 ptas.

Warning

If you drive a foreign or rental car to and around Barcelona, take extra care. Groups of delinquents are known to zero in on them occasionally. They get you to pull over indicating you have a problem with a tyre or whatever. While you and one of them are busy examining the problem, the guy's sidekick is busy emptying your car.

This is becoming a growing problem at the airport, where there have also been reports of false rental-car company employees approaching people with the story that they will park the car for them. The car (and anything the poor victim hasn't taken out) disappears. Rental-car company employees do *not* park cars for customers.

TAXI

Taxis are black-and-yellow (with the exception of the black-and-cream taxis in Palma de Mallorca, Barcelona's taxis are the only ones in Spain to differ from the national standard all-white jobbies) and cost 300 ptas flagfall plus meter charges. These work out to about 105 ptas per kilometre (30 ptas more from 10 pm to 6 am and all day Saturday, Sunday and holidays). A further 300 ptas is added for all trips to/from the airport, and 125 ptas for luggage bigger than 55x35x35cm. The trip from Estació Sants to Plaça de Catalunya, about 3km, costs about 700 ptas.

You can call a taxi on ☎ 93 225 00 00, ☎ 93 330 03 00, ☎ 93 266 39 39 or ☎ 93 490 22 22. General information is available on ☎ 010. Radio Taxi Móvil (☎ 93 358 11 11) has taxis adapted for wheelchair users.

A green light on the roof means the taxi is free (*lliure/libre* in the Catalan/Castilian sign usually placed in the lower passenger side of the windscreen). With 11,000 taxis in action, you rarely have to wait too long to grab one. There is a taxi rank by the Monument a Colom at the bottom of La Rambla (Map 5).

BICYCLE & MOPED

The moped rules in Barcelona, although plenty of people zip around on bicycles.

Plaça de Sant Jaume – the Barri Gòtic's heart

CHRISTOPHER GROENHOUT

Pick up your own Picasso on La Rambla

MARTIN MOOS

Barcelonins say it with flowers.

OLIVER STREWE

Mercat de la Boqueria – a feast for the eyes

NEIL SETCHFIELD

Cable cars dangle precariously over the harbour.

ANDERS BLOMQVIST

Fantasy meets history at the wax museum.

The haywire roof of Fundació Antoni Tàpies

Palau de la Generalitat and the Catalan flag

Església de Santa Maria del Pi's rose window

Josep Vilaseca's Modernista Arc de Triomf

Ascend Monument a Colom for sea views.

Bike lanes have been laid out along quite a few main roads (for instance along Gran Via de les Corts Catalanes, Avinguda Diagonal, Carrer d'Aragó, Avinguda de la Meridiana and Carrer de la Marina), and most of the town is pretty flat. Otherwise, dodging around in the traffic can be a little hairy. A bicycle path has also been traced out along much of the waterfront from Port Olímpic towards the Riu Besòs. New routes are being planned all the time, and there are several scenic itineraries mapped out for bike-riders in the Collserola parkland.

You can occasionally pick up a cycle route map at the tourist office on Plaça de Catalunya.

Bicycles on Public Transport
You can transport your bicycle on the metro except during rush hours on weekdays (ie, not between 6.30 and 9.30 am, and 4.30 and 8.30 pm). On weekends and holidays, and throughout July and August, there are no restrictions. You can also use FGC trains (except the Plaça d'Espanya–Igualada line), except from opening time until 9.30 am at the weekend. Finally you can transport your bike on rodalies from 10 am to 3 pm on weekdays and all day on weekends and holidays.

Bicycle Rental
Several outlets rent out bicycles. Un Menys (Map 6; ☎ 93 268 21 05), Carrer de l'Esparteria 3, charges 2000 ptas for a whole day, 1500 ptas for half a day or 600 ptas an hour. Scenic (Map 5; ☎ 93 221 16 66), Carrer de la Marina 22, charges 750 ptas an hour or 3000 ptas for a whole day. Another option is the car park and bicycle rental place (look for the Bicicletas sign) at Passeig de Picasso 40 (Map 6; ☎ 93 319 18 85). They rent out cycles for 400 ptas an hour or 2000 ptas per day. There are several other rental outlets in the vicinity.

Moped Rental
For nipping about town, you could make your own two-stroke contribution to the city's noise pollution by renting out a small cylinder scooter. On average it will cost you 4000 ptas per day (plus 16% IVA). You are not supposed to take scooters beyond the city limits. You can rent them at Vanguard (Map 3; ☎ 93 439 38 80), Carrer de Londres 31.

WALKING
The Barri Gòtic and surrounding areas are ideal for walking, but you'll need to use public transport to reach farther-flung sights (such as the Sagrada Família, the Monestir de Pedralbes, Montjuïc and Tibidabo) more efficiently.

Although drivers here are generally more considerate than drivers in, say, Madrid, do not take it for granted that cars will stop at crossings. In fact, play it safe and assume they won't. Drivers do, however, tend to respect red lights.

One of the great rules of wandering around cities is 'look up' – you never know what you may see. Unfortunately, 'look down' is in some respects a safer bet in Barcelona, especially in the centre, liberally besprinkled with dog-do.

ORGANISED TOURS
Bicycle Tours
Un Menys bicycle store (Map 6; ☎ 93 268 21 05), Carrer de la Esparteria 3, organises bicycle tours around the old centre of town, La Barceloneta and Port Olímpic. Daytime tours take place on Saturday and Sunday, starting at the store at 10 am and finishing at 12.30 pm. The 2500 ptas price includes a stop for a drink in Port Vell. The night version is on Tuesday and Saturday, starting at 8.30 pm and finishing at midnight. The 6000 ptas price tag includes a drink stop and a meal along the Barceloneta waterfront. If you have a large group, they will do these tours on other days of the week too.

Other Tours
The Bus Turístic (see Public Transport in this chapter) is better value than conventional tours for getting around the sights, but if you want a guided trip, try Julià Tours (Map 4; ☎ 93 317 64 54) at Ronda de la Universitat 5, and Pullmantur (Map 2; ☎ 93 318 02 41) at Carrer del Bruc 645. Both do

GETTING AROUND

daily city tours by coach, plus out-of-town trips to Montserrat, Vilafranca del Penedès, the Costa Brava and Andorra. Their city tours cost about 4750 ptas for a half-day, 10,500 ptas for a full day.

A walking tour of the Ciutat Vella on Saturday and Sunday mornings departs from the Oficina d'Informació de Turisme de Barcelona on Plaça de Catalunya (Map 6; English at 10 am, Spanish and Catalan at noon). The price is 1000 ptas.

La Casa Elizalde (Map 2; ☎ 93 488 05 90), Carrer de València 302, organises courses and all sorts of other activities across the city. Also on offer are some Barcelona walks (which generally occupy a morning and cost 775 ptas a head) and one-day or weekend excursions outside the city. They are generally aimed at locals but if you can deal with Catalan (you may find this the majority language), they can be informative.

For other guide services and tailor-made options, get in touch with the Barcelona Guide Bureau (☎ 93 310 77 78, fax 93 268 22 11).

GETTING AROUND

Walking Tours

Before we get into the nitty-gritty of what there is to see and do in Barcelona, for which see the following chapter, we set out below some thematic itineraries to guide you through the best of what the city has to offer.

To see a decent chunk of Barcelona and give it any justice you will need a good week and plenty of energy. Quite a few attractions are well dispersed throughout the city, so you'd be wise to use public transport to save some shoe leather.

We suggest three thematic walks. The first two take you around the Ciutat Vella (old city), stopping off at main points of interest spanning Roman times to the 18th century. The second walk follows on where the first left off, and together they form a single circuit – too much for one day if you intend to do anything more than march past and join the dots. This is not the idea!

The third walk is devoted entirely to Modernisme, which for many visitors is what Barcelona is all about.

You will notice a few overlaps between the Modernisme walk and the Ciutat Vella circuit, so you may want to combine elements of the tours, or come up with your own. The walks are designed to get you oriented and they thread together many of the sights of old and (relatively) new Barcelona.

Sights preceded by an asterisk are dealt with in greater detail in the Things to See & Do chapter.

Quite a few sights beyond the thematic and/or geographical scope of these tours are mentioned only in passing or not at all – you can read more about them in the Things to See & Do chapter. Conversely, several minor sites get just a quick mention here. Happy yomping!

CIUTAT VELLA CIRCUITS

A walking tour of the medieval rabbit warren that is Old Barcelona will necessarily weave and wind and bend back on itself. If you intend to stop at any of the sights

along the way, you'll need to allow at least two long hard days to complete both walks (especially the first one).

Walk 1: Barri Gòtic & La Ribera

In this walk we explore the very heart of the city. This is where the Romans built their outpost, upon the core of which medieval Barcelona slowly grew – it remains the secular and religious centre of the city to this day.

Plaça de Sant Jaume This square (1 on map) is the heart of Barcelona and seems a reasonable place to start.

The north-western and south-eastern sides of the square are lined by the *Palau de la Generalitat (2) and *Ajuntament (3), the seats of regional and city government, respectively. Just north of the medieval square, and possibly incorporating some of it, lay the original forum of Roman Barcino, opposite which stood the temple on a slight rise known as Mont Taber. Together they formed the centre of civic and religious life. The town's two main roads crossed through the forum. From roughly north to south ran the *decumanus* (now Carrer del Bisbe Irurita), intersected by the *cardo* – a classic plan for a Roman settlement, as seen right across the empire. It was a military camp turned into a town – you can learn more about it in the Museu d'Història de la Ciutat (see under Barri Gòtic).

Jewish Quarter & Around From Plaça de Sant Jaume, head west along Carrer del Call, the main street in the former Jewish quarter *(Call)* in medieval Barcelona (Carrer de Ferran, the straight street just below it, also leading towards La Rambla, was only rammed through in 1823). At No 5, the jewellery shop just past Carrer de Ramon del Call, you can see remnants of the Roman walls and south-western gate. A block north up here you reach Carrer de Marlet. At No 1 is a Hebrew inscription in the wall, one of the few overt reminders of the area's former identity. According to the Castilian translation underneath (1820), a holy rabbi, Samuel Hasareri, must have lived or died here. What is truly intriguing is the apparent date of his death (692 AD).

The next junction is with Carrer dels Banys Nous, where the Jewish community was permitted to build new public baths just beyond the then city walls (before Jaume I raised new walls along the present day Rambla). From here the street changes name to Carrer de la Boqueria. Take the next right and follow it into Plaça de Sant Josep Oriol. The Gothic church in front of you is *Santa Maria del Pi (4; entrance in

Rough Justice

At the junction of Baixada de Santa Eulàlia and Carrer de Sant Sever you may notice a devotional niche and a ceramic plaque quoting a passage from one of the works of the 19th-century Catalan cleric and writer Jacint Verdaguer. He talks of one of the many tortures of Santa Eulàlia, joint patron saint of Barcelona. Supposedly born into the pagan world of Roman Barcino before Christianity became the official religion of the empire, Eulàlia was so appalled by the licentious living of her contemporaries that she became a Christian.

This apparently was not considered good form, and the locals took time off to demonstrate the extent of their disapproval. Flung into a tower in the Call, she subsequently underwent a series of highly unpleasant trials – apparently one of them was to be stuffed into a barrel (some versions say with nails hammered into it) which was rolled down the hill of what is now Baixada de Santa Eulàlia. She eventually died at the stake (no-one can agree where) and her purported remains lie buried in the crypt of the Catedral. At least that's what we think. Many experts actually identify her with a like-named saint from Mérida (Extremadura, western Spain) and there is no shortage of doubting Thomases who claim the whole story is a load of old tosh.

the adjoining square). Opposite it, at No 4, stands the **Palau de Fiveller** (5), a one-time private mansion dating to 1571.

Wend your way back east down Carrer de l'Ave Maria, dogleg left up Carrer dels Banys Nous and first right up Baixada de Santa Eulàlia (we are back in the Call). Where the street name changes to Carrer de Sant Sever, you'll see a tiny lane to your left. Head down this into a quiet, leafy, but a tad neglected square, which boasts the rather obscure **Museu del Calçat** (6), or footwear museum. It opens 11 am to 2 pm Tuesday to Sunday; admission costs 200 ptas. The church before you is the baroque **Església de Sant Felip Neri** (7), completed in 1752. It adjoins the *Palau Episcopal** (8; or Palau del Bisbat). Follow Carrer de Montjuïc del Bisbe, surely one of the narrowest lanes in Barcelona, into Carrer del Bisbe Irurita.

The Catedral You are facing the entrance into the shady cloister of the *Catedral** (9). You *could* turn right and head back to Plaça de Sant Jaume, passing first the modest **Església de Sant Sever** (10) and then the main Gothic facade of the Palau de la Generalitat.

Roman Route However, we will turn left (north-west) and head out through the old city gates (parts of the Roman originals are still extant) where Carrer del Bisbe Irurita leads into Plaça Nova. (For the record, the south-western gates stood on Carrer del Call. To the south-east, the entrance to Barcino was on what is now Carrer de Regomir, while the north-eastern exit was about where Carrer de la Llibreteria runs into Baixada de la Llibreteria.)

Proceed up Carrer dels Arcs and a short way along Avinguda del Portal de l'Àngel before hanging a left into Carrer de la Canuda. It is speculated that this was part of the old Roman branch road of the Via Augusta (that linked Rome to Cádiz) into Barcelona. Proceed along it until you hit Plaça de la Vila de Madrid. Here you will see a small **Roman cemetery** (11) with a few sad looking tombs.

euro currency converter 1000 ptas = €6.01

In Search of Guifré el Pelós Take Carrer de Bertrellans north a block to Carrer de Santa Anna. Turn right and you'll find almost immediately to your left a lane leads into a surprisingly tranquil square backed by the unassuming **Església de Santa Anna** (12). It originally dates to the 12th century, but little remains of the original Romanesque structure. The Gothic cloister is a shady haven – if you can get in.

Back on Carrer de Santa Anna, cross Avinguda del Portal de l'Àngel and continue down Carrer Comtal. Taking a right down Carrer de N'Amargos is interesting if only to see the plaque at No 8. It claims that the palace garden walls of the first Count of Barcelona, Guifré el Pelós (Willy the Hairy – see History in the Facts about Barcelona chapter) stood here. Carrer de N'Amargos was also the first in the city to get gas lighting.

Back to the Catedral Turn right at Carrer de Montsió and at Avinguda del Portal de l'Àngel take a left and retrace your steps to Plaça Nova and the Catedral. The narrow old streets around the Catedral are beautifully traffic free and dotted with buskers playing classical guitar or Catalan folk songs.

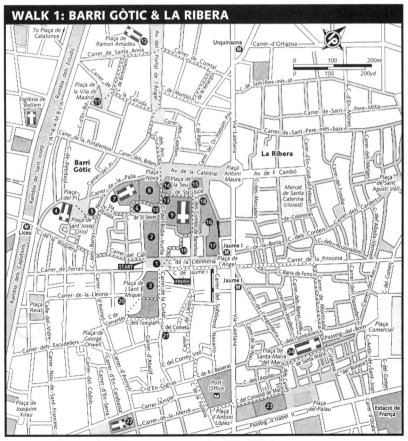

WALK 1: BARRI GÒTIC & LA RIBERA

Re-enter the Roman gates (note on your left the remnants of the aqueducts that supplied Roman Barcino with water) and take the first left. You are on Carrer de Santa Llúcia. On your right is the Romanesque *Capella de Santa Llúcia (13; wedged onto the Catedral) dedicated to the saint of the same name. On your left is *Casa de l'Ardiaca (14). Farther ahead on your right is the main entrance to the Catedral. The building directly ahead of you is the *Casa de la Pia Almoina (15).

The lane heading south-east down the eastern flank of the Catedral, Carrer dels Comtes de Barcelona, will lead you to the complex of buildings making up the former Palau Reial Major. Turn left into the courtyard known as *Plaça del Rei (16); access to the complex (which includes an underground tour of this sector of Roman Barcino) is through the *Museu d'Història de la Ciutat (17) and the *Museu Frederic Marès (18). When you're through, leave Plaça del Rei via the street you entered it from, cross over Carrer dels Comtes de Barcelona and take the next left to dogleg your way down Carrer del Paradis for a quick look at what's left of the *Temple Romà Augusti (19), Barcino's Roman temple. This brings you back to Plaça de Sant Jaume, and this might be a jolly good moment to take a breather.

Southern Barri Gòtic From Plaça de Sant Jaume, head south-east down Carrer de la Ciutat along the only remaining Gothic facade of the Ajuntament. Turn right around the building and you end up in the rather nondescript Plaça de Sant Miquel. The onetime Roman baths here have long since been covered up. Still in one piece, however, is the charming 15th-century **Casa Centelles** (20), on the corner of Baixada de Sant Miquel. You can wander into the fine Gothic-Renaissance courtyard if the gates are open, but that's as far as you'll get.

Head north-east again along Carrer dels Templaris and make a right down Carrer de la Ciutat. Where it becomes Carrer de Regomir you will notice the site of Roman Barcino's southernmost **city gate** and parts of the 3rd- and 4th-century city wall. To get

a closer look, walk up a side passage and enter the Centre Cívic Pati Llimona. Here they stage art shows and the like and you can wander in for free from 9 am to 2 pm and 4.30 to 8.30 pm daily.

Just beyond the gate at No 13 is another 15th century mansion, **Casa Gualbes** (21). Just for fun, backtrack a little and turn into Carrer del Cometa and then left into Carrer de Palma. Follow this into the charming little Plaça de Sant Just, flanked by a Gothic church of the same name and a lovely spot for a rest and coffee.

From the square you can now take another street back down towards the waterfront, Carrer de Lledó. It's a rundown old lane, but once was a fine medieval residential street. Follow it (don't mind the changes of name en route) all the way down to **Carrer de la Mercè**. The baroque church of the same name, **Església de la Mercè** (22; home to Barcelona's most celebrated patron saint), lies three blocks south-west.

La Ribera You are going to head northeast, cross Via Laietana into La Ribera, and stroll along Carrer del Consolat de Mar past **La Llotja** (23), the city's medieval stock exchange. The fine Gothic interior built in the 14th century is encased in a neo-classical facade. Picasso and Miró both attended art school in this building. It is now the seat of Barcelona's Chamber of Commerce and normally it is possible to arrange visits on Friday from 10 am to 2 pm. At the time of writing it was, however, closed indefinitely for building work. For information on the latest situation call ☎ 93 416 93 00.

When you see Carrer dels Canvis on your left, take this to reach Plaça de Santa Maria del Mar. The area is sprinkled with appealing little bars and places to eat, and dominated by the Gothic *Església de Santa Maria del Mar (24). Wander along its eastern flank and around the apse you'll find yourself in *Carrer de Montcada, a fine medieval street bursting with mansions, museums, shops and a couple of choice watering holes. This is a good area to hang about and you may well want to save any further leg-stretching for another day.

If not, the remainder of our route takes you back across the Barri Gòtic along Carrer de la Princesa, over Via Laietana, and along Carrer de Jaume I back to Plaça de Sant Jaume.

Walk 2: El Raval

Beginning at **Plaça de Sant Jaume** (1 on map), follow Carrer de Ferran until it spills on to La Rambla; you'll see ***Gran Teatre del Liceu** (2; see the Entertainment chapter) virtually in front of you. Our objective now is to reach the waterfront.

As you wander down La Rambla you can duck to the right down Carrer Nou de la Rambla (carved through El Raval at the end of the 18th century to give quicker access to Montjuïc from the centre) to see Gaudí's ***Palau Güell** (3; see Walk 3 and under El Raval in the Things to See & Do chapter) or to the left for ***Plaça Reial** (4). Farther down La Rambla on the left is the ***Museu de Cera** (5; wax museum) and right on the

waterfront traffic circle the 19th-century ***Monument a Colom** (6; known to Anglos as Columbus). Over to your right are the great Gothic shipyards, the ***Drassanes** (7), which house the fine ***Museu Marítim**.

From here each sight requires a bit of legwork. Head west along Avinguda de les Drassanes and on to Carrer de Sant Pau. A few blocks towards Avinguda del Paral.lel is the Romanesque ***Església de Sant Pau del Camp** (8). You then backtrack most of the way along Carrer de Sant Pau towards La Rambla, turning left up Carrer de l'Arc de Sant Agustí. **Església de Sant Agustí** (9) is where the city's main Good Friday procession begins. At Carrer de l'Hospital head west for the ***Antic Hospital de la Santa Creu** (10).

For a change of scene and a departure from the medieval side of Barcelona's life, you can wander from the hospital across Plaça de la Gardunya into the back end of the bustling ***Mercat de la Boqueria** (11)

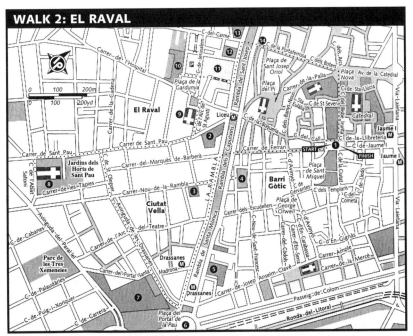

before re-emerging on La Rambla. To the left (heading towards Plaça de Catalunya) are, firstly, the 18th-century ***Palau de la Virreina** (12) and then, across Carrer del Carme, the baroque ***Església de Betlem** (13). Cross the road to No 118 – the Llibreria & Informaciò Cultural de la Generalitat de Catalunya, housed in a former mansion, the **Casa de Comillas** (14), which was built in 1774. It was one of many such houses of the well-to-do that went up along La Rambla in the late 18th and early 19th centuries.

Should you want to return to the centre of the Barri Gòtic and the starting point of this series of walks, simply head down Carrer de la Portaferrissa – you'll emerge onto Plaça Nova near the Catedral. Follow Carrer del Bisbe Irurita south-east to return to Plaça de Sant Jaume.

MODERNISME CIRCUIT

If you wanted to see every vaguely Modernista building or facade in Barcelona, you'd probably need a week. The itinerary that follows is by no means exhaustive but would definitely be exhausting if you tried to do it in a day, so you may want to spread things out or be selective.

On the assumption that you are feeling methodical, chronologically inclined and have nosed around the Ciutat Vella, we'll start this meander there too. Where possible, completion dates of buildings are given.

Walk 3: Modernista Architecture

*Palau Güell (1), on Carrer Nou de la Rambla in El Raval, is our starting point. It is an early job done by Gaudí (1886) for his main patron, the industrialist Eusebi Güell. Walk a few paces east on to La Rambla and turn left (north). Within a couple of blocks you pass the **Antiga Casa Figueras** (2) at No 83, with its elaborate tilework and, virtually across the road, **Casa Quadros** (3), lavishly decorated in oriental style with outward-jutting dragon and umbrellas (which tell you what this place once sold). Make a quick detour down Carrer de Sant Pau and peer inside the restaurant of the

Fonda Espanya (4; 1903, now part of the Hotel España – see the Places to Stay chapter). Ramon Casas had a hand in the decoration.

*Mercat de la Boqueria (5) is on your left as you proceed up La Rambla. It is one of several covered markets that can be considered Modernista constructions, although it was built over a long period – 1840 to 1914. Cross the boulevard and head northeast along Carrer de Santa Anna, take a right on to Avinguda del Portal de l'Àngel and then turn left into Carrer de Montsió. Here you can admire **Casa Martí** (6) – Els Quatre Gats restaurant – which, along with being *the* hangout for Modernista artists and other hip souls from 1897 to 1903, was in fact one of Puig i Cadafalch's first creations (1896).

Take the first left (Passatge del Patriarca), then make a right turn down Carrer Comtal. This takes you into the busy boulevard Via Laietana. Head north a few paces and cross to the little lane called Carrer de Ramon Mas. Spare a moment to admire the **Caixa de Pensions** (7), Via Laietana 56. This largely neo-Gothic fantasy was headquarters to the bank of the same name from 1914 to 1917. Follow Carrer de Ramon Mas (it turns right down Carrer de Francesc de Paula into Carrer de Sant Pere més alt), to stand before Domènech i Montaner's ***Palau de la Música Catalana** (8). Now backtrack to Via Laietana and cruise north along Carrer de les Jonqueres and cross Plaça d'Urquinaona. As you head up Carrer de Roger de Llúria you will pass the **Cases Cabot** (9; 1905) at Nos 8–14, designed by Josep Vilaseca. The first doorway has fine decoration. Around the corner is Gaudí's **Casa Calvet** (10; 1900), Carrer de Casp 48. Inspired by the baroque, the main attraction is the staircase inside.

We continue up to Gran Via de les Corts Catalanes where, at No 654, we pass Enric Sagnier's **Casa Mulleras** (11; 1904), the best feature of which is the gallery on the facade. Farther west, Josep Vilaseca's **Casa Pia Batlló** (12; 1906), Rambla de Catalunya 17, is most interesting for its use of ironwork.

Cross Gran Via and head north-west a couple of blocks along Rambla de Catalunya, turn right into Carrer del Consell de Cent and on a block to the corner of Passeig de Gràcia. Here is *Casa Lleo Morera (13; 1905), first of the Manzana de la Discordia buildings. The other two, *Casa Amatller (14) and *Casa Batlló (15), are around the corner to your left.

The next left into Carrer d'Aragó takes you to the *Fundació Antoni Tàpies (16), originally built by Domènech i Montaner for the publishers Editorial Montaner i Simon (1885). Continue up Passeig de Gràcia – you will probably have noticed the Modernista street lamps along it. You will pass Casa Enric Batlló (17) at No 75, another apartment building by Vilaseca. Cross at Carrer de Provença for Gaudí's masterpiece, *La Pedrera (18; formerly called the Casa Milà) before turning right at the next block into Carrer de Rosselló. On the corner of Carrer de Pau Claris is Puig i Cadafalch's *Palau Quadras (19).

Across Avinguda Diagonal is the Casa Comalat (20; 1911) by Salvador Valeri. The Gaudí influence on this Modernista latecomer is obvious. Head around the back to Carrer de Còrsega to see a lighter, more playful facade. If you can sneak in, you can admire the fine mosaics and stained glass inside. Heading east a couple of blocks down Avinguda Diagonal you reach *Casa de les Punxes (21).

At this point you've probably had more than enough for one day. If you are a diehard, another half dozen or so buildings can be seen around here and farther west up the Diagonal. On the walking-tour map they are Nos 22–26: Domènech i Montaner's Casa Fuster (22; 1910); Sagnier's Església de Pompeia (23; 1915); Puig i Cadafalch's Casa Serra (24; 1903); Manuel Sayrach's Casa Sayrach (25; 1918); and Puig i Cadafalch's Casa Company (26; 1911).

A further cluster of minor Modernista creations lies sprinkled south of Diagonal between Carrer de Roger de Llúria and Passeig de Sant Joan. On the walking tour map they are Nos 27–32. However, you still have some major Modernista sights to deal with and, as it is preferable to see them, you might be better off leaving this lot for another day or forgetting about them altogether.

Should you get around to them, from Casa de les Punxes (21) drop down Carrer del Bruc to Carrer de Mallorca. Casa Thomas (27; 1898), at No 291 by Domènech i Montaner, is your first port of call. It is one of his earlier efforts – the ceramic details are a trademark. Less than a block away, Palau Montaner (28) was finished off by the same architect in 1893. Jeroni Granell's Casa (29; 1903), Carrer de Girona 122, is a colourful companion. Virtually across the road at No 113 is Domènech i Montaner's Casa Lamadrid (30; 1902). Casa Llopis i Bofill (31; 1902), Carrer de València 339, is an interesting block of flats by Antoni Gallissà – the facade is particularly striking. Puig i Cadafalch's Casa Macaya (32; 1901), Passeig de Sant Joan 108, has a wonderful courtyard, if you can get a look inside.

Gaudí Beyond the Walk

Separate excursions should be planned for Gaudí's Parc Güell in the north-west of the city, Finca Güell (better known as the Palau Reial) and, out of town, the Colònia Güell.

Other buildings well worth going to include Casa Vicenç (1888, Gaudí), Carrer de les Carolines 22 (FGC Plaça Molina). Its angular appearance is enough proof that this is early Gaudí, but it is awash with colour and shape that make it stand out in any case.

Gaudí also added some touches to the Col.legi de les Teresianes school in 1889 – the most distinctive features are the parabolic arches. It is possible to visit the school on Saturday mornings (but not in July or August), but you have to call ☎ 93 212 33 54 to arrange it. Gaudí fanatics might want to reach Bellesguard (Map 1), a house he built in 1909 on the site of the ancient palace of the Catalan King Martí I. It's quite a walk from the nearest FGC station, Plaça de John F Kennedy.

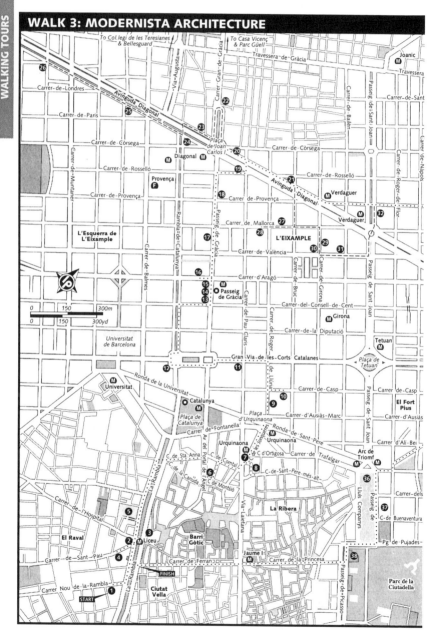

WALK 3: MODERNISTA ARCHITECTURE

However, let's assume you don't want to run around here yet. You have reached Casa de les Punxes (21), and those who don't want to head straight for a footbath will probably have their hearts set on Gaudí's *La Sagrada Família (33). To save on toe power you could jump on the metro at Verdaguer station and travel one stop on line 5.

Another stop on line 5 takes you to the *Hospital de la Santa Creu i de Sant Pau (34). Or you could walk up along Avinguda de Gaudí, which sports some fine Modernista street lamps.

Even if you are not interested in bullfighting, you might want to cast your eye briefly over the *Plaça de Braus Monumental (35; 1915), five blocks or one metro stop south-east of the Sagrada Família (metro Monumental), on the corner of Gran Via de les Corts Catalanes and Carrer de la Marina. It was built by Ignasi Mas and is the larger of the city's two bullfighting rings. The other, Les Arenes, on Plaça d'Espanya, was built around the same time but is no longer in use. Both edifices play with Islamic themes, but you could swear that Mas had a dash of Dalí's blood in his veins – the arena is topped by ceramic-clad eggs!

From the Plaça de Braus Monumental, walk two blocks south-east to Carrer de Ribes, where you swing south towards the *Arc de Triomf (36), built by Vilaseca for the Universal Exhibition in 1888. Heading south-east again along Passeig de Lluís Companys towards the Parc de la Ciutadella you pass on your left the Palau de Justicia (37; 1915), a rather austere, modern building done largely by Sagnier.

At Passeig de Pujades you swing right and then left into Passeig de Picasso. On your left is Domènech i Montaner's *Castell dels Tres Dragons (38), now the Museu de Zoologia.

From here you could return to the starting point by heading south-west along Carrer de la Princesa, Plaça de Sant Jaume and Carrer de Ferran until you reach La Rambla.

Things to See & Do

Barcelona offers a rich palette of sights with something to interest everyone: from the remains of Roman Barcino to the early opus of Picasso; from a grand medieval seafaring museum to one of Europe's most impressive aquariums; from the monuments of the Modernistas to the modern art of Miró.

Museum and art gallery opening hours vary considerably, but as a rule of thumb you should be OK between about 10 am and 6 pm in most places (many shut for lunch from around 2 to 4 pm). Most museums and galleries close all day Monday and Sunday afternoon from 2 pm. Each year there is talk of night-time opening in some museums during the summer – check with the tourist office for the latest details.

Explanations tend to be in Catalan, although English gets a fairly good run – sometimes better than Castilian!

Tickets & Discounts
Admission prices also vary, but 400 ptas to 900 ptas covers the range of most. Students generally pay a little over half, as do senior citizens (aged 65 and over) with appropriate ID and children under 12.

Possession of a Bus Turístic ticket (see the Getting Around chapter) entitles you to discounts to some museums.

The Ruta del Modernisme ticket (see the boxed text later in this chapter) entitles you to discounted admission to several key Modernista sights. It is good value.

Articket gives you admission to six important art galleries for 2496 ptas (to be cute, they actually price this at €15). The galleries included are the Museu Nacional d'Art de Catalunya, the Museu d'Art Contemporani de Barcelona (MACBA), the Fundació Antoni Tàpies, the Cultura Contemporània de Barcelona (CCCB), the Fundació Joan Miró and La Pedrera.

You can pick up the ticket through Telentrada (call ☎ 902 10 12 12 or log onto www.telentrada.com), at the tourist office

Highlights

- Behold the inspired magic of Gaudí's unfinished masterpiece, La Sagrada Família
- Take courage and 'run the fire' during the madness of the Festa de la Mercè in September
- Savour fine seafood in one of Barcelona's quality restaurants
- Board a full-size replica of Don Juan's galley in the swash-buckling Museu Marítim
- Ferret out the many hidden bars secreted away throughout the Ciutat Vella
- Ride the city's only surviving tram up to Tibidabo and feast on the views
- Sip a summer's evening flute of *cava* on the weird roof of La Pedrera
- Go underground at the Museu d'Història de la Ciutat to discover Barcelona's Roman origins
- Take a stroll down La Rambla – any time of day or night
- Indulge in a drink or three at a summertime terrace on Gràcia's Plaça del Sol

in Plaça de Catalunya or at branches of the Caixa Catalunya bank.

If you intend to get around Barcelona fast and want to visit multiple museums in the blink of an eye, the Barcelona Card might come in handy. It costs 2500/3000/3500 ptas for 24/48/72 hours. You get free transport and up to 50% off admission prices to many museums and other sights, as well as minor discounts on purchases at a limited number of shops and restaurants. The card is available at the main tourist office, where you should have a look at the pamphlet first to see whether the discounted sights are what you were hoping to see.

LA RAMBLA (Map 6)

Spain's most famous street, although clearly very much the preserve of visitors, is still a worthy place to first take the city's pulse. Flanked by narrow traffic lanes, the middle of La Rambla is a broad, tree-lined pedestrian boulevard, crowded every day until the wee hours with a cross-section of Barcelona's varied populace and out-of-towners.

Dotted with cafes, restaurants, kiosks and newsstands that sport reams of international newspapers and pornography, and enlivened by buskers, pavement artists, mimes and living statues, La Rambla rarely allows a dull moment.

La Rambla gets its name from a seasonal stream (*raml* in Arabic) that once ran here. It was outside the city walls until the 14th century, and built up with monastic buildings and subsequently mansions of the well-to-do from the 16th to the early 19th centuries. Unofficially, it's divided into five sections – this explains why to many people the boulevard also goes by the name of Las Ramblas – but street numbers are in a single sequence starting at the bottom (waterside) end.

Rambla de Canaletes

A block to the east at the end of this first stretch of La Rambla along Carrer de la Canuda is Plaça de la Vila de Madrid, with a sunken garden where some **Roman tombs** have been exposed (see also the Walking Tours chapter). Also on this part of La Rambla is a turn-of-the-century drinking fountain, the water of which supposedly emerges from what were once known as the springs of Canaletes. It used to be said of people who lived in Barcelona that they 'drank the waters of Les Canaletes'. Nowadays they say that anyone who drinks from the fountain will return to Barcelona, which is not such a bad prospect.

Rambla dels Estudis

This second stretch, from below Carrer de Santa Anna to Carrer de la Portaferrissa, is also called Rambla dels Ocells (birds) because of its twittering bird market.

Rambla de Sant Josep

This section, from Carrer de la Portaferrissa to Plaça de la Boqueria, is lined with verdant **flower stalls**, which give it the alternative name Rambla de les Flors (flowers).

The **Palau de la Virreina**, La Rambla de Sant Josep 99, is a grand 18th-century rococo mansion housing an arts/entertainment information and ticket office run by the *Ajuntament* (town hall). Just across Carrer del Carme, the **Església de Betlem** was constructed in baroque style for the Jesuits in the late 17th and early 18th centuries to replace an earlier church destroyed by fire in 1671. Fire was a bit of a theme for this site. The church was once considered the most splendid of Barcelona's few baroque offerings, but leftist arsonists torched it in 1936.

Continuing towards the waterfront from Palau de la Virreina, you are confronted by the bustling sound, smell and taste-fest of the **Mercat de la Boqueria**. It is possibly La Rambla's most interesting building, not so much for its Modernista-influenced design as for the action of the food market.

Barcelona seems to take pride in being a pleasure centre and in the **Museu de l'Eròtica** (☎ 93 318 98 65, fax 93 301 0896), at No 96, you can observe how people have been enjoying themselves since ancient times – lots of Karma Sutra and flickering porn flicks from the 1920s. The centre opens 10 am to midnight daily; admission costs 975 ptas. You can visit their Web site at www.eroticamuseum.com.

Plaça de la Boqueria, where four side streets meet just north of Liceu metro station, presents the opportunity to walk all over a Miró – the colourful **Mosaïc de Miró** in the pavement, with one tile signed by the artist.

Rambla dels Caputxins

Also called Rambla del Centre, this stretch runs from Plaça de la Boqueria to Carrer dels Escudellers. The latter street is named after the potters' guild, founded in the 13th century, whose members lived and worked here (their raw materials came principally from Sicily). On the western side of La Rambla is the side facade of the **Gran Teatre**

THINGS TO SEE & DO

del Liceu, Barcelona's famous 19th-century opera house, reopened in late 1999 after being gutted by fire in 1994. The Liceu launched such Catalan stars as Josep (aka José) Carreras and Montserrat Caballé.

On the eastern side of Rambla dels Caputxins, farther south, is the entrance to the palm-shaded Plaça Reial (see the Barri Gòtic section). Below this point La Rambla gets seedier, with a few strip clubs and peep shows.

Rambla de Santa Mònica

The final stretch of La Rambla widens out to approach the Columbus monument overlooking Port Vell. It is named after the Convento de Santa Mònica that once stood on the western flank of the street. It has been converted into an art gallery and cultural centre, the Centre d'Art Santa Mònica.

On the eastern side, at the end of narrow Passatge de la Banca, is the Museu de Cera (wax museum). Inside are about 300 wax figures, ranging from tableaux of a Gitano (gypsy) cave, a bullring medical room and a hall of horror, to statues of Cleopatra, Franco and even Yasser Arafat. Also in the roll call are several good and great Catalans, such as writer Ramon Llull. It opens 10 am to 1.30 pm and 4 to 7.30 pm Monday to Friday, 11 am to 2 pm and 4.30 to 8.30 pm on weekends and holidays. Admission costs 1100 ptas.

Monument a Colom (Map 5)

The goings on around the bottom of La Rambla and the harbour beyond it, are supervised by the tall Columbus monument, built for the Universal Exhibition in 1888. It was in Barcelona that Columbus gave the delighted Catholic Monarchs a report of his first discoveries in the Americas, but that's about the extent of his involvement with the place. Or is it? It was popularly believed in the 19th century that Columbus was one of Barcelona's most illustrious sons, although it is commonly accepted that he was born and raised in Genoa (that town's senior officials attended the inauguration of the monument). Then, in 1998, a Catalan historian announced he had evidence to prove

Columbus was in fact a Catalan, which would put the mockers on claims that a little cottage preserved in downtown Genoa is his birthplace. At any rate, Columbus died penniless and forgotten in 1506 in Valladolid, central Spain.

You can ascend by lift (250 ptas), 9 am to 8.30 pm daily (June to September). It opens 10 am to 7.30 pm (with a break from 2 to 3.30 pm Monday to Friday) in April and May, while final closing time is 6.30 pm throughout the rest of the year.

Museu Marítim (Map 5)

West of the Monument a Colom on Avinguda de les Drassanes stand the Reials Drassanes (royal shipyards), a rare work of non-religious monumental Gothic architecture that now houses the Museu Marítim – a fascinating tribute to the seafaring exploits that shaped much of Barcelona's history.

The shipyards were, in their heyday, among the greatest in all Europe. Begun in the 13th century and completed by 1378, the buildings demonstrate that the Catalan Gothic penchant for broad, stout construction had some useful applications. Look up at the ceilings and you feel you are looking at the upturned hulls of so many galleys. The long arched (the arches reach 13m at their highest) bays sloped off as slipways directly into the water – which lapped the seaward side of the Drassanes until at least the end of the 18th century.

By then, shipbuilding here had ceased and the buildings were being used for artillery production and as a training ground, ammunition dump and barracks. Only in 1935 was the site handed over to the Ajuntament, which had already decided to convert it into a maritime museum. This finally happened in 1941 after civil war had returned them briefly to the role of arms factory.

Much of the building remained neglected, however, and only in 1987 was an ambitious plan put into effect to restore the shipyards to their medieval glory and install what is one of the city's most imaginative and captivating museums. Plans are afoot to invest four billion pesetas to improve the museum and create a 'cultural axis' along the waterfront between Montjuïc and the Museu d'Història de Catalunya. This would include education and information centres in the Moll de la Fusta area. The plan also contemplates creating a kind of pond around the Drassanes and thus 'returning' it to its watery context. Sounds potentially cheesy, but we'll see. The work is due for completion in 2004.

The first few sections of the museum include models, charts and a collection of *mascarons* (the figureheads that once adorned the prow of sailing ships). Sailors hoped these figures would help steer their vessels clear of unwanted nastiness. Here also is material devoted to one of the world's first successful submariners, Narcis Monturiol i Estarriol.

From these first rooms you enter the main bays of the shipyards, dominated by a full size replica (made in the 1970s) of Don John (Juan) of Austria's flagship, which he took into battle against the Turks off Lepanto (Italy) in 1571. The result of this, the last great sea struggle between fleets of galleys (under sail or otherwise), was a famous (if ultimately fruitless) victory for the Christians. This part of the museum is full

---

Taking a Dive

Would the real Captain Nemo please stand up? Narcis Monturiol i Estarriol (1819–85) was a curious character with, from all appearances, a generous heart. His interests were wide-ranging. As an editor of publications defending workers' and women's rights he ran into trouble with the authorities and their censor's scissors. He also followed closely attempts to set up some (rather pitiful in retrospect) utopian societies in the Americas.

His optimism reached its high point in a rather different field – scientific invention. The bee in his bonnet was the submarine. By the beginning of the 19th century several attempts had been made to take vessels below the sea, some of them successful. But these projects did not attract funds and generally ended where they had started, on the drawing board.

MICK WELDON

In 1856 Monturiol got to work on his first wooden, fish-shaped sub, the *Ictíneo*. It was about 6m long – a cramped little underwater beast – but it worked. The screws were driven by the crew's muscle power and a shortage of air made the dives fairly brief affairs, but Monturiol made more than 50 dives in the couple of years after he launched the sub in 1859.

He became an overnight celebrity but got no money from the navy. Undeterred, Monturiol sank himself further into debt by designing *Ictíneo II*. This time he really did come up with a first. Seventeen metres long, its screws were steam driven and Monturiol had worked out a system for renewing the oxygen inside the vessel. Nothing like it had been built before. It trialled in 1864 but again attracted no money, either from the navy or from private industry. Everyone had something nice to say about it, but Monturiol had spent a huge sum of money on it. In 1868, his creditors lost patience and had it broken up for scrap, a blow from which Monturiol never really recovered.

of vessels (some real but mostly models) of all types and epochs, from coastal fishing skips to giants of the steam age. You can wander through life-sized dioramas on board a sailing ship, read captains' logs and watch videos (in Catalan) on different aspects of sailing history.

Best of all, head for Àmbit (area) 12, pick up the audio phones and follow the red lights. This wonderful little tour takes you amidships of Don Juan's galley, where audiovisuals help you to imagine the ghastly life of the slaves, prisoners and volunteers (!) who at full steam could haul this vessel along at nine knots. They remained chained to their seats, four to an oar, at all times. Here they worked, drank lots (fresh water was stored below decks, where the infirmary was also located), ate, slept and went to the loo. It seems unlikely they could have greatly enjoyed their maritime adventures. The tour takes you on to a dockside scene in Havana at the time when Barcelona's merchants were doing a brisk business in late-19th-century Cuba; you also board a steam liner and join Narcis Monturiol on his underwater experiments.

The museum opens 10 am to 7 pm daily. Admission costs 800 ptas (students and seniors 600 ptas). Admission is free from 3 pm on the first Saturday of the month. Many of the explanations are in Catalan only, but scattered about the various sections are sheets in several languages explaining key points.

BARRI GÒTIC (Map 6)

The 'Gothic quarter' is the nucleus of old Barcelona. The medieval city was elevated on the Roman core, which in succeeding centuries slowly spread north, south and west. The Barri Gòtic is a classic warren of narrow, winding streets and unexpected little squares, and now home to a dense concentration of budget hotels, bars, cafes and restaurants. Few of its great buildings date from after the early 15th century – the decline Barcelona went into at that time curtailed grand projects for several centuries.

The Barri Gòtic stretches from La Rambla in the west to Via Laietana in the east,

and roughly from Carrer de la Portaferrissa in the north to Carrer de la Mercè in the south. Carrer de Jaume I and Carrer de Ferran (the latter, which was named after King Fernando VII, was sliced through the city in 1823) form a kind of halfway line: these streets and those to their north tend to be dotted with chic little shops and feel 100% safe; those to their south become darker and a little seedier – albeit still full of perfectly respectable places to eat, drink and stay.

Plaça de Sant Jaume

In the 2000 or so years since the Romans settled here, the area around this square (oft remodelled) has been the focus of Barcelona's civic life. Facing each other across it are the Palau de la Generalitat (seat of Catalunya's government) on the northern side and the Ajuntament to the south. Both have fine Gothic interiors which, unhappily, the general public can only enter at limited times.

Palau de la Generalitat Founded in the early 15th century to house Catalunya's parliament, the palace was extended over the centuries as its importance (and bureaucracy) grew. It is open to the public only on 23 April, the Dia de Sant Jordi (St George, Catalunya's patron saint), and on 24 September (Festes de la Mercè).

At any time, however, you can admire the original Gothic main entrance on Carrer del Bisbe Irurita (designed by medieval architect Marc Saffont). Of lesser interest are the facades around the back on Carrer de Sant Sever and on Carrer de Sant Honorat, but at least they too preserve something of the feeling of the building's ancient roots. The modern main entrance on Plaça de Sant Jaume is a late Renaissance job with neoclassical leanings – nothing to write home about. If you wander by in the evening, squint up through the windows into the Saló de Sant Jordi and you will get some idea of the sumptuousness of the interior.

If you *do* get inside, you're in for a treat. Normally you will have to enter from the rear (Carrer de Sant Sever). The first rooms you pass through are characterised by low vaulted ceilings. From here you pass upstairs to the raised courtyard known as the **Pati dels Tarongers**, a modest Gothic orangery. The 16th-century Sala Daurada i de Sessions, one of the rooms leading off the patio, is a splendid meeting hall lit up by huge chandeliers. Still more imposing is the Renaissance Saló de Sant Jordi, whose murals were added this century – many an occasion of pomp and circumstance takes place here. Finally you descend the staircase of the Gothic Pati Central to leave by what was, in the beginning, the building's main entrance.

Ajuntament Facing the Palau de la Generalitat across the square, and otherwise known as the Casa de la Ciutat, the town hall has been the seat of city power for centuries. The Consell de Cent, from medieval times the ruling council of the city, first sat here in the 14th century, but the building has lamentably undergone many changes since the days of Barcelona's Gothic-era splendour.

Only the original, now disused, entrance on Carrer de la Ciutat retains its Gothic ornament. The main 19th-century neoclassical facade on the square is a charmless riposte to the Palau de la Generalitat and the remaining sides of the building are recent and utterly depressing.

Inside, however, it is quite another story. To *get* inside, you have to turn up on Saturday or Sunday between 10 am and 2 pm; admission is free. You enter a courtyard and will probably be directed to the right (pick up a brochure on the way) to the **Escala d'Honor**, a majestic staircase that leads you up to the Gothic gallery.

From here you enter the **Saló de Cent**, the hall in which the town council once held its plenary sessions. The broad vaulting is pure Catalan Gothic and the wooden artesonado ceiling demonstrates fine work. In fact, however, much of what you see is comparatively recent. The building was badly damaged in a bombardment in 1842 and has been repaired and tampered with repeatedly. The wooden neo-Gothic seating was added at the beginning of the 20th century,

as was the grand alabaster *retablo* (retable, or altarpiece) at the back. To the right you enter the small **Saló de la Reina Regente**, built in 1860, where the Ajuntament now sits. To the left of the Saló de Cent you reach the Saló de les Croniques – the murals recount Catalan exploits in Greece and the Near East in Catalunya's merchant empire-building days.

As you head down the other set of stairs to the courtyard, you may notice several statues of women – the least recognisable as such is Joan Miró's *Dona*.

Catedral & Around

Approached from Avinguda de la Catedral, Barcelona's central place of worship presents a magnificent image. The richly decorated main (north-western) facade, laced with gargoyles and all the stone intricacies you would expect of northern European Gothic, sets it quite apart from other churches in Barcelona. The facade was actually added in 1870, although based on a 1408 design. The rest of the building was built between 1298 to 1460. The remaining facades are sparse in decoration, and the octagonal, flat-roofed towers are a clear reminder that, even here, Catalan Gothic architectural principles prevailed.

The interior – open 8.30 am to 1.30 pm and 4 to 7.30 pm (5 to 7.30 pm at the weekend) – is a broad, soaringly high space divided into a central nave and two aisles by lines of elegant, slim pillars. The cathedral was one of the few churches in Barcelona spared by the anarchists in the civil war, so its ornamentation, never over-lavish, is intact.

In the first chapel on the right from the north-western entrance, the main Crucifixion figure above the altar is the **Sant Crist de Lepant**. It is said Don Juan's flagship bore it into battle at Lepanto. Farther along this same wall, past the south-western transept, are the wooden **coffins** of Count Ramon Berenguer I and his wife Almodis, founders of the 11th-century Romanesque predecessor of the present cathedral.

Smack in the middle of the central nave is the late-14th-century **coro**, or choirstalls. Although this central placement of the

THINGS TO SEE & DO

choirstalls can be seen in great churches elsewhere in Europe, it is pretty much a standard across the Iberian peninsula.

A broad staircase before the main altar leads to the **crypt**. It contains the tomb of Santa Eulàlia, one of Barcelona's two patron saints. The carving on the alabaster sarcophagus, executed by Pisan artisans, recounts some of her tortures and, along the top strip, the removal of her body to its present resting place.

You can visit the cathedral's **roof** and tower by an *ascensor* (lift), which rises every half hour from 10.30 am to 12.30 pm and 4.30 to 6.30 pm Monday to Saturday, from the Capella de les Animes del Purgatori near the north-eastern transept. Tickets cost 200 ptas.

From the south-western transept, exit to the lovely **cloister**, with its trees, fountains and flock of geese (there have been geese here for centuries, and nobody has yet come up with a convincing reason why). One of the cloister chapels commemorates 930 priests, monks and nuns martyred in the civil war.

Along the northern flank of the cloister you can enter the **Sala Capitular** (chapter house) for 100 ptas. Although bathed in rich reds of carpet and cosseted by fine timber seating, the few artworks here gathered are of minor interest. Among them figure a *Pietat* by Bartolomeo Bermejo. A couple of doors down in the north-western corner of the cloister is the **Capella de Santa Llúcia**, one of the few bits of Romanesque Barcelona still intact. Walk out the door on to Carrer de Santa Llúcia and turn around to look at the exterior – you can see that, although incorporated into the Catedral, it is in fact a separate building.

Turn on your heels and you are facing the 16th-century **Casa de l'Ardiaca** (archdeacon's house), which now serves as an archive. In office hours you may wander into the supremely serene courtyard, cooled by trees and a fountain. Climb the stairs to the next level, from where you can look down into the courtyard and across to the Catedral. Inside the building you can see parts of the Roman wall (open 9 am to 9 pm Monday to Friday, to 2 pm on Saturday).

Measure for Measure

Have a close look at the external wall of the Romanesque Capella de Santa Llúcia. At about waist level you can make out the inscription *'A 2 Canas lo Pou'*. The *cana* was a unit of measurement (eight palms or 1.55m) once in common use by tailors. Apparently a well *(pou)* was situated about 3m from where you stand. If you inspect the corner of the same building, you'll notice two vertical grooves etched into the stone – they measure 2 canas. The story goes that if, after having bought some material, you discovered you had been cheated by the tailor, you could search for the local gendarmes who in turn would have the good salesman accompany them to this spot to verify whether the cana he was using gave the full measure. Of course, the tailor may have kept a proper cana hidden away for just such occasions.

Across Carrer del Bisbe Irurita is the 17th-century **Palau Episcopal** or Palau del Bisbat (bishop's palace). Virtually nothing remains of the original 13th-century structure. As noted in the Walking Tours chapter, the Roman city's north-western gate stood here, and you can see the lower segments of the Roman towers that stood on either side of the gate at the base of the Palau Episcopal and Casa de l'Ardiaca. In fact, the lower part of the entire north-western wall of the Casa de l'Ardiaca is of Roman origin – you can also make out part of the first arch of the one-time Roman aqueducts, which supplied the ancient town with water.

Casa de la Pia Almoina The Roman walls continued across present-day Plaça de la Seu into what subsequently became the Casa de la Pia Almoina. In the 11th century the city's main centre of charity was located here, although the much-crumbled remains of the present building (still undergoing restoration) date to the 15th century. It houses the **Museu Diocesà** (diocesan museum) and for 300 ptas you can see a sparse collection of medieval religious art. Otherwise there's little there, unless a temporary exposition is on, in which case you may pay more to enter. The museum opens 10 am to 2 pm and 5 to 8 pm Tuesday to Saturday, 11 am to 2 pm on Sunday.

Temple Romà d'Augusti Opposite the south-eastern end of the Catedral, narrow Carrer del Paradis leads towards Plaça de Sant Jaume. Inside No 10 are four columns of Barcelona's main Roman temple, dedicated to Caesar Augustus and built to worship his imperial highness in the 1st century AD. You are now standing on the highest point of Roman Barcino – Mont Taber. Though it is generally said that this mound is 15m high, a plaque outside No 10 insists it is 16.9m. You can visit (free) anytime the door is open. This tends to be in the morning only, from around 10 am to 2 pm, although there is no timetable and you may have to take pot luck.

Plaça del Rei & Around
Plaça del Rei is the courtyard of what was the Palau Reial Major, the palace of the counts of Barcelona and monarchs of Aragón. It's surrounded by tall, centuries-old buildings, most of which are now open to visitors as the Museu d'Història de la Ciutat (city history museum).

Museu d'Història de la Ciutat You enter this museum, one of the most intriguing in Barcelona, in **Casa Padellàs** on Carrer del Veguer.

When you enter Casa Padellàs, built for a 15th-century noble family, you find yourself in a courtyard typical of Barcelona's Gothic mansions, with an external staircase up to the 1st floor.

Buy your tickets inside on the ground floor, then pass through a few small rooms housing a handful of ancient artefacts from Roman and pre-Roman days. Enter the video room (the informative show takes 28 minutes), then get the elevator down to a remarkable piece of Barcelona – a whole stretch of the excavated Roman town. The elevator is cute. Instead of the floor number

it has the year 1996. You get out at Year 12 (presumably 12 BC) in…Barcino.

As you wander around the ruins you can inspect part of the *cardo* or main cross-road, a defensive tower, shops, houses (a few with floor mosaics intact), public baths and storage areas for wine and *garum* (a kind of fish sauce that was a staple throughout the Roman empire). The walk takes you right under the Catedral so you can see what little remains of its Romanesque and Visigothic predecessors (the latter consists of a baptismal font).

Once you are through, you will emerge at a hall and ticket office set up on the northern side of Plaça del Rei. To your right is the **Saló del Tinell**, the banqueting hall of the royal palace and a fine example of Catalan Gothic (built 1359–70). Its broad arches and bare walls give a sense of solidity and solemnity that would have made an appropriate setting for Fernando and Isabel to hear Columbus' first reports of the New World. The hall is sometimes used for temporary exhibitions, which may mean an extra charge for admission. It also may mean that your peaceful contemplation of its architectural majesty is somewhat obstructed.

As you back out of the Saló you end up in the **Capella Reial de Santa Àgata**, the palace chapel, also built in the 14th century. Outside, a spindly bell tower rises from the north-eastern side of Plaça del Rei. Inside all is bare except for the 15th-century altarpiece and the magnificent *techumbre* (wooden ceiling). The altarpiece is considered one of Jaume Huguet's finest surviving works. The stained glass is a recent addition.

Head into Plaça del Rei down the fan-shaped stairs and bear left to the entrance to the multi-tiered **Mirador del Rei Martí** (lookout tower of King Martin), built in 1555. It is part of the museum and leads you to the gallery above the square. You can also climb to the top of the tower, which dominates Plaça del Rei and affords excellent views over the city.

The museum opens 10 am to 2 pm and 4 to 8 pm Tuesday to Saturday, and 10 am to

THINGS TO SEE & DO

2 pm on Sunday. Admission costs 500 ptas (free on the first Saturday of the month from 4 to 8 pm). You can pay an extra 200 ptas to watch the entertaining 3D video tracing the history of the city, before you commence your visit proper. It's also possible to join guided evening tours for 1000 ptas. Since most of the explanations in the museum are in Catalan and/or Castilian (and very occasionally in English), it is worth asking for the pamphlet in your language to give you some clues as to what you will be looking at.

Palau del Lloctinent The south-western side of Plaça del Rei is taken up by this palace, built in the 1550s as the residence of the Spanish viceroy of Catalunya. It is worth wandering in (from Carrer dels Comtes de Barcelona) and upstairs – the building is somewhat rundown but boasts a fine wooden ceiling and pleasing courtyard (admission is free).

Until 1993 it housed the Arxiu de la Corona d'Aragón, a unique collection documenting the history of the kingdom prior to unity under Fernando and Isabel. The archive is now at Carrer dels Almogàvers 77. When you walk back outside, have a look at the walls of the Catedral. See all the grooves cut into the stone? It appears the viceroy's soldiers who were housed here used the church walls to sharpen their weapons.

Museu Frederic Marès A short distance up Carrer dels Comtes de Barcelona, this museum is housed in yet another building of the Palau Reial Major. Frederic Marès i Deulovol (1893–1991) was a rich sculptor, traveller and obsessive collector. He specialised in medieval Spanish sculpture, huge quantities of which are displayed on the ground and 1st floors – including some lovely polychrome wooden sculptures of the Crucifixion and the Virgin.

The top two floors hold a mind-boggling array of knick-knacks, from toy soldiers and cribs to scissors and 19th-century playing cards, from early still cameras to pipes, from fine ceramics to a room that once

served as Marès' study and library, now crammed with his sculpture.

The museum opens from 10 am daily, except Monday (until 2 pm on Sunday and holidays, 5 pm on Tuesday and Thursday and 7 pm on the remaining days). Admission costs 400 ptas but is free on the first Sunday of the month.

Roman Walls
From Plaça del Rei it's worth a little detour to see the two best surviving stretches of Barcelona's Roman walls. One is on the south-western side of Plaça Ramon de Berenguer el Gran, with the Capella Reial de Santa Àgata atop them. The other is a little farther south, by the northern end of Carrer del Sotstinent Navarro. They date from the 3rd and 4th centuries, when the Romans rebuilt their walls after the first attacks by Germanic tribes from the north.

Plaça de Sant Josep Oriol & Around
This small plaza, not far off La Rambla, is the prettiest in the Barri Gòtic. Its bars and cafes attract buskers and artists and make it a lively place to hang out for a while. It is surrounded by quaint little streets, many of them dotted with other appealing cafes, restaurants and shops.

Looming large over the plaza itself is the **Església de Santa Maria del Pi**, a Gothic church built in the 14th to 16th centuries. It opens 8.30 am to 1 pm and 4.30 to 9 pm (9 am to 2 pm and 5 to 9 pm on Sunday and holidays). The beautiful rose window above its entrance on Plaça del Pi is claimed by some to be the world's biggest. The interior of the church was gutted by fire in 1936 and most of the stained glass is modern. The third chapel on the left is dedicated to Sant Josep Oriol, with a map showing spots in the church where he worked numerous miracles.

The area between Carrer dels Banys Nous and Plaça de Sant Jaume is known as the **Call**, Barcelona's former Jewish quarter and centre of learning from at least the 11th century, until anti-Semitism saw Jews expelled in the late 15th century (see also the

Walking Tours chapter). Even before the expulsion, Jews were not exactly privileged citizens. As in many medieval centres they were obliged to wear a special identifying mark on their garments and had trouble getting permission to expand their ghetto as the Call's population increased.

Plaça Reial & Around

Just south of Carrer de Ferran, near its La Rambla end, is Plaça Reial, a large, traffic-free plaza whose 19th-century neo-classical facades hide numerous eateries, bars, nightspots and budget places to stay.

Residents here have a rough time of it, with noise a virtual constant as punters crowd in and out of restaurants, bars and clubs at all hours. It could be (and was) worse. Until the area was cleaned up in the 1980s, it had a fearsome reputation for poverty, crime and drugs. Indeed, the whole area between Carrer d'Avinyó and La Rambla was once a red-light zone and a notorious den of low life.

The plaza retains a restless atmosphere, where unsuspecting tourists, respectable citizens, ragged buskers and down-and-outs come face to face. Don't be put off, but watch your bags and pockets. The lampposts by the central fountain are Antoni Gaudí's first known works.

This southern half of the Barri Gòtic is imbued with the memory of Picasso, who lived as a teenager with his family in Carrer de la Mercè, had his first studio in Carrer de la Plata (now a rather cheesy restaurant) and was a regular visitor to a brothel at Carrer d'Avinyó 27. That experience may have inspired his 1907 painting *Les Demoiselles d'Avignon*.

EL RAVAL

West of La Rambla, the Ciutat Vella spreads to Ronda de Sant Antoni, Ronda de Sant Pau and Avinguda del Paral.lel, which together trace the line of Barcelona's 14th-century walls. Known as El Raval, from an Arabic word that denoted the one-time suburban sprawl *extra muros*, the area contains one of the city's most dispiriting slums, the seedy red-light zone of the Barri Xinès.

For centuries it has been home to whores, louche lads and, at times, a bohemian collection of interlopers. In the 1920s and '30s especially, it was a popular playground with Barcelonins of many classes busy at night with the activity in taverns, *cafés concerts*, cabarets and brothels. In the harsh light of day the tawdriness and poverty is more evident, hardly surprising given the concentration of people living in often less than ideal circumstances. Carrer Nou de la Rambla, where Picasso lived for a while, was particularly lively. By the 1950s brothels had been outlawed and many of the bars had shut down. In later years drug abuse became an increasing problem, and the physiognomy of the area changed with the waves of impecunious migrants, mainly from North Africa and the Indian subcontinent, who moved into cheap and often dank lodgings.

Past and present lend the Barri Xinès a certain fascination, but this is not the place to bring your Rolex. It's not overly dangerous but, among the mixed bag of whores and pimps, transvestites and transsexuals, drug abusers of all persuasions and a picaresque assortment of local low life, the percentage of dodgy characters with a keen eye for prosperous pockets is quite high.

El Raval has not been completely abandoned to its fate. Various projects, including one to create a huge new shady rambla north of Carrer de Sant Pau, are signs that some day the area may yet be turned around (although town planners have been scratching their heads about just how to achieve this since the late 19th century). The northern half of El Raval is already notably less seedy, and an increasingly bohemian set is moving in to take advantage of low rents and the mushrooming of hip new cafes and bars. From an outsider's point of view, it would in some respects be a shame to sanitise it all – but local residents probably feel differently!

Església de Sant Pau del Camp (Map 5)

Back in the 9th century, when monks founded the monastery and church of Sant

Pau del Camp (St Paul in the Fields), it was a good walk from the city gates amid fields and gardens. Today you see only the church and cloister erected in the 12th century. Sadly neglected amid the worst squalor El Raval has to offer, this is one of the best of Barcelona's few Romanesque remnants. The doorway to the church in fact bears some rare Visigothic decoration, predating the Muslim invasion of Spain. The cloister opens 5 to 8 pm (closed Tuesday, Sunday and public holidays).

Antic Hospital de la Santa Creu (Map 6)

Almost directly north from the Església de Sant Pau del Camp stands what was, in the 15th century, the city's main hospital. The Antic Hospital de la Santa Creu today houses the Biblioteca de Catalunya (Catalunya's national library) and the Institut d'Estudis Catalans. The library is the single most complete collection of documents (estimated at around three million) tracing the region's long history. In its medieval heyday, the hospital was deemed one of Europe's best, where the sick got comparatively (for the times) good care and abandoned children and lunatics were also taken in – presumably they were housed in separate wards. Parts of what you see today were added in the 16th and 17th centuries. The hospital, construction of which began in 1401 during the reign of Martí, lies on what was the main entrance to the city from the road to Madrid.

As you enter the main courtyard, you can't help being reminded you are in El Raval. Dilapidated, it serves as a kind of park to all and sundry – round old ladies gossiping and walking their little dogs, the occasional drunk taking a snooze, outmoded young punks having a snack. Earnest students and academics from other parts of town head for the library, which opens 9 am to 8 pm Monday to Friday, and 9 am to 2 pm on Saturday. Inside you can admire fine Catalan Gothic vaulting in the ceiling. The **chapel** of the former hospital is worth poking your nose into as well. It opens noon to 2 pm and 4 to 8 pm Tuesday to Saturday, 11 am to 2 pm on Sunday. It is often used for temporary exhibitions.

Palau Güell (Map 6)

A few steps off La Rambla at Carrer Nou de la Rambla 3–5, the Palau Güell is one of the few Modernista buildings in the Ciutat Vella. Gaudí built it in the late 1880s for his most important patron, the industrialist Eusebi Güell. It was intended as a guest wing and social annexe to Güell's main mansion on La Rambla. It lacks some of Gaudí's later playfulness but is still a characteristic riot of styles (Gothic, Islamic, Art Nouveau) and materials. After the civil war, police occupied it and tortured political prisoners in the basement.

Visitors will be taken on a compulsory guided tour of the place, which is a compendium of Gaudí's earlier architectural ideas. When you enter the building, turn around to face the inside of the main entrance – it is a parabolic arch, the predominant form throughout the building, and characteristic of other Gaudí constructions.

You will first be taken downstairs to the low-vaulted brick stables. Even the solid upwards-fanning pillars are of slim brick – at the time considered by more conventional designers an ignoble material best hidden from view. *Au contraire*, said Gaudí and the Modernistas – just look at the great works of Islamic and Mudéjar architecture spread across Spain, all in unclad brick.

From the ground floor you are led up dark grey marble stairs to the next floor, whose main feature are backlit mirrors posing as windows to increase the impression of space. Up another floor and you reach the main hall and its annexes. The hall is like a four-sided empty parabolic pyramid – each wall an arch stretching up three floors and coming together to form a dome that reaches the ceiling. The chapel that once filled one of the walls was partly destroyed in the civil war.

The adjoining rooms boast varying themes on artesonado ceilings – finely carved wood, drawing on a long tradition with its roots in Islamic design. The liberal use of wrought iron in decoration, for example in the one-time gas lamps and ceiling ornamentation, is another reaffirmation of the value of 'ignoble' materials.

The whole effect, while a masterful insight into Modernista ideas and in particular those of Gaudí, is a little gloomy until you emerge onto the flat roof to be confronted by a riot of tiled colour and fanciful design in the building's chimney pots.

The Palau Güell opens 10 am to 1.30 pm and 4 to 6.30 pm, except Sunday, and tours usually start on the hour. Admission costs 400 ptas (students 200 ptas). If you have a Ruta del Modernisme ticket, you pay half-price. See the boxed text 'Ruta del Modernisme' later in this chapter.

Picasso – who hated Gaudí's work – began his Blue Period in 1902 in a studio across the street at Carrer Nou de la Rambla 6.

Museu d'Art Contemporani de Barcelona & Around (Map 6)

One thing that gave the northern half of El Raval a fillip was the opening, in 1995, on Plaça dels Àngels of the vast white Museu d'Art Contemporani de Barcelona (MACBA).

The ground and first floors are given over to exhibitions from the gallery's own collections. They tend to change things here a lot, so it is difficult to give clear hints on what or whom you might see. Works start with artists such as Antoni Tàpies, Joan Brossa, Paul Klee and Alexander Calder. Such artists as Miquel Barceló and Ferran García Sevilla, protagonists of neo-expressionism who emerged in the 1980s, also generally get a run. Other contemporary Catalan artists whose work you may well come across include Susana Solano, Juan Muñoz and Carlos Pazos, but on the whole the collection offers a broadly international outlook.

The gallery also presents temporary exhibitions and boasts a good art bookshop. Opening hours are 11 am to 7.30 pm Monday to Friday (closed Tuesday), 10 am to 8 pm Saturday, 10 am to 3 pm on Sunday and holidays. Admission costs 775 ptas (350 ptas on non-holiday Wednesdays).

On Carrer de Montalegre behind the museum you will find the **Centre de Cultura Contemporània de Barcelona**, or CCCB (Map 4), a complex of auditoriums and exhibition and conference halls opened in 1994 in what had been an 18th-century hospice. The big courtyard, with a vast glass wall on one side, is spectacular. With 4500 sq metres of exposition space in four display areas, the centre hosts a constantly changing program of exhibitions with 'the city' as their core theme. Often staged in conjunction with other European museums and galleries, the exhibitions range broadly from architectural studies to photo exhibits. For instance, a major exposition during 2000 was entitled *La Fundació de la Ciutat – Mesopotàmia, Grècia i Roma* (The Founding of the City – Mesopotamia, Greece & Rome). The centre organises all sorts of other activities too, from folk music performances to art lectures.

LA RIBERA (Map 6)

La Ribera is the area of the Ciutat Vella north-east of the Barri Gòtic, from which it's divided by noisy Via Laietana, driven through this part of the city in 1907. La Ribera, whose name refers to the waterfront that once lay much further inland than today and was the main commercial dockland of medieval Barcelona, preserves a network of intriguing, narrow streets. They are peppered with some major sights, good bars and restaurants, and the area lacks the seedy character of some parts of the Barri Gòtic.

Palau de la Música Catalana

This concert hall at Carrer de Sant Pere més alt 11 is one of the high points of Modernista architecture. It's not exactly a symphony, more a series of crescendos in tile, brick, sculptured stone and stained glass. Built between 1905 and 1908 by Lluís Domènech i Montaner for the Orfeo Català musical society, with the help of some of the best Catalan artisans of the time, it was conceived as a temple for the Catalan Renaixença (Renaissance).

You can see some of its splendours, such as the main facade with its mosaics, floral capitals and the sculpture cluster representing Catalan popular music from the outside, and you can glimpse lovely tiled pillars inside the ticket office entrance on Carrer de

Sant Francesc de Paula. Best, however, is the richly colourful auditorium upstairs, with its ceiling of blue and gold stained glass and, above a bust of Beethoven, a towering sculpture of Wagner's Valkyries (Wagner was top of the Renaissance charts).

To see this, you need to attend a concert or join a guided tour. These tours, which take 50 minutes, take place every half hour from 10 am to 3.30 pm daily. You can buy the tickets from Les Muses del Palau's shop, at Carrer de Sant Pere més alt 1, up to one week in advance. They cost 700 ptas. For information call ☎ 93 268 10 00. You can get in for half-price with a Ruta del Modernisme ticket.

Carrer de Montcada

Possibly an early example of deliberate town planning, this medieval high street was driven down towards the sea from the road that in the 12th century led north from the city walls. It would, in time, become the best address in town for the city's merchant class, and the bulk of the great mansions that remain intact today date back (albeit often tampered with later) to the 14th century. This area was the commercial heartland of medieval Barcelona.

Capella d'En Marcús On the little square of the same name that caps the top (north-western) end of Carrer de Montcada lies the often unnoticed chapel of this 12th-century alms house. Erected on land that at the time lay beyond the city walls, the complex was a halfway house for poor wayfarers and also served as a small hospital. Construction was financed as a private work of charity by a wealthy businessman, Bernat Marcús. Although its original Romanesque elements are recognisable, the tiny chapel has been much meddled with over the centuries.

Mercat de Santa Caterina The big produce market a block west of the Capella d'En Marcús was knocked down in 1999 but will be rebuilt some time in the future. In the meantime archaeologists are busy studying one of the most important finds in recent years. For the market was erected over the site of what was once a sprawling Dominican convent.

Museu Picasso Barcelona's most visited museum, the Museu Picasso occupies three of the many fine medieval stone mansions on Carrer de Montcada, at Nos 15–19. It is worth wandering in just to admire the courtyard and internal staircase of the first of these, but few people do so without subsequently devoting a couple of hours to the collection.

Although Picasso never visited Spain during the Franco years, he always had a soft spot for Catalunya and in 1962 agreed to the idea of his old Barcelona friend and secretary Jaume Sabartés that a Picasso museum be founded here. Sabartés' collection was combined with works already owned by the city. Later, Picasso himself made large donations (including many early works and a bequest of graphics) to the museum, and in 1981 his widow, Jacqueline Roque, contributed 141 ceramics.

The collection is strongest on Picasso's earliest years, up until 1904, but there is enough material from subsequent periods to give you a deep impression of the man's versatility and genius. Above all, you feel that Picasso is always one step ahead of himself, let alone anyone else, in his search for new forms of expression.

The collection starts, naturally enough, at the beginning, with sketches, oils and doodling from Picasso's earliest years in Málaga and La Coruña – most of it done around 1893–5. Some of his self-portraits and the portraits of his father, which date from 1896, are evidence enough of his precocious talent. *Retrato de la Tía Pepa* (Portrait of Aunt Pepa), done in Málaga in 1897, is a key painting.

On the second floor you are in a pivotal year of the master's life – 1900. By now he is gaining confidence and abandoning the strictures of academic painting. This was the year of his first exhibition in Els Quatre Gats and his first trip to Paris. The lines are fluid and alive, and soon he embarks on his first conscious thematic adventure, the Blue Period. From this point he distanced himself increasingly from simply depicting scenes of life in Barcelona or Paris, from the streets to the cabarets, to interpreting them more symbolically. The blue-tinted glasses through which he regards the world lend to many of his paintings in this period a melancholy air – some of the titles, such as *The Defenceless*, confirm the tendency.

From here on the collection is less comprehensive. There are a handful of examples from his subsequent Pink Period (Paris) and a modest selection of Cubist paintings.

More significant is the section from rooms 22 to 26. From 1954 to 1962 Picasso was obsessed by the idea of researching and 'rediscovering' the greats, in particular Velázquez. In 1957 he executed a series of renditions of the latter's masterpiece, *Las Meninas* (which hangs in El Prado, Madrid). It is as though Picasso has looked at the original Velázquez painting through a prism reflecting all the styles he had worked through until then. The series includes studies of single characters from the original work through to depictions of the work as a whole. Room 24 contains eight appealing treatments of *Pichones* (pigeons).

Finally, on the top floor (rooms 28–36) is a series of lithographs done in Picasso's last years, the so-called Suite 156.

The museum opens 10 am to 8 pm Tuesday to Saturday and holidays, and 10 am to 3 pm on Sunday. Admission costs 725 ptas (free on the first Sunday of each month). There are additional charges for special exhibitions.

Museu Tèxtil i d'Indumentària This Textile & Costume Museum occupies the 13th-century Palau dels Marquesos de Lló at Carrer de Montcada 12, and part of the Palau Nadal next door (both buildings underwent repeated alterations into the 18th century). Its 4000 items range from 4th-century Coptic textiles to 20th-century local embroidery, but best is the big collection of clothing from the 16th century to the 1930s. The items in the museum were collected over a period of more than 100 years. Opening hours are 10 am to 8 pm Tuesday to Saturday, 10 am to 3 pm on Sunday and holidays. Admission costs 400 ptas or 700 ptas if you combine it with the Museu Barbier-Mueller d'Art Precolombí next door (both museums are free on the first Saturday of each month). The old courtyard is graced with an agreeable cafe.

Museu Barbier-Mueller d'Art Precolombí Occupying the rest of the Palau Nadal at No 14, this museum holds part of one of the most prestigious collections of pre-Colombian art in the world. The artefacts from South American 'primitive' cultures come from the treasure-trove of Swiss businessman Josef Mueller (who died in 1977) and his son-in-law Jean-Paul Barbier, who directs the Musée Barbier-Mueller in Geneva.

All the rooms have been blacked out, with only the artefacts on display eerily lit up in the gloom. The first room you enter is given over to South American gold jewellery. From then on you pass through a series of rooms containing ceramics, jewellery, statues, textiles and other objects. Explanations are in several languages including English.

It opens 10 am to 8 pm Tuesday to Saturday, 10 am to 3 pm on Sunday and holidays. Admission costs 500 ptas (700 ptas when combined with the Museu Tèxtil i d'Indumentària).

Along Carrer de Montcada Several other mansions on the street are now commercial art galleries where you're welcome to browse (they often stage exhibitions). The biggest is the **Galeria Maeght** at No 25 in the 16th-century Palau dels Cervelló. For more tips on art galleries, turn to the Shopping chapter. If you can get a peek into the baroque courtyard of the originally medieval Palau de Dalmases at No 20 (now a hideously expensive place to sip wine; see the Entertainment chapter), do so – it is one of the finest on the strip.

Església de Santa Maria del Mar

Carrer de Montcada opens at its southeastern end into **Passeig del Born**, a plaza

THINGS TO SEE & DO

where jousting tournaments took place in the Middle Ages and which was Barcelona's main square from the 13th to 18th centuries. They used to say *roda el món i torna al Born* (go around the world and return to the Born) and the merchants and shipowners who lived and dealt around here no doubt saw the area as the navel of their world.

At the southern end of Passeig del Born stands one of Barcelona's finest Catalan Gothic churches, Santa Maria del Mar. Built in the 14th century, Santa Maria was lacking in superfluous decoration even before anarchists gutted it in 1909 and 1936. This only serves to highlight its fine proportions, purity of line and sense of space. The apse features a beautiful slim arcade and some of the 15th- to 18th-century stained glass is particularly fetching. The church opens 9 am to 1.30 pm and 4.30 to 8 pm daily. On Monday nights at 6 pm you can attend the Llum i Misteri show, a kind of sound and light performance with live organ music and a brief commentary (in Catalan, Castilian and English) on the place of the church in the history of this part of the city. It costs 1500 ptas and lasts 50 minutes.

PARC DE LA CIUTADELLA (Map 5)

East of La Ribera and north of La Barceloneta, Parc de la Ciutadella is perfect if you just need a bit of space and greenery, but also has a couple of more specific attractions.

After the War of the Spanish Succession, Felipe V built a huge fort (La Ciutadella) to keep watch over Barcelona. It became a much loathed symbol of everything Catalans hated about Madrid and was later used as a political prison. Only in 1869 did the central government allow its demolition (you can see a diorama of the fortress in the Museu Militar on Montjuïc). The site was turned into a park and used as the main site for the Universal Exhibition of 1888. It opens 8 am to 8 pm daily (to 9 pm from April to September).

The single most impressive thing in the park is the monumental **Cascada** (waterfall)

near the Passeig de Pujades entrance, created in 1875–81 by Josep Fontsère with the help of the young Gaudí. It's a dramatic combination of classical statuary, rugged rocks, greenery and thundering water. Nearby, you can hire little rowboats to paddle about the small lake – a potential diversion for recalcitrant kids.

Museu Nacional d'Art Modern de Catalunya

In the south-east of the park, next door to the **Parlament de Catalunya**, where the regional parliament meets, this art gallery is housed in the fort's former arsenal. By the time you read this, it is possible (although dates were not yet fixed) that the collection will have been put into storage. The museum buildings are to be handed over to the parliament and the collection is destined to be transferred to the Museu Nacional d'Art de Catalunya in Montjuïc, possibly by 2003.

The collection consists of Catalan art from the mid-19th century to the mid-20th century. Most of the paintings are of comparatively little interest, spanning Catalan Realisme, Anecdotisme, Modernisme (Ramon Casas and Santiago Rusiñol are each represented by about a dozen paintings, among the most interesting, Casas' depiction of himself and Pere Romeu on a tandem bicycle. Romeu was the director of Els Quatre Gats, the Barcelona tavern where Modernista artists and hangers on hung out) and into Noucentisme.

Among the Noucentistas, perhaps the work of Joaquim Sunyer is the most striking on show. Three fairly minor works by Dalí have managed to find their way in here too.

More attention-grabbing are the many items of Modernista interior and, in the case of iron grills created by Gaudí for the Casa Vicenç, exterior design. They include furniture, lampshades, doors and so on. The museum opens 10 am to 7 pm Tuesday to Saturday, 10 am to 2.30 pm on Sunday and holidays. Admission costs 500 ptas; if you have the Ruta del Modernisme ticket, you get in for half-price.

Zoo

The southern end of the park is occupied by a large Parc Zoològic (zoo; ☎ 93 225 67 80), best known for its albino gorilla Floquet de Neu (Snowflake, or Copito de Nieve in Castilian), who was orphaned by poachers in Guinea (Africa) in the 1960s. Floquet is claimed to be the only albino gorilla in the world and is something of a symbol for the zoo. It opens 10 am to 7.30 pm daily (to 5 pm in winter). Admission costs 1550 ptas.

Barcelona Globus

If you want to get a bird's eye view of the city, you might consider a short ride in what is claimed to be the largest helium balloon in the world, moored near the zoo. Up to 35 passengers may clamber into the gondola for the 15-minute up and down trip (to an altitude of 150 metres). It operates 10 am to 7 pm (to 9 pm in summer) Monday to Saturday, to 9 pm on Sunday and holidays (11 pm in summer). The ride costs 2000 ptas. For more information call ☎ 93 342 97 90. Could be one for the kids.

Around the Park

Along the Passeig de Picasso side of the park are several buildings constructed for, or just before, the Universal Exhibition. The one at the top end is the most interesting. Known as the **Castell dels Tres Dragons**, it is a product of the medieval imagination of Domènech i Montaner, who put the castle trimmings on a pioneering steel frame. The coats of arms are all invented and the whole building exudes a rather playful air. It was used as a cafe-restaurant during the exhibition. Now it houses the **Museu de Zoologia** (Map 6), open 10 am to 2 pm Tuesday to Sunday (to 6.30 pm Thursday). Admission costs 400 ptas. If you like stuffed animals, model elephants and the inevitable skeletons of huge ex-living things, this rather fusty old institution is the place for you.

Then comes L'Hivernacle, one of two arboretums, a mini botanical garden with a pleasant cafe in its midst. Next is the **Museu de Geologia**. Most people would have to have rocks in their heads to spend too much

time in here, but then again, budding geologists may well want to examine the stones, minerals and fossils on display. Admission times and price are as for the Museu de Zoologia. The museum is followed by L'Umbracle, another arboretum.

North-west of the park along Passeig de Lluís Companys is the imposing Modernista **Arc de Triomf** (Map 6), designed by Josep Vilaseca as an entrance to the Universal Exhibition, with unusual, almost Islamic-style brickwork. Just what the triumph was is a trifle hard to guess. It is difficult to put yourself back into the clothes and feelings of Barcelonins in the late 1880s. The exhibition was an (at times farcical and certainly very expensive) attempt to put this middle-ranking and much-ignored city on the world map. The wheels of industry were turning (albeit not at the pace of great European centres further north) and the loss of Cuba, (see History in the Facts about Barcelona chapter), which would have a devastating impact on Barcelona's trade and manufacturing, was 10 years off. The town fathers were obviously feeling in good spirits, even if no particular 'victory' offered itself as cause for erecting triumphal arches!

Màgic BCN

This 40-minute special effects 'ride' gives you the impression of travelling by train through scenes and countryside all over the world. It's quite clever and will doubtless appeal to the kiddies. It operates at 6 and 7 pm every day, with extra sessions at 11 am, noon and 1 pm at the weekend. Check these hours as they change with startling frequency. The ride costs 875 ptas (children under 12, 625 ptas). Màgic BCN is at Passeig de Lluís Companys 10–12.

PORT VELL (Map 5)

Barcelona's old port at the bottom of La Rambla, once such an eyesore that it caused public protests, has been transformed beyond recognition since the 1980s. Instead of warehouses, railyards and dumps, you are confronted by chic shopping, harbourside munching, movies-on-sea, discos and Irish pubs, parking for yachts and a huge aquarium. All these elements and more have left the 'old port' looking brand spanking new.

For a view of the harbour from the water, you can take a **golondrina** excursion boat (☎ 93 442 31 06) from Moll de les Drassanes in front of the Monument a Colom. A 35-minute trip to the breakwater *(rompeolas)* and lighthouse *(faro)* on the seaward side of the harbour costs 500 ptas; a one-hour and 20-minute trip to Port Olímpic costs 1300 ptas (those aged under 19, 900 ptas). This latter trip is on a glass-bottomed catamaran. The number of departures depends largely on season and demand. Breakwater trips normally go at least hourly in the daytime, Port Olímpic trips at least three times daily. North-east from the golondrina quay stretches the palm-lined promenade **Moll de la Fusta**.

At the centre of the redeveloped harbour is the **Moll d'Espanya**, a former wharf linked to Moll de la Fusta by a wave-shaped footbridge, the **Rambla de Mar**, which rotates to let boats enter the marina behind it.

At the end of Moll d'Espanya is the glossy Maremàgnum shopping and eating complex, but the major attraction is **L'Aquàrium** (☎ 93 221 74 74) behind it – an ultra-modern aquarium that opened in 1995. It's claimed to be Europe's biggest and to have the world's best Mediterranean collection. It is divided into 21 tanks, of which the 80m-long shark tunnel is a highlight. All up, some 8000 fish (including 11 sharks) have taken up residence here. Admission is a steep 1450 ptas (four to 12-year-olds and pensioners 950 ptas). It opens 9.30 am to 9 pm (until 11 pm in July and August). Beyond L'Aquàrium is the Imax Port Vell big-screen cinema.

The **cable car** *(telefèric* or *funicular aereo)* strung across the harbour to Montjuïc provides another view of the city. You can get tickets at Miramar (Montjuïc) and the Torre de Sant Sebastià (in La Barceloneta). Access to the Torre de Jaume I, halfway along, was suspended at the time of writing. A return ticket from Miramar to Sant Sebastià will cost 1200 ptas, or 1000 ptas one way. The cable car operates daily from 10.30 am to 7 pm (to 5.30 pm in winter).

LA BARCELONETA & PORT OLÍMPIC

It used to be said that Barcelona had 'turned its back on the sea', but an ambitious Olympics-inspired redevelopment program has returned to life a long stretch of coast north-east of Port Vell.

La Barceloneta is a mid-18th century sailors' and fishermen's quarter laid out by the French engineer Prosper Verboom to replace housing destroyed to make way for the Ciutadella. The narrow grid system was quite an innovation in its time, although the dreary five and six-storey apartment blocks that make up the area today are hardly enticing. By the 19th century it was a pretty squalid spot, especially in hard times (read the first few chapters of Eduardo Mendoza's *City of Marvels* to get an idea of what it must have been like). La Barceloneta is still known for its seafood restaurants, of which several good ones survive (see the Places to Eat chapter), although many disappeared in the coastal redevelopment programs that came with the Olympics.

A Raw Prawn

The cheerful-looking outsized prawn that dominates one of the (now closed) waterfront restaurants along the Moll de la Fusta has become the object of heated debate. Created by the Catalan designer Javier Mariscal around the time of the 1992 Olympics, the *gamba de Mariscal* may go the way of the dodo as the Ajuntament shuts down the eateries and bars in the area – to be replaced by municipal offices. What was the Gambrinus restaurant above which the friendly crustacean hovers is destined one day to become the information office of an expanded new Museu Marítim for the city. The Ajuntament wants the prawn to stay where it is, but the restaurant owner wants hard cash for it. The restaurant owners have had several offers for it – including from a Japanese company. For the time being, the prawn remains unmoved.

Museu d'Història de Catalunya (Map 5)

The Palau de Mar building facing the harbour once served as warehouses, but was transformed in the 1990s into something quite different. Below the seaward arcades is a string of good restaurants. Inside is the Museum of Catalonian History.

The permanent display covers the 2nd and 3rd floors, taking you, as the bumph says, on a 'voyage through history' from the Stone Age through to the early 1980s. The museum is a busy hodgepodge of dioramas, artefacts, videos, models, documents and interactive bits. It is an entertaining and informative (although a little uneven) exploration of 2000 years of Catalan history. See how the Romans lived, listen to Arab poetry from the time of the Muslim occupation of the city, peer into the dwelling of a Dark Ages family in the Pyrenees, mount a knight's horse and try to lift a suit of armour, or descend into an air-raid shelter from the civil war.

Labelling is in Catalan, but you can ask for a brochure (returnable) with some explanations in your own language (quite a few tongues are catered for). The museum opens 10 am to 7 pm Tuesday to Thursday, to 8 pm Friday and Saturday, and from 10 am to 2.30 pm on Sunday and holidays. Admission costs 500 ptas.

Beaches & Port Olímpic

Barcelona's fishing fleet ties up along the Moll del Rellotge, south of the museum. On La Barceloneta's seaward side are Platja de Sant Sebastià and Platja de la Barceloneta, the first of Barcelona's **beaches** (Map 1), once dirty and unused, but now cleaned up and popular on summer weekends. **Passeig Marítim**, a 1.25km promenade from La Barceloneta to Port Olímpic – through an area formerly full of railway sidings and warehouses – makes for a pleasant stroll if you manage to dodge the rollerbladers.

Port Olímpic (Map 1) was built for the Olympic sailing events and is now a classy marina surrounded by bars and restaurants. An eye-catcher on the approach from La Barceloneta is the giant copper *Peix* (Fish) sculpture by Frank Gehry. The area behind Port Olímpic – dominated by Barcelona's two tallest skyscrapers, the luxury Hotel Arts

THINGS TO SEE & DO

Buffalo Barna

Back in December 1889, a curious crowd moved into what was vacant ground on the block bounded by Carrer de Muntaner, Còrsega, Rosselló and Aribau.

Sioux, Cheyennes and Arapahos, accompanied by Mexican bandits and cowboys, who had arrived in Barcelona by steamship from Marseilles, erected tents and tepees. Buffalo Bill had arrived in town with his Wild West Show, bringing 184 people, 159 horses and 20 buffaloes.

William Frederick Cody (1846–1917), explorer, guide and tracker for General Custer, had quite a record. An expert shot, he had been a sheriff, member of the Pony Express, was obsessed by buffalo hunting and was reputedly a Freemason. He came to Europe to try to make a buck out of his Exhibition of American Indian and Frontier Life.

Barcelona had recently put itself on the map with the Universal Exhibition of 1888, so it seemed only natural to pay a visit. The show stayed there for five weeks, but not everything went according to plan. In between displays of Indian attacks on wagon trains and cowboys whooping it up, torrential rains forced numerous cancellations, a tepee was destroyed by fire and a 'flu epidemic killed one of the showmasters and left several Indians under the weather.

When Bill and his circus headed off for Naples, two of his crew were left behind in the Hospital de la Santa Creu. One of them is reputed to have died here and ended up buried on Montjuïc, but nobody knows for certain. Cody & Co never returned to Spain. Bill's boast that with 30,000 Indians he could expel the Spanish army from Cuba probably didn't go down well. (The US Navy took care of the problem 10 years later in any case.)

Barcelona and Torre Mapfre office block – is the Vila Olímpica, formerly the living quarters for the Olympic participants, now mostly sold off as expensive apartments.

To the north-east, more beaches stretch towards the Riu Besòs (which marks the city's north-eastern boundary). The initial (southernmost) stretch of Platja de Mar Bella is a nudist strip, although punters not wishing to reveal all seem to mingle comfortably enough with the in-the-altogether crowd. All these beaches are kept clean and the water is perfectly decent.

Behind Platja de Nova Mar Bella and beyond to the Besòs rise the serried skeletal hulks of what will be the hotels, conference centres and pricey apartments of the Front Marítim, Barcelona's future luxury residential district.

L'EIXAMPLE

L'Eixample (el Ensanche in Castilian, meaning the Enlargement), stretching one to 1.5km north, east and west of Plaça de Catalunya, was the city's 19th-century answer to overcrowding in the confines of the medieval city.

Work on l'Eixample began in 1869 to a design by the architect Ildefons Cerdà, who specified a grid of wide streets with plazas formed by their chamfered (cut-off) corners. Cerdà also planned numerous green spaces but these didn't survive the intense demand for l'Eixample real estate.

L'Eixample has been inhabited from the start by the city's middle classes, many of whom still think it's the best thing about Barcelona. Along its grid of straight streets are the majority of the city's most expensive shops and hotels, a range of eateries and several nightspots. The main sightseeing objective is Modernista architecture, the best of which – apart from La Sagrada Família – is clustered on or near l'Eixample's main avenue, Passeig de Gràcia.

Manzana de la Discordia (Map 2)

The so-called 'Apple (read Block) of Discord' on the western side of Passeig de Gràcia, between Carrer del Consell de Cent and

> ## How Do You Like Them Apples?
>
> Despite the Catalanisation of most Barcelona names in recent decades, the Manzana de la Discordia has kept its Spanish name to preserve a pun on *manzana*, which means both 'block' and 'apple'. According to Greek mythology, the original Apple of Discord was tossed onto Mt Olympus by Eris (Discord), with orders that it be given to the most beautiful goddess, sparking jealousies that helped start the Trojan War. The pun won't transfer into Catalan, whose word for block is *illa*, and for apple *poma*.

Carrer d'Aragó, gets its name from three houses remodelled in highly contrasting manner between 1898 and 1906 by three of the leading Modernista architects.

At No 35, on the corner of Carrer del Consell de Cent, is **Casa Lleo Morera**, Domènech i Montaner's contribution, with Art Nouveau carving outside and a bright, tiled lobby in which floral motifs predominate. You can no longer visit the 1st floor, which is giddy with swirling sculptures, rich mosaics and whimsical decoration.

Casa Amatller located at No 41, by Puig i Cadafalch, combines Gothic window frames with a stepped gable borrowed (deliberately) from urban architecture of the Netherlands. The pillared entrance hall and the staircase lit by stained glass are like the inside of some romantic castle. You can wander around the ground floor and pick up a Ruta del Modernisme ticket here – see the boxed text on this value ticket.

Casa Batlló, next door at No 43, is one of Barcelona's gems. Of course it's by Gaudí. The facade, sprinkled with bits of blue, mauve and green tile and studded with wave-shaped window frames and balconies, rises to an uneven blue tiled roof with a solitary tower. The roof represents Sant Jordi (St George) and the dragon, and if you stare long enough at the building, it seems almost to be a living being. You might fluke your way into the foyer (but not beyond) if the main entrance is open.

While here you may want to pop into the **Museu del Parfum** (Map 2), Passeig de Gràcia 39, in the Regia store. It contains everything from ancient scent receptacles to classic Eau de Cologne bottles. It opens 10 am to 8.30 pm Monday to Friday, and 10.30 am to 2 pm and 5 to 8.30 pm Saturday.

Fundació Antoni Tàpies (Map 2)

Round the corner from the Manzana de la Discordia, at Carrer d'Aragó 255, this is both a pioneering Modernista building (completed in 1885) and the major collection of a leading 20th-century Catalan artist.

The building, designed by Domènech i Montaner for the publishing house Editorial Montaner i Simón, combines a brick-covered iron frame with Islamic inspired decoration. Tàpies saw fit to crown the building with the meanderings of his own mind – to some it looks like a pile of coiled barbed wire, to others…well.

Antoni Tàpies, whose experimental art has often carried political messages – he opposed Francoism in the 1960s and '70s – launched the Fundació in 1984 to promote contemporary art, donating a large part of his own work. The core collection spans the whole arc of Tàpies' creation, and also includes some contributions from other contemporary artists. The Fundació houses an important research library devoted principally to Tàpies, but again embracing a wider range of contemporary art.

The Fundació opens 10 am to 8 pm, Tuesday to Sunday; admission costs 700 ptas (students 350 ptas).

La Pedrera (Map 2)

Back on Passeig de Gràcia, at No 92, is another Gaudí masterpiece, built between 1905 and 1910 as a combined apartment and office block. Formally called the Casa Milà after the businessman who commissioned it, it's better known as La Pedrera (the quarry) because of its uneven grey stone facade, which ripples round the corner of Carrer de Provença. The wave effect is emphasised by elaborate wrought-iron balconies.

The Fundació Caixa Catalunya office (☎ 93 484 59 95) has opened the place up

THINGS TO SEE & DO

to visitors, organising it as the Espai Gaudí (Gaudí Space) and guiding visitors through the building and up onto the roof, with its giant chimney pots looking like multi-coloured medieval knights. Gaudí wanted to put a tall statue of the Virgin up here too: when the Milà family said no, fearing it might make the building a target for anarchists, Gaudí resigned from the project in disgust. One floor below the roof, where you can appreciate Gaudí's taste for McDonald's M-style arches (if McDonald's had existed in those days, would he have come up with something else?), is a modest museum dedicated to his work. You can see models and videos dealing with each of his buildings.

Downstairs on the next floor you can inspect an apartment (El Pis de la Pedrera). It is fascinating to wander around this elegantly furnished home, done up in the style a well-to-do family might have enjoyed at the turn of the century. The sensuous curves and unexpected touches in everything from light fittings to bedsteads, from doorhandles to the balconies can hardly fail to induce a heartfelt desire to move in at once. The lower floors of the building often host temporary expositions.

La Pedrera opens 10 am to 8 pm daily. Guided visits take place at 6 pm; 11 am on weekends and holidays. You can elect to pay 600 ptas just to see the Espai Gaudí and the roof terrace *or* the apartment. It is worth paying the full 1000 ptas to see both if you have failed to purchase a Ruta del Modernisme pass.

From July to September, the place is opened up on Friday and Saturday evenings (9 pm to midnight). The roof is lit up in an eerie fashion and, while you are taking in the night views of Barcelona, you also get to sip a flute of cava and listen to live music in the background (1500 ptas).

Palau Quadras & Casa de les Punxes (Map 2)

Within a few blocks north and east of La Pedrera are two of Puig i Cadafalch's major buildings. The nearer is the Palau del Baró de Quadras at Avinguda Diagonal 373, created between 1902 and 1904 with detailed neo-Gothic carvings on the facade and fine stained glass. It houses the **Museu de la Música**, with an international collection of instruments. The displays include one of the most important collections of guitars in the world, as well as a series of organs dating as far back as the 16th century. Also housed here is a research library and a *fonoteca*, or library of music recordings. It opens 10 am to 2 pm Tuesday to Sunday. It opens until 8 pm on Wednesday from late September to late June. Admission costs 400 ptas. On the third Sunday of most months you can usually hear some of the museum's instruments being played from noon. Often the choice of instrument is put into a thematic context. In 1999–2000 it was the saxophone.

The Casa Terrades is on the other side of Avinguda Diagonal, 1½ blocks east at No 420. This apartment block of 1903–05, like a castle in a fairy tale, is better known as the Casa de les Punxes (House of the Spikes) because of its pointed turrets.

La Sagrada Família (Map 2)

If you only have time for one sightseeing outing in Barcelona, this should probably be it. La Sagrada Família inspires awe by its sheer verticality and, in the true manner of the great medieval cathedrals it emulates, it's still not half built after more than 100 years. If it's ever finished, the topmost tower will be more than half as high again as those standing today.

The Temple Expiatori de la Sagrada Família (Expiatory Temple of the Holy Family) was the project to which Antoni Gaudí dedicated the latter part of his life.

It stands in the east of l'Eixample and opens to visitors daily from 9 am. It closes at 8 pm from April to the end of August; at 7 pm in March, September and October; and 6 pm from November to February.

The admission charge of 800 ptas (students 600 ptas) includes a good museum in the crypt. What you're visiting is a building site, but the completed sections and the museum can be explored at leisure. Up to four times daily 50-minute guided tours are offered at 500 ptas a head. The entrance is by the south-western facade fronting Carrer de Sardenya and Plaça de la Sagrada Família. Inside is a bookstall where you should invest 500 ptas in the *Official Guide* if you want a detailed account of the church's sculpture and symbolism. Once inside, you can spend a further 200 ptas per ride on lifts to take you up inside one of the towers on each side of the church.

To get your bearings, you need to realise that this facade, and the opposite one facing Plaça de Gaudí, each with four sky-scraping towers, are at the *sides* of the church. The main facade, as yet unbuilt, will be at the south-eastern end, on Carrer de Mallorca.

Nativity Facade This, the north-eastern facade, is the building's artistic pinnacle, mostly done under Gaudí's personal supervision and much of it with his own hands. You can climb high up inside some of the four towers by a combination of lifts (when they're working) and narrow spiral staircases – a vertiginous experience. The towers are destined to hold tubular bells capable of playing complicated music at great volume. Their upper parts are decorated with mosaics spelling out '*Sanctus, Sanctus, Sanctus, Hosanna in Excelsis,*

STAEVEN VALLAK

DAMIEN SIMONIS

DALE BUCKTON

SIMON BRACKEN

MANFRED GOTTSCHALK

Even in its half-finished state, Gaudí's Sagrada Família is awe inspiring. When building work is completed there will be a total of 18 towers, with one – representing Christ – over 170m high.

MANFRED GOTTSCHALK

Relaxing on Rambla de Mar and Moll d'Espanya – the waterside extension of La Rambla

GUY MOBERLY

DAMIEN SIMONIS

Homenatge a La Barceloneta   Lichtenstein's Barcelona's Head

NEIL SETCHFIELD

Frank Gehry's *Peix* (Fish) dominates Port Olímpic.

DAMIEN SIMONIS

Dona i Ocell by Joan Miró

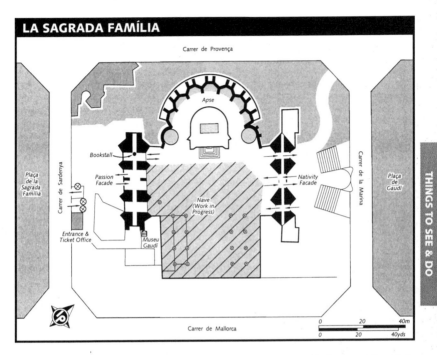

LA SAGRADA FAMÍLIA

Carrer de Provença

Apse

Bookstall

Passion
Facade

Nave
(Work in
Progress)

Nativity
Facade

Carrer de Sardenya

Plaça
de la
Sagrada
Família

Entrance &
Ticket Office

Museu
Gaudí

Carrer de la Marina

Plaça
de
Gaudí

Carrer de Mallorca

| 0 | 20 | 40m |
| 0 | 20 | 40yds |

THINGS TO SEE & DO

Amen, Alleluia'. Asked why he lavished so much care on the tops of the spires, which no one would see from close up, Gaudí answered: 'The angels will see them.'

Beneath the towers is a tall, three-part portal on the theme of Christ's birth and childhood. It seems to lean outwards as you stand beneath looking up. Gaudí used real people and animals as models for many of the sculptures.

The three sections of the portal represent, from left to right, Hope, Charity and Faith. Among the forest of sculpture on the Charity portal, you can make out, low down, the manger surrounded by an ox, an ass, the shepherds and kings, with angel musicians above. Directly above the blue stained-glass window is the Archangel Gabriel's Annunciation to Mary. At the top is a green cypress tree, symbolic refuge in a storm for the white doves of peace dotted over it.

Lower sculptures on the Hope portal show the flight into Egypt and the massacre of the innocents, with Jesus and Joseph in their carpenters' workshop just above. Sculpture on the Faith portal includes, in the centre of the lower group, the child Jesus explaining the Scriptures to the priests.

Interior The semicircular apse wall at the north-western end of the church was the first part to be finished (in 1894). From the altar steps you can look down the nave at the work in progress, with the walls and columns near completion and the roofs begun. The main Glory Facade will, like the north-eastern and south-western facades, be crowned by four towers – the total of 12 representing the 12 apostles. Further decoration will make the whole building a microcosmic symbol of the Christian church, with Christ represented by the massive 170m central tower above the transept and the five remaining planned towers symbolising the Virgin Mary and the four Evangelists.

Gaudí – God's Architect

The idea for La Sagrada Família came from a rich publisher, Josep Marià Bocabella i Verdaguer, the man behind the emergence of an arch-conservative society dedicated to Sant Josep (St Joseph). The society came together in part as a response to calls from Pope Pius IX for a renewal of the Catholic faith, which he saw threatened in a Europe flooded with ideas of liberalism, democracy, modernity and other such iniquitous nonsense.

The Pope had concrete cause for concern. Garibaldi's victories in Italy had left the Vatican virtually bereft of secular power. Liberalism in Spain seemed equally pernicious.

Among the Pope's exhortations was a renewal of devotion to Jesus, Mary and Joseph, the Holy Family, or *Sagrada Família*. And so Bocabella had an inspired idea. What decadent, liberal Barcelona needed was a great church raised to the Holy Family, where contrite citizens could expiate their sins. The society raised the cash and the first stone of a neo-Gothic structure was laid in 1882. The original architect soon quit, and into the breech stepped Antoni Gaudí in 1884.

MICK WELDON

Gaudí devoted everything to the Sagrada Família – a project that was to be his last

He was given a free hand. He conceived a structure that drew on Gothic roots, and embellished it with his own very particular spin.

Gaudí, born into an artisan family in Reus, southern Catalunya, and trained as a metalsmith, was already a successful architect. Up to 1910 he worked on numerous buildings in Barcelona and elsewhere – beyond Catalunya he left three monuments, one each in Comillas (Cantabria), Astorga and León. After abandoning the more-or-less finished Pedrera on Passeig de Gràcia for the Milà family, he began to narrow his efforts.

True, he continued to work for Eusebi Güell, his chief patron and wealthy industrialist, on two ambitious projects that never reached completion: the Parc Güell and Colònia Güell (see those sections later in this chapter for more on both – the crypt of the church in the latter provides many clues as to how Gaudí aimed to approach technical challenges in his masterwork). Funds for both projects had petered out by 1916, by which time his only interest seemed to be La Sagrada Família.

A conservative and moderate Catalanist, Gaudí became increasingly religious and came to view his great church, into which he poured all the architectural and design knowledge he had accumulated, as a sacred mission. As Bocabella's

Gaudí – God's Architect

Josephine society and Barcelona's wealthy tired of the project and having to cough up money for what seemed a bottomless pit, Gaudí resigned himself, with suitably religious stoicism, to a long struggle. He invested everything he had into it, and ran craft workshops on site to nurture a skilled workforce to carry out the kind of decoration he wanted. He was probably deep in thought about how to proceed next when he was run over by a tram on the corner of Gran Via de les Corts Catalanes and Carrer de Bailèn in 1926. He was so ragged and poor that at first no one recognised him. He died three days later and the whole city turned out for his funeral.

As he worked on La Sagrada Família, Gaudí evolved steadily grander and more original ideas for it. He stuck to the basic Gothic cross-shaped ground plan with an apse, but eventually devised a temple 95m long and 60m wide, able to seat 13,000 people, with a central tower 170m high and another 17 of 100m or more. With his characteristic dislike for straight lines (there were none in nature, he said), Gaudí gave his towers swelling outlines inspired by the weird peaks of the holy mountain Montserrat outside Barcelona, and encrusted them with a tangle of sculpture that seems an outgrowth of the stone.

The Passion Facade, sculpted by Josep Subirachs

At Gaudí's death only the crypt, the apse walls, one portal and one tower had been finished. Three more towers were added by 1930 – completing the north-eastern (Nativity) facade – but in 1936 anarchists burned and smashed everything they could in La Sagrada Família, including the workshops, models and plans.

Work restarted in 1952 using restored models and photographs of drawings, with only limited guidance on how Gaudí had thought of solving the huge technical problems of the building. Between 1954 and 1976 the south-western (Passion) facade, with four more towers, was completed, with only some decorative detail work outstanding. The nave, started in 1978, is coming along nicely.

Constant controversy has dogged the building program. Some say the quality of the new work and its materials – concrete instead of stone – are inferior to the earlier parts; others claim that, in the absence of detailed plans, the shell should have been left as a monument to Gaudí; yet others simply oppose all the expenditure (although the funding is private). The chief architect, Jordi Bonet, and his supporters, aside from their desire to see Gaudí's mighty vision made real, argue that their task is a sacred one – this is a church intended to atone for sin and appeal for God's mercy on Catalunya. The way things are going, it might be finished by 2020 – a truly medieval construction timetable.

Gaudí's own story is far from over. The rector of La Sagrada Família, Lluís Bonet Armengol (the architect's brother), is promoting Gaudí's beatification. In March 2000 the Vatican decided to proceed with the examination of the case for canonising him. Even before becoming a saint, Gaudí has started attracting pilgrims, as devotees come to pray at his tomb in the crypt of the Sagrada Família. Says Bonet Armengol, Gaudí's contemporaries 'knew he was God's architect'.

In 2002 Barcelona intends to squeeze every tourist peseta it can out of the 150th anniversary of Gaudí's birth. That year has already been dubbed by the city's promoters the 'year of architecture and Gaudí'.

Passion Facade This south-western facade, on the theme of Christ's last days and death, has been constructed since the 1950s with, like the Nativity Facade, four needling towers and a large, sculpture-bedecked portal. The sculptor, Josep Subirachs, has not attempted to imitate Gaudí's work but has produced strong images of his own. The sculptures, on three levels, are in an S-shaped sequence starting with the Last Supper at bottom left and ending with Christ's burial at top right.

Museu Gaudí Open the same times as the church, the museum includes interesting material on Gaudí's life and other work, as well as models, photos and other material on La Sagrada Família. You can see a good example of his plumb-line models which showed him the stresses and strains he could get away with in construction.

Hospital de la Santa Creu i de Sant Pau (Map 1)

The hospital is Domènech i Montaner's Modernista masterpiece – a huge construction that today still serves as one of the city's most important hospitals. The architect wanted to create a unique environment that would hopefully cheer up the patients. The whole complex, made up of 48 pavilions, is lavishly decorated and no pavilion is the same as another.

Among the many artists who contributed statuary, ceramics and artwork was the prolific Eusebi Arnau. You can wander around the grounds at any time, and it is well worth the stroll up Avinguda de Gaudí from La Sagrada Família.

Museu Taurino (Map 1)

Housed in the Plaça de Braus Monumental bullring on Gran Via de les Corts Catalanes, this bullfighting museum displays bulls' heads, old posters, *trajes de luces* (bullfighters' gear) and other memorabilia. You also get to wander around the ring and corrals. It opens 10.30 am to 2 pm and 4 to 7 pm daily from April to early October; on fight days it opens 10.30 am to 1 pm only. Admission costs 375 ptas.

Museu Egipci (Map 2)

This private collection, with some 500 objects on display, was shifted from its former rather cramped home to an airy seven-floor exhibition space at Carrer de València 284 in May 2000. The hotel magnate Jordi Clos continues to collect material and his museum is divided into different thematic areas (the pharaoh, religion, daily life, etc). In the basement floor is an exhibition area and library, in which various volumes (including some original editions of works by Carter, the Egyptologist who led the Tutankhamen excavations) are on display.

The museum opens 10 am to 2 pm and 4 to 8 pm Monday to Saturday, 10 am to 2 pm on Sunday. Admission costs 900 ptas (students and seniors 700 ptas).

Fundación Francisco Godia (Map 2)

This recently opened private collection contains an intriguing mix of medieval art, ceramics and modern paintings. It is at Carrer de València 284 (☎ 93 272 31 80), next door to the Museu Egipci, and opens 10 am to 8 pm daily, except Tuesday. Admission costs 700 ptas (students 350 ptas).

GRÀCIA (Map 2)

Once a separate village north of l'Eixample and then in the 19th century an industrial district famous for its republican and liberal ideas, Gràcia was incorporated into the city of Barcelona in 1897. In the 1960s and '70s it became fashionable among radical and bohemian types, and even today retains some of that flavour – plenty of hip local luminaries make sure they get around the bars and cafes of Gràcia.

The district's interest lies in the atmosphere of its narrow streets (don't even think about trying to park a car here!), small plazas and the bars and restaurants on them. An evening or night-time wander is the best way to savour these. Diagonal and Fontana are the nearest metro stations to central Gràcia.

The liveliest plazas are **Plaça del Sol**, **Plaça de Rius i Taulet** with its clock tower (thus also known as Plaça del Rellotge – a popular meeting point), and the tree-lined **Plaça de la Virreina** with the 17th-century Església de Sant Josep. The local council at one point looked set to get rid of the trees, but thankfully the neighbours took up arms and put a stop to such nonsense. Gràcia isn't exactly going to win any green awards as it is! On **Plaça de Rovira i Trias** you can sit on a bench next to a statue of Antoni Rovira, Ildefons Cerdà's rival in the competition to design l'Eixample in the late 19th century. Rovira's design has been laid out in the pavement so you can see what you think of it.

Three blocks east of Plaça de Rius i Taulet you can shop for groceries in a big covered market. West of Gràcia's main street, Carrer Gran de Gràcia, an early Gaudí house, the turreted, vaguely Mudéjar **Casa Vicenç** stands at Carrer de les Carolines 22.

MONTJUÏC

Montjuïc, the hill overlooking the city centre from the south-west, is home to some fine art galleries and leisure attractions, soothing parks and the main group of 1992 Olympic sites.

The name Montjuïc (Jewish Mountain) indicates there was once a Jewish settlement here. Before Montjuïc was turned into parks in the 1890s, its woodlands had provided food-growing and breathing space for the people of the cramped Ciutat Vella. Montjuïc also has a darker history: its castle was used by the Madrid government to bombard the city after political disturbances in 1842, and as a political prison up to the Franco era. The first main burst of building on Montjuïc came in the 1920s when it was chosen as the stage for Barcelona's 1929 World Exhibition. The Estadi Olímpic, the Poble Espanyol and some museums all date from this time. Montjuïc got a face-lift and more buildings for the 1992 Olympics.

Abundant roads and paths, with occasional escalators, plus buses and even a chair lift allow you to visit Montjuïc's sights in any order you choose. The five main attractions are the Poble Espanyol, the Museu Nacional d'Art de Catalunya, the Estadi Olímpic, the Fundació Joan Miró and the views from the castle. Visiting them all would make for an extremely full day.

Getting There & Away

You *could* walk from the Ciutat Vella (the foot of La Rambla is 700m from the eastern end of Montjuïc). Local bus Nos 50 and 61 make their way up here from Plaça d'Espanya and other parts of town. The Bus Turístic (see Getting Around) also makes several stops on Montjuïc.

In some respects, unfortunately, the most reliable way to get to where you want to go on Montjuïc is one of those silly little road trains. The Tren Turístic operates daily from late June to at least mid-September and during Easter. Otherwise it sometimes operates on weekends – ask at the tourist office. It leaves Plaça d'Espanya every half hour from 11 am to 8.30 pm and stops at all the museums and other points of interest. It costs 500 ptas, wherever you decide to get off.

Another way of saving your legs is the funicular railway from the Paral.lel metro station to Estació Parc Montjuïc. This goes daily from 11 am to 10 pm from mid-June to mid-September, 10.45 am to 8 pm during the Christmas and Easter holiday periods, 10.45 am to 8 pm on Saturday, Sunday and holidays only during the rest of the year. Tickets cost 250/375 ptas one way/return.

From Estació Parc Montjuïc, the Telefèric de Montjuïc chair lift will carry you yet higher, to an upper entrance of the now closed Parc d'Atraccions (Mirador stop) and then the castle (Castell stop). This operates daily from 11.30 am to 9.30 pm from mid-June to the end of September, 11 am to 2.45 pm and 4 to 7.30 pm in October and the Christmas and Easter periods, 11 am to 2.45 pm and 4 to 7.30 pm on Saturday, Sunday and holidays only during the rest of the year. Tickets cost 475/675 ptas one way/return.

A further option is the *funicular aereo* the cable car that runs between Miramar and Torre de Sant Sebastià (La Barceloneta). See Port Vell earlier in this chapter.

THINGS TO SEE & DO

Around Plaça d'Espanya (Map 4)

The approach to Montjuïc from Plaça d'Espanya gives you the full benefit of the landscaping on the hill's northern side and allows Montjuïc to unfold before you from the bottom up. On Plaça d'Espanya's northern side is the big **Plaça de Braus Les Arenes** bullring, built in 1900 but no longer used for bullfights. The Beatles played here in 1966. Behind the bullring is the **Parc Joan Miró**, created in the 1980s – worth a quick detour for Miró's giant, highly phallic sculpture *Dona i Ocell* (Woman and Bird) in the western corner. Actually, locals know the park (which apart from Miró is a fairly sad affair) as the Parc de l'Escorxador (abattoir park), as that's what once stood here – not surprising given the proximity to the bullring.

Just south of Estació Sants is the rather odd **Parc d'Espanya Industrial**. Looked at in the most favourable light possible it is supposed to be an inventive public space, full of metallic towers and other ingenious things. It is actually a dispiriting cement structure and about the only useful thing about it is the sports centre.

Fountains (Map 7)

Avinguda de la Reina Maria Cristina, lined with modern exhibition and congress halls, leads from Plaça d'Espanya towards Montjuïc. On the hill ahead of you is the Palau Nacional de Montjuïc, and stretching up a series of terraces below it are Montjuïc's fountains, starting with the biggest, La Font Màgica. This comes alive with a music and light show on summer evenings – a unique performance in which the water at times looks like seething fireworks or a mystical cauldron of colour. Depending on the music they choose, it can be quite moving. And it's free! Well worth the effort of getting here. On the last evening of the Festes de la Mercè in September they put on a particularly spectacular display including fireworks. The regular show lasts about 15 minutes and takes place every half hour from 9.30 to 11.30 pm, Thursday to Sunday, from June to September. During the rest of the year it happens from 7 to 9 pm on Friday and Saturday.

Pavelló Mies van der Rohe (Map 7)

Just to the west of the Font Màgica is a strange building indeed. In 1929 Ludwig Mies van der Rohe erected here the Pavelló Alemany (German pavilion) for the World Exhibition. Now known by the name of its architect, it was actually removed after the show. Decades later a society was formed to rebuild what was in hindsight considered a gem. Rebuilt in the 1980s, it is a curious structure made up of interlocking planes – walls of marble or glass, ponds of water, ceilings and just plain nothing. This is Mies van der Rohe's temple to the new urban environment but at the time it passed unnoticed. Opinion as to whether it should have been rebuilt or not is divided, just as it is on whether the 400 ptas admission fee is worth paying. Modern architecture buffs will love it. The pavilion opens 10 am to 8 pm.

Museu Nacional d'Art de Catalunya (Map 7)

The Palau Nacional, built in the 1920s for the World Exhibition, houses the Museu Nacional d'Art de Catalunya. The building itself is quite overwhelming and, although designed by Catalan architects, is interpreted by some as an expression of central Castilian dominance over all Spain, including Catalunya (the World Exhibition was held in 1929, under the dictatorship of Miguel Primo de Rivera).

The museum's two main permanent expositions cover Romanesque and Gothic art. The former is by far the most interesting, and one of the most important concentrations of early medieval art in the world. It consists of frescoes, woodcarvings and painted altar frontals (low-relief wooden panels that were forerunners of the elaborate altarpieces adorning later churches) transferred from country churches across northern Catalunya early in the 20th century. The insides of several churches have been recreated and the frescoes – in some cases fragmentary, in others extraordinarily complete and alive with colour – have been placed as they were when *in situ*. The Gothic collection includes art from outside Catalunya and is less extensive. Most of the explanations are in Catalan, but you can pick up a catalogue style booklet that at least gives you an idea of what you are looking at.

The first thing you see as you enter the Romanesque section is a remake of the apse of the church of Sant Pere de la Seu d'Urgell, dominated by a beautiful fresco from the early 12th century. In this first hall (Àmbit I) there are coins from the early days of the Comtes de Barcelona, capitals from columns used in Muslim monuments and some finely decorated altar frontals.

In Àmbit III, the frescoes from the church of Sant Pere d'Àger are particularly striking (item No 31). The depiction of Christ on wood from the church of Sant Martí de Tost (No 47 in Àmbit IV) is in a near perfect state of preservation – the vividness of the colours can only make you wonder what some of the more faded, grander frescos must once have looked like. Another good piece is No 49, an altar frontal depicting Christ and the Apostles.

One of the star attractions is the fresco of Mary and the Christ Child from the apse of the church of Santa Maria de Taüll (No 102 in Àmbit VII). In Àmbit X, have a look at No 116, an altar frontal in which the martyrdom of several saints figures among the main themes – here you can see the medieval mind at work, depicting holy individuals who apparently contemplate their own slow deaths with supreme indifference – whether boiling in water, having nails slammed into the head, being sliced up by sword or, a personal favourite, being sawn in half from head to toe!

Moving right along, the Gothic art section reveals clearly the development of painting – from two-dimensional and disembodied didactic painting to a more impassioned, human depiction of religious figures and events. In these halls you can see Catalan Gothic painting (look out

especially for the work of Bernat Martorell in Àmbit XI and Jaume Huguet in Àmbit XII), and that of other Spanish and Mediterranean regions. If the saintly suffering theme appeals to you, look out for the depiction of the martyrdom of Santa Llúcia and Sant Vicenç in Àmbit III.

The museum opens 10 am to 7 pm Tuesday to Saturday (to 9 pm Thursday), 10 am to 2.30 pm on Sunday and holidays. Admission costs 800 ptas (free on the first Thursday of the month).

Poble Espanyol (Map 7)

This 'Spanish Village' in the north-west of Montjuïc – 10 minutes walk from Plaça d'Espanya or the Museu Nacional d'Art de Catalunya – is both a cheesy souvenirhunters' haunt and an intriguing scrapbook of Spanish architecture. Built for the Spanish crafts section of the 1929 exhibition, it's composed of plazas and streets lined with surprisingly good copies of characteristic buildings from all the country's regions.

You enter from Avinguda del Marquès de Comillas, beneath a towered medieval gate from Ávila. Inside, to the right, is an information office with free maps. Straight ahead from the gate is a Plaza Mayor, or town square, surrounded with mainly Castilian and Aragonese buildings. Elsewhere you'll find an Andalucían *barrio*, a Basque street, Galician and Catalan quarters and even – at the eastern end – a Dominican monastery. The buildings house dozens of moderate to expensive restaurants, cafes, bars, craft shops and workshops, and a few souvenir stores.

The Poble Espanyol opens from 9 am daily (to 8 pm Monday; to 2 am Tuesday to Thursday; to 4 am Friday and Saturday; and to midnight Sunday). Admission costs 975 ptas (1200 ptas combined with Galería Olímpica – see later in this section; students and children aged seven to 14, 550 ptas). After 9 pm on days other than Friday and Saturday, it's free. At night, the restaurants, bars and discos become a lively corner of Barcelona nightlife. If you want more information or a guided tour, call ☎ 93 325 78 66 or email ⓔ info@poble-espanyol.com.

euro currency converter €1 = 166 ptas

Museu Etnològic & Museu d'Arqueologia (Map 7)

Down the hill east of the Museu Nacional d'Art, these museums are worth a visit if their subjects interest you, although neither is very excitingly presented and most of the explanatory material is in Catalan.

The Museu Etnològic (Ethnology Museum) on Passeig de Santa Madrona organises extensive temporary exhibitions on a range of cultures from other continents. It opens 10 am to 3 pm (to 7 pm Tuesday and Thursday, except in summer), daily but Monday. Admission costs 400 ptas.

The Museu d'Arqueologia (archaeology museum), at the corner of Passeig de Santa Madrona and Passeig de l'Exposició, covers Catalunya and related cultures elsewhere in Spain. Items range from copies of pre-Neanderthal skulls to lovely Carthaginian necklaces and jewel-studded Visigothic crosses. There's good material on the Balearic Islands (rooms X to XIII) and Empúries (Emporion), the Greek and Roman city on the Costa Brava (rooms XIV and parts of XVII). The Roman finds upstairs were mostly dug up in Barcelona. It opens 9.30 am to 7 pm, Tuesday to Saturday; 10 am to 2.30 pm on Sunday (400 ptas).

Anella Olímpica (Map 7)

The 'Olympic Ring' is the group of sports installations where the main events of the 1992 Olympics were held, on the ridge above the Museu Nacional d'Art de Catalunya. Westernmost is the **Institut Nacional d'Educació Física de Catalunya** (INEFC), a kind of sports university, designed by Ricard Bofill. Past a circular arena, the Plaça d'Europa, with the **Torre Calatrava** communications tower behind it, is the **Piscines Bernat Picornell** building, where the swimming events were held (now open to the public – see the Swimming & Gym section under Activities later). Next comes a pleasant little park, the Jardí d'Aclimatació.

Estadi Olímpic (Map 7) The main stadium of the Olympic Games, admission free, opens 10 am to 6 pm (as late as 8 pm in summer) daily; enter at the northern end.

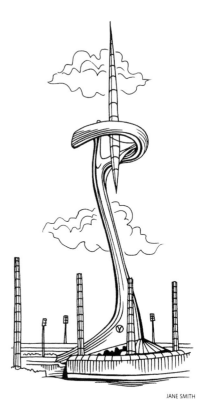

JANE SMITH

Space-age Torre Calatrava takes the design of communication transmitters to a new level

If you saw some of the Olympics on TV, the 65,000 capacity stadium may seem surprisingly small.

So may the Olympic flame-holder rising at the northern end, into which a long-range archer spectacularly deposited a flaming arrow in the opening ceremony. (Well, nearly. The archer actually missed, but the clever organisers had foreseen this possibility. The flame-holder was alive with gas, so the arrow only had to pass within 2m of it to set the thing on fire. A gleeful Barcelona TV crew was waiting on the other side for just such a 'failure'.)

The stadium was opened in 1929 but completely restored for 1992. At its southern end (enter from outside) is the **Galería Olímpica**, which has an exhibition, including videos, on the 1992 games. You will need to be quite a fan of all things Olympian to get anything out of this. One favourite item are the models of the standard daily diet of cyclists and gymnasts – there's something intriguing about looking at a plate of plastic pasta. Or you can behold the splendours of an athlete's bed made up with duvet and pillow cases sporting Barcelona's Olympic mascot, Cobi. Speaking of which, a whole display is dedicated to Cobi. The gallery opens 10 am to 1 pm and 4 to 6 pm Monday to Friday (to 8 pm in summer) and holidays from 10 am to 2 pm. Admission costs 400 ptas.

West of the stadium is the 17,000 capacity **Palau Sant Jordi**, an indoor sports, concert and exhibition hall opened in 1990 and designed by the Japanese architect Arata Isozaki.

Nou Jardí Botànic (Map 7)

South across the road from the Estadi is this new botanical garden, built on what was an old municipal dump. The theme is 'Mediterranean' fauna and the collection includes some 2000 species thriving in areas around the world with a climate similar to that of the Med.

The trees and plants you see come from the Eastern Mediterranean, Spain (including the Balearic and Canary Islands), North Africa, Australia, California, Chile and South Africa. It opens 10 am to 5 pm, or 3 pm from November to March and in July and August. Admission costs 200 ptas and you can use the same ticket to make a second visit.

Cementiri del Sud-Ouest (Map 7)

On the hill south of the Anella Olímpica you can see the top of a huge cemetery, the Cementiri del Sud-Ouest or Cementiri Nou, which extends down the southern side of the hill. Opened in 1883, it's an odd combination of elaborate architect-designed tombs for rich families and small niches for the rest. It includes the graves of numerous Catalan artists and politicians.

Fundació Joan Miró (Map 7)

Barcelona's gallery for one of the greatest Catalan artists of the 20th century, Joan Miró, is 400m north-east, downhill, from the Estadi Olímpic. Miró established the foundation in 1971. Its light-filled buildings were designed by his close friend and architect Josep Lluís Sert, who also built Miró's Mallorca studios.

This, the greatest single collection of the artist's work, comprises around 300 of his paintings, 153 sculptures, some textiles and more than 7000 drawings spanning his entire life, of which only a part is ever on display. The exhibits tend to concentrate on Miró's more settled last 20 years, but there are some important exceptions. The ground floor Sala (room) Joan Prats shows the younger Miró moving away, under surrealist influence, from his *relative* realism (for instance his 1917 painting of the *Ermita de Sant Joan d'Horta*), then starting to work towards his own recognisable style. This section includes the 1939–44 Barcelona series of tortured lithographs – Miró's comment on the Spanish Civil War.

The Sala Pilar Juncosa (named after his wife), upstairs, also displays works from the 1930s and '40s. After this room, the bulk of what you see is from his latter years – mostly paintings, but some sculpture (especially some playful items on the outdoor terrace). While some of the paintings are classics of the style for which he is best known, with an almost childlike delight in primary colours, in the 1970s he opted for an exploration of more muted greens, browns and black.

Another interesting section is devoted to the 'Miró Papers', which include many preparatory drawings and sketches, some on bits of newspaper or cigarette packets. *A Joan Miró* is a collection of work by other contemporary artists, donated in tribute to Miró. The Fundació also has a contemporary art library open to the public, a good specialist art bookshop and a cafe. It also stages exhibitions and recitals of contemporary art and music.

The gallery opens 10 am to 7 pm (an hour longer in summer), Tuesday to Saturday

THINGS TO SEE & DO

(to 9.30 pm Thursday), 10 am to 2.30 pm on Sunday and holidays. Admission costs 800 ptas.

Castell de Montjuïc & Around (Map 7)

The south-east of Montjuïc is dominated by the Castell (castle). Near the bottom of the ruined remains of what was the Parc d'Atraccions (amusement park) are the Estació Parc Montjuïc funicular/telefèric station and the ornamental **Jardins de Mossèn Cinto Verdaguer**. The one-time amusement park is destined to become part of a larger botanical garden.

From the **Jardins del Mirador** opposite the Mirador telefèric station there are fine views over the port of Barcelona.

The Castell de Montjuïc dates in its present form from the late 17th and 18th centuries. For most of its existence it has been used to watch over the city and as a political prison and killing ground. Anarchists were executed here around the turn of the century, fascists during the civil war and Republicans after it – most notoriously Lluís Companys in 1940. The army finally handed it over to the city in 1960. The castle is surrounded by a network of ditches and walls, and today houses the **Museu Militar**. You enter an artillery-lined courtyard, off which rooms are filled with a ragbag of weapons old and new, as well as uniforms, yellowing maps and so on. Stairs lead down to another series of halls lined with more of the same, along with castle models, a couple of portraits of General Franco and even an equestrian statue of him. In Room (*sala*) 18 are some tombstones, some dating to the 11th century, from the one-time Jewish cemetery on Montjuïc (open 9.30 am to 8 pm, daily except Monday). Admission to the museum costs 250 ptas. Best of all are the excellent views from the castle area of the port and city below. You can eat amid the artillery at the museum cafe.

Towards the foot of this part of Montjuïc, above the thundering traffic of the main road to Tarragona, the **Jardins de Mossèn Costa i Llobera** have a good collection of tropical and desert plants – including a veritable forest of cacti; the gardens are open 10 am to sunset and admission is free.

PARC GÜELL (Map 1)

North of Gràcia and about 4km from Plaça de Catalunya, Parc Güell is where Gaudí turned his hand to landscape gardening. It's a strange, enchanting place where his passion for natural forms really took flight – to the point where the artificial almost seems more natural than the natural.

Parc Güell originated in 1900 when Count Eusebi Güell bought a tree-covered hillside (then outside Barcelona) and hired Gaudí to create a miniature garden city of houses for the wealthy, in landscaped grounds. The project was a commercial flop and was abandoned in 1914 – but not before Gaudí had created 3km of roads and walks, steps and a plaza in his inimitable manner, plus the two gatehouses. In 1922 the city bought the estate for use as a public park.

The simplest way to Parc Güell is to take the metro to Lesseps, then walk 10 to 15 minutes: follow the signs north-east along Travessera de Dalt, then left up Carrer de Larrard, which brings you out almost at the park's two Hansel and Gretel-style gatehouses on Carrer d'Olot.

The park opens daily from 9 am: to 9 pm from June to September; to 8 pm April, May and October; to 7 pm March and November; and to 6 pm other months (admission is free). It's extremely popular, and its quaint nooks and crannies are irresistible to photographers – who on busy days have trouble keeping out of each other's pictures.

The steps up from the entrance, guarded by a mosaic dragon/lizard, lead to the **Sala Hipóstila**, a forest of 84 stone columns (some of them leaning), intended as a market. To the left from here curves a gallery whose twisted stonework columns and roof give the effect of a cloister beneath tree roots – a motif repeated in several places in the park. On top of the Sala Hipóstila is a broad open space whose centrepiece is the **Banc de Trenadis**, a tiled bench curving sinuously around its perimeter.

The spired house to the right is the **Casa**

Museu Gaudí, where Gaudí lived for most of his last 20 years (1906–26). It contains furniture by him and other memorabilia. It opens 10 am to 8 pm daily from May to September; to 7 pm in March, April and October and to 6 pm the rest of the year. As a rule it opens only from 10 am to 2 pm on Sunday and may close between 2 and 4 pm in the off-season. Admission costs 300 ptas.

Much of the park is still wooded but full of pathways. The best views are from the cross-topped **Turo del Calvari** in the southwestern corner.

TIBIDABO

Tibidabo (542m) is the highest hill in the wooded range that forms the backdrop to Barcelona. It's a good place for some fresh air (it's often a few degrees cooler than the city) and, if the air's clear, it has views over the city and inland as far as Montserrat. Tibidabo gets its name from the devil, who, trying to tempt Christ, took him to a high place and said, in the Latin version: *'Haec omnia tibi dabo si cadens adoraberis me.'* ('All this I will give you if you will fall down and worship me.')

Getting There & Away

First, get an FGC train to Avinguda de Tibidabo from Catalunya station on Plaça de Catalunya – a 10 minute ride for 150 ptas. Outside Avinguda de Tibidabo station, hop on the *tramvia blau*, Barcelona's last surviving tram, which runs up between fancy turn-of-the century mansions to Plaça del Doctor Andreu (275/400 ptas one way/return). The tram runs daily in summer, and on Saturday, Sunday and holidays the rest of the year, every 15 or 30 minutes from 9 am to 9.30 pm. On other days a bus (150 ptas) serves the route at similar times. From Plaça del Doctor Andreu the Tibidabo funicular railway climbs through the woods to Plaça de Tibidabo at the top of the hill (300/400 ptas, one way/return), every 15–30 minutes from 7.15 am to 9.45 pm daily. If you're feeling active, you can walk up or down through the woods instead. The funicular only operates when the Parc d'Atraccions is open.

The cheaper alternative is bus No T2, the 'Tibibús', from Plaça de Catalunya to Plaça de Tibidabo (230 ptas). This runs on Saturday, Sunday and holidays year round, every 30 minutes from 10.30 am. From late June to early September it runs Monday to Friday too, every hour from 10.30 am. The last bus down leaves Tibidabo 30 minutes after the Parc d'Atraccions closes.

Temple del Sagrat Cor

The Church of the Sacred Heart, looming above the top funicular station, is meant to be Barcelona's answer to Paris' Sacré Coeur. It's certainly equally visible, and even more vilified by aesthetes (perhaps with good reason). It's actually two churches, one on top of the other. The top one is surmounted by a giant Christ and has a lift to the roof (100 ptas). Visiting times to the church are 8 am to 7 pm daily.

Parc d'Atraccions

The reason most Barcelonins come up to Tibidabo (☎ 93 211 79 42) is for some thrills (but hopefully no spills) in this funfair, close to the top funicular station. Admission costs 800 ptas plus extra for each ride, 1200 ptas for admission and six rides, or 2500 ptas with access to all rides – including seven minutes in the Hotel Krueger, an *hospedaje* of horrors inhabited by actors playing out their Dracula, Hannibal Lecter and other fantasies. The funfair's opening times change with the season, so check with a tourist office: in summer it's usually open from noon until late at night daily; in winter it may open on Saturday, Sunday and holidays only, from about noon to 7 pm. A cloud is hanging over the ageing fun park, and at the time of writing it was unclear if it would be open for much longer.

Torre de Collserola

The 288m Torre de Collserola telecommunications tower (☎ 93 406 93 54 for information) was built in 1990–92. The external glass lift to the visitors' observation area, 115m up, is as hair-raising as anything at the Parc d'Atraccions. From the top they say you can see for 70km on a clear day. It

THINGS TO SEE & DO

opens 11 am to 2.30 pm and 3.30 to 6 pm Wednesday to Friday and 11 am to 6 pm on weekends and holidays. These hours can be extended to 8 pm in summer. It closes in January. The ride up costs 500 ptas.

To get there take the same transport as for Tibidabo to Plaça de Tibidabo, then walk about 600m west along the Camí de Vallvidrera al Tibidabo.

Museu de la Ciencia (Map 1)

This is one of those interactive science museums where you get to twiddle knobs and press buttons and so discover how the world around you works. There is also a planetarium. In the coming years museum space will grow and in it a small sample of tropical jungle will be planted. This could be a good one for young kids, but it's awkwardly placed at Carrer de Teodor Roviralta 55 near the Ronda de Dalt. Opening times are 10 am to 8 pm Tuesday to Sunday; admission costs 500 ptas (free on the first Sunday of the month). Bus No 60 stops close by.

CAMP NOU (Map 1)

Among Barcelona's most visited museums – hard on the heels of the Museu Picasso – comes the Museu del Futbol Club Barcelona at the club's giant Camp Nou (sometimes also known as Nou Camp) stadium, 3.5km west of Plaça de Catalunya (metro Collblanc). Barça is one of Europe's top football clubs and its museum is a hit with football fans the world over.

Camp Nou, built in the 1950s and enlarged for the 1982 World Cup, is one of the world's biggest stadiums, holding 120,000 people, and the club has a world record membership of 110,000. Soccer fans who can't get to a game (see the Entertainment chapter) should find the museum (on the Carrer d'Aristides Maillol side of the stadium) worthwhile. The best bits are the photo section, the goal videos, and the views out over the stadium. Among the quirkier paraphernalia are old sports board games, a 19th-century leather football, the life-size diorama of old-time dressing rooms, posters and magazines from way back and the *futbolín* (table soccer) collection.

It opens 10 am to 6.30 pm Monday to Saturday (Tuesday to Saturday from October to March), 10 am to 2 pm on Sunday and holidays. Admission costs 500 ptas.

PEDRALBES (Map 1)

This is a wealthy residential area north of Camp Nou.

Palau Reial de Pedralbes

Close to Palau Reial metro station, across Avinguda Diagonal from the main campus of the Universitat de Barcelona, is the entrance to the **Parc del Palau Reial**, a verdant park open daily. In the park is the Palau Reial de Pedralbes, an early-20th-century building that belonged to the family of Eusebi Güell (Gaudí's patron) until they handed it over to the city in 1926 to serve as a royal residence – among its guests have been King Alfonso XIII, the president of Catalunya and General Franco.

Today it houses the **Museu de Ceràmica**, with a good collection of Spanish ceramics from the 13th to 19th centuries, including work by Picasso and Miró. Spain inherited from the Muslims, and then further refined, a strong tradition in ceramics – here you can compare some exquisite work (tiles, porcelain tableware and the like) from some of the greatest centres of pottery production across Spain, including Talavera de la Reina in Castilla, Manises and Paterna in Valencia, and Teruel in Aragón. Upstairs is a display of fanciful modern ceramics from this century – here they have ceased to be a tool with aesthetic value and are purely decorative.

Across the corridor, the **Museu de les Arts Decoratives** brings together an eclectic assortment of furnishings, ornaments, and knick-knacks dating as far back as the Romanesque period (early Middle Ages). The plush and somewhat stuffy elegance of Empire and Isabelline-style divans can be neatly compared with some of the more tasteless ideas to emerge on the subject of seating in the 1970s.

Both museums open 10 am to 6 pm Tuesday to Saturday, 10 am to 3 pm Sunday and holidays. Admission costs 400 ptas for each museum or 700 ptas for both.

Over by Avinguda de Pedralbes are the Gaudí-designed stables and porter's lodge for the **Finca Güell**, as the Güell estate here was called. They were done in the mid-1880s, when Gaudí was strongly impressed by Islamic architecture. They can't be visited, although there is nothing to stop you admiring Gaudí's wrought-iron dragon gate from the outside.

Museu-Monestir de Pedralbes

This peaceful old convent, now a museum of monastic life also housing part of the Thyssen-Bornemisza art collection, stands at the top of Avinguda de Pedralbes, about a 10-minute walk from Finca Güell. The easiest way here, if you are not walking up from Finca Güell, is to get the suburban FGC train to Reina Elisenda (the end of the line) from Catalunya station and then either walk (about 10 minutes) or pick up one of the buses running along Passeig de la Reina Elisenda de Montcada (such as Nos 22, 64 & 75).

The convent, founded in 1326, still houses a community of nuns who inhabit separate closed quarters. The museum entrance is on Plaça del Monestir, a divinely quiet corner of Barcelona; it opens 10 am to 2 pm Tuesday to Sunday. Admission costs 700 ptas or 400 ptas only for either the monastery *or* the Thyssen-Bornemisza collection.

The architectural highlight is the large, elegant, three-storey cloister, a jewel of Catalan Gothic, built in the early 14th century. You will be gently persuaded to head around it to your right, and the first chapel you come across is the Capella de Sant Miquel, whose murals were done in 1346 by Ferrer Bassá, one of Catalunya's earliest documented painters.

As you head around the cloister, you can peer into a restored refectory, a kitchen, stables, stores and a reconstruction of the old infirmary – all giving a good idea of convent life. Perhaps the hardest thing to imagine is spending your days in the cells on the ground and first floors. Here the devout nuns would spend much of their days in prayer and devotional reading.

The Col.lecció Thyssen-Bornemisza (entry from the ground floor), quartered in the (painstakingly restored) one-time dormitories of the nuns and the Saló Principal, is part of a wide-ranging art collection acquired by Spain in 1993. Most of it went to the Museo Thyssen-Bornemisza in Madrid; what's here is mainly religious work by European masters including Canaletto, Titian, Tintoretto, Rubens, Zurbarán and Velázquez. Around 70 paintings and eight sculptures are on display. Together with the Madrid collection, they represent an extraordinarily eclectic approach to art procurement (if you get a chance to go to Madrid, the collection there, virtually across the road from El Prado, is a must). The sculptures and 17 of the paintings were produced by mostly anonymous medieval Italian artists. Next come around 20 pieces belonging to the early Renaissance period in Germany (including Cranach the Elder), accompanied by another 16 from northern Italy stretching into the 16th century. The collection is capped by about a dozen late baroque works.

THE OUTSKIRTS
Jardins del Laberint d'Horta

Laid out in the twilight years of the 18th century by Antoni Desvalls, Marquès d'Alfarras i de Llupià, the carefully manicured park remained a private family idyll until the 1970s, when it was opened to the public. Many a fine party and theatrical performance was held here over the years, but now it serves as kind of museum-park. The gardens take their name from a maze in their centre, but other paths take you past a pleasant artificial lake *(estany)*, waterfalls, a neoclassical pavilion and a false cemetery. The latter is inspired by 19th-century romanticism, often characterised by an obsession with a swooning, anaemic vision of death.

The gardens open 10 am to sunset daily (which means anything from 6 pm in January to 9 pm in August). Admission costs 250 ptas. To get there you can take the metro to Montbau (Line 3); from there you still have about a 15-minute walk east along the Ronda de Dalt freeway to the gardens, on Carrer dels Germans Desvalls s/n.

THINGS TO SEE & DO

Colònia Güell

Apart from La Sagrada Família, the last grand project Gaudí would turn his hand to was the creation of a kind of Utopian workers' complex outside Barcelona at Santa Coloma de Cervelló. His main role was to erect the colony's church – workers' housing and the local co-op were in the hands of other architects. He first thought about it in 1898, but work on the church's crypt started in 1908. It proceeded for eight years, at which point interest in the whole idea fizzled. The crypt today still serves as a working church.

This structure is an important part of Gaudí's oeuvre, little visited by tourists and yet a key to understanding what the master had in mind for his magnum opus, La Sagrada Família. The mostly brick-clad columns that support the ribbed vaults in the ceiling are inclined in much the way you might expect trees in a forest to lean at all angles (reminiscent also of Parc Güell, which Gaudí was working on at much the same time). Gaudí had worked out the angles in such a way that their load would be transmitted from the ceiling to the earth without the help of extra buttressing. Similar thinking lay behind his plans for La Sagrada Família, whose final Gothic inspired structure would tower above anything ever done in the Middle Ages but not require so much as one buttress to hold it all up.

Down to the wavy design of the pews, Gaudí's hand is visible (you can see an example of the seating in the Museu Nacional d'Art Modern de Catalunya in the Parc de la Ciutadella too). The primary colours in the curvaceous plant-shaped stained-glass windows are another reminder of the era in which the crypt was built.

The easiest way to get there is to take an FGC train (the S3, 150 ptas) from Plaça d'Espanya and get off at Molí Nou station, the last stop (train No S33 leaves roughly hourly, usually at a quarter past the hour, for Santa Coloma station, one further on). When you reach the station, exit by the underpass and turn right (north) up the BV-2002 road towards Santa Coloma de Cervelló. It's a 15-minute walk (the first five minutes on

this traffic-choked road will be equivalent to your year's air pollution intake). You will walk along the walls of a light industrial complex called Recinto Colonia Güell, at the corner of which you turn left – follow this road as it veers to the right and you enter the small settlement – some of the houses and shops are unmistakable leftovers of the Modernistas' planned workers' village. Keep straight uphill to reach the crypt.

Alternatively, you could get off the train one stop earlier at Sant Boi de Llobregat and catch the L76 bus right to Santa Coloma, but this will end up taking longer.

The Colònia Güell opens from 10 am to 1.15 pm and 4 to 6 pm daily, mornings only on Thursday and holidays. If in doubt call ahead on ☎ 93 640 29 36. Admission costs 100 ptas.

Sant Cugat del Vallès

When the marauding Muslims tramped through the one-time Roman encampment turned Visigothic monastery of Sant Cugat del Vallès in the 8th century, they razed the lot to the ground. These things happen, so after the Christians got back in the saddle, work on a new monastic complex was stoically begun. What you see today is a combination of Romanesque and Gothic buildings. The lower floor of the cloister is a fine demonstration of Romanesque and the principal reason for making the effort to come here (Sant Cugat may have been a favourite summer getaway for Barcelonins at the turn of the 19th century, but those days are long gone). The Gothic church and upper storey of the cloister also repay some quiet contemplation. The monastery opens 9 am to noon and 4 to 8 pm daily; admission is free.

To get here, take the FGC train from Plaça de Catalunya (lines S1, S2, S5 or S55) to Sant Cugat del Vallès (285 ptas, 25 minutes). If you go on the second or fourth Sunday of the month, you may catch a *clàssic tren*, a vintage electric job from the 1920s that will take you up to the sounds of live jazz or classical music. Tickets are the same price as for normal trains. For more information call FGC on ☎ 93 205 15 15.

From the Sant Cugat train station you could wait for a local circle line bus, but the walk is hardly taxing. Head left out of the station along Avinguda d'Alfonso Sala Conde de Egara and turn right down Carrer de Ruis i Taulet, followed by a left into Carrer de Santiago Rusiñol, which leads to the monastery.

ACTIVITIES

For information on where you can practise sports in Barcelona, try the Servei d'Informació Esportiva (☎ 93 402 30 00), Avinguda de l'Estadi 30–40 (in the same complex as the Piscines Bernat Picornell on Montjuïc). It opens 8.30 am to 3 pm on weekdays (Map 7).

Swimming & Gym

The Olympic pool on Montjuïc (Map 7), the Piscines Bernat Picornell (☎ 93 423 40 41), opens to the public from 7 am until midnight Monday to Friday, until 9 pm Saturday, and 7.30 am to 4.30 pm Sunday. It costs 1200 ptas, including use of the good gym inside. Access to the outdoor pool alone costs 650 ptas in summer *only*. It opens 10 am to 6 pm (9 am to 9 pm in summer) Monday to Saturday and 10 am to 2.30 pm (9 am to 8 pm) on Sundays. If you are about for any length of time and want regular access to the pool, gym and other facilities, think about taking out membership. You need to have a local bank account, as the monthly charge is made by direct debit *(domiciliació bancària)*. You pay 3875 ptas to join and the same each month.

The nearby open-air Piscina Municipal de Montjuïc, used for diving and water polo in the 1992 Olympic Games, has a rather forlorn air about it and opens weekends only in July and August (550 ptas, 10 am to 6 pm).

Another pool option for lap swimmers are the Banys Sant Sebastià (Map 1; ☎ 93 221 00 10), down by La Barceloneta beach. The main (indoor) pool opens daily from 7 am to 10.30 pm, Sunday from 8 am to 5 pm. Admission costs 1025 ptas, which includes use of the gym. You can also become a member under conditions similar to those outlined above.

Bowling

Bowling Barcelona (Map 3; ☎ 93 330 50 48), Carrer de Sabino Arana 6 (metro Maria Cristina), is the place to come if you like launching round objects at pins.

Squash

You can sweat it out on the court at a few places in Barcelona. Try the Poliesportiu Perill (Map 2; ☎ 93 459 44 30) at Carrer de Perill 16–22 (metro Diagonal).

Table Tennis

Ping Pong habitués can find out where the handiest place to play is by calling the Federació Catalana de Tennis de Taula (☎ 93 280 03 00). The Poliesportiu Municipal l'Espanya Industrial next to the so-called park of the same name in Sants (metro Sants-Estació) has tables.

Tennis

For more conventional tennis, there are several options in Barcelona. About the most pleasant and relatively convenient is the Tennis Municipal Pompeia (Map 7; ☎ 93 423 97 47), Avinguda del Marquès de Comillas 29–41, on Montjuïc.

COURSES

The CIAJ (Centre d'Informació i Assessorament per a Joves) youth information service (Map 6; ☎ 93 402 78 00), Carrer de Ferran 32, in the Barri Gòtic has information on various courses available throughout the city. It opens 10 am to 2 pm and 4 to 8 pm Monday to Friday.

Language Courses

Some of the best-value Spanish language courses are offered by the Universitat de Barcelona, which runs intensive courses (40-hours tuition over periods ranging from two weeks to a month; 45,000 ptas) year round. Longer Spanish courses, and courses in Catalan, are also available.

For more information you can ask at the university's Informació office at Gran Via de les Corts Catalanes 585 (Map 4). It opens 9 am to 2 pm Monday to Friday. Otherwise try (for Spanish) its Instituto de Estudios

Hispánicos (☎ 93 403 55 19, fax 93 403 54 33), or (for Catalan) its Servei de Llengua Catalana (☎ 93 403 54 77, fax 93 403 54 84) – both are in the same building as the information office.

The university-run Escola Oficial d'Idiomes de Barcelona (Map 6; ☎ 93 324 93 30, fax 93 934 93 51) at Avinguda de les Drassanes s/n (metro Drassanes) is another place offering economical 80-hour summer Spanish courses, as well as longer part-time courses in Spanish and Catalan.

Across Catalunya there are more than 220 schools where you can learn Catalan. Pick up a list at the Llibreria & Informaciò Cultural de la Generalitat de Catalunya (Map 6; ☎ 93 302 64 62), Rambla dels Estudis 118. International House (Map 6; ☎ 93 268 45 11, fax 93 268 02 39, e ihbarcelona@bcn.ihes.com) is at Carrer de Trafalgar 14. Intensive courses start at around 50,000 ptas per week. They can also organise accommodation.

Advertisements for courses and private tuition are posted at the university, Come In bookshop at Carrer de Provença 203 (Map 2) and the British Council (Map 3).

Other Courses

Check out course lists at CIAJ. These examples and many other courses are really aimed at people hanging around for a while. In most cases reasonable Spanish, if not Catalan, will be required.

La Cafetera de l'Esbart Català de Dansaires
(Map 6; ☎ 93 303 10 01, Passatge del Crèdit 8). This group organises courses in Catalan dance for anyone from beginners to advanced, and is of special interest to professionals. Usually the sessions are held on Monday.

Institut del Teatre
(Map 6; ☎ 93 268 20 78, Carrer de Sant Pere més baix 7). The institute offers serious courses in various aspects of theatre – for long-termers with a view to breaking into theatre.

Centre Cívic Drassanes
(Map 6; ☎ 93 441 22 80, Carrer Nou de la Rambla 43). This civic centre puts on all sorts of courses and workshops ranging from didgeridoo to Windows 98.

Barcelona Centre d'Imatge
(☎ 93 311 92 73, Carrer de Pons i Gallarza 25). Various levels offered in photography.

Àrea Espai de Dança i Creació
(Map 1; ☎ 93 210 78 50, Carrer d'Alegre de Dalt 55 bis). One of the best spots in town to learn contemporary dance – some English is spoken.

Conceived as a miniature garden city for Barcelona's wealthy, Parc Güell is another unfinished Gaudí creation. It's an enchanting place to escape to from the hustle and bustle of the city.

Temple del Sagrat Cor's spire

Detail from the Temple del Sagrat Cor, Tibidabo

Medieval meets modern at Tibidabo – the Temple del Sagrat Cor and Parc d'Atraccions

La Font Màgica, Montjuïc, comes alive with lights and music.

The monumental Cascada

Places to Stay

Barcelona attracts more tourists with every passing year, so it's getting squeezy. The peak (high season) periods are Setmana Santa (Easter week), summer (especially July and August), during the Festes de la Mercè (second half of September), Christmas and New Year, and finding a room then can be a pain. Local tourism authorities happily claim an average year-round room-occupation rate of 80%. With a little searching you'll usually find something, but you will need patience. Arrive in the morning – checkout time is generally midday.

Seasons, Reservations & Prices

Prices may vary with the season. Some places have separate price structures for the high season *(temporada alta)*, mid-season *(temporada media)* and the low season *(temporada baja)*, all usually displayed on a notice in reception or close by. (Hoteliers are not bound by these displayed prices. They are free to charge less, which they quite often do, or more, which happens fairly rarely.)

The bad news is that prices in many places seem to be rising exponentially, well out of line with inflation. This means that, while the prices in this guide are correct at the time of going to press, there is a fair chance they may have already risen by the time you have the book in your hands. Always check before committing yourself. Many smaller places will insist you pay in advance each day.

Taxes

Virtually all accommodation prices are subject to IVA, the Spanish version of value-added tax, which is 7%. This is often included in the quoted price at cheaper places, but less often at more expensive ones. To check, ask: *'¿Está incluido el IVA?'* ('Is IVA included?') In some cases you will only be charged IVA if you ask for a receipt.

PLACES TO STAY – BUDGET
Camping

The nearest camp site is the big *Cala Gogó (☎/fax 93 379 46 00, Carretera de la Platja s/n, El Prat de Llobregat)*, 9km south-west of the city centre, near the airport. It opens mid-March to mid-October and charges 3400 ptas for a site, car and two adults. You can get there by bus No 65 from Plaça d'Espanya, or by RENFE train from Plaça de Catalunya to El Prat, then a 'Prat Platja' bus.

There are some better – but still vast – sites a few kilometres farther out, to the south-west on the coastal C-246 road, the Autovía de Castelldefels. All are reachable by bus No L95 from the corner of Ronda de la Universitat and Rambla de Catalunya. They include (with prices for a car, a tent and two adults):

El Toro Bravo (☎ 93 637 34 62, Carretera C-246, Km 11, Viladecans). Although it's a tad shabby, it opens year round and costs 3400 ptas.

Filipinas (☎ 93 658 28 95, Carretera C-246, Km 12, Viladecans). Also open year round, it is one of the best for value for money; it costs 3400 ptas.

La Ballena Alegre (☎/fax 93 658 05 04, Carretera C-246, Km 12.4, Viladecans). Open from April to the end of September, it is also good, costing 4300 ptas.

Eleven kilometres north-east of the city, *Camping Masnou (☎ 93 555 15 03, Camí Fabra 33, El Masnou)* is open year round. It's 200m from El Masnou train station (reached by suburban *rodalies/cercanías* trains from Catalunya station on Plaça de Catalunya) and charges 2740 ptas for a car, tent and two adults.

All are inconvenient if you want late nights in Barcelona, because the only way back late at night is by taxi.

Youth & Backpacker Hostels

Barcelona has four HI hostels and several non-HI hostels. All require you to rent sheets (150 ptas to 350 ptas) if you don't have any and some lock their gates in the early hours so aren't suitable if you plan to party on late. Except at the Kabul, which doesn't take bookings, it's advisable to call ahead in summer. Most have washing machines.

The non-HI *Youth Hostel Kabul* (*Map 6; ☎ 93 318 51 90, fax 93 301 40 34, Plaça Reial 17*) is in the Barri Gòtic. It's a rough and ready place but does have, as its leaflets say, a 'great party atmosphere' and no curfew. The price is 2000 ptas, plus 1000 ptas key deposit. Safes are available for valuables. There's room for 130 people in bare bunk rooms holding up to 10 each. Remember to take your key with you when you go out for the night – one reader reported having trouble being let back in without it.

The biggest and most comfortable hostel is the 183-place *Alberg Mare de Déu de Montserrat* (*Map 1; ☎ 93 210 51 51, fax 93 210 07 98, Passeig Mare de Déu del Coll 41–51*). It's 4km north of the centre, a 10-minute walk from Vallcarca metro or a 20-minute ride from Plaça de Catalunya on bus No 28, which stops almost outside the gate. The main building is a former private mansion with a Mudéjar-style lobby. Most rooms sleep six. A hostel card is needed: if you're under 25 or have an ISIC card, B&B costs 1900 ptas; otherwise it's 2500 ptas. The hostel is in HI's International Booking Network (IBN), which enables you to book through about 200 other HI hostels and booking centres around the world. You can also book through the central booking service of Catalunya's official youth hostels organisation, the Xarxa d'Albergs de Joventut (*☎ 93 483 83 63, fax 93 483 83 50*). (Note: the other Barcelona hostels, even the HI ones, are not in the Xarxa.)

Alberg Juvenil Palau (*Map 6; ☎ 93 412 50 80, Carrer del Palau 6*) in the Barri Gòtic has a friendly atmosphere and just 40 places in separate-sex bunk rooms. It costs 1600 ptas, which includes breakfast.

Hostal de Joves (*Map 1; ☎ 93 300 31 04, Passeig de Pujades 29*) faces the northern end of Parc de la Ciutadella, a few minutes' walk from the Estació de França and Arc de

Triomf metro station. It has 68 bunk places in small, rather grim dorms. The price is 1500 ptas including breakfast.

Another handy but spartan place off Carrer de la Boqueria is the *Albergue Arco* (*Map 6; ☎ 93 301 31 93, Carrer de l'Arc de Santa Eulàlia 1*). It opens 24 hours a day and a bed in a separate-sex dorm costs 1400 ptas.

Alberg Pere Tarrès (*Map 3; ☎ 93 410 23 09, fax 93 419 62 68, Carrer de Numància 149*), 1km north of Estació Sants, has 92 places in dorms of four to eight bunks. B&B costs from 1500 ptas to 2000 ptas, depending on age and whether you have a hostel card. The gates are shut from 11 am to 3 pm and from 11 pm to 8.30 am (they're opened briefly to let guests in at 2 am).

The small and distant *Alberg Studio* (*Map 1; ☎ 93 205 09 61, fax 93 205 09 00, Carrer de la Duquessa d'Orleans 58*), off Passeig de la Reina Elisenda de Montcada, 4km north-west of Plaça de Catalunya, opens only from 1 July to 30 September, and has 50 places. It stays open 24 hours and charges 1700 ptas. FGC trains run to nearby Reina Elisenda station from Catalunya station.

Hostales, Pensiones & Hotels

Town authorities are particularly parsimonious with licences to open small pensiones and hostales. This means that, as more travellers stream into the city each year, finding a room at budget rates becomes tougher. Many of the places below are often full, so you may want to let your fingers do the walking. As prices go up, the definition of 'budget' blurs. We have set a cut-off point at 6000/9000 ptas for singles/doubles. Anything at that price and heading upwards is in the Mid-Range (or Top End) section. The prices given are for the high season.

Bathrooms are often in the corridor and shared at these places. Prices sometimes fall a little in the low season or if you stay for a week or more.

La Rambla At the top of La Rambla, above Restaurante Nuria, *Pensión Noya* (*Map 6; ☎ 93 301 48 31, Rambla de Canaletes 133*) has 15 smallish but clean rooms (shower and loo in the corridor) at 3000/6000 ptas for singles/doubles in high season. Front rooms overlooking La Rambla can be noisy.

Down near the bottom of La Rambla, time seems to have passed by the *Hostal Marítima (Map 6;* ☎ *93 302 31 52, Rambla de Santa Monica 4),* once a backpackers' stalwart. Still, the rooms are adequate and clean, and the price hasn't changed in years – 2000 ptas per person. The entrance is on Passatge de la Banca leading to the Museu de Cera.

Barri Gòtic This central, atmospheric area has many of the better budget places. A few of those listed below are not, strictly speaking, in the Barri Gòtic but within a couple of minutes walk of it.

Hostal Lausanne (Map 6; ☎ *93 302 11 39, Avinguda del Portal de l'Àngel 24)* is a friendly, helpful place with good security. Popularity has made prices sneak up, but on balance this remains a good place. Clean doubles without bathroom cost 5500 ptas. Getting a single seems impossible.

Hostal Fontanella (Map 6; ☎*/fax 93 317 59 43, Via Laietana 71)* is a friendly, immaculate place, with 10 (in some cases smallish) rooms costing 3000/5000 ptas or 4000/6900 ptas with bathroom.

An excellent deal is the friendly *Hostal Campi (Map 6;* ☎ *93 301 35 45, fax 93 301 41 33, Carrer de la Canuda 4).* Singles/doubles without bathroom cost 2700/5000 ptas. If you can afford them, the best rooms are the doubles with shower and loo. They are extremely roomy and bright and cost 6000 ptas.

Hostal-Residencia Rembrandt (Map 6; ☎*/fax 93 318 10 11, 23 Carrer de la Portaferrissa)* is so popular that it was completely booked for July and August at the time of writing. The rooms are good and cost 3000/5000 ptas, or 4000/7000 ptas with bathroom.

Hostal Paris (Map 6; ☎*/fax 93 301 37 85, Carrer del Cardenal Casañas 4)* has 42 mostly large rooms in a rambling, shambolic old place. Singles without bathroom can start as low as 3000 ptas, and the most you'll pay is 7500 ptas for a double with

bathroom. The place is basic and often full of backpackers.

Hostal Galerias Maldà (Map 6; ☎ *93 317 30 02, Carrer del Pi 5),* upstairs in the arcade, is a rambling family house with 21 rooms, some of them really big. It's one of the cheapest places in town, at 1500/3000 ptas, and has one great single set in a kind of tower.

Pensión Europa (Map 6; ☎ *93 318 76 20, 18 Carrer de la Boqueria)* has simply furnished and clean singles costing 2800 ptas and better doubles without/with own bathroom costing 5600/6800 ptas. There's a big sitting room with a TV. It's not a bad deal but can get noisy when full.

Pensión Bienestar (Map 6; ☎ *93 318 72 83, Carrer d'En Quintana 3)* is a quiet, backstreet cheapy. Rooms are nothing special but they are fine for the money. The beds are a little past their prime. Singles/doubles cost 2000/3600 ptas.

Pensión Fernando (Map 6; ☎ *93 301 79 93, Carrer de l'Arc del Remedio 4)* is on Carrer de Ferran, in spite of the address. Again, you have the option of dorms here, at 2300 ptas per person (if you get lucky you'll be in a room that has its own shower and loo). At least one of these rooms is designed for wheelchair access. There are lockers in the dorm rooms (which start at four beds). Otherwise, you can take a double/triple for 7000/8500 ptas. You can catch some rays on the roof.

An OK deal, smack in the heart of the old Jewish quarter, is *Hotel Call (Map 6;* ☎ *93 302 11 23, fax 93 301 34 86, Carrer de l'Arc de Sant Ramon del Call 4).* The rooms are comfortable and all have bathroom and phone. Some, however, are terribly small. Still, it is reasonable value at 3425/4815 ptas for a single/double.

Hotel Rey Don Jaime I (Map 6; ☎*/fax 93 310 62 08, Carrer de Jaume I 11)* is not a bad deal in the upper budget range if you can get a quiet room – the street noise can be a bit much in the front. Rooms with shower and loo cost 5300/8000 ptas.

Pensió Colom 3 (Map 6; ☎ *93 318 06 31, Carrer de Colom 3),* almost on Plaça Reial, is an unofficial hostel with dorm beds (double bunks) costing 1500 ptas. They also have doubles/triples for 8000/ 10,800 ptas, or 9100/12,100 ptas with bathroom – they are overpriced. The place has washing machines and pool tables.

If you want a nice double on the square, head instead to **Pension Villanueva** *(Map 6; ☎ 91 301 50 84, Plaça Reial 2).* Prices start at 2500/3500 ptas for basic singles/ doubles and range up to 7500 ptas for the best rooms, spacious doubles with own bathroom and looking onto the square.

Hotel Barcelona House *(Map 6; ☎ 93 301 82 95, fax 93 412 41 29, Carrer dels Escudellers 19)* is a newish place in the middle of the Gothic action. It has reasonable, comfortable rooms. The doubles are quite OK at 8667 ptas, while the singles are less inspiring for 3745 ptas.

Hostal Levante *(Map 6; ☎ 93 317 95 65, Baixada de Sant Miquel 2),* off Plaça de Sant Miquel, is a large, bright hostal with rooms of all shapes and sizes. Smallish singles start at 3500 ptas, while doubles without/with private bathroom go for 5500/6500 ptas. Try for the one with the balcony. The owners have some apartments nearby too, which can work out well for groups of four or more – ask at the reception.

Casa Huéspedes Mari-Luz *(Map 6; ☎ 93 317 34 63, Carrer del Palau 4)* is another fine budget option. The bright, sunny rooms with wooden beams in the ceiling are well kept and the management chirpy. The place has a genuinely social atmosphere. You have the option of sleeping in a room for four or more people at 2000 ptas per person, or taking a double room, which can cost 5500 ptas or 5800 ptas.

Lone travellers have a hard time of it in many Barcelona digs, but **Pensión Alamar** *(Map 6; ☎ 93 302 50 12, Carrer de la Comtessa de Sobradiel 1)* seems to specialise in them. They only have one double among the 13 small but well-kept rooms. You pay 2500 ptas per person, which is fair.

Moving a little further towards the waterfront, **Hostal El Cantón** *(Map 6; ☎ 93 317 30 19, Carrer Nou de Sant Francesc 40)* is another good budget bet. Singles/doubles/ triples without bathroom cost 2000/4000/

5700 ptas. If you opt for those with bathroom you are looking at 2600/5800/7800 ptas. Some of these are spacious with sparkling new bathrooms, fan, fridge and balcony.

Not quite as good but handy for the waterfront is **Hostal Nilo** *(Map 6; ☎ 93 317 90 44, Carrer de Josep Anselm Clavé 7).* Perfectly acceptable singles/doubles cost 2700/4400 ptas, or 4000/5500 ptas with bathroom.

El Raval On the fringe of the Barri Xinès, **Hotel Peninsular** *(Map 6; ☎ 93 302 31 38, fax 93 412 36 99, Carrer de Sant Pau 34)* is a bit of an oasis. Once part of a convent, it has a plant-draped atrium extending the full height and most of the length of the hotel. The 80 rooms are clean and (mostly) spacious but otherwise nothing particularly special. Rooms start at 3500/6000, or 5000/ 7500 ptas with bathroom. Continental breakfast is included and the good news (in a sense) is that they don't take bookings.

Hostal Residencia Opera *(Map 6; ☎ 93 318 82 01, Carrer de Sant Pau 20)* is a bit tatty, but it's worth trying if other places are full. Rooms cost 3500/5000 ptas, or 4000/ 6000 ptas with bathroom.

A much better option, but one that is perennially full and nudging up into the mid-range price bracket, is **Hostal Mare Nostrum** *(Map 6; ☎ 93 318 53 40, fax 93 412 30 69, Carrer de Sant Pau 2).* Bright doubles with/without bathroom cost 8975/ 7500 ptas plus IVA. They have a couple of singles for 5850 ptas. Rooms are attractive and come with TV, air-con and heating. Breakfast costs 550 ptas, which is not bad considering you get full views of La Rambla from your table.

Hostal La Terrassa *(Map 6; ☎ 93 302 51 74, fax 93 301 21 88, Carrer de la Junta del Comerç 11)* is a big hostal with basic singles/doubles that are OK for what you pay: 2400/3800 ptas without own bathroom. Doubles with bathroom come in at 4600 ptas. You can sun yourself in the patio out the back.

La Ribera With about 20 clean rooms, singles/doubles at **Pensión Lourdes** *(Map 6;*

☎ *93 319 33 72, Carrer de la Princesa 14)* cost 3500/4700 ptas. Doubles with private bathroom cost 6700 ptas.

L'Eixample A few cheapies are spread strategically across this upmarket part of the city north of Plaça de Catalunya.

Hostal Goya (Map 5; ☎ 93 302 25 65, fax 93 412 04 35, Carrer de Pau Claris 74), has 12 nice, good-sized rooms at 3100/4500 ptas. Doubles with private shower and loo cost 5600 ptas. *Hostal Palacios (Map 2; ☎/fax 93 301 37 92, Gran Via de les Corts Catalanes 629 bis)* has 25 decent rooms. Singles without bathroom cost 3500 ptas. A few singles with shower cost 4500 ptas and doubles with the whole shebang cost 7500 ptas exactly.

You should check out *Hostal Oliva (Map 2; ☎ 93 488 01 62, fax 93 488 17 89, Passeig de Gràcia 32)* just for the quaint old lift, which you will want to take up to the 4th floor. The rooms are basically well kept, but some of those without private bathroom have little room for anything but the bed. Singles/doubles cost 4000/6200 ptas, doubles with bathroom cost 7200 ptas.

A leafier location is *Hostal Neutral (Map 2; ☎ 93 487 63 90, fax 93 487 68 48, Rambla de Catalunya 42)*. Doubles with own bathroom cost 6530 ptas. Those without cost 5460 ptas. They have no singles.

Pensión Aribau (Map 4; ☎ 93 453 11 06, Carrer d'Aribau 37) offers reasonable singles/doubles for 3500/6500 ptas. The singles only have a basin but do come with a TV, while the doubles have shower, loo, TV and even a fridge.

Near Estació Sants A five-minute walk south-west of the station, *Hostal Sans (Map 1; ☎ 93 331 37 00, fax 93 331 37 04, Carrer de Antoni de Capmany 82)* is a modern place with rooms costing 2900/4600 ptas, or 4500/5500 ptas with bathroom.

Hostal Sofia (Map 4; ☎ 93 419 50 40, fax 93 430 69 43, Avinguda de Roma 1–3) is just across the square in front of the station and rather more expensive. The 12 sparkling clean rooms cost 5000/8000 ptas, or 7000/10,000 ptas with bathroom.

Gràcia If you want to stay out of the tourist core of Barcelona and mix with more of a local crowd, you might want to try staying up in Gràcia. You have a handful of choices here. *Hostal San Medín (Map 2; ☎ 93 217 30 68, fax 93 415 44 10, Carrer Gran de Gràcia 125)* is a simple place with spartan but clean rooms going for 3500/6500 ptas, 4500/7500 ptas with bathroom. Another good one farther down the road is *Pensión Norma (Map 2; ☎ 93 237 44 78, Carrer Gran de Gràcia 87)*. You can get rooms without bathroom for 4000/6000 ptas or doubles with en suite for 7000 ptas.

PLACES TO STAY – MID-RANGE

All of the rooms in this range have private bathrooms.

La Rambla

Hotel Continental (Map 6; ☎ 93 301 25 70, fax 93 302 73 60, Rambla de Canaletes 138) has 35 pleasant, well-decorated rooms, all with cable TV, microwave, fridge, safe and fan. Room rates, including a good breakfast, start at 6900/9000 ptas in summer and rise for doubles with Rambla views. It seems OK to us, but some readers have reported being disappointed.

Hotel Cuatro Naciones (Map 6; ☎ 93 317 36 24, fax 93 302 69 85, La Rambla 40) has adequate rooms for 7490/10,700 ptas, which includes breakfast and IVA. It was built in 1849 and was once – a long time ago – Barcelona's top hotel. Buffalo Bill preferred it to a wagon when he was in town back in 1889.

Hotel Oriente (Map 6; ☎ 93 302 25 58, fax 93 412 38 19, La Rambla 45) is famous for its Modernista design and has a fine sky-lit restaurant and other public rooms, but staff can be offhand. The bedrooms are slightly past their prime but still comfortable, with tiled floors and bathrooms, safes and TV. Singles/doubles, pushing the limits of mid-range pricing, cost 10,700/17,120 ptas plus IVA.

Barri Gòtic

For decent rooms, all with bath, try *Hotel Roma Reial (Map 6; ☎ 93 302 03 66, fax 93*

PLACES TO STAY

301 18 39, Plaça Reial 11), costing 6000/9000 ptas in the high season.

Hotel Comercio *(Map 6; ☎ 93 318 74 20, fax 93 318 73 74, Carrer dels Escudellers 15)* is not a bad little mid-range hotel run by the same people who own the Hotel Roma Reial. The rooms have all the usual amenities and you can't get much closer to the action in the depths of Barri Gòtic. Singles/doubles/triples cost 6000/9000/12,000 ptas.

At **Hotel Jardi** *(Map 6; ☎ 93 301 59 00, Plaça de Sant Josep Oriol 1)* doubles with a balcony over the lovely square cost around 8000 ptas. At the time of writing they were refurbishing some of the rooms, including their singles. It is a good little hotel and may well be better when the work is finished.

Hotel Nouvel *(Map 6; ☎ 93 301 82 74, fax 93 301 83 70, Carrer de Santa Anna 18–20)* has some elegant Modernista touches and good air-con rooms with satellite TV costing 10,300/15,750 ptas plus IVA. Prices include breakfast.

El Raval

With some lovely Modernista touches – stained glass and murals in its public rooms, Gaudíesque window mouldings – **Hotel Mesón de Castilla** *(Map 4; ☎ 93 318 21 82, fax 93 412 40 20, Carrer de Valldonzella 5)* has 56 good, quaintly decorated rooms. It costs 11,600/14,800 ptas plus IVA, including breakfast. There's easy parking too.

Hotel España *(Map 6; ☎ 93 318 17 58, fax 93 317 11 34, Carrer de Sant Pau 9–11)* is famous for its two marvellous dining rooms designed by the Modernista architect Lluís Domènech i Montaner. One has big sea-life murals by Ramon Casas, the other has floral tiling and a wood-beamed roof. The 60 plus simple but comfortable rooms cost 5700/10,800 ptas including breakfast.

Not as interesting but a quite reasonable option is **Hotel Principal** *(Map 6; ☎ 93 318 89 70, fax 93 412 08 19, Carrer de la Junta del Comerç 8)* where functional rooms with TV, air-con and safe cost 7900/10,200 ptas. Breakfast is included. They run the **Hotel Joventut**, virtually next door, at the same rates.

Near Parc de la Ciutadella

A good bet here is **Hotel Triunfo** *(Map 6; ☎/fax 93 315 08 60, Passeig de Picasso 22)*. Singles/doubles with heating and air-con, TV, phone and private bathroom cost 6500/10,500 ptas. The best rooms are those that look across to the park (mostly singles). Some of the other rooms are a little poky, so try to see a few before choosing.

L'Eixample

A fine choice for a bit of old-fashioned style is **Hotel Gran Via** *(Map 2; ☎ 93 318 19 00, fax 93 318 99 97, Gran Via de les Corts Catalanes 642)* with 53 good-sized rooms costing 10,000/14,000 ptas plus IVA and a big, elegant lounge opening onto a roof terrace. Breakfast is available for 1100 ptas.

PLACES TO STAY – TOP END

Someone has neglected to tell these people that inflation in Spain is running at under 3%. In a little more than two years some hotels have lifted their official rates to Joe Public by as much as 50%! If you get lucky and turn up when business people aren't in town, you can get some good offers – always ask. You must add 7% IVA to the rates below, except where otherwise indicated.

La Rambla

The top hotel on La Rambla is elegant **Le Meridien** *(Map 6; ☎ 93 318 62 00, fax 93 301 77 76,* [e] *lemeridien@meridienbarcelona .com, Rambla dels Estudis 111)*. Its top floor presidential suite is where the likes of Michael Jackson, Madonna and Julio Iglesias stay. Normal singles/doubles cost 38,000/42,000 ptas, but occasionally they put on specials at 26,000 ptas per room (single or double use).

El Raval

The **Hotel San Agustín** *(Map 6; ☎ 93 318 16 58, fax 93 317 29 28, Plaça de Sant Agustí 3)* has a little more character, if only because of its location on a quiet square. Rooms, all with air-con, heating and satellite TV, cost 12,500/17,500 ptas, including breakfast.

Right at the top end of this *barri* and a brief stroll away from La Rambla and Plaça de Catalunya, **Hotel Lleó** *(Map 4; ☎ 93 318 13 12, fax 93 412 26 57, Carrer de Pelai 22)* is a fine mid to high-cost establishment with comfortable rooms, wheelchair access and a bar. Singles/doubles cost 14,000/18,500 ptas.

Barri Gòtic

Looking old on the outside, **Hotel Suizo** *(Map 6; ☎ 93 310 61 08, fax 93 310 40 81, Plaça de l'Àngel 12)* is quite modern within and has a restaurant and snack bar. Rooms – comfortable, if unspectacular – cost 14,250/18,500 ptas plus IVA.

Hotel Colón *(Map 6; ☎ 93 301 14 04, fax 93 317 29 15, Avinguda de la Catedral 7)* is a better choice (if you can afford it) for its location facing the cathedral. The 146 comfortable and elegant rooms cost 17,500/26,300 ptas.

L'Eixample

Hotel Balmes *(Map 2; ☎ 93 451 19 14, fax 93 451 00 49, Carrer de Mallorca 216)* is a good, modern hotel with white bricks much in evidence in the interior. Average-sized rooms with air-con, nice tiled bathrooms and satellite TV, are comparatively good value at 14,500/24,400 ptas. There's garage parking, a coffee shop, a garden with bar and swimming pool and a restaurant.

Hotel Regente *(Map 2; ☎ 93 487 59 89, fax 93 487 32 27, Rambla de Catalunya 76)* is also a reasonable deal. Rooms with air-con and satellite TV cost 19,400/22,200 ptas. The rooms feature wood panelling and have a nice feel.

The **St Moritz Hotel** *(Map 2; ☎ 93 412 15 00, fax 93 412 12 36, Carrer de la Diputació 262 bis)* is another upmarket hotel with 92 rooms at 20,900/24,900 ptas. It has a restaurant and a pleasant terrace bar.

Hotel Majèstic *(Map 2; ☎ 93 488 17 17, fax 93 488 18 80, Passeig de Gràcia 70)*, is a sprawling, comfortable place with a nice line in modern art on the walls and a rooftop swimming pool. The 300 plus rooms, all air-con with satellite TV, cost up to 30,000/36,000 ptas.

The **Comtes** (or **Condes**) **de Barcelona Hotel** *(Map 2; ☎ 93 488 22 00, fax 93 488 06 14, Passeig de Gràcia 73–75)* is one of Barcelona's best hotels. It has two separate buildings facing each other across Carrer de Mallorca. The older one occupies the Casa Enric Batlló, built in the 1890s but now stylishly modernised. The air-con, sound-proofed rooms, with marble bathrooms, start at 29,000/31,000 ptas.

Hotel Ritz *(Map 2; ☎ 93 318 52 00, fax 93 318 01 48, Gran Via de les Corts Catalanes 668)* is the top choice for old-fashioned elegance, luxury, individuality and first-class service. It has been going since 1919. Room rates (regardless of whether single or double occupancy) start at 45,000 ptas. A suite with one bedroom and tiled step-down 'Roman bath' costs 140,000 ptas.

A less expensive choice for old-style elegance is **Hotel Avenida Palace** *(Map 5; ☎ 93 301 96 00, fax 93 318 12 34, Gran Via de les Corts Catalanes 605)*. Singles/doubles are fine at 26,475/34,050 ptas with breakfast and IVA included.

Alternatively, if you can cough up 29,000/34,900 ptas, consider the elegant **Hotel Ducs de Bergara** *(Map 5; ☎ 93 301 51 51, fax 93 317 34 42, Carrer de Bergara 11)*. The building is a fine Modernista piece with an 18th-century artesonado ceiling and some nice Art Deco touches. Oh, and there's a pool too.

One of the classiest addresses in town is the **Hotel Claris** *(Map 2; ☎ 93 487 62 62, fax 93 487 87 36, Carrer de Pau Claris 150)*. Of course you pay for the pleasure, to the tune of 36,000/42,900 ptas. Suites cost up to 125,000 ptas, whilst breakfast costs another 2800 ptas. It was recently awarded Best City Hotel in Europe, and houses a permanent collection of Egyptian art.

Port Olímpic

Barcelona's most fashionable, if rather impersonal, lodgings is the **Hotel Arts Barcelona** *(Map 1; ☎ 93 221 10 00, fax 93 221 10 70, Carrer de la Marina 19–21)*, in one of the two sky-high towers that dominate the Port Olímpic. It has over 450 rooms and charges from 50,000 ptas for a double.

PLACES TO STAY

LONG-TERM RENTALS

The Universitat de Barcelona, Gran Via de les Corts Catalanes 585 (Map 4; ☎ 93 402 11 00); CIAJ, Carrer de Ferran 32 (Map 6; ☎ 93 402 78 00) and the British Council (Map 3; ☎ 93 241 99 77, see Facts for the Visitor) have notice boards with ads for flat shares. You can also try International House (Map 6; ☎ 93 268 45 11, fax 93 268 02 39, [e] ihbarcelona@bcn.ihes.com), at Carrer de Trafalgar 14. Young people and students should check out the options at Punt d'Informació Juvenil, Carrer de Calàbria 147 (Map 4; ☎ 93 483 83 84).

The free English-language monthly *Barcelona Metropolitan* (see Newspapers & Magazines in the Facts for the Visitor chapter) carries rental classifieds.

Otherwise, get a hold of *Anuntis*, the weekly classifieds paper. The last few pages of the *Suplement Immobiliària* (real estate supplement) carry ads for shared accommodation under the rubrique *lloguer/hostes i vivendes a compartir*. Ads tend to be in Castilian rather than Catalan. Rooms can come as cheap as 25,000 ptas per month, but for something halfway decent, not too far from the centre, you're looking at a minimum of 35,000 ptas. You need to add bills (gas, electricity, water, phone and comunidad – building maintenance charges).

Places to Eat

FOOD

Eating, especially if you are not hamstrung by a rigidly tight budget, is a highlight of any stay in Barcelona. After a day spent trying to fathom the genius of Gaudí or the peculiarities of Picasso, what better counterpoint than hunkering down for a protracted stay at the tables of Barcelona's delightfully varied restaurants?

Food terminology in this chapter is given in Catalan/Castilian or Catalan alone, except in the few cases where the Castilian term is used in both languages. The idea is to reflect what you are most likely to see and hear in the streets of Barcelona, not to descend into the murky depths of linguistic polemics.

When to Eat

You may not arrive in Barcelona with jetlag, but your tummy will think it has abandoned all known time zones.

Breakfast *(esmorzar/desayuno)* is generally a no-nonsense affair, taken at a bar on the way to work. Lunchtime *(dinar/comida)* is basically from 2 to 4 pm and is the main meal of the day. No local would contemplate chomping into dinner *(sopar/cena)* before 9.30 pm. Most (but not all) kitchens close by midnight.

Don't panic! If your gastric juices can't hold out, you can easily track down bar snacks or fast food (local and international) outside these times. And, anxious to ring up every tourist dollar possible, plenty of restaurants cater for northern European intestinal habits – although you often pay for this with mediocre food and the almost exclusive company of other tourists.

Where to Eat

Many bars and some cafes offer some form of solid sustenance. This can range from *entrepans/bocadillos* (filled rolls) and *tapes/tapas* (bar snacks) through to more substantive *raciones* (basically a bigger version of a tapas dish), and full meals in *menjadors/comedores* (sit-down restaurants) out the back. *Cerveseries/cervezerías* (beer bars), *tavernes/tabernas* (taverns), *tascas* (snack bars) and *cellers/bodegas* (cellars) are just some of the kinds of establishment in this category.

For a full meal you are most likely to end up in a *restaurant/restaurante*, but other names will pop out at you. A *marisquería* specialises in seafood, while a *mesón* (a 'big table') might indicate (but not always!) a more modest eatery.

What to Eat

Breakfast A coffee with some sort of pastry *(pasta/bollo)* is the typical breakfast. You may get a croissant or some cream-filled number (such as a *canya*). Some people prefer a savoury start – you could go for a *bikini/sandwich mixto* – a toasted ham and cheese. A Spanish *tostada* is simply buttered toast (you might order something to go with it). The Catalan version, a *torrada*, is usually more of an open toasted sandwich with something on it besides butter (depending on what you ask for). Some people go for an all-Spanish favourite, *xurros amb xocolata/churros con chocolate*, a lightly deep-fried stick of plain pastry immersed in thick, gooey hot chocolate. They are sold at stands around town and for many are an early-morning, post-disco, pre-hangover cure.

JANE SMITH

Xurros amb xocolata – the Catalan's chocolaty way to start the day!

PLACES TO EAT

Lunch & Dinner Many straightforward Spanish dishes are available here as elsewhere in the country. The travellers' friend is the *menú del día*, a set price meal usually comprising three courses, with a drink thrown in. This is often only available for lunch and can range from around 900 ptas to 5000 ptas at posh establishments. A *plat combinat/plato combinado* is a simpler version still – a one-course meal consisting of basic nutrients – the 'meat-and-three-veg' style of cooking. You'll see pictures of this stuff everywhere. It's filling and cheap but has little to recommend it in culinary terms.

You'll pay more for your meals if you order a la carte, but the food will be better. The menu *(la carta)* begins with starters such as *amanides/ensaladas* (salads), *sopes/sopas* (soups) and *entremeses* (hors d'oeuvres). The latter can range from a mound of potato salad with olives, asparagus, anchovies and a selection of cold meats – almost a meal in itself – to simpler cold meats, slices of cheese and olives.

The hungry Catalan, after a starter, will order a first then second course. The latter are often listed under headings such as: *pollastre/pollo* (chicken); *carn/carne* (meat); *mariscs/mariscos* (seafood); *peix/pescado* (fish); *arròs/arroz* (rice); *ous/huevos* (eggs); and *verdures/verduras* (vegetables). Meat may be subdivided into *porc/cerdo* (pork), *vedella/ternera* (beef) and *anyell/cordero* (lamb).

Postres (desserts) have a lower profile; *gelats/helados* (ice cream), fruit and flans are often the only choices in cheaper places. Sugar addicts should look out for local specialities, such as *crema Catalana*, where possible.

Catalan Cuisine Basques may well disagree, but Catalunya has a reputation for producing some of Spain's finest cuisine. Catalunya is geographically diverse and therefore provides a variety of fresh, high-quality seafood (though, due to high demand, much seafood is now crated in from other parts of Spain and even Europe),

meat, poultry, game, fruit and vegetables. These can come in unusual and delicious combinations: meat and seafood (a genre known as *mar i muntanya* – 'sea and mountain'), poultry and fruit, fish and nuts. Quality Catalan food tends to require a greater fiscal effort.

The essence of Catalan food lies in its sauces for meat and fish. These sauces may not be mentioned on menus as they're so ubiquitous. There are five main types: *sofregit* (fried onion, tomato and garlic); *samfaina* or *chanfaina* (sofregit plus red pepper and aubergine or courgette); *picada* (based on ground almonds, usually with garlic, parsley, pine or hazel nuts, and sometimes breadcrumbs); *allioli* (pounded garlic with olive oil, often with egg yolk added to make more of a mayonnaise); and *romesco* (an almond, tomato, olive oil, garlic and vinegar sauce, also used as a salad dressing).

Catalans find it hard to understand why other people put butter on bread when *pa amb tomàquet* – bread sliced, then rubbed with tomato, olive oil, garlic and salt – is so easy.

Some typical dishes are listed in the Language chapter at the end of the book.

Other good things to look out for include *oca* (goose) and *canalons* (Catalan cannelloni). Wild mushrooms are a Catalan passion – people disappear into the forests in autumn to pick them. There are many, many types of *bolets*; the large succulent *rovellons* are a favourite.

JANE SMITH

Head to La Barceloneta for a taste of Barcelona's best seafood.

International Cuisine

Barcelona can't compete with New York, Sydney, London or Paris, but it does offer a fair smattering of foreign restaurants. In case you want a break from the local stuff, a few of the better addresses are sprinkled in among the recommendations below.

DRINKS
Nonalcoholic

Clear, cold water from a public fountain or tap is a Spanish favourite – but check that it's *potable* (fit to drink). For tap water in restaurants, ask for *aigua d'aixeta/agua de grifo*. *Aigua/agua mineral* (bottled water) comes in innumerable brands, either *amb/con gas* (fizzy) or *sense/sin gas* (still). A 1.5L bottle of still mineral water costs around 80 ptas in a supermarket, but out and about you may be charged as much as 200 ptas.

Coffee In Spain coffee is strong and slightly bitter. A *cafè amb llet/café con leche* (generally drunk at breakfast only) is about 50% coffee, 50% hot milk. Ask for *grande* or *doble* if you want a large cup, *en got/en vaso* if you want a smaller shot in a glass, or *sombra* if you want lots of milk. A *café solo* is an espresso (short black); *cafè tallat/café cortado* is an espresso with a little milk. For iced coffee, ask for *cafè amb gel/café con hielo*; you'll get a glass of ice and a hot cup of coffee, to be poured over the ice – which, surprisingly, doesn't all melt straight away!

Tea As in the rest of Spain, Barcelonins prefer coffee, but increasingly it is possible to get hold of many different styles of tea and *infusión de hierbas* (herbal concoctions). Locals tend to drink tea black. If you want milk, ask for it to come separately (*a parte*) to avoid ending up with a cup of tea-flavoured watery milk.

Soft Drinks *Suc de taronja/zumo de naranja* (orange juice) is the main freshly squeezed juice available. It's often served with sugar. To make sure you are getting the real thing, ask for the juice to be *natural*, otherwise you run the risk of getting a puny little bottle of runny concentrate.

Refrescs/refrescos (soft drinks) include the usual international brands of soft drinks, local brands such as Kas, and *granissat/granizado* (iced fruit crush).

A *batido* is a flavoured milk drink or milk shake. *Orxata/horchata* is a Valencian drink of Islamic origin. Made from the juice of *chufa* (tiger nuts), sugar and water, it is sweet and tastes like soya milk with a hint of cinnamon. You'll come across it both fresh and bottled: Chufi is a delicious brand. A naughtier version is called a *cubanito* and involves sticking in a blob of chocolate ice-cream.

Alcoholic

Wine Spain is a wine-drinking country and *vi/vino* (wine) accompanies almost every meal. Spanish wine is robust because of the sunny climate. It comes *blanc/blanco* (white), *negro/tinto* (red), or *rosat/rosado* (rosé). In general it is cheap, although there is no shortage of expensive wines. A 500 ptas bottle of wine, bought from a supermarket or wine merchant, will be quite drinkable. The same money in a restaurant will get you a very mediocre drop. Cheap *vi de taula/vino de mesa* (table wine) can sell for less than 200 ptas a litre, but wines at that price can be pretty rank.

Catalunya's whites are better than its reds, but the area is best known for *cava*, the fine local version of Champagne (see the Excursions chapter for more on Catalunya's main wine and cava region and how to identify quality wines).

You can order wine by the glass *(copa)* in bars and restaurants. At lunch or dinner it is common to order a *vi/vino de la casa* (house wine) – usually by the litre or half litre.

Beer The most common way to order *cervesa/cerveza* (beer) is to ask for a *canya*, which is a small draught beer (*cervesa/cerveza de barril*). A larger beer (about 300ml) is sometimes called a *tubo* (which comes in a straight glass). A pint is a *jarra*. If you just ask for a cerveza you may get bottled beer, which is more expensive. A small bottle of beer is called a *flascó/botellín*. The local brew is Estrella Damm (of which there are several variants, including the potent and

PLACES TO EAT

JANE SMITH

Fruity *sangría* will leave you feeling
refreshed after a day in the sun

flavoursome Voll Dam), while San Miguel,
made in western Catalunya's Lleida, is also
widely drunk. The Damm company produces
15% of all Spain's beer, as does San Miguel.

A *clara* is a shandy – a beer with a hefty
dash of lemonade.

Other Drinks *Sangría* is a wine and fruit
punch, sometimes laced with brandy. It's
refreshing going down but can leave you
with a sore head. You'll see jugs of it on tables in restaurants. *Tinto de verano* is a mix
of wine and Casera, a brand of lemonade, or
sweet, bubbly water. You don't see it so
much in Barcelona, although it is common
in other parts of Spain.

There is no shortage of imported and
Spanish-produced top-shelf stuff – *coñac*
(brandy) is popular.

PLACES TO EAT – BUDGET

One traveller's budget restaurant may be another's splurge, so these categories are a little arbitrary. Those hoping to satisfy their
hunger for around 1000 ptas could try the
following places (in a few cases you can
opt to spend a little more – say up to around
2000 ptas – and broaden your range of
choices). Remember that, although most
places recommended for tapas are placed
in the budget category, if you eat a lot of
tapas – which on average can cost 150 ptas
to 300 ptas – by the time you're on your
fourth or fifth (and the accompanying
drinks) you'll have well and truly crashed
the 1000-ptas barrier!

La Rambla

Opposite the Liceu opera house, *Cafè de
l'Òpera (Map 6;* ☎ *93 317 75 85, La Rambla 74)*, is La Rambla's most interesting
cafe, with elegant 1920s decor. It gets busy
at night (see Bars in the Entertainment
chapter), but is quieter for morning coffee
and croissants.

Barri Gòtic

This area is peppered with good eateries,
some of them excellent value.

Pastry Shops & Coffee Bars Tempting
pastry and/or chocolate shops, often combined with coffee bars, abound. There's a
special concentration along Carrer and
Baixada de la Llibreteria, north-east off
Plaça de Sant Jaume. Among the least re-
sistible pastry/chocolate places are: *Santa
Clara (Map 6; Carrer de la Llibreteria 21)*
and *La Colmena (Map 6)*, on the corner
of Baixada de la Llibreteria and Plaça de
l'Àngel. Two places with particularly good
coffee in this area are *Bon Mercat (Map 6)*,
on the corner of Baixada de la Llibreteria
and Carrer de la Freneria, and *Il Caffè di
Roma (Map 6; Plaça de l'Àngel)*, which is
part of a chain you'll see all over town.

*Xocolateria La Xicra (Map 6; Plaça de
Sant Josep Oriol 2)* has great cakes, various
coffees, teas and *xocolata* (hot chocolate,
250 ptas) so thick it's listed on the menu
under desserts. Nearby, two other good
places to sit down for a coffee and croissant
are *Granja La Pallaresa (Map 6; Carrer de
Petritxol 11)* and *Croissanterie del Pi (Map
6; Carrer del Pi 14)*.

A great little place to sip a wide variety
of teas and herbal infusions is *Salterio
(Map 6; Carrer de Sant Domènec del Call
4)*, just off Carrer de Ferran.

Takeaway Felafel & Kebabs A takeaway counter doing good felafel costing
250 ptas is *Disco-Bar Real (Map 6)* on the
corner of Plaça Reial and Carrer de Colom.
*Buen Bocado (Map 6; Carrer dels Escud-
ellers 31)* has felafel for 300 ptas and
shawarma for 425 ptas. It only opens in the
evenings, until 2 am. The nameless *felafel*

& *kebab takeaway (Map 6; Carrer dels Escudellers)*, just to the east of Carrer dels Obradors, is a bit cheaper.

Restaurants A tiny little vegetarian snack hutch, *Joy (Map 6; Carrer Ample 3)*, does tea and banana cake at 200 ptas, which ain't bad for breakfast. *Self-Naturista (Map 6; ☎ 93 318 26 84, Carrer de Santa Anna 13)* is a popular self-service vegetarian restaurant with a four-course lunch *menú* for 965 ptas. Mains don't cost more than 700 ptas.

At the southern end of Plaça Reial, *Restaurante Senshe Tawakal (Map 6; Carrer del Vidre)* serves lentils and vegetables, or chicken and chips for 450 ptas, and couscous for 550 ptas. Carrer de la Mercè (Map 6), running roughly south-west from the main post office is a good place to hunt around for great little northern Spanish *tascas* and *sidrerías* (cider bars). Most of these are run by immigrants from Galicia and Asturias. *Tasca El Corral*, at No 19, and *Sidrería La Socarrena*, at No 21, are both worth checking out, but there are many others. *Bar Celta*, No 16, is cheap – you can fill up on tapas for under 1000 ptas.

A cross between a cafe of a century gone by and a hippy hangout, *La Cerería (Map 6; ☎ 93 301 85 10, Baixada de Sant Miquel 3–5)* is a cooperative that offers some tasty vegetarian cooking, great desserts and low prices. The fruit shakes are good too. It opens 9 am to 10 pm.

La Verónica (Map 6; ☎ 93 412 11 22, Carrer d'Avinyó 20) shines out like a beacon around here, its red decor and bright white lighting hard to miss. Inside they serve reasonable pizzas at affordable prices in an atmosphere that could be described as fashionably camp. At lunchtime there's a set meal costing 1000 ptas. It's closed on Monday.

Close by, the *Venus Delicatessen (Map 6; ☎ 93 301 15 85, Carrer d'Avinyó 25)* is less in your face and serves a tempting range of rather small dishes. The little marble-top tables for two form the perfect base for a fat slice of cheesecake. It's open noon to midnight Monday to Saturday.

International Cuisine Just in off La Rambla, *The Bagel Shop (Map 6; ☎ 93 412 48 38, Carrer de la Canuda 25)* is the only place in town where your lox and cream cheese bagel will be the genuine article. It's open on Sunday mornings for a hangover breakfast, which is not bad at 700 ptas.

Sushi-Ya (Map 6; ☎ 93 412 72 49, Carrer d'En Quintana 4) is a simple place for cheap Japanese food. The sushi set meal costs 1175 ptas, which is hard to argue with in terms of price, and you can take food away. Don't expect top Japanese cuisine, but it makes an affordable change.

Wagamama (Map 6; ☎ 610 27 73 18, Carrer d'Escudellers 39) is a cool new place to get into good noodle dishes (up to 900 ptas) until 1 am (daily). It also serves weird and wonderful salads and mixed fruit drinks.

El Raval

Grungy but cheap, *Restaurant Els Tres Bots (Map 6; Carrer de Sant Pau 42)* has a *menú* costing 875 ptas. Along the road, *Restaurante Pollo Rico (Map 6; Carrer de Sant Pau 31)* has a downstairs bar where you can get a quarter chicken, an omelette or a veal steak with chips, bread and wine, starting at 500 ptas; its slightly more expensive upstairs restaurant is a bit more salubrious.

Bar Kasparo (Map 6; ☎ 93 302 20 72, Plaça de Vicenç Martorell 4) is a relaxed Australian-run place where you can get great mixed salads and other healthy light food – perfect in summer on this quiet, pedestrianised square.

Buenas Migas (Map 6; ☎ 93 412 16 86, Plaça del Bonsuccés 6) is a charming hole in the wall where you can pick up a decent version of focaccia, as well as pizza slices and other tasty snacks.

Another hip little establishment is *Ra (Map 6; ☎ 93 301 41 63, Plaça de la Gardunya)*, which looks a beach bar that got lost and ended up in the car park. It offers a vaguely vegetarian menu, with a couple of meat options thrown in. The food is OK but unexceptional. It is, however, cheap (*menú del día* for 995 ptas) and the atmosphere

PLACES TO EAT

decidedly groovy. You can get fruit shakes and breakfast here too. It opens Monday to Saturday.

The charming *El Convent (Map 6; ☎ 93 302 31 12, Carrer de Jerusalem 3)*, elegantly lodged in what was once a religious institution, offers a good set menu costing 965 ptas. The *ensalada de arroz con gambitos* (rice salad with shrimps) is a tasty first course.

International Cuisine Tasty curries and biryanis are available from *Kashmir Restaurant Tandoori (Map 6; Carrer de Sant Pau 39)* for around 800 ptas. It is one of a growing number of curry houses around here, reflecting a growing wave of mainly Pakistani immigration into El Raval.

Sant Antoni

The haven of *orxata* in Barcelona, *Horchatería Sirvent (Map 4; ☎ 93 441 27 20, Carrer del Parlament 56)* serves up the best you'll try without catching the Euromed down to this drink's spiritual home, Valencia. You can get it by the glass or take it away by the bottle. This place also sells ice cream, *granissat* and *turrón* (nougat). It's closed on Sunday.

La Ribera

Vegetarians should head for *Comme-Bio*, aka *La Botiga (Map 6; ☎ 93 319 89 68, Via Laietana 28)*, a modern, chemical- and additive-free vegetarian restaurant and wholefood shop. Its good, four-course *menú* (1125 ptas) includes a help-yourself salad bar; many a la carte dishes, including pizzas and spinach-and-Roquefort crepes, cost around 900 ptas, or you can go for a set dinner menu of 1850 ptas. There's another branch at Gran Via de les Corts Catalanes 603 (Map 5).

Lluna Plena (Map 6; ☎ 93 310 54 29, Carrer de Montcada 2) is an unclad brick, cellar-style place with good Catalan and Spanish food. It's packed for its four-course 1050 ptas lunch *menú* and is closed on Sunday night and Monday.

Restaurante Mar de la Ribera (Map 6; ☎ 93 315 13 36, Carrer dels Sombrerers 7),

right by Santa Maria del Mar, does a decent three-course *menú* for 1000 ptas, including half a bottle of wine. It's a pleasant place with ceramics and paintings on the walls.

Several more eateries are sprinkled in among the bars on and around Passeig del Born and Plaça de les Olles, east of Santa Maria del Mar.

Restaurant L'Econòmic (Map 6; Plaça de Sant Agustí Vell 13) is a popular local hangout where a full set lunch comes in at 1000 ptas, unless you want to try the classier 3000 ptas version.

International Cuisine Offering a strange mix of food is *Café Kafka (Map 6; ☎ 93 310 05 26, Carrer de Fusina 7)* – their Sudanese chef prepares Arab dishes while the Filipino cook does a range of Southeast-Asian-style food. Prices are moderate.

For Greek food, *Dionisos (Map 6; ☎ 93 319 75 77, Avinguda del Marquès de l'Argentera 27)* is a breezy little spot on the edge of the Passeig del Born hubbub.

L'Eixample

A good place to start a visit to l'Eixample is at the ninth-floor cafeteria at *El Corte Inglés* department store on Plaça de Catalunya (Map 5). It's reasonably priced and has tremendous views.

Tapas, Snacks & Coffee For an excellent coffee on Passeig de Gràcia pop into *Cafè Torino (Map 2; Passeig de Gràcia 59)*, on the corner of Carrer de València – a neat, friendly place, popular with a mildly chic, young clientele.

You'll find a number of glossy but informal tapas places near the bottom end of Passeig de Gràcia. *Quasi Queviures (Qu Qu; Map 2; ☎ 93 317 45 12, Passeig de Gràcia 24)* has a big choice including sausages and hams, pâtés and smoked fish. Many tapas cost over 400 ptas, but portions are decent. *Ba-Ba-Reeba (Map 2; ☎ 93 302 21 29, Passeig de Gràcia 28)* is similar but less Catalan. *Cerveseria Tapa Tapa (Map 2; ☎ 93 488 33 69 Passeig de Gràcia 44)*, on the corner of Carrer del Consell de Cent, is another big, bright place with a great range of tapas costing from 250 ptas. Some of these places can feel a little barn-like and are owned by the same people.

Lizarran (Map 2; Carrer de Mallorca 257) is a lively spot with reasonable tapas. It is part of a chain but, as chains go, the quality isn't bad.

Restaurants Economical *plats combinats* – for example, chicken, chips and *berenjena* (aubergine), or *botifarra* (pork sausage), beans and red pepper – are available from *Bar Estudiantil (Map 4; Plaça de la Universitat)*, each for around 600 ptas. This place opens until late into the night and is a genuine student hangout.

El Café de Internet (Map 2; ☎ 93 302 11 54, Gran Via de les Corts Catalanes 656) has a double bill of food and the Internet. Before, during or after your meal or snack, you can use an Internet terminal upstairs. Downstairs you can munch your way through a buffet lunch costing 1200 ptas, including a drink.

L'Hostal de Rita (Map 2; ☎ 93 451 87 07, Carrer d'Aragó 279), a block east of Passeig de Gràcia, is an excellent mid-range restaurant. The 995-ptas four-course lunch *menú* is a good deal. A la carte mains cost 700 ptas to 1000 ptas. Expect to queue.

The same people own *Restaurant Madrid Barcelona (Map 2; ☎ 93 215 70 27, Carrer d'Aragó 282)* virtually over the road. Mains come in at under 1000 ptas, although if you have wine and dessert you are likely to end up with a bill of 2000 ptas. It is so popular that they set up odd little cardboard stools outside for customers who are waiting for a table.

FrescCo (Map 2; ☎ 93 301 68 37, Carrer de València 263), half a block east of Passeig de Gràcia, packs 'em in with its all-you-can-eat buffet of salads, soups, pizza, pasta, fruit, ice cream and drinks for 1175 ptas. It is part of a chain.

La Flauta (Map 4; ☎ 93 323 70 38, Carrer d'Aribau 23) is known for its fine tapas and tasty baguettes with all manner of fillings.

If you want to fill up on *orxata* or great milk shakes, drop by *La Valenciana (Map 4; ☎ 93 453 11 38, Carrer d'Aribau 1)*.

Around La Sagrada Família

This area is not a great culinary cubby hole but if starvation strikes during your visit, *La Baguetina Catalana (Map 2)*, on the corner of Carrer de Provença and Carrer de Sardenya, does good baguettes for 300 ptas to 400 ptas, while *Celler del Trabucaire (Map 2; ☎ 93 245 71 89, Carrer de Mallorca 420)* has an appetising range of tapas and raciones. Look for the large 'La Casa del Jamón' sign.

Gràcia

Bar Candanchu (Map 2; ☎ 93 237 73 62, Plaça de Rius i Taulet 9) has a restaurant with many *plats combinats* and paella for 1250 ptas. *Mario Pizza*, on the same square, does pizzas for 900 ptas to 1100 ptas.

A good down-to-earth Lebanese place is *Sannin (Map 1; ☎ 93 285 00 51, Carrer de l'Encarnació 44)*. A full meal of old favourites like shawarma, hummus, tabbouleh, dessert and drinks need not cost much more than 1500 ptas.

Sarrià

The best place in Barcelona for *patatas bravas* (potato bits dripping with a slightly spicy tomato sauce mixed with mayonnaise) is *Bar Tomàs (Map 1; ☎ 93 203 10 77, Carrer Major de Sarrià 49, FGC Sarrià)*. The place itself is an unassuming bar – it does other tapas as well. It is closed on Wednesday.

Restaurant Chains

There are a few local restaurant chains where you can get a quick, decent snack or meal with minimum effort. A few of the branches are listed below.

Bocatta sells hot and cold baguettes with a big range of fillings, costing 360 ptas to 695 ptas. There are branches at Carrer de Santa Anna 11 (Map 6), Plaça de Sant Jaume (Map 6), the corner of Carrer de Comtal and Carrer de N'Amargos (Map 6) and Rambla de Catalunya between Carrer de Mallorca and Carrer de València (Map 2). Most branches open 8 am to midnight daily.

Pans & Company provides similar fare and prices to Bocatta. There are branches at

La Rambla 123 (Map 6), Carrer de Ferran 14 (Map 6), Carrer dels Arcs off Plaça Nova (Map 6), Ronda de la Universitat 7 (Map 4), Rambla de Catalunya 13 (Map 5), Passeig de Gràcia 39 (Map 2) and Carrer de Provença 278 (Map 2).

Pastafiore serves pizza and pasta: a half *(media)* pizza costs 395 ptas to 575 ptas, but you'll need a whole *(entera)* one for 550 ptas to 865 ptas if you're hungry; pasta costs around 475 ptas to 675 ptas but tends to be less appetising (any resemblance to Italian food is purely coincidental). There are branches at Rambla de Canaletes 125 (Map 6), Carrer de Provença 278 (Map 2) and Travessera de Gràcia 60 (Map 2).

Self-Catering

There's great fresh food of all types at the *Mercat de la Boqueria* (Map 6) on La Rambla, open 8 am to 8 pm Monday to Saturday. In La Ribera, *Mercat de Santa Caterina* (Map 6), which has been temporarily shifted to Passeig de Lluís Companys, is another good shopping choice. In Gràcia there's a big covered *food market* (Map 2) just off Travessera de Gràcia.

Champion (Map 6), near the northern end of La Rambla, is a convenient central supermarket.

PLACES TO EAT – MID-RANGE

Opening your purse wider will improve your options greatly. At the places listed below you can expect to pay anything from 2000 ptas to 3500 ptas for a full evening meal with all the trimmings.

Plaça de Catalunya

Right on the square, *Café Zurich (Map 6; ☎ 93 317 91 53, Carrer de Pelai 39)*, has been resuscitated after years of closure. It is an old-style cafe, great for the morning paper, but a little more expensive than the average cafe.

Barri Gòtic

A Basque favourite is *Irati (Map 6; ☎ 93 302 30 84, Carrer del Cardenal Cassañas 17)*. The set lunch menu costs 1500 ptas, or you can enjoy the great tapas and a glass

of beer or six (but watch how your debts mount!). It is closed on Sunday night and Monday. A couple of doors down is the psychedelic *Juicy Jones (Map 6; ☎ 93 302 43 30, Carrer del Cardenal Cassañas 7)*, where a vegetarian set menu costs around 1100 ptas, or you can just sip the juices (around 375 ptas). It is closed on Sunday.

Mesón Jesús (Map 6; ☎ 93 317 46 98, Carrer dels Cecs de la Boqueria 4), between Plaça de Sant Josep Oriol and Carrer de la Boqueria, is a cosy, homely place. It does a good 1400 ptas three-course set *menú* and is closed Saturday night and Sunday.

Can Culleretes (Map 6; ☎ 93 317 30 22, Carrer d'En Quintana 5) is Barcelona's oldest restaurant, founded in 1786. It's still going strong, with old-fashioned decor and good Catalan food. A three-course *menú*, including half a bottle of wine, will cost around 2500 ptas. It is closed Sunday nights and Monday.

Les Quinze Nits (Map 6; ☎ 93 317 30 75, Plaça Reial 6) is a stylish, bistro-like restaurant, on the borderline between smart and casual, with a long menu of good Catalan and Spanish dishes at reasonable prices. Three courses with wine and coffee typically come to about 2500 ptas. The problem is you almost always have to queue for ages and, while the place is good, it is not *that* good!

El Taxidermista (Map 6; ☎ 93 412 45 36, Plaça Reial 8) is a rather slick new joint offering Les Quinze Nits some local competition. The cooking demonstrates a little Mediterranean sparkle and the lunch set menu is not bad at 1200 ptas. In the evening you're looking at about 3000 ptas. The kitchen closes by midnight but the place stays open as a cafe until 2.30 am. It closes altogether on Monday.

La Fonda Escudellers (Map 6; ☎ 93 301 75 15), on the corner of Carrer dels Escudellers and Passatge dels Escudellers, is run by the same people as Les Quinze Nits and has similar ambience and standards. You will be directed efficiently to one of the three floors from the entrance and the food is better than in many places around town that charge double.

A warm glow at Los Caracoles

Sip Spanish beer by the sea

Locals prefer to munch their tapas whilst propping up the bar.

Eating out is a highlight of any trip to Barcelona.

Ponder the spirit of Barcelona.

Atmospheric Els Quatre Gats restaurant was a hang-out of the Modernistas and a haunt of Picasso.

Decision time at Los Caracoles – little has changed since it opened as a tavern in the 19th century.

Restaurant Pitarra (*Map 6;* ☎ *93 301 16 47, Carrer d'Avinyó 56*) serves up quality Catalan food. The old house was where the late-19th-century playwright Serafí Pitarra did most of his work, hence the restaurant's name. It's a little expensive, with mains costing up to 1975 ptas. It is closed on Sunday.

A recent addition to the glam gastronomy circuit is *Slokai* (*Map 6;* ☎ *93 317 90 94, Carrer del Palau 5*). It's as much about being seen as eating well, although some of the dishes are interesting. It closes Saturday lunchtime and Sunday.

El Salón (*Map 6;* ☎ *93 315 21 59, Carrer de l'Hostal d'En Sol 6*) is one of the city's more popular eateries – even on a Monday night you are advised to book ahead or get in early for either the 9 pm or 11 pm shift! The problem with the first shift is that they oblige you to finish up by 11 pm – a tad rude. It's closed on Sunday.

International Cuisine The best Italian food in town can be had at *Ristorante Il Mercante di Venezia* (*Map 6;* ☎ *93 317 18 28, Carrer de Josep Anselm Clavé 11*), where mains cost about 1200 ptas. It's closed on Monday.

The nearby *Le Tre Venezie* (*Map 6;* ☎ *93 342 42 52, Plaça del Duc de Medinaceli 4*), run by the same people, offers a good range of pasta and risotto dishes. The *pappardelle all'anatra* (a broad ribbon pasta with duck) is not bad. You can also have breakfast. It's closed on Tuesday.

Margarita Blue (*Map 6;* ☎ *93 317 71 76, Carrer de Josep Anselm Clavé 6*) does imaginative versions of Mexican food and doubles as a bar.

El Paraguayo (*Map 6;* ☎ *93 302 14 41, Carrer del Parc 1*), just off Carrer Ample, is a great place for succulent slabs of meat bigger than your head. Try the *entraña*; the word means 'entrails' but the meal is in fact a juicy slice of prime beef folded over onto itself and accompanied by a herb sauce. The *dulce de leche* (a South American version of caramel) desserts are to die for. Expect to pay around 2000 ptas a head. It's closed on Monday.

El Raval

Urban revival is bringing new life into El Raval, one of the poorest quarters of old Barcelona. Several tempting places have popped up, attracting a hip, young clientele.

Salsitas (*Map 6;* ☎ *93 318 08 40, Carrer Nou de la Rambla 22*) is the place to go for your post bingeing brunch a la East Village. Eggs Benedict anyone? It opens from the unlikely time of 8 am to 1 pm on weekend mornings.

Rita Blue (*Map 6;* ☎ *93 412 34 38, Plaça de St Agustí 3*) is a pleasant designer restaurant with a whiff of New York in the air, but be prepared to wait at the bar. The food is a tempting mix of Mediterranean dishes with a hint of the exotic. For instance you could order Mexican *fajitas* with Tandoori chicken. The lighting is perfect and the service efficient. Expect to pay up to 3000 ptas a head. It opens all week, but for dinner only at the weekend.

Poble Sec

The recently renovated *Restaurant Elche* (*Map 7;* ☎ *93 441 30 89, Carrer de Vila i Vilà 71*), does some of Barcelona's best paella and good *fideuá* (similar to paella, but made with vermicelli noodles). Several varieties are on offer, mostly costing around 1300 ptas to 1800 ptas per person (two people minimum).

International Cuisine If you fancy Moroccan or other North African dishes, try *Restaurant Kasbah* (*Map 7;* ☎ *93 329 83 84, Carrer de Vila i Vilà 82*), which is not a bad little place. A variety of *tajines* (a spicy stew) cost 1000 ptas each, or you can try the limited French menu. The restaurant closes on Monday.

La Ribera

For an old-style Catalan restaurant try *Pla de la Garsa* (*Map 6;* ☎ *93 315 24 13, Carrer dels Assaonadors 13*), decorated with attractive tiles, lamps and paintings. The 1200 ptas lunch *menú* gives you three courses plus good wine and cheese. It's closed on Monday.

For a bit of a splurge on superb, mainly Catalan and French, cooking you can't do much better than **Senyor Parellada** (Map 6; ☎ 93 310 50 94, Carrer de l'Argenteria 37), an informally chic restaurant. Book for dinner. Mains start at around 2000 ptas. You might start with *carpaccio de salmó* (thin strips of garnished uncooked salmon), followed by *anec amb figues* (duck with figs). It's closed on Sunday and holidays.

Centre Cultural Euskal Etxea (Map 6; ☎ 93 310 21 85, Placeta de Montcada 1) is a fine San Sebastián-style bar where you can wash down the scrummy tapas with glasses of the Basque wine, *txacoli*. If you plan to make this your main meal, be prepared to part with 2000 ptas to 3000 ptas. It is closed on Sunday night and Monday.

Sagardi (Map 6; ☎ 93 319 99 93, Carrer de l'Argenteria 64) is a brand spanking new addition to Barcelona's Basque contingent. It's a little too spotless to make a convincing Basque cider bar, but the food is good (the entrance to the restaurant is off Carrer de Basea) and thank heavens US-style chain food outlets are not the only kind of eatery spreading like ivy. You can expect to pay up to 4000 ptas for a full meal.

Little Italy (Map 6; ☎ 93 319 79 73, Carrer del Rec 30) offers a stylish mix of Mediterranean dishes, some of them (mostly the first courses) vaguely Italian. The lunch set meal costs 1750 ptas, otherwise you are looking at around 2000 ptas for a main. Try to stop by on a Wednesday or Thursday evening, when jazz musos appear at around 10 pm. The place closes on Sunday.

La Flauta Mágica (Map 6; ☎ 93 268 46 94, Carrer dels Banys Vells 18) is the place to go for inventive vegetarian cuisine at mid-range prices (around 3000 ptas a head). It opens for dinner only.

You'll struggle to get into **L'Ou Com Balla** (Map 6; ☎ 93 310 53 78, Carrer dels Banys Vells 20) without a reservation. It presents a sometimes exquisite choice of local, sort-of-Moroccan and more-or-less French dishes in an inviting space with low lighting and well chosen ambient music. A meal can cost about 3500 ptas. It's open for dinner only. If you miss out here they send you across the road to **El Pebre Blau** (Map 6; ☎ 93 319 13 08, Carrer dels Banys Vells 21), which has the

same menu; the setting is a little less personal and the queues shorter.

International Cuisine A nice change from Spanish cuisine can be found at **Restaurante Bunga Raya** (Map 6; ☎ 93 319 31 69, Carrer dels Assaonadors 7), with its Malaysian and Indonesian food. It has a set menu costing 1795 ptas and closes on Monday.

Gades (Map 6; ☎ 93 310 44 55, Carrer de l'Esparteria 10) is a smart address for fondue, of which they do nearly a dozen varieties for 1700 ptas. The bare brick walls and vaults lend the place an elegantly muted atmosphere. It closes on Sunday.

Habana Vieja (Map 6; ☎ 93 268 25 04, Carrer dels Banys Vells 2) is the spot to seek out if you are yearning for *picadillo*, *ropa vieja* and other Cuban meat dishes. Prices are moderate. It's closed on Sunday.

L'Eixample

The **Centro Asturiano** (Map 2; ☎ 93 215 30 10, Passeig de Gràcia 78) is a great little club tucked away up on the first floor. It opens its doors to the lunchtime rabble for the solid 1200 ptas *menú del día*. The open air interior patio is a wonderful spot to eat, but you can go inside too. It's closed on Sunday.

Restaurant de l'Escola de Restauració i Hostalatge (Map 4; ☎ 93 453 29 03, Muntaner 70–72) is where many cooks learn their trade – and in general they appear to be learning it rather well. Meals are modestly priced and the menu varies regularly.

International Cuisine There's one in every major city, and for American-style portions of American-style food, the **Hard Rock Cafe** (Map 6; ☎ 93 270 23 05, Plaça de Catalunya 21) may well be the place for you. You can buy the T-shirt next door.

For some of the better-quality Chinese food in Barcelona (the city has plenty of the cheap and cheerful variety), try **Swan** (Map 2; ☎ 93 488 09 77, Carrer de la Diputació 269).

Practically next door is a new arrival in Barcelona, **Thai Gardens** (Map 2; ☎ 93 487 98 98, Carrer de la Diputació 273). You can

PLACES TO EAT

pop in for a limited set lunch menu costing 1500 ptas or try the more extensive evening spread for 4500 ptas. There's takeaway too – except on Sunday, when the place is closed.

Gràcia

A rustic spot specialising in *torrades*, grilled meats and salads is *Taverna El Glop* (*Map 2; ☎ 93 213 70 58, Carrer de Sant Lluís 24*). Locals say it's a bit passé, and branches are opening elsewhere in town, but the food remains good. A meal with drinks costs from 2500 ptas to 3000 ptas. It's closed on Monday.

La Singular (*Map 2; ☎ 93 237 50 98, Carrer de Franciso Giner 50*) does fantastic salads (with salmon, tuna or pâté) as mains. If you throw in a few tapas and have wine and coffee you'll be looking at 2500 ptas a head. It's closed on Wednesday.

La Gula (*Map 2; ☎ 93 415 29 86, Carrer de Franciso Giner 6*) specialises in rice dishes, for which you will pay about 2000 ptas a head.

Port Vell & La Barceloneta

In the Maremàgnum complex on the Moll d'Espanya, a couple of popular waterside eateries are *Tapasbar* (*Map 5; ☎ 93 225 81 80*) and *El Chipirón* (*Map 5; ☎ 93 225 80 40*). Both specialise in (average) seafood. Several fast-food places lurk here, too.

Fronting the Palau de Mar is a line of al fresco dining options mostly specialising in (finer) seafood. One of the best is *La Gavina* (*Map 5; ☎ 93 221 05 95*), where you can expect to pay around 4000 ptas a head for a full meal with wine. When the chefs are on form, their *fideuá* is scrummy.

Restaurant Set (7) Portes (*Map 6; ☎ 93 319 30 33, Passeig d'Isabel II 14*) is a classic, founded in 1836. The old world atmosphere is reinforced by the decor of wood panelling, tiles, mirrors and plaques naming some of the famous – such as Orson Welles – who have eaten here. Paella (from 1475 ptas to 2225 ptas) is the speciality. It's near-essential to book.

La Barceloneta has some good seafood restaurants. Many, such as *El Rey de la Gamba* (*Map 5; ☎ 93 221 64 17, Passeig de Joan de Borbó 46*), are on the waterfront road facing Port Vell. Most main dishes cost 1000 ptas to 2000 ptas plus IVA. One of the best along this strip is *Puda Can Manel* (*Map 5; ☎ 93 221 50 13, Passeig de Joan de Borbó 60–61*). The paella is fine at 1400 ptas a head; the *crema Catalana* for dessert, however, is not so hot. You will pay around 3500 ptas per person. It is closed on Monday.

Port Olímpic

The harbour here is lined on two sides by dozens of *restaurants* and *tapas bars* (*Map 1*), extremely popular in spring and summer. They are not cheap and mostly rely on the frenetic portside activity for atmosphere. One of the more economical places is *La Taverna del Cel Ros* (*Map 1; ☎ 93 221 00 33*), which does a reasonable *fideuá* for 1375 ptas. It's closed on Thursday. The irritating thing around here is the touting waiters – seriously good eateries don't need to tout for business.

Tibidabo

Plaça del Doctor Andreu at the foot of the Tibidabo funicular is a good place to halt on your way to or from Tibidabo. The best views are from the *Mirablau Terrazza* (*Map 1*), an open-air cafe by the tramvia blau stop. A couple of more expensive restaurants across the street are the only alternative.

PLACES TO EAT – TOP END

Although Barcelona is not to be compared with the likes of London, it is possible to part company with more serious sums of money. Eating at the following restaurants will see your wallet lightened by anything from 4000 ptas upwards. In some cases, if you choose carefully, you might bring the bill down just a tad.

Barri Gòtic

A turn-of-the-century artists' lair (see the boxed text 'The Coolest Cats in Town' on the next page) now reincarnated as a fairly expensive restaurant, *Els Quatre Gats* (*Map 6; ☎ 93 302 41 40, Carrer de Montsió 3 bis*) has somewhat dismissive service. It was restored to its original appearance a few years ago and displays reproductions of some of its former customers' portraits, painted by other former customers. Starters/ snacks such as *esqueixada* (salad of salted cod with tomato, red pepper, onion and white beans) cost close to 1000 ptas, and mains cost around 3000 ptas. Just have a drink if you only want to sample the atmosphere. It's closed for Sunday lunch.

Les Quatre Barres (Map 6; ☎ 93 302 50 60, Carrer d'En Quintana 6) serves up excellent Catalan food – costing 3000 ptas or 4000 ptas for a meal with drinks. The set lunch costs 1380 ptas. It closes all day Sunday and Monday night.

El Gran Café (Map 6; ☎ 93 318 79 86, Carrer d'Avinyó 9) has classy Modernista decor and good Catalan/French food. A la

The Coolest Cats in Town

Modernisme has survived in the imagination as a wholly architectural and design phenomenon. In its time, however, it was a much broader, albeit in some respects effete, artistic 'movement'. On canvas, Ramon Casas and Santiago Rusiñol were the leading lights, although neither could really pretend to greatness. Casas was something of a dandy, and a well-lined one at that. He and Rusiñol had both spent time in Parisian artistic circles, as had many other hopefuls and hangers-on. Among their pals were Miguel Utrillo, another painter, and Pere Romeu. The latter was an intriguing character who had given up painting and developed an interest in shadow puppetry. His hobbies ranged from swimming to cycling, from cabaret to sports cars.

From 1892 until 1899 Rusiñol, who thought he had developed new, symbolic ways of expression through his art, organised *festes modernistes* down in what was destined to become the eternal playground of Sitges. Somehow, these eccentric little get-togethers of artists, musicians, writers and party-goers seemed a little insubstantial and so, in 1897, it was decided to establish a permanent base.

Casas had the dosh, so he bought an early Modernista house (Josep Puig i Cadafalch's first creation) on Carrer de Montsió and entrusted its management to Romeu. It became a restaurant, bar and meeting place for the luminaries of Barcelona Modernisme, and came to be known as Els Quatre Gats, (the Four Cats). In Catalan the expression means 'a handful of people'. That handful consisted of Casas, Rusiñol, Romeu and Utrillo, who proceeded to organise all sorts of cultural

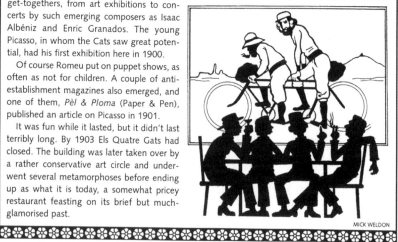

get-togethers, from art exhibitions to concerts by such emerging composers as Isaac Albéniz and Enric Granados. The young Picasso, in whom the Cats saw great potential, had his first exhibition here in 1900.

Of course Romeu put on puppet shows, as often as not for children. A couple of anti-establishment magazines also emerged, and one of them, *Pèl & Ploma* (Paper & Pen), published an article on Picasso in 1901.

It was fun while it lasted, but it didn't last terribly long. By 1903 Els Quatre Gats had closed. The building was later taken over by a rather conservative art circle and underwent several metamorphoses before ending up as what it is today, a somewhat pricey restaurant feasting on its brief but much-glamorised past.

MICK WELDON

carte main dishes cost 1200 ptas to 3000 ptas. It is closed on Sunday and public holidays.

Los Caracoles (Map 6; ☎ 93 302 31 85, Carrer dels Escudellers 14) started life as a tavern in the 19th century and is one of Barcelona's best-known restaurants – although it's now frequented by tourists rather than by the celebrities whose photos adorn its walls. It's still good and lively, and offers a big choice of seafood, fish, rice and meat. Try the snails.

La Ribera

With great tapas and a small dining room with good seafood, a three-course Catalan meal with drinks will cost around 3500 ptas at *Cal Pep (Map 6; ☎ 93 310 79 61, Plaça de les Olles 8)*. It is closed on Sunday, holidays and at lunchtime on Monday.

For the best fondue in town, go straight to *La Carassa (Map 6; ☎ 93 310 33 06, Carrer de Brosoli 1)*. It's a cosy, intimate place, but so popular that there are often two shifts, one at 9 pm and another at 11 pm. If you get in for the first, they'll boot you out at 11 pm to make way for the next round. It opens Monday to Saturday.

L'Eixample

You could easily miss *Tragaluz (Map 2; ☎ 93 487 01 96, Passatge de la Concepció 5)*, but don't. It serves inventive Mediterranean cuisine (with an Italian leaning) and mouth-watering desserts – what about the *tarta de manzana con helado de dulce de leche* (apple pie with caramel ice cream)?! A meal costs about 5000 ptas a head with wine. Directly across the road is *El Japonés*, the restaurant's Japanese branch. They open until midnight.

Gargantúa i Pantagruel (Map 4; ☎ 93 453 20 20, Carrer d'Aragó 214) is warm and inviting and serves quality Catalan country cooking – you can watch your meat being grilled. Expect to spend about 3500 ptas.

Barcelona's first Japanese restaurant is still one of its best. *Yamadori (Map 4; ☎ 93 453 92 64, Carrer d'Aribau 68)* will set you back about 5000 ptas. It opens Monday to Saturday.

Gràcia

Reputedly the place where shellfish is about as good as it gets in all Barcelona is *Botafumeiro (Map 2; ☎ 93 218 42 30, Carrer Gran de Gràcia 81)*. It would want to be, as you will abandon the best part of 10,000 ptas a head for the pleasure.

Considerably more modest but a local classic of Catalan cuisine – try the *botifarra amb mongetes* (pork sausage with fried white beans) – *Cal Juanito (Map 2; ☎ 93 213 30 43, Carrer de Ramon i Cajal 3)* is a delightful place with tiled decor, wooden rafters and walls covered in plates signed by all the great and good who have munched here over the decades. It costs about 4500 ptas a head and closes on Sunday evening and Monday.

Restaurant Roig Robí (Map 2; ☎ 93 218 92 22, Carrer de Seneca 20) is one of the city's more highly regarded top-end spots. Grab a quiet table by the windows or, in summer, in the little internal courtyard. The *mandonguilles de merluza amb bolets i sipia* (cod meatballs with mushrooms and cuttlefish) are delicious. Expect to pay from 7000 ptas upwards for a full meal.

La Barceloneta

For a real treat (and splurge) make for *Can Solé (Map 5; ☎ 93 221 50 12, Carrer de Sant Carles 4)*. The food is superb, the desserts are to die for and the service is little short of amazing – when you're half way through your fish, they come and remove it and discreetly strip away all the bones for you. Expect to pay about 5000 ptas for four courses, wine and coffee. It's closed on Sunday night and Monday.

Poble Nou

On a small square still surrounded by local fishermen's houses in Poble Nou, *Restaurant Els Pescadors (Map 1; ☎ 93 225 20 18; Plaça de Prim 1)* is a fine seafood place. The mainly seafood menu is excellent and diners are attracted from far and wide to this otherwise fairly grubby, post-industrial part of town. You'll pay about 4500 ptas for a full meal.

PLACES TO EAT

Entertainment

To get clued in to what's on, pick up a copy of the *Guía del Ocio* (125 ptas), the city's weekly entertainment rag. It is not as complete as it could be but it is a good starting point.

For a better take on what's hip and what's not in bars and clubs, you need to dig up freebie mags and booklets distributed around some of the town's cooler bars. They include *Micro* and *Go Barcelona*, both much better than *Guía del Ocio* for a real grip on the club and music scene.

BARS

You could write a book on Barcelona's bars (but it might not be good for your health), which run the gamut from wood-panelled wine cellars to bright waterfront places and trendy haunts sporting gimmicky modern designs. Each is a different scene. Some bars are very local, some are full of foreigners, some are favoured by students, others by the well-dressed middle classes. Some play great music, others are places for a quiet talk.

You can pay anything up to 500 ptas for a bottle of beer (in terms of quantity, draught costs less) – a lot depends on where and at what time you buy it. Mixed drinks tend to start at 400 ptas.

Most bars are at their liveliest from around 11 pm and tend to close between 2 and 3 am. Thursday to Saturday are the busiest nights of the week. The following places should keep you busy for a while and you'll soon start discovering your own favourite nooks.

La Rambla

Opposite the Liceu opera house, *Cafè de l'Òpera* (Map 6; La Rambla 74), is the busiest and classiest place on an otherwise largely tacky strip. It was founded in 1876 and has been in action since at least 1929. It is pleasant for an early evening tipple before getting serious. See the Places to Eat chapter for more details

Barri Gòtic

A characterful little bar, *Bar del Pi* (Map 6; Plaça de Sant Josep Oriol) has a mixed local clientele. You can sip an early evening aperitif outside on one of the Barri Gòtic's nicest plazas.

Bar Pilarica (Map 6; Carrer de la Dagueria 26) must be the smallest bar in Barcelona but it's groovy for a passing drink. For something more spacious, try *Cafè de l'Acadèmia* (Map 6; Plaça de Sant Just), facing the church. This place also happens to be a decent restaurant.

The smell of dope in *B.O.2* (Map 6; ☎ 93 317 02 66, Carrer de Sant Domènec del Call 14) can be so thick that knives would be useless. Still, if you want to swallow beer to the accompaniment of old rock concert videos, this is not a bad little dive to skive in until about 3 am. A quite different option open Wednesday to Saturday until the same time is *Paradise* (Map 6; Carrer del Paradis), a little reggae hideaway.

Glaciar (Map 6; ☎ 93 302 11 63, Plaça Reial 3) gets busy with a young crowd of foreigners and locals in the evening and stays open until 2 or 3 am. The more basic *Bar Reixas* (Map 6) in the opposite corner of the square is also popular. You can get cheap drinks at nearby *Restaurante Senshe Tawakal* (Map 6); see the Places to Eat chapter for details.

Tiny *Bar Malpaso* (Map 6; Carrer d'En Rauric 20), just off Plaça Reial, is packed at night with a young, casual crowd and plays great Latin and African music, although frequently the DJs indulge in one musical theme or another – it takes a while to get into gear. Another hip low-lit place with a more varied, often gay, clientele is *Schilling* (Map 6; ☎ 93 317 67 87, Carrer de Ferran 23). Mixed drinks cost about 700 ptas at both.

The decor at *Al Limón Negro* (Map 6; Carrer dels Escudellers Blancs 3) keeps changing, but it remains a laid-back place for a few tipples until well into the night.

A few yards closer to the waterfront you can raise the red lantern at **Shanghai** (Map 6; Carrer de N'Aglá 9), a humming but cosy place for a beer…or sake.

Thiossan (Map 6; Carrer del Vidre 3) is a cool Senegalese haunt where you can get a bite to eat or just sit in mellow contentment listening to the African rhythms and allowing soothing ales to do their work.

Zoo (Map 6; ☎ 93 302 77 28, Carrer dels Escudellers 33) is a busy little watering hole in the heart of the Barri Gòtic. They'll cater to foreigners' desires for sangría but the place gets quite a few locals in too. Out the back is quite an interesting little restaurant should hunger overtake your thirst.

Dot (Map 6; Carrer Nou de Sant Francesc 7) is one of the hippest hang-outs in this part of town. It generally opens until about 3 am, a little later on Friday and Saturday, and each night the musical theme changes, from 'space funk' on Friday and drum 'n' bass on Saturday to easy listening on Sunday.

On the corner of Carrer d'Avinyó and Carrer de Milans is a rather hip new **bar** for the lovers of self-conscious grunge. A short saunter to the west brings you onto Plaça de George Orwell, surrounded by little bars, at their best when the terraces are in action in summer.

Parnasse (Map 6; ☎ 93 310 12 47, Carrer d'En Gignàs 21) is tucked away in the backstreets near the main post office. You can drink anything from malt whisky to Screaming Orgasms.

Bar Center Point (Map 6; ☎ 619 35 39 45, Passeig de Colom 11) is an odd little bar down near the old port. During the week it stays open until 3 am but on Friday and Saturday it's happening until 6 am. They occasionally get in a DJ and the session has been known to go on into broad daylight.

People in need of an early morning heart-starter (or pre-sleep hair of the dog) can call in at **Bar Los de Extremadura** (Map 6; Carrer Ample 51), which has little to recommend it except that it is open for a tipple from about 6 am.

El Raval

This area has a number of old harbour-style bars – dark, wood-panelled and bare except for the odd mirror and vast arrays of bottles behind the bar. These now tend to be bohemian hang-outs rather than dens of low life and are atmospheric places to drink.

However, barely in off La Rambla is something altogether different. To pass by **Boadas** (Map 6; ☎ 93 318 88 26, Carrer dels Tallers 1) you'd hardly think of pushing open the door. Do it. Inside is one of the city's oldest and best cocktail bars. The bow-tied waiters have been serving up dry martinis and other poison since 1933. Joan Miró, among others, used to tipple in here. A drink will cost you about 700 ptas.

A rather different story is **L'Ovella Negra** (Map 6; ☎ 93 317 10 87, Carrer de les Sitges 5), or The Black Sheep to Anglos. It's a noisy, fun, barn-like tavern with a young crowd, pool and futbolín (table football).

One not to miss is **Bar Marsella** (Map 6; Carrer de Sant Pau 65), which opened its doors in 1820 and still specialises in absenta (absinthe), a beverage hard to find because of its supposed narcotic qualities. Your glass of absinthe comes with a lump of sugar, a fork and a little bottle of mineral water. Hold the sugar on the fork, over your glass, and drip the water onto the sugar so that it dissolves into the absinthe, which turns yellow. The result should be a warm glow in you and a mellow atmosphere in the bar – at weekends it is so crammed that mellow is not the word that springs to mind.

Nearby is **The Quiet Man** (Map 6; ☎ 93 412 12 19, Carrer del Marquès de Barberà 11), a relaxed Irish pub attracting both locals and foreigners. There's live music some nights. Another Irish joint is the **Shamrock** (Map 4; ☎ 93 412 46 36, Carrer dels Tallers 72).

Another good place is **Casa Almirall** (Map 6; Carrer de Joaquim Costa 33), which has been going since the 1860s; it's dark and intriguing (although slightly less so since it was spruced up in early 2000), with Modernista decor and a mixed clientele. This is a busy little corner of Barcelona. At the **Granja de Gavà** (Map 6; Carrer de

Joaquim Costa 37), look inside for the out-sized statue of a big lady with banana. In this one-time *bodega* (wine cellar), now a rel-axed little bar, the Barcelona writer Terenci Moix was born in 1942. Next door is **Benidorm** *(Map 6; Carrer de Joaquim Costa 39)*, which is something of a throwback to the 1970s. A lone mirror ball brings flashes of light to the red walls of what could almost be someone's lounge. A good mix of music attracts a combination of foreigners and local journalism students. It shuts around 2.30 am.

Café Que Pone Muebles Navarro *(Map 6; ☎ 907 18 80 96, Carrer de la Riera Alta 4–6)* is an art-gallery-cum-lounge-cum-bar where you can get great cheesecake! It at-tracts an arty, studenty, hip kinda crowd and opens until at least midnight (closed Mon-day). Interestingly, the name translates as 'cafe where the sign says Navarran furniture'.

Salsitas *(Map 6; ☎ 93 318 08 40, Carrer Nou de la Rambla 22)* – see also Places to Eat – apart from being a restaurant, also converts into a music bar with DJs until 3 am. It has a vaguely camp feel but is open to one and all.

Bar Pastís *(Map 6; ☎ 93 318 79 80, Car-rer de Santa Mònica 4)* is a tiny old bar with a French cabaret theme (lots of Piaf in the background). It's been going, on and off, since the end of WWII. Tuesday is live tango night – you'll need to be in here be-fore 9 pm to have a hope of sitting, getting near the bar or anything much else.

If you still need a drink by 2.30 am, when all or most of these places have shut their doors, and you don't want a club or disco, your best bet (except on Sunday) is the **London Bar** *(Map 6; ☎ 93 318 52 61, Car-rer Nou de la Rambla 36)*. It opens until 5 am and occasionally stages some off-the-wall music acts; a bottled beer costs about 500 ptas. This is a classic of the *barri* (dis-trict) and has been open since 1909. It started as a hang-out for circus hands (!) and in later years was frequented by the likes of Picasso, Miró and Hemingway in search of some local colour.

At **Kentucky** *(Map 6; Carrer de l'Arc del Teatre)*, all sorts of local types collect at the long American-style bar and mix with stray foreigners. Beer costs 300 ptas; it's tacky and always packed – perfect!

Still haven't had enough? Or are you just emerging from the clubs? Need a little more fuel or a slow landing? Head for **Bar Au-rora** *(Map 6; ☎ 93 442 30 44, Carrer de l'Aurora 7)*. It starts getting punters in at 6 am at weekends.

La Ribera

The city's best known *cava* bar – **El Xam-panyet** *(Map 6; Carrer de Montcada 22)* – is a small, cosy place with tiled walls, good *tapas* and cava by the glass.

Next door the baroque magnificence of the **Palau de Dalmases** *(Map 6; Carrer de Montcada 20)* is matched by the Peter Greenaway-style luxury inside. You almost feel you should don a powdered wig to sip on your cocktails here, and on Thursday night you'll have live classical music play-ing in the background. The snag is price – a glass of no-name wine will cost 1000 ptas (cocktails cost 1500 ptas)!

El Nus *(Map 6; Carrer dels Mirallers 5)* is a small, dim, chic bar in the narrow old streets near the Església de Santa Maria del Mar, done out with pictures of its Maharishi-lookalike owner. It's good for a quiet drink after dinner.

Along and near Passeig del Born, which links Església de Santa Maria del Mar and the former fresh-produce market El Born, you'll find stacks of bars. Worth a try are **El Copetín** *(Map 6; Passeig del Born 19)*, for cocktails, and **Miramelindo** *(Map 6; Pas-seig del Born 15)*, a spacious tavern where you can hear yourself talk as well as drink.

Sitting at a small table by candle light be-neath the brick vaults of **La Tinaja** *(Map 6; Carrer de l'Esparteria 9)*, once a ware-house, is a pleasurable way to sip on wine and indulge in a few snacks – something you can do daily from 5 pm to 2 am.

Mudanzas *(Map 6; Carrer de la Vidri-eria 15)* has been around for a lot longer. It's a popular little bar and you can often hear live music here. Around the corner, shady Plaça de les Olles is a charming lit-tle hideaway square in summer when the *terrasses* are in operation.

In a class of its own is nearby wine bar *La Vinya del Senyor (Map 6; Plaça de Santa Maria del Mar)*. Come here to taste a selection of wines and cavas, accompanied by simple snacks.

It's difficult to know how to classify *Abaixadors 10 (Map 6; Carrer dels Abaixadors 10)*. You climb upstairs to a place divided up into several spaces – a lowlit theatre-bar where you can hear good music until about 3.30 am, and another brighter bar with restaurant attached. Once upon a time this was one of Barcelona's more intimate dance locales. It opens Wednesday to Sunday and the main drawback is the admission charge – up to 1000 ptas (which includes a drink).

If you should head north off Passeig del Born, you probably would never think to trudge up Carrer del Rec. Do it. *Borneo (Map 6; Carrer del Rec 49)* is a laid-back bar with wide windows onto the street. Across the road and a few doors up is *Gimlet (Map 6; Carrer del Rec 24)*, where they do some mean cocktails (which here, as in other cocktail bars, cost about 750 ptas).

Closer to the Parc de la Ciutadella, *Suborn (Map 6; ☎ 93 310 11 10, Carrer de la Ribera 18)* is several things to several people. After dabbling in original cuisine in the earlier part of the evening, the place gradually turns into a groovy little bar where you can dance to whatever the guest DJ is spinning. It stays open until at least 2.30 am, except on Monday, when it is well shut.

Beaches & Port Olímpic

All the beaches have at least one little *chiringuito*, a covered beach bar where you can get drinks, ice-creams and occasionally even snacks. They generally stay open until about 8 pm. A particularly hip one, apparently known as *DJ Zone* (although no sign clues you in) is located at the southern end of Platja de Mar Bella (Map 1).

The Port Olímpic yacht harbour is lined with bars and discos, all with tables out front in the open air; some have good music inside too. Unfortunately, the area is a little artificial and touristy.

L'Eixample

In general it is safe to say that the 19th-century expanse that is l'Eixample is not a good place to go looking for nightlife. One or two options are worth looking for, however.

La Bodegueta (Map 2; Rambla de Catalunya 100) is a classic wine cellar. Bottles and barrels line the walls and wooden stools surround the marble tables.

La Fira (Map 2; Carrer de Provença 171) is a designer bar with a difference. You enter through a hall of distorting mirrors and inside you'll find that everything is fairground paraphernalia. It sounds corny but the atmosphere is fun.

Gràcia

Two lively bars in Gràcia are *Café del Sol (Map 2; ☎ 93 415 56 63, Plaça del Sol 16)* and *Mirasol (Map 2; ☎ 93 238 01 13, Plaça del Sol 4)*. The former has a vaguely bohemian crowd, and tapas and tables outside. The outside part shuts by 2 am, inside you have another hour's drinking. Just off the square, *La Ñola (Map 2; Carrer del Planeta 39)*, is another bustling neighbourhood bar.

The main spot on Plaça de Rius i Taulet, and very pleasant too, is *Bar Chirito de Oro (Map 2)*.

A gentle designer haunt imitating a village bar, with benches at low tables, is *Café Salambó (Map 2; Carrer de Torrijos 51)*. It has an upper level with pool tables and there's food too – the three-course *menú* costs 1150 ptas.

Farther up the hill are *bars* and *cafes* with potential, around the corner of Carrer de Torrijos and Carrer de la Perla. A block north, *Café la Virreina (Map 2; ☎ 93 237 98 80, Plaça de la Virreina)*, is a relaxed place with a mixed-ages crowd, 1970s rock music, cheap hot *bocadillos* (filled rolls), and tables outside on the leafy square.

Western Gràcia/Avinguda Diagonal

The area around Carrer de Marià Cubí gets busy with locals at the weekend. It's a little on the *pijo* (posh) side, but can be fun all the same. And it's not likely to be filled with tourists! Don't bother earlier in the week, as the area tends to be dead.

Mas i Mas (Map 3; ☎ 93 209 45 02, Carrer de Marià Cubí 199) is one of the area's best-known drinkeries. Another must is **Universal** (Map 3; ☎ 93 201 35 96, Carrer de Marià Cubí 182). It opens Monday to Saturday until 4.30 am and sometimes has live music. The street is lined with bars of various types and should keep you well occupied for a night. Nearby are some discos for carrying on later into the night (see Discos (Clubs) later in this chapter).

Poble Nou

Here's another part of town that the flood of foreigners doesn't reach – Carrer de Zamora (metro Marina or Bogatell) is the place to head. If you like your bars barnlike, the *Megataverna Ovella Negra (Map 1; ☎ 93 309 59 38, Carrer de Zamora 78)*, is the place to be from Thursday to Saturday until 3 am. There's a handful of other bars around here.

LIVE MUSIC

There's a good choice most nights of the week. Many venues double as bars and/or clubs. In the latter case, if you paid to see an act, the dancing after will come free. Starting times are rarely before 10 pm, more often around midnight. Admission charges range from nothing to 1500 ptas or so – the higher prices often include a drink.

To see big name acts, either Spanish or from abroad, you will probably pay more. They often perform at venues such as the 17,000-capacity Palau Sant Jordi on Montjuïc or the Teatre Mercat de les Flors (at the foot of Montjuïc).

To find out what's on, look in *Guía del Ocio's* 'Música' section, and check posters and leaflets in places such as Glaciar bar on Plaça Reial. Here are some of the most reliable places, both for music and general liveliness.

Barri Gòtic

The **Barcelona Pipa Club** (Map 6; Plaça Reial 3) generally has jazz from around midnight from Thursday to Saturday. Admission usually costs 1000 ptas. It's like

someone's flat inside and stays open until 2 or 3 am. You buzz at the door and head two floors up.

Harlem Jazz Club (Map 6; ☎ 93 310 07 55, Carrer de la Comtessa de Sobradiel 8) is a stalwart stop on the Barcelona jazz circuit, although they sometimes get in other acts (including some rock and Latin). You can usually see something here nightly (except Monday) from about 11 pm to 2 am. Admission is generally free, except on Friday and Saturday, when you pay around 700 ptas for your first drink.

Jamboree (Map 6; ☎ 93 301 75 64, Plaça Reial 17) offers varied jazz and funk most nights. Admission (which generally includes a drink) costs up to 2000 ptas; the place becomes a disco after the live stuff ends. It sometimes closes on Sunday.

Sala Tarantos (Map 6), next door to Jamboree, sometimes puts on reasonable flamenco – most often Friday and Saturday at midnight. Admission costs around 1500 ptas.

Sidecar (Map 6; 93 302 15 86, Carrer de Heures 4–6), just off Plaça Reial, presents pop and rock bands of various denominations several nights a week, usually starting 11 pm and winding up around 3 am. Admission ranges up to 1000 ptas.

La Ribera

For jazz, tango and other music sessions, try *El Foro* (Map 6; ☎ 93 310 10 20, Carrer de la Princesa 53) from Wednesday through to the weekend; it usually opens at 11 pm. This place, with restaurant and bar upstairs and club downstairs, attracts a broad range of acts and punters – admission prices depend greatly on the nature of the event.

Poble Sec

The place for world music – chiefly African, Latin and Spanish – is *Club Apolo* (Map 5, ☎ 93 441 40 01, Carrer Nou de la Rambla 113), from 10.30 pm several nights a week. It costs 2000 ptas for big name bands, who are followed by live salsa or (on Friday and Saturday) a disco. The latter also goes by the name of *Nitsaclub*; the cover charge ranges from 1500 ptas to 1800 ptas depending on the DJ.

Gràcia

Teatreneu (Map 2; ☎ 93 284 77 33, *Carrer de Terol 26*) occasionally stages concerts, ranging from techno to acid jazz. Check if anything is on the program.

Western Gràcia/Avinguda Diagonal

The first two of the following are within a few blocks of Avinguda Diagonal; the nearest stations are Diagonal (metro), Hospital Clínic (metro) and Gràcia (FGC).

La Boîte (Map 3; ☎ 93 419 59 50, *Avinguda Diagonal 477*) offers jazz or blues, with the occasional jam session several nights a week at midnight. Admission costs 1200 ptas to 2500 ptas. Later on the place becomes a disco.

Luz de Gas (Map 2; ☎ 93 209 77 11, *Carrer de Muntaner 246*) has live soul, country, salsa, rock, jazz or pop most nights at midnight or 1 am. Admission usually costs 1500 ptas.

Cova del Drac (Map 3; ☎ 93 200 70 32, *Carrer de Vallmajor 33*) is a good spot for jazz sessions most nights of the week. Admission is free but drinking is very expensive. Your first mixed drink (which includes cover charge) can cost 1600 ptas, while follow-ups cost 600 ptas. A taxi is the best way here. It opens Tuesday to Sunday.

El Clot

One of the city's big clubs that allows rock bands on stage a few nights a week is *Savannah* (Map 1; ☎ 93 231 38 77, *Carrer de la Muntanya 16; metro Clot*). Often starting around 10.30 pm, admission usually costs 1000 ptas to 1300 ptas.

DISCOS (CLUBS)

Barcelona's discos come alive from about 2 or 3 am until 5 or 6 am, and are best on Friday and Saturday. Some have live bands, often starting around midnight, to fill the place before the real action begins (see Live Music earlier in this chapter). Disco cover charges range from nothing to as much as 3000 ptas. It depends partly on how busy the place is and whether the bouncers like your look. If you go early, you'll often pay less. Drinks are expensive, of course: anything up to 800 ptas for a beer. Some discos ask for smart dress and won't let you in wearing sneakers or runners.

Guía del Ocio lists many discos in its 'Tarde & Noche' section. Where's hot changes as fast as it does everywhere else but among the following places are some *de toda la vida* (that is, classics that don't die).

Barri Gòtic

Jamboree (Map 6), see Live Music earlier in this chapter, becomes a crowded dance scene from around 1.30 am, after the live stuff finishes. It has two spaces – one for Latin rhythms, one for rock – till 5 am or so. Admission costs from nothing to 1500 ptas.

Karma (Map 6; ☎ 93 302 56 80, *Plaça Reial 10*) is a young, student-type basement place with good music open from around 11 pm to 4 am. You usually pay 1000 ptas, which covers a drink. It can get so packed you can barely move – thank God for the air-conditioning!

El Raval

A fun disco, *Moog* (Map 6; ☎ 93 318 59 66, *Carrer de l'Arc del Teatre 3*) plays Latin and dance hits from as far back as the 1970s upstairs; downstairs it has strobe lights and techno. It opens until about 7 am at weekends. Admission costs 1000 ptas (as do the mixed drinks).

A more recent arrival is the Bongo Lounge DJ team at the *Paloma* (Map 4; ☎ 93 301 68 97, *Carrer del Tigre 27*) on Thursday and Friday night from about 2.30 am. This is one of the city's last functioning old-time dance-halls, but on these nights a strange metamorphosis takes place as the big band gives way to DJs spinning techno. It is a remarkable place from another age. Admission costs 800 ptas but drinks cost a hefty 1000 ptas. The fun ends around 6 am.

La Ribera

For a sassy salsa place, where early in the week you can sip on piña coladas and other South American mixes and dance on the luridly decorated dance floor, try *Luz de*

Luna (Map 6; ☎ 93 310 75 42, *Carrer del Comerç 21*). Mid-week, it fills up from around 2 am but closes by about 4 am. On Friday and Saturday you can shake and wiggle until 6 am. Cocktails cost around 600 ptas.

A more straightforward dance place is *Magic* (Map 6; ☎ 93 310 72 67, *Passeig de Picasso 40*). It opens Wednesday to Sunday from 11 pm to 5 am. They sometimes get live acts but it's basically a disco.

Woman Caballero (Map 6; ☎ 93 300 40 17) is the latest reincarnation of a Barcelona classic, the former Fellini, in the basement of Estació França. Clubbers make for the Sala 02 on Friday, Saturday and pre-holiday nights. The action starts at 2 am and DJs from all over the country and abroad spin everything from techno to 'minifunk' and 'industrial minimalism'. Admission costs 2000 ptas. In the Sala Gran Dadà and Sala Privè you can see all sorts of performers, from dance groups to magicians!

Poble Sec

Continuing the world theme, *Club Apolo* (Map 5), plays a range of ethnic, funk, house, soul and R&B from 1.30 am to groove to on Friday and Saturday. Salsa is the theme on Wednesday and Thursday. Admission costs 1500 ptas to 1800 ptas depending on the live act or DJs. See also Live Music earlier in this chapter.

Port Vell

A bevy of bars and discos open in the Maremàgnum complex until the wee hours. In July and August, most of the action is here and spreads along the waterfront. One of the places to watch for is *Boîte Nayandei* (Map 5; ☎ 93 225 80 10), open nightly until 5 am.

Other possibilities range from Irish pubs to salsa spots such as *Mojito Bar* (Map 5; ☎ 93 225 80 14). With such a concentration of places you can chop and change if you want, although cover charges on some are a disincentive. All in all, the crowd in the noisier discos is young to very young, but 'older' folks will find company in some of the less over-the-top establishments. Mixed

drinks in these places begin around the 800 ptas mark, beer 500 ptas (you may be offered flyers for a free *second* drink in some places).

L'Eixample

A big 1980s designer bar, *Nick Havanna* (Map 2; ☎ 93 215 65 91, *Carrer del Rosselló 208*) has become home to one of the city's club hits, Row. Row's DJ team mixes up a set of vanguard house Thursday to Saturday – it has become something of a favourite with Barcelona's clubbers. The place is generally busy until about 5 am. Admission is free but drinks are cheeky.

Satanassa (Map 4; ☎ 93 451 00 52, *Carrer d'Aribau 27*) is an 'antidesign' haunt of androgynous people (with a notable gay leaning), with gaudy erotic murals. It opens from 11 pm to 4 or 5 am. Admission is free.

Velvet (Map 2; ☎ 93 217 67 14, *Carrer de Balmes 161*) is a smallish, designer bar and disco inspired by the film *Blue Velvet*, with 1960s music. It is busy with a fairly straight crowd. Admission is free.

Zoo Club (Map 4; ☎ 93 323 68 20, *Carrer de Balmes 51*) is relatively new on the Barcelona scene. The standard fare is house but it's an accessible club that attracts a heterodox and generally off-their-heads clientele. It opens at 11.30 pm and keeps hopping until 5 am from Wednesday to Saturday. Admission generally costs 2000 ptas (which includes the first of your tipples).

Mond Club (Map 2; ☎ 93 457 38 77, *Carrer de Còrsega 363*) hosts an indie night on Friday in what was once a dance hall, the Sala Cibeles.

Fuse (Map 2; ☎ 93 481 31 74, *Carrer de Roger de Llúria 40*) is fast becoming one of Barcelona's most popular dance havens. The DJs spin an eclectic mix of house and related rhythms, and at weekends you may find yourself emerging on the streets at…10 am.

Montjuïc

The Poble Espanyol has several bars that get lively. The most original is *Torres de Ávila* (Map 7; ☎ 93 424 93 09), inside the tall entrance towers themselves. Created by the top Barcelona designer Javier Mariscal (who was responsible for the Olympics mascot Cobi in 1992), it has several levels and all sorts of surreal touches, including an egg-shaped room and glass lifts that you fear will shoot you through the roof. It opens from 10 pm to 4 am; admission costs 1000 ptas.

When it starts dying down you could move to *Terrazza (Map 7; ☎ 93 423 12 85, Avinguda del Marquès de Comillas)*. It is one of the most popular summertime dance spots in town, open on Friday and Saturday nights. It's out the back of the Poble Espanyol. In winter it goes indoors and becomes *Discothèque.*

Around Avinguda Diagonal

West of Via Augusta, *Otto Zutz (Map 2; ☎ 93 238 07 22, Carrer de Lincoln 15)*, is for beautiful people (the bouncers will decide how beautiful you are) and those who favour wearing black. Admission costs 2000 ptas and a beer 800 ptas.

La Boîte (Map 3), becomes a club after the nightly jazz or blues session (see Live Music earlier in this chapter).

The Music Box (Map 3; ☎ 93 209 35 89, Avinguda Diagonal 618) is farther west and a favourite with the Carrer de Marià Cubí bar crowd (see Bars earlier in this chapter). This thumping disco hits its straps from about 2 to 5 am at the weekend (earlier in the week it is not so hot).

Fiesta Bori (Map 3; ☎ 93 414 54 61, Carrer de Bori i Fontestà) is the place to go if you are sick of salsa. Here you can get lessons in line dancing from 11 pm to 1 am and then practice into the wee hours! It closes on Sunday.

Up & Down (Map 3; ☎ 93 205 51 94, Carrer de Numància 179) opens Tuesday to Saturday. Wednesday night is curious as it's *sevillanas* (a flamenco-like southern-Spanish folk dance) night. There's not much point in arriving before 1 am at this club – the upstairs half is for an older clientele while bright young solvent Barcelonins head downstairs and try to score with one another.

Gràcia

Maintaining a hard-rock warehouse-type scene, *KGB (Map 1; ☎ 93 210 59 06, Carrer de Ca l'Alegre de Dalt 55)* stays open until 8 am for tireless all-nighters.

Tibidabo

A bar with great views and a small disco floor, *Mirablau (Map 1; Plaça del Doctor Andreu)* keeps going until about 5 am.

El Clot

Playing good dance music, *Savannah (Map 1)*, opens nightly until midnight on Sunday, 3 am Tuesday to Thursday and 5 am on Friday and Saturday. See also Live Music earlier in this chapter.

GAY & LESBIAN VENUES

Three good gay bars, virtually next door to each other, are *Punto BCN (Map 4; ☎ 93 453 61 23, Carrer de Muntaner 63–65)*, *Dietrich (Map 4; Carrer del Consell de Cent 255)* and *Este Bar (Map 4; Carrer del Consell de Cent 257)* around the corner. Punto BCN is a relaxed place to meet a 30-something plus crowd, while Este Bar is perhaps a tad more self-conscious. Dietrich is more of a theatre-cafe, often with very camp entertainment. It is a big, friendly space and opens until about 3 am. This local concentration of bars (and some clubs – see later in this section) has earned this part of town the sobriquet of 'Gaixample'.

Café de la Calle (Map 2; Carrer de Vic 11) is a cosy meeting place for lesbians and gay men. *Antinous (Map 6; ☎ 93 301 90 70, Carrer de Josep Anselm Clavé 6)* is a gay bookshop and cafe.

If *Bar La Concha (Map 6; Carrer de la Guàrdia 14)* in El Raval were a theme bar, the theme would be the actress from Castilla-La Mancha, Sara Montiel. The place is covered in more than 250 photos of her, which seem to be the big attraction for a largely gay and transvestite crowd. The music ranges from paso dobles (the Spanish quickstep) to modern Spanish hits, and the place opens until 3 am.

A good lesbian bar is *Bahía (Map 2; Carrer de Seneca 12)*, open until about

2.30 am. Another nearby is **Member's** *(Map 2; ☎ 93 237 12 04, Carrer de Seneca 3)*. Both are open to all comers. More exclusively lesbian is **La Rosa** *(Map 3; ☎ 93 414 61 66, Passatge de Brusi 39)*.

Discos (Clubs)

The two top gay discos are **Metro** *(Map 4; ☎ 93 323 52 27, Carrer de Sepúlveda 185)*, near Plaça de la Universitat, and **Martin's** *(Map 2; ☎ 93 218 71 67, Passeig de Gràcia 130)*. Metro attracts some lesbians and heteros as well as gay men; it's packed for its regular Monday-night cabarets. Martin's is gay men only. Both open from midnight to 5 am and have dark rooms.

Popular with a young, cruisy gay crowd is **Arena** *(Map 4; ☎ 93 487 83 42, Carrer de Balmes 32)*. It has a dark room, opens at midnight and closes around 5 am. Round the corner, **Arena Clasic** *(Map 4; ☎ 93 487 83 42, Carrer de la Diputació 233)* is a little more sedate. **Arena VIP** *(Map 4; Gran Via de les Corts Catalanes 593)* is a more mixed mainstream place with a gay flavour. It opens at midnight and you will probably leave about dawn.

Another good one that doesn't get started

Castles in the Air

It's a little difficult to know how to classify making human castles, but to many a Catalan, the *castellers* are as serious in their sport as any footballer.

The 'building' of *castells* is particularly popular in central and southern Catalunya and the number of this activity's fans is growing. *Colles* (teams) from various parts of Catalunya compete in the summer and you are most likely to see castellers in town *festes majors* (festivals).

Erecting human towers is not a new pastime. The golden age of this activity was in the 1880s when the most daring castellers raised nine human storeys. Now, 62 colles have been registered by the Coordinadora de Colles Castelleres. Of these, two teams, la Vella and Jove dels Xiquets de Valls, can trace their roots back a century. Castle fever is spreading – teams have 'sprung up' in Mallorca and France, and as far away as Mexico and Argentina.

It's very much an amateur sport. The club will pay team members' travel costs and supply a team jersey, but that's as far as the remuneration goes. It was once an exclusively male preserve but women now form up to a quarter of some colles.

The 'Castles'

The idea is to build human layers of a castle and then to successfully undo it without everyone tumbling in a heap. This is much easier said than done. The first level of the *tronco* (trunk) is a wide and solid scrum of people, together known as the *pinya*. The most popular teams 'playing' at home can get a thousand people volunteering to be part of the pinya!

Above this you build your castle. About the best any team has recorded is a *quatre de nou* or *tres de nou*: a four-by-nine or three-by-nine castle. That means nine storeys of people, three or four in the core levels tapering to two then one person at the top. Often the base pinya does not provide enough buttressing, so you get more of the same on the second level. That is called the *folre*. Hence, very often the result is, say, a *quatre de nou amb folre* (a four-by-nine with folre). Teams who, on those rare occasions, can do without the folre get extra merit. Sometimes a team will add some support to the third level *(manilles)*. When one is built without any extra support at the lower levels it is termed *net* (clean).

If all goes well, the whole structure is topped off by a kid *(anxaneta)* who serves as a pinnacle, or *agulla*. When the anxaneta waves his arm the castle is complete. If it can be dismantled without collapsing in a heap, the castle is *descarregat*.

There are more permutations of this activity than crenellations on your average stone castle. Teams sometimes concentrate on a level, say seven, ranging from a *nou de set* (nine people by seven

until about 3 am is *Salvation (Map 5; ☎ 93 318 06 86, Ronda de Sant Pere 19–21)*. It opens on Friday and Saturday.

CLASSICAL MUSIC & OPERA

Guía del Ocio has ample listings, but the monthly *Informatiu Musical* leaflet has the best coverage of classical music (as well as other genres). You can pick it up at tourist offices and the Palau de la Virreina arts information office (Map 6; ☎ 93 301 77 75) at La Rambla de Sant Josep 99, which also sells tickets for many events. You will see from the leaflet that recitals take place all over the city and beyond – in theatres, museums, monasteries and so on.

Amid much ceremony Barcelona's great opera house, the *Gran Teatre del Liceu (Map 6; ☎ 93 485 99 13, La Rambla 51–59)* reopened in September 1999, more than five years after being destroyed by fire. The reconstruction cost around 17 billion ptas but directors say that it is now one of the most technologically advanced theatres in the world. Let's hope the fire extinguishing systems have been improved.

Apart from opera, you can see world-class dance companies strut their stuff or

---

Castles in the Air

storeys) through to the really tricky two- and one-person levels. Those involving two castellers per storey are *torres* (towers) and those with one per level are *pilars* (pillars). It is rare to get either above six or seven storeys. To keep team members humming, someone usually belts out some strident tunes on a *gralla*, similar to a kazoo.

It is tempting to think the sky's the limit on what castellers can achieve, but perhaps it is more prosaically a question of human strength and persistence. The virtually unthinkable, *castells de deu* (10 levels) had not been achieved since the 19th century until 1998. Other challenges include the *quatre de nou sense folre* (a four-by-nine without folre), also unheard of in more than 100 years, and the *tres de vuit aixecat per sota*. The latter is tough because the upper levels are formed *first* and then lifted up by three teams who form the bottom levels. Until 1999, no team had managed this feat since the 19th century.

JANE SMITH

When & Where

You don't often see castellers in action in Barcelona, although teams converge on Plaça de Catalunya in June for noncompetitive displays (for the exact dates check with the tourist office) and occasionally for festivals in the city's districts. One of the best teams to look for is Els Castellers de Vilafranca del Penedès (see the Excursions chapter), which appears at festivals all over Catalunya. In Vilafranca, the main festival takes place around the end of August.

The standard afternoon program involves three competing teams, each with four castles to make – around three hours of sweaty work. The action takes place in town squares – just turn up and join the crowd. The season lasts roughly from February to December. Every two years there is a championship day at Tarragona's bullring, usually around October. The next meeting is due in 2002.

---

attend classical music concerts and recitals. Tickets can cost anything from 500 ptas to 1000 ptas for the cheapest seats, and up to 11,000 ptas for the best spot for a night at the opera. You will need to book well in advance for the big shows. You can do so through ServiCaixa on ☎ 902 33 22 11. Take a peek at the Liceu's Web site at www.liceubarcelona.com.

The chief venue for classical and choral music is the **Palau de la Música Catalana** *(Map 6; ☎ 93 295 72 00, Carrer de Sant Pere més alt 11)* in La Ribera, which has a busy and wide-ranging program. Attending a concert here is also a fine way to see the gorgeous interior of this Modernista building. You could easily find yourself paying from 5000 ptas to 15,000 ptas for the more prestigious international performances.

In the late 1990s, Barcelona's impressive (if rather bland compared with the Palau) new home for serious music lovers, **L'Auditori** *(Map 1; ☎ 93 247 93 00, Carrer de Lepant 50)*, swung into action. It puts on plenty of orchestral, chamber, religious and other music throughout the year. You can often hear fine performances (Catalan Jordi Savall's baroque music for instance) for around 2000 ptas to 3000 ptas.

The **Palau Sant Jordi** *(Map 7)* on Montjuïc is used for bigger concerts and the **Teatre Mercat de les Flors** *(Map 7; ☎ 93 318 85 99, Carrer de Lleida 59)*, at the foot of Montjuïc, is an important venue for music, dance and drama.

The easiest way to get hold of tickets for most of the above venues and other theatres throughout the city is through the Caixa de Catalunya's Tel-Entrada service on ☎ 902 10 12 12, or on the Internet at www.telentrada.com. There's also a *venta de localidades* (ticket office) on the ground floor of the Corte Inglés on Plaça de Catalunya and another at the FNAC store on the same square.

To get half price on some tickets, you can buy them personally at the Caixa de Catalunya desk in the tourist office at Plaça de Catalunya. To qualify you must purchase the tickets in person no more than three hours before the start of the show you wish

to see. The system is known as Tiquet-3. In the *Guía del Ocio* shows for which you can get such tickets are marked with an asterisk.

CINEMAS

Foreign films, shown with subtitles and original soundtrack rather than dubbed, are marked 'v.o.' *(versión original)* in movie listings. Cinemas to check for these include:

Alexis *(Map 2; ☎ 93 215 05 06, Rambla de Catalunya 90)*
Arkadín *(Map 2; ☎ 93 405 22 22, Travessera de Gràcia 103)*
Casablanca *(Map 2; ☎ 93 218 43 45, Passeig de Gràcia 115)*
Icària-Yelmo *(Map 1; ☎ 93 221 75 85, Carrer de Salvador Espriu 61)*
Maldà *(Map 6; ☎ 93 317 85 29, Carrer del Pi 5)*
Renoir-Les Corts *(Map 3; ☎ 93 490 55 10, Carrer de Eugeni d'Ors 1)*
Verdi *(Map 2; ☎ 93 237 05 16, Carrer de Verdi 32)*

The **Filmoteca** *(Map 3; ☎ 93 410 75 70, Avinguda de Sarrià 3)* specialises in film seasons that concentrate on particular directors, styles and eras of film. If you want to see old classics in the original language, then **Méliès Cinemes** *(Map 4; ☎ 93 451 00 51, Carrer de Villarroel 102)* is for you.

A ticket usually costs from 600 ptas to 750 ptas but most cinemas have a weekly *día del espectador* (viewer's day), often Monday or Wednesday, when they charge 400 ptas to 600 ptas.

THEATRE

Theatre is nearly all in Catalan or Spanish (*Guía del Ocio* specifies which). For all that's happening in theatre head for the arts information office in Palau de la Virreina on La Rambla. Look for the many leaflets and the monthly listings guide *Teatre BCN*.

The **Teatre Lliure** *(Map 2; ☎ 93 218 92 51, Carrer de Montseny 47)* in Gràcia is dedicated to theatre in Catalan – if you get into the language you can see anything from the classics to the latest avant-garde productions. Actors play on a stage in the middle of the theatre, surrounded by the audience. The Palau de l'Agricultura on Montjuïc (opposite the Museu d'Arqueologia) is being

Passionate flamenco features in the line up.

Una cervesa…or two or three more?

The party begins when the sun goes down.

Start the evening with refreshing *sangría*

Opera aficionados head for Gran Teatre del Liceu.

Bullfighting at Plaça de Braus Monumental

Shopping in l'Eixample's grand boulevards

Take home some eye-catching Catalan ceramics

Chocoholics should head for the *Xocolaterias*.

With over 100 different types of *cava*, you'll be spoilt for choice in Barcelona's luxury shops.

restructured to house what will one day be the centre of an expanded Teatre Lliure.

Artenbrut (Map 2; ☎ 93 457 97 05, *Carrer del Perill 9–11*) concentrates more on new and rising directors. Performances are usually in Catalan and occasionally in Castilian. *Teatre Malic* (Map 6; ☎ 93 310 70 35, *Carrer de la Fusina 3*) is a relatively small spot that offers a packed program including music, alternative theatre and a mix of better known local talent and emerging genius.

Teatre Tantarantana (Map 5; ☎ 93 285 79 00, *Carrer de les Flors 22*), apart from staging all sorts of contemporary theatre, also puts on kids' shows, including pantomime, puppets and so on. These shows start at 6 pm.

Originally destined to become *the* home of Catalan theatre, Ricard Bofill's ultra neoclassical *Teatre Nacional de Catalunya* (Map 1; ☎ 93 306 57 06, *Plaça de les Arts 1, metro Glòries*) opened its doors in 1997. So far it has put on a mixed bag of (not always exciting) theatre but it is worth keeping an eye on the program.

The *Teatre Victòria* (Map 5; ☎ 93 443 29 29, *Avinguda del Paral.lel 67–69*) often stages ballet and contemporary dance but otherwise is used by well-known companies such as Tricicle. This trio of comic mimes has been doing the rounds with their version of 'intelligent humour' for 20 years. The good thing about these guys is that anyone can enjoy the fun because language is not an issue.

The *Teatre Principal* (Map 6; ☎ 93 301 47 50, *La Rambla 27*), opened again in 1998 after a long absence and tends to stage a hodgepodge of theatre and musicals.

Keep your eyes peeled for any of the eccentric (if not downright crazed) performances of Barcelona's La Fura dels Baus theatre group. They have won worldwide acclaim for their brand of startling, often acrobatic, theatre in which the audience is frequently dragged into the chaos.

Teatre Romea (Map 6; ☎ 93 317 71 89, *Carrer de l'Hospital 51*) had new life breathed into it in 2000 and puts on a range of interesting plays, some in Catalan and some in Spanish. A Catalan version of *A Streetcar Named Desire* followed a Spanish classic, Calderón de la Barca's *La Vida es Sueño* that year.

DANCE
Sardana

The *sardana*, Catalunya's national dance, is danced every week – except sometimes in August – on Plaça de la Seu in front of the cathedral at 6.30 pm on Saturday and noon on Sunday. These are not shows for tourists but feature ordinary Catalans doing something they enjoy. The dancers join hands to form ever-widening circles, placing their bags or coats in the centre. The dance is intricate but, in true Catalan style, hardly flamboyant. The steps and the accompanying brass and reed music are rather sedate; at times jolly, at times melancholy, rising to occasional crescendos, then quietening down again. It's a bit of an acquired taste. For more details see the boxed text 'A Slow Number' in the Facts about Barcelona chapter.

Flamenco

Although quite a few important flamenco artists grew up in the gitano barrios of Barcelona, seeing good performances of this essentially Andalucían dance and music here is not so easy. A few tacky *tablaos*, where punters see flamenco while eating dinner, are scattered about. On occasion class acts perform here, but you need to be in the know – otherwise it's rather second class and touristy. *El Tablao de Carmen* (☎ 93 325 68 95, *Carrer dels Arcs 9*) is in the Poble Espanyol (Map 7) while the *Tablao Cordobés* (Map 6; ☎ 93 317 66 53) is at La Rambla 35. Book ahead.

Another place to keep your eye on is *Sala Tarantos* (Map 6; see *Live Music* earlier in this chapter).

CASINO

The *Gran Casino de Barcelona* (Map 1; ☎ 93 225 78 78, *Carrer de la Marina 19–21*), Port Olímpic, is the place for you if you feel either lucky or unfairly endowed in the fiscal department. Apart from the usual one-armed bandits and more sophisticated games, there are restaurants, bars and a disco. It opens from 1 pm to 5 am daily.

ENTERTAINMENT

The Boots of Barça

In 1895, a group of English residents kicked off a local football tournament in Barcelona. This odd activity, imported from Perfidious Albion, caught on. The first local club to be formed was Palamós (still in 2nd division) in 1898. On 29 November of the following year, FC Barcelona came into being.

Competition didn't really get going until the following year when three more groups formed. These were L'Hispània, l'Irish and the Societat Espanyola de Futbol (which kept changing its name but always retained the 'Espanyol' bit). Interestingly, the latter was the only one to permit only Spanish players. The bulk of FC Barcelona's players were English, German and Swiss, with only a few token Catalans. Some would mutter that things haven't changed much today! L'Hispània was mostly Scottish and there are no prizes for guessing who filled the ranks of l'Irish.

In November 1900, the dozen or so teams that then existed formed a league, with four of them (including FC Barcelona) in the first division. The Copa Macaya, Catalunya's first championship, which was fought out the following month, saw the Scots of L'Hispània take the honours. Thus began Catalan football.

In the meantime, football was spreading across the rest of Spain. In 1902 the first national championships, the Campeonato de Copa de España (later known as the Copa del Rey, Spain's equivalent of the British FA Cup) were staged. Barcelona went under to Biscaia 2–1.

By 1910, FC Barcelona was the premier club in a rapidly growing local league. The red and blue colours were already well known and the first signs of professionalism in the game emerged – paid transfers of players were recorded and Espanyol's management charged spectators. Barça had 560 members (about 110,000 today), who were all mighty chuffed at the team's victory at that year's national championship.

Antagonism between Catalan FC Barcelona and Castilian Spanish Espanyol (not to mention from Madrid's premier team, Real Madrid) was often cause for violent contests before the civil war – FC Barcelona fans will tell you it was a constant struggle against dodgy decisions in the national league. After Franco's victory in 1939, things didn't get any easier, but massive migration in the 1950s and '60s brought new players and supporters – it was one way for newcomers to integrate into local society.

Barça remains one of Spain's great teams – one of only three (along with Real Madrid and Athletic de Bilbao) never to have been relegated to 2nd division. Since the *Liga* (league) got fully under way in 1928, Barça has emerged champion 16 times, second only to arch-rivals Real Madrid (27 victories). Between them the two have virtually monopolised the game – only seven other teams have managed to come out on top (three of them only once or twice) in more than 60 years of competition.

Outside the first division championship, Barcelona has emerged the top cup-winning team in Spain. The side has grabbed 24 Copas del Rey (Real Madrid has won 17), four UEFA Cups (Real Madrid has taken two) and four Cup Winner's Cups (Real Madrid has yet to lay its hands on this trophy). The European Champions League has been more of a struggle. Barcelona took it in 1998, but lags well behind Real Madrid's record eight trophies.

The end of the 1999–2000 season was frustrating for Barça fans. Not only did the side run second in the league, but it was edged out of the Champions League by rivals Valencia in the semifinals. Then Dutch coach Louis van Gaal bowed out, leading to uncertainty about whether or not big-name international players would stay with the side.

SPECTATOR SPORTS
Football

Barcelona Football Club has not only one of Europe's best teams, Barça, but also one of its best stadiums – the 120,000-capacity Camp Nou in the west of the city (Map 1; metro Collblanc). Games are quite an occasion as long as the opposition is good enough to fire up the home team and the crowd. Check the daily press for upcoming games. Tickets, available at the stadium and through some banks, cost from around 3000 ptas to 8000 ptas – the cheapest are in the one small standing section, a long, long way above the pitch. For more information call ☎ 93 496 36 00. The city's other club, Espanyol, based at the Estadi Olímpic on Montjuïc (Map 7), traditionally plays a quiet second fiddle (in the top division) to Barça, although lately the players have been improving their game. A local derby, or better still a match against arch-rivals, Real Madrid, is a guarantee that sparks will fly, although getting tickets can be difficult.

Bullfights

Death in the Afternoon is not a favourite Catalan theme, but there are some fights on Sunday afternoon in summer at the Plaça de Braus Monumental, on the corner of Gran Via de les Corts Catalanes and Carrer de la Marina (Map 1; metro Monumental). The 'fun' usually starts at 6 pm. Tickets are available at the arena from 10.30 am to 2 pm and 6 to 7 pm from Wednesday to Saturday, from 10 am on Sunday, or by phoning ☎ 902 33 22 11. Prices range from 2500 ptas to 12,000 ptas – the latter is for the front row in the shade – any closer and you'd be fighting the bulls yourself.

See the Treatment of Animals section in the Facts about Barcelona chapter for details of organisations that can provide further information about bullfighting.

Toro, Toro, Toro For many, bullfighting is a sickening affair; others view it as a noble battle. Whichever way you look at it, there is little doubt about the cruelty of it or about the risks that *toreros* (bullfighters) run. The *corrida* (bullfight) is a spectacle with a long

history – even the Romans enjoyed a good bullfight.

The corrida is about many things – death, bravery, performance. It is certainly bloody and cruel and there is nothing worse than to see a matador and his sidekicks mess up the kill. *La lidia*, as the art of bullfighting is also known, took off in an organised fashion in Spain in the mid-18th century. In the 1830s, Pedro Romero, the greatest torero of the time was, at the age of 77, appointed director of the Escuela de Tauromaquia de Sevilla, the country's first bullfighters' college. It was around this time, too, that breeders succeeded in creating the first reliable breeds of *toro bravo* (fighting bull).

The Fight As a rule, six bulls and three matadors are on the day's card. If any are considered not up to scratch they are booed off (the president will display a green handkerchief) and replacements brought on. Each fight takes about 15 to 20 minutes.

Traditionally, young men have aspired to the ring in the hope of fame and fortune, much like boxers. Most attain neither. Only champion matadors make good money, and some make a loss for the matador must rent or buy his outfit and equipment, pay for the right to fight a bull and pay his *cuadrilla* (team).

You will notice the team is made up of quite a few people. Firstly, there are several *peones*, junior bullfighters under the orders of the main torero, who is the matador. The peones come out to distract the bull with great capes, manoeuvre him into the desired position and so on.

Then come the *picadores*, mounted on horseback. Charged by the bull, which tries to eviscerate the (nowadays) heavily padded and blind-folded horse, the picador shoves his lance into the withers of the bull. The peones then return to the scene to measure their courage against the (it is hoped) charging bull.

The picador is followed by the *banderilleros*. Two banderilleros will each successively race towards the charging bull and attempt to plunge a pair of colourfully decorated *banderillas* (short prods with harpoon-style ends) into the bull – again aiming for the withers.

The dress of the matador could be that of a flamenco dancer. At its most extravagant, the *traje de luces* (suit of lights) can be an extraordinary display of bright, spangly colour. All the toreros, with the occasional exception of the matadors, wear the black *montera* (the Mickey Mouse-ears hat). The torero's standard weapons are the *estoque* or *espada* (sword) and the heavy silk and percale *capa* (cape). You will notice, however, that the matador, and the matador alone, uses a different cape with the sword – a smaller piece of cloth held with a bar of wood called the *muleta* and used for a number of different passes, or *faenas*.

How well he is doing can be judged by the cries from the crowd. The various moves must be carried out in certain parts of the stadium, which is divided into three parts: the *medios* (centre), *tercios* (an intermediate, chalked-off ring) and *tablas* (the outer ring).

When the bull seems tired and unlikely to give a lot more, the matador chooses his moment for the kill. Placing himself head-on he aims to sink the sword cleanly into the animal's neck *(estocada)* for an instant kill. It's easier said than done.

The sad carcass is dragged out by a team of dray-horses and the sand raked in preparation for the next bull. The meat ends up in the butcher's.

Shopping

Although perhaps not in the same league as London, Paris or Milan, Barcelona is certainly among Europe's cities of style. It is a natural magnet for the fashion-conscious and there is no shortage of design outlets for even the most tireless consumer.

Everything from books to jewels, *haute couture* (local and international) designer furniture, *cava* and condoms is on offer. Several markets animate squares around the centre of town.

Most of the mainstream stores can be found on a shopping 'axis' that looks something like the hands of a clock set at a quarter to five. From the waterfront it leads up La Rambla through Plaça de Catalunya and on up Passeig de Gràcia (see Map 1). At Avinguda Diagonal you turn left.

From here as far as Plaça de la Reina Maria Cristina (especially the final stretch from Plaça de Francesc Macià) the Diagonal is jammed with places where you can empty your bank account.The T1 Tombbus service has been laid on for the ardent shopper (see the Getting Around chapter) and eventually a tram may run the length of Avinguda Diagonal too.

The best shopping areas in central Barcelona are Passeig de Gràcia and the streets to its south-west (including the Bulevard Rosa arcade, Map 2, just north of Carrer d'Aragó), and Barri Gòtic streets such as Carrer de la Portaferrissa, Carrer de la Boqueria, Carrer del Call, Carrer de la Llibreteria and Carrer de Ferran, and around Plaça de Sant Josep Oriol (all Map 6).

Department store bargain-hunters should note that the winter sales officially start on or around 10 January and their summer equivalents on or around 5 July.

The big department stores (like El Corte Inglés) and shopping complexes (such as El Triangle) tend to open in the morning from 9 or 10 am through to 9 or 10 pm at night, Monday to Saturday. Smaller shops often close for a few hours at lunchtime (around 2 to 4 pm).

ANTIQUES

If you can't break away from the old town, Carrer de Banys Nous in the Barri Gòtic (Map 6) is lined with antique shops and is a good area to start. The side streets in the immediate area, including Carrer de la Palla, also hide a bevy of antique shops. While you're wandering along Carrer de la Palla, glance up at No 21 – it was once the Hospital de Sant Saver – founded back in 1462. There are alternatives. Bulevard dels Antiquaris, Passeig de Gracìa 55 (Map 2; part of the Bulevard Rosa arcade complex) is jammed with antique shops, most of a general nature (furnishings, paintings, decorative items) with a few specialists: Brahuer (jewellery), Govary's (porcelain dolls), Dalmau (wooden picture frames) and Victory (crystal).

ART

You could start hunting for art in several places. Along Carrer de Montcada (Map 6) are several galleries, the biggest being Galeria Maeght at No 25. Others include the Galeria Surrealista, next door to the Museu Picasso, the Sala Montcada of the Fundació La Caixa at No 16, Galeria Beaskoa next door and Galeria Montcada (jammed in next to the Palau de Dalmases).

Predictably enough, the presence of the Museu d'Arte Contemporanea de Barcelona in El Raval is turning the surrounding area into an artsy zone. You'll find a half dozen small galleries and designer stores on Carrer del Doctor Dou, Carrer d'Elisabets and Carrer dels Àngels (Map 6).

The classiest concentration of galleries – about a dozen of them – is on the short stretch of Carrer del Consell de Cent between Rambla de Catalunya and Carrer de Balmes (Map 2). A particularly interesting place is the Galeria Victor Saavedra (Map 2; ☎ 93 238 51 61), Carrer d'Enric Granados 97. Saavedra, himself an artist, has been promoting all sorts of artists from around Europe since the late 1980s.

The *Guía del Ocio* guide (for more on this useful publication, see the Entertainment chapter) carries a limited list of art galleries.

ART PRINTS & POSTERS

For many, a big Miró print or a Picasso poster would make the perfect gift. The Fundació Joan Miró (Map 7), Museu Picasso (Map 6) and Museu d'Art Contemporàni de Barcelona (Map 6; MACBA) are all well stocked. The souvenir shops in the main tourist office and Palau de la Virreina, La Rambla de Sant Josep 99 (Map 6), also carry limited offerings.

For high-quality postcards of Barcelona, prints and the like, Estamperia d'Art (Map 6; ☎ 93 318 68 30), Plaça del Pi 1, is a good place to investigate.

BARÇA

For some, football is the meaning of life. If you fall into that category your idea of shopping heaven may well be La Botiga del Barça, Carrer de Arístides Maillol s/n (Map 1; near the team's Museu del Futbol at the Camp Nou stadium) and their branch (☎ 93 225 80 45) in the Maremàgnum complex (Map 5). There you can get shirts, keyrings, footballs, the works – anything you could think of featuring the famous red and blue colours.

BOOKS

There is no shortage of decent bookshops in Barcelona but the local product is pricey, largely due to high printing costs in Spain. Those keen on Catalan have come to the right place. A wealth of specialist bookshops cater to particular requirements and several outlets sell general literature in other European languages too.

La Rambla

Llibreria & Informaciò Cultural de la Generalitat de Catalunya (Map 6; ☎ 93 302 64 62) Rambla dels Estudis 118. A good first stop for books and pamphlets on all things Catalan, although a lot of it is highly specialised and technical.
Llibreria de la Virreina (Map 6; ☎ 93 301 77 75) Palau de la Virreina, La Rambla de Sant Josep 99.

An assortment of art/architecture and art history books, many with at least some relevance to Barcelona.

Barri Gòtic & El Raval

Antinous (Map 6; ☎ 93 301 90 70) Carrer Josep Anselm Clavé 6. Good gay bookshop and cafe.
Cómplices (Map 6; ☎ 93 412 72 83) Carrer de Cervantes 2. Gay and lesbian books.
Documenta (Map 6; ☎ 93 317 25 27) Carrer del Cardenal Casañas 4. Novels in English and French, and maps.
MACBA (Map 6; ☎ 93 412 08 10) Plaça dels Àngels. This place is an excellent source of books on a whole range of visual arts and architectural subjects.
Próleg (Map 6; ☎ 93 319 24 25) Carrer de la Dagueria 13. Women's bookshop.
Quera (Map 6; ☎ 93 318 07 43) Carrer de Petritxol 2. Specialist in maps and guides, including for walking and trekking.

L'Eixample

Alibri (Map 4; ☎ 93 317 05 78) Carrer de Balmes 26. One of the city's best general bookstores, with a wealth of material and foreign language books too.
Altaïr (Map 2; ☎ 93 454 29 66) Carrer de Balmes 71. Great travel bookshop with maps, guides and travel literature.
Come In (Map 2; ☎ 93 453 12 04) Carrer de Provença 203. Specialist in English-language teaching books; also plenty of novels and books on Spain, in English and French.
The English Bookshop (Map 4; ☎ 93 425 44 66) Carrer de Entença 63. A good range of literature, teaching material and children's books.
Happy Books (Map 2; ☎ 93 317 07 68) Passeig de Gràcia 77. This place has a bit of everything. The big advantage is the discount prices if you can find what you want. There's another branch at Carrer de Pelai 20 (Map 4).
Laie (Map 2; ☎ 93 518 17 39) Carrer de Pau Claris 85. Novels and books on architecture, art and film in English, French, Spanish and Catalan.
Llibreria Bosch (Map 4; ☎ 93 317 53 08) Ronda de la Universitat 11. Another of the city's stalwarts.
Librería Francesa (Map 2; ☎ 93 215 14 17) Passeig de Gràcia 91. Lots of novels and guide books in French.

Gràcia

Acció Llibres (Map 2; ☎ 93 237 17 15) Carrer de Xiquets de Valls 2. Some adventure sports titles.

euro currency converter 1000 ptas = €6.01

Bookstore (Map 1; ☎ 93 237 95 19) Carrer de la Granja 13. Second-hand English-language books.

CAMPING & OUTDOOR EQUIPMENT

One of the better shops for walking and camping gear (including a decent range of tents) is La Tenda (Map 2; ☎ 93 488 33 60), Carrer de Pau Claris 118–120. They have plenty of walkers' maps for Catalunya and beyond.

CANDLES

Even if you are not interested in all the mounds of wax, you may want to pop in to Cereria Subirà (Map 6; ☎ 93 315 26 06), Baixada de la Llibreteria 7, just to say you have been in the oldest shop in Barcelona. It started trading in 1761.

CERAMICS

A couple of interesting ceramics and pottery shops owned by the same people are hidden north of the Catedral. Ceràmiques i Terrisses Cadí (Map 6; ☎ 93 317 73 85), Carrer de les Magdalenes 23, has a diverse range of plates, jugs and so on. The owners will either be here or in the twin store (simply called Ceramica) across the road.

CLOTHING & FABRICS

If you are after international fashion, Avinguda Diagonal (Maps 2 and 3) is the place to look. Calvin Klein is at No 484 (Map 2), Giorgio Armani at Nos 490 (Map 2) and 620 (Map 3), Gianni Versace at No 606 (Map 3) and Gucci at No 415 (Map 2). Jean Pierre Bua, at No 469 (Map 3), hosts designers ranging from Jean Paul Gaultier through to Helmut Lang.

Max Mara (Map 2; ☎ 93 488 17 77) fans will want to head for Passeig de Gràcia 23.

Loewe (Map 3; ☎ 93 216 04 00), at Avinguda Diagonal 570, is one of Spain's leading and oldest fashion stores, founded in 1846. There's another branch, opened in 1943, in the Modernista Casa Lleo Morera on Passeig de Gràcia (Map 2). You could also try Ortiga (Map 3), Carrer de Bori i Fontestà 10, for prêt-a-porter evening dresses. Adolfo Domínguez, Passeig de Gràcia 32 (Map 2), is a star name in Spanish fashion and Gonzalo Comella, on the corner of Passeig de Gràcia and Carrer de Casp, is known for men's clothing.

Zara is another well-known local name for women's fashion. It is a chain and you'll find several across town including branches in l'Illa del Diagonal shopping complex (see Department Stores below), Avinguda Diagonal 584 (Map 3), Passeig de Gràcia 16 (Map 5) and at Avinguda del Portal de l'Àngel 24 (Map 6). Antonio Miró, Carrer del Consell de Cent 349 (Map 2), concentrates on light, natural fibres to produce smart, unpretentious men's and women's fashion – jackets are a strong point. Jeanne Weis (Map 6; ☎ 93 301 04 12) at Carrer d'En Rauric 8, north of Carrer de Ferran (Barri Gòtic) has some nice lines in African printed fabrics, cushions and shirts.

CONDOMS

Barcelona even has several exotic condom shops, one of them on one of the prettiest squares of the Barri Gòtic – La Condoneria (Map 6; ☎ 93 302 77 21) at Plaça de Sant Josep Oriol 3. Here you can purchase condoms of every colour and shape you could dream of (and some that might never have occurred to you).

CRAFTS

If you want to take a look at high quality Catalan crafts *(artesania)* to get some inspiration for future shopping expeditions, pop into the Centre Català d'Artesania (Map 2; ☎ 93 467 46 60) at Passeig de Gràcia 55. It is dedicated to promoting and maintaining Catalan craft traditions.

Natura Selection (Map 2; ☎ 93 488 19 72), Carrer del Consell de Cent 304 (l'Eixample), has a big stock of ethnic bags (leather and cloth), jewellery, pots, drums, candles, carvings, glass, baskets, tablecloths, rugs and more. Casa Miranda (Map 6; ☎ 93 301 83 29), Carrer de Banys Nous 15, has woven baskets of all shapes and sizes.

Another eye-catching arts and crafts store with odds and ends imported from various corners of the planet is Ètnia (Map 6; ☎ 93 268 32 39) at Carrer del Rec 51.

SHOPPING

DESIGN

Vinçon (Map 2; ☎ 93 215 60 50), Passeig de Gràcia 96, has the slickest designs in furniture and household goods, both local and imported. Not surprising really, since the building belonged to the turn-of-the-century artist Ramon Casas – painter and leading member of the *quatre gats* (see boxed text 'The Coolest Cats in Town' in the Places to Eat chapter).

Bd Ediciones de Diseño (Map 2; ☎ 93 458 69 09), Carrer de Mallorca 291, is worth a look, even if you have left your credit cards at home. Here you will find a collection of pieces for the home by some of Barcelona's leading designers. Opened in 1972, this prize-winning store is located in a Modernista house built by Domènech i Montaner and restored in 1979.

When hanging around La Ribera, design-buffs should also mark off a little time for Aspectes (Map 6; ☎ 93 319 52 85), Carrer del Rec 28, which has a broad range of stuff from furniture to Art Deco knick-knacks for the home. The Art*quitect* (Map 6; ☎ 93 268 23 86) showroom at Carrer del Comerç 31, is interesting for those enthusiastic about building design.

FOOD & DRINK

Serious champagne sippers should pop by Xampany (Map 4; ☎ 606 33 60 42), Carrer de València 200. It stocks over 100 types and brands of *cava* and all the associated drinking utensils you can imagine.

If coffee is more your tipple, head for El Magnífico (Map 6; ☎ 93 319 60 81), Carrer de l'Argenteria 64. These guys have been roasting all sorts of coffee for most of this century. Nuts to you at Casa Gispert (Map 6; ☎ 93 319 75 35), Carrer dels Sombrerers 23, where they've been toasting almonds and selling all manner of dried fruit since 1851.

Xocolateria Valor (Map 2; ☎ 93 487 62 46), Rambla de Catalunya 46, is a relative newcomer to Barcelona, but for more than 100 years this Alicante-based confectioner has been responsible for tooth decay in countless willing victims. You can buy to take away or try anything from ice cream to milk shakes on the spot.

FURNITURE

You probably won't be looking to purchase furniture while in Barcelona but if you happen to be in the area you should drop into La Maison Coloniale (Map 4; ☎ 93 443 22 22), Carrer de Sant Antoni Abat 61. The colonial-style furniture is exquisite, and so is the setting – what remains of the 15th-century Gothic Església de Sant Antoni Abat, largely destroyed in the Civil War.

JEWELLERY

Joyería Bagués (Map 2; ☎ 93 216 01 74), Passeig de Gràcia 41, in the Casa Amatller, is a reliable name in high quality rocks. If you want to check out a more international name, try Cartier (Map 2; ☎ 93 488 00 62) at Carrer del Consell de Cent 351. For gold jewellery, Vasari, Passeig de Gràcia 73 (Map 2), is reliable.

If you wander down along the museum trail on Carrer de Montcada, you'll find several silver specialists on the same street.

LLADRÓ & MAJORICA

These are possibly the two best known Spanish brand names in the world. Lladró porcelain is coveted as much as the Majorica pearls that compete with it for display space in several stores around Barcelona. García (Map 5; ☎ 93 302 69 89), La Rambla 4, is a handy spot to take a look at these products.

For a broader and higher quality selection of Majorica jewellery, head for the Majorica store (Map 2; ☎ 93 416 09 06) at the intersection of Avinguda Diagonal and Carrer de Còrsega.

MUSIC

One of the biggest record stores is Planet Music (Map 2; ☎ 93 451 42 88), with more than 50,000 CDs, at Carrer de Mallorca 214. They have other branches around town.

Several small shops specialising in indie and other niche music can be found on or around Carrer de Sitges and especially on Carrer dels Tallers (El Raval), which boasts a dozen music stores. Castelló (Maps 4 and 6; ☎ 93 318 20 41), at Nos 3 (classical music), 7 and 79, is a large family business that has been going since 1935; it is said to account for a fifth of the retail record business in Catalunya. Rock & Blues (Map 6; ☎ 93 412 59 86), at No 10, is a haven for vinyl and rare records. CD-Drome (Map 4; ☎ 93 317 46 46), nearby at Carrer de Valldonzella 3, specialises in house, hip-hop, trip-hop and other hops. Daily Record (Map 6; ☎ 93 301 77 55), at Carrer de Sitges 9, is another interesting outlet.

If you like medieval and baroque music, pop into the delightful Eutherpe (Map 6; ☎ 93 412 63 05), Carrer de Elisabets 18, in El Raval. They mix the CDs with a tempting collection of art books.

MUSICAL INSTRUMENTS
New-Phono (Map 6; ☎ 93 315 12 04), Carrer Ample 37 in the Barri Gòtic, has been selling instruments under one name or another since 1834. The shop is housed in what was once the stables of a noble family.

PERFUME
Regia (Map 2; ☎ 93 216 01 21), Passeig de Gràcia 39, is reputed to be one of the best perfume stores in the city.

PHOTOGRAPHY
Arpi (Map 6; ☎ 93 301 74 04), La Rambla 38, has five floors given over to all things photographic (still, video and cinema). It is a standard port of call for professional snappers. For a good second-hand collection, try Casanova (Map 4; ☎ 93 302 73 63), Carrer de Pelai 18.

SHOES
There's a gaggle of relatively economical shoe shops on Avinguda del Portal de l'Àngel, off Plaça de Catalunya (Map 6).

Camper (Map 2; ☎ 93 215 63 90), Carrer de València 249, something of a classic shoe merchant in Spain, has a good range.

SOUVENIRS
If you're in the mood for a little kitsch, the easiest thing to do is head for La Rambla. The place is lined with shops that will sell you all sorts of junk. However, before you flash your cash at La Rambla's merchants,

have a look inside Barcelona Original, the souvenir boutique in the building of the Oficina d'Informació Turisme de Barcelona at Plaça de Catalunya. It has an interesting range of quality stuff, including ceramics, watches, art prints, coffee table books and the like. Most of the major museums and art galleries have shops attached where you can 'buy the T-shirt' and other more substantial gifts.

WHERE TO SHOP
Department Stores
The single best place to look for anything you need is the El Corte Inglés department store (Map 5; ☎ 93 306 38 00) on Plaça de Catalunya. It has another important branch north-west of town on Plaça de la Reina Maria Cristina and a third on Avinguda Diagonal (both on Map 3).

Marks & Spencer (☎ 93 419 94 36) recently opened a branch on Plaça de Catalunya (Map 6). You can also find them at Avinguda Diagonal 545 (Map 3).

A couple of doors down at Avinguda Diagonal 549 is FNAC (Map 3), the French-owned store specialising in CDs, tapes, videos and books. Actually, the two shops form part of a huge shopping mall – l'Illa del Diagonal – considered to be one of the city's more interesting post-Olympic architectural developments (Map 3).

Back on Plaça de Catalunya, the city's latest shopping centre, El Triangle (Map 5), is finally open for business. Here you'll find another branch of FNAC (Map 5) among the tenants.

If you like shopping emporia, the Centre Comercial de les Glòries (Map 1), by the massive roundabout and metro stop of the same name, is probably for you. It counts 250,000 sq m of space in the grounds of the former Hispano Olivetti factory and is also home to a range of bars and eateries to take your mind off shopping for a while.

Late-Night Stores
The concept of the 24-hour general store has yet to reach Barcelona, but an approximation is VIPS, an import from Madrid. It's at Rambla de Catalunya (Map 5) and opens

Monday to Thursday from 8 am to just 8 pm (!), picking up its act for the rest of the week by closing at 3 am. In Madrid the chain thrives, but in Barcelona it hasn't really caught on. The 7-eleven store at Carrer de Roger de Llúria 2 (Map 2) opens 7 am to 3 am daily.

Markets

Large Els Encants Vells (the old charms) flea market (also known as the Fira de Bellcaire) is held every Monday, Wednesday, Friday and Saturday from 8 am to 7 pm (8 pm in summer) next to Plaça de les Glòries Catalanes (Map 1; metro Glòries). The markets moved here in August 1928 from Avinguda Mistral, near Plaça d'Espanya, because the sight of such a jumble sale did not fit in with the town fathers' visions for the 1929 World Exhibition. There are plans to shift them again – out to the edge of the city along the Ronda de Dalt in Vall d'Hebron – by 2002. You can find everything here – all at *preus de ganga* (bargain-basement prices).

In the Barri Gòtic, there's a crafts market in Plaça de Sant Josep Oriol on Thursday and Friday, an antiques market in Plaça Nova on Thursday, and a coin and stamp collectors' market in Plaça Reial on Sunday morning (all on Map 6). On the western edge of El Raval, Mercat de Sant Antoni (Map 4; metro Sant Antoni) dedicates Sunday morning to old maps, stamps, books and cards.

Excursions

Catalunya, the autonomous region of which Barcelona is the capital, offers a little of everything: tacky package coastal resorts and remote cliff-side beaches; skiing and trekking; a plethora of towns and villages boasting jewels of Romanesque and Gothic art and architecture; ancient ruins to the north and south of Barcelona; and one of Europe's top gay party towns. What appears in this chapter is merely a taste of what is accessible on day trips out of Barcelona. Lonely Planet's *Spain* and *Catalunya & the Costa Brava* contain many more hints on heading farther afield.

The cost of train journeys given in this chapter are for second-class, one-way fares, unless otherwise stated.

ACCOMMODATION

This chapter is designed for the day-tripper, so no accommodation information is provided. If you plan to do overnight trips, approach each town's tourist office for accommodation listings.

For the record, the 26 member hostels of Catalunya's official youth hostel network, Xarxa d'Albergs de Joventut, all share a central booking service (☎ 93 483 83 63, fax 93 483 83 50) at Turisme Juvenil de Catalunya, Carrer de Rocafort 116–122, Barcelona (Map 4).

At Xarxa hostels you need a Hostelling International (HI) card. With a few minor exceptions, all have the same price structure: if you're under 25 or have an ISIC, B&B costs 1675/1900/2250 ptas in the low/mid/high season; otherwise it's 2200/2500/2800 ptas, respectively. Lunch or dinner costs 850 ptas and sheets 350 ptas. For 300 ptas you can stay in the hostel during the day.

Catalunya has a wide network of *cases de pagès*. These are farmhouses and other rural lodgings that often provide good and economical accommodation in country areas. You can pick up a complete guide to them at the regional tourist office in the Palau Robert in Barcelona.

NORTH OF BARCELONA
Girona
postcode 17080 • pop 71,858

Northern Catalunya's largest city, Girona (Gerona), sits in a valley 36km inland from the Costa Brava. Its impressive medieval centre seems to struggle uphill above the Riu Onyar.

The Roman town of Gerunda lay on the Via Augusta, the highway from Rome to Cádiz (Carrer de la Força in Girona's old town follows it in part). Taken from the Muslims by the Franks in 797, Girona became the capital of one of Catalunya's most important counties, falling under the sway of Barcelona in the late 9th century.

Information The tourist office (☎ 972 22 65 75) is towards the southern end of the old town, at Rambla de la Llibertat 1. It opens 8 am to 8 pm Monday to Friday, 8 am to 2 pm and 4 to 8 pm on Saturday, and 9 am to 2 pm on Sunday.

Catedral The fine baroque facade of the cathedral stands at the head of a majestic flight of steps rising from Plaça de la Catedral. Most of the building, however, is much older. Repeatedly rebuilt and altered down the centuries, it has Europe's widest Gothic nave (23m). The cathedral's museum, through the door marked 'Claustre Tresor', contains the masterly Romanesque *Tapís de la Creació* (Tapestry of the Creation). The 500 ptas fee for the museum also admits you to the beautiful 12th-century Romanesque cloister.

Other Things to See Next door to the cathedral, in the 12th- to 16th-century Palau Episcopal, the collection of the **Museu d'Art** (art museum) ranges from Romanesque woodcarvings through to early 20th-century painting. It opens 10 am to 6 pm (to 7 pm in summer) Tuesday to Saturday, and 10 am to 2 pm on Sunday and holidays. Admission costs 300 ptas.

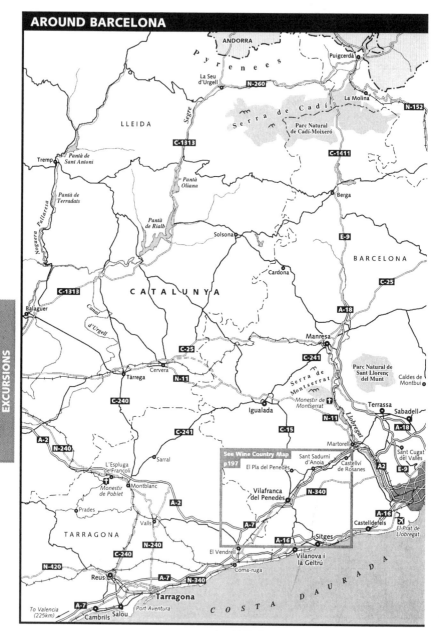

AROUND BARCELONA

ANDORRA
P   Y   R   E   N   E   E   S
Puigcerdà
La Seu
d'Urgell
N-260
La Molina
N-152
LLEIDA
Segre
Serra   de   Cadí
Parc Natural
de Cadí-Moixeró
C-1313
C-1411
Tremp
Pantà de
Sant Antoni
Pantà
Oliana
Berga
Pantà de
Terradets
Noguera Pallaresa
Pantà
de Rialb
E-9
Solsona
BARCELONA
Cardona
C-25
Balaguer
C-1313
C   A   T   A   L   U   N   Y   A
Canal
d'Urgell
A-18
Manresa
C-25
C-241
Tàrrega
Cervera
N-11
Parc Natural de
Sant Llorenç
del Munt
Caldes de
Montbui
C-240
Serra   de
Montserrat
Terrassa
Sabadell
Igualada
Monestir de
Montserrat
A-18
A-2
N-240
C-241
C-15
N-11
Llobregat
Sarral
L'Espluga
de Francolí
See Wine Country Map
p197
Sant Sadurní
d'Anoia
Martorell
Sant Cugat
del Vallès
Monestir
de Poblet
Montblanc
El Pla del Penedès
Castellví
de Rosanes
A-2
E-9
Prades
A-2
Vilafranca
del Penedès
N-340
A-16
Valls
Casteldefels
TARRAGONA
C-240
N-240
El Vendrell
A-7
Sitges
A-16
El Prat de
Llobregat
N-420
Reus
Coma-ruga
Vilanova i
la Geltrú
C   O   S   T   A   D   A   U   R   A   D   A
To Valencia
(225km)
A-7
A-7
N-340
Port Aventura
Tarragona
Cambrils   Salou

EXCURSIONS

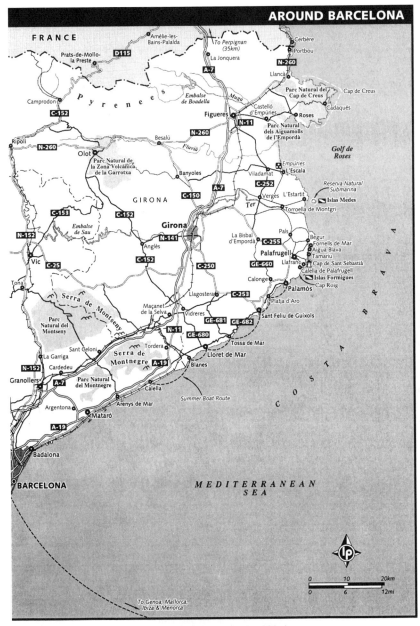

AROUND BARCELONA

FRANCE

Amélie-les-Bains-Palalda
To Perpignan (35km)
Cerbère
Portbou
Prats-de-Mollo-la Preste
D115
La Jonquera
N-260
A-7
Llançà
Camprodon
C-152
P y r e n e e s
Embalse de Boadella
Muga
Parc Natural del Cap de Creus
Cap de Creus
Castelló d'Empúries
Cadaqués
Figueres
N-II
Roses
Ripoll
N-260
Besalú
N-260
Fluvià
Parc Natural dels Aiguamolls de l'Empordà
Olot
Parc Natural de la Zona Volcànica de la Garrotxa
Banyoles
Viladamat
Empúries
L'Escala
Golf de Roses
GIRONA
C-150
A-7
C-252
Verges
L'Estartit
Reserva Natural Submarina
C-153
C-152
Ter
Torroella de Montgrí
Islas Medes
Girona
Embalse de Sau
N-152
N-141
La Bisbal d'Empordà
Pals
Begur
C-255
Fornells de Mar
Aigua Blava
Tamariu
Anglès
Palafrugell
Cap de Sant Sebastià
Vic
C-25
C-152
C-250
GE-660
Llafranc
Calella de Palafrugell
Tona
Calonge
Islas Formigues
Palamós
Cap Roig
Serra de Montseny
Llagostera
C-253
Platja d'Aro
Parc Natural del Montseny
Maçanet de la Selva
Vidreres
Sant Feliu de Guíxols
La Garriga
Sant Celoni
N-II
GE-681
GE-682
Tordera
GE-680
Tossa de Mar
N-152
Cardedeu
Serra de Montnegre
A-19
Lloret de Mar
Granollers
A-7
Parc Natural del Montnegre
Blanes
C O S T A   B R A V A
Calella
Argentona
Summer Boat Route
Arenys de Mar
Mataró
A-19
Badalona
BARCELONA
M E D I T E R R A N E A N
S E A

EXCURSIONS

0   10   20km
0   6   12mi

To Genoa, Mallorca, Ibiza & Menorca

euro currency converter €1 = 166 ptas

Girona's second great church, **Església de Sant Feliu**, stands downhill from the cathedral. The 17th-century main facade, with its landmark single tower, is on Plaça de Sant Feliu, but the entrance is at the side. The nave has 13th-century Romanesque arches but 14th- to 16th-century Gothic upper levels.

The **Banys Àrabs** (Arab baths) on Carrer de Ferran Catòlic are actually a Christian affair from the 12th-century in Romanesque style, although they're modelled on earlier Muslim and Roman bathhouses. Summer opening hours are 10 am to 7 pm Tuesday to Saturday and 10 am to 2 pm on Sunday and holidays; it opens 10 am to 2 pm Tuesday to Sunday the rest of the year. Admission costs 200 ptas.

Across the street from the Banys Àrabs, steps lead up into lovely gardens that follow the city walls up to the 18th-century Portal de Sant Cristòfol gate, from which you can walk back down to the cathedral. This quick circuit is known as the **Passeig Arqueològic**.

Down across the little Riu Galligants, the **Monestir de Sant Pere de Galligants** – an 11th- and 12th-century Romanesque monastery – has a lovely cloister. It houses Girona's **Museu Arqueològic** (archaeology museum). It opens 10.30 am to 1.30 pm and 4 to 7 pm (10 am to 2 pm and 4 to 6 pm in winter) Tuesday to Saturday, 10 am to 2 pm on Sunday and holidays. Admission costs 300 ptas.

Until 1492, Girona was home to Catalunya's second most important medieval Jewish community (after Barcelona). The **Jewish quarter** *(Call)* was centred on Carrer de la Força. For an idea of medieval Jewish life and culture, visit the **Centre Bonastruc Ça Porta**, entered from a narrow alley off the upper side of Carrer de la Força. Named after Jewish Girona's most illustrious figure, a 13th-century Cabbalist philosopher and mystic, the centre – a warren of rooms and stairways around a courtyard – has exhibitions and a cafe. It opens 10 am to 8 pm (to 6 pm in winter) Monday to Saturday, 10 am to 3 pm on Sunday and holidays. Admission costs 200 ptas.

You can walk along a good length of the top of the city walls – **Passeig de la Muralla** – from Plaça de Josep Ferrater i Mora, just south of the Universitat de Girona building at the top of the old town, down to Plaça del General Marvà near Plaça de Catalunya.

Places to Eat For a great range of *tapas* costing from 325 ptas, try *Tapa't (Carrer de la Cort Reial)*. You can tuck into some vegetarian goodies at *La Polenta (Carrer de la Cort Reial 6)*, where mains cost up to 1200 ptas.

A great little Basque tavern and restaurant is *Zanpanzar (☎ 972 21 28 43, Carrer de la Cort Reial 10–12)*. It's usually packed with locals, and offers *pintxos* (Basque tapas) and some fine meat dishes. Round off with *goxua intxaursaltsarekin*, a Basque tart consisting of biscuit, apple and an amazing nut sauce. Expect to fork out about 3000 ptas per head.

For tempting savoury and sweet crepes, head for *La Crêperie Bretonne (☎ 972 21 81 20, Carrer de la Cort Reial 14)*. This is the local branch of a popular eatery in Perpignan (southern France). They keep cooking until midnight (except on Sunday, when the restaurant is closed).

Cafè Le Bistrot (☎ 972 21 88 03, Pujada de Sant Domènec), with one of the most picturesque stairways in the old town, is a treat. Vaguely bohemian, it serves up salads, *pizzes de pagès* (little bread-based pizzas) and crepes for between 500 ptas and 700 ptas.

Getting There & Away Barcelona Bus (☎ 972 20 24 32) runs to/from Barcelona's Estació del Nord (1450 ptas, 1¼ hours) and Figueres (580 ptas, 50 minutes) three to seven times daily. SARFA (☎ 972 20 17 96) runs buses to most parts of the Costa Brava.

Girona is on the railway between Barcelona, Figueres and Portbou on the French border. There are around 20 trains per day to Figueres (330 ptas to 380 ptas, 30–40 minutes) and Barcelona (790 ptas to 910 ptas, 1½ hours), and about 15 to Portbou and/or Cerbère (515 ptas to 595 ptas).

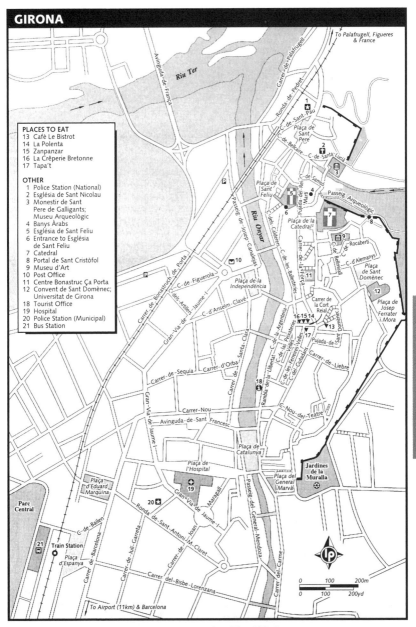

GIRONA

PLACES TO EAT
13 Cafè Le Bistrot
14 La Polenta
15 Zanpanzar
16 La Crêperie Bretonne
17 Tapa't

OTHER
1   Police Station (National)
2   Església de Sant Nicolau
3   Monestir de Sant
    Pere de Galligants;
    Museu Arqueològic
4   Banys Àrabs
5   Església de Sant Feliu
6   Entrance to Església
    de Sant Feliu
7   Catedral
8   Portal de Sant Cristòfol
9   Museu d'Art
10 Post Office
11 Centre Bonastruc Ça Porta
12 Convent de Sant Domènec;
    Universitat de Girona
18 Tourist Office
19 Hospital
20 Police Station (Municipal)
21 Bus Station

EXCURSIONS

Figueres
postcode 17600 • pop 33,600

Another 40km north from Girona along the A-7 *autopista*, or by train, is Figueres (Figueras), a bit of a dive with a one-man show – Salvador Dalí. In the 1960s and '70s he created the extraordinary Teatre-Museu Dalí here, the town of his birth.

Information The tourist office (☎ 972 50 31 55) on Plaça del Sol opens 9 am to 9 pm Monday to Saturday, and 9 am to 3 pm on Sunday, from June to mid-September; and from 8.30 am to 3 pm and 4.30 to 7.30 pm Monday to Friday, 9.30 am to 1.30 pm and 3.30 to 7.30 pm on Saturday during the rest of the year.

Teatre-Museu Dalí Salvador Dalí was born in Figueres in 1904 and went to school here. Although his career took him for spells to Madrid, Barcelona, Paris and the USA, he remained true to his roots and lived well over half his adult life at Port Lligat, near Cadaqués on the coast east of Figueres. Between 1961 and 1974 Dalí converted Figueres' former municipal theatre, ruined by a fire at the end of the civil war in 1939, into the Teatre-Museu Dalí.

Even on the outside, the building aims to surprise, from the collection of bizarre sculptures at the entrance on Plaça de Gala i Salvador Dalí to the pink wall along Pujada del Castell, topped by a row of Dalí's trademark egg shapes and what appear to be female gymnast sculptures.

Inside, the ground floor (Level 1) includes a semicircular garden area on the site of the original theatre stalls. In its centre is a classic piece of weirdness called *Taxi Plujós* (Rainy Taxi), composed of an early Cadillac – said to have belonged to Al Capone – and a pile of tractor tyres, both surmounted by statues, with a fishing boat balanced precariously above the tyres. Put a coin in the slot and water washes all over the inside of the car. The Sala de Peixateries (Fish Shop Room) off here holds a collection of Dalí oils, including the famous *Autoretrat Tou amb Tall de Bacon Fregit* (Self-Portrait with Fried Bacon) and *Retrat*

de Picasso (Portrait of Picasso). Beneath the former stage of the theatre is the crypt, with Dalí's plain tomb.

The stage area (Level 2), topped by a glass geodesic dome, was conceived of as Dalí's Sistine Chapel. The large backdrop – egg, head, breasts, rocks, trees – was part of a ballet set, one of Dalí's many ventures into the performing arts. If proof were needed of Dalí's acute sense of the absurd, the painting *Gala Mirando el Mar Mediterráneo* (Gala Looking at the Mediterranean Sea) appears, from the other end of the room, with the help of coin-operated viewfinders, to be a portrait of Abraham Lincoln.

One floor up (Level 3) you come across the Sala de Mae West, a living-room whose components, viewed from the right spot, make up a portrait of Ms West – a sofa for her lips, two fireplaces for nostrils, two impressionist paintings of Paris for eyes.

The museum opens 9 am to 7.15 pm daily from July to September; and 10.30 am to 5.15 pm (closed Monday except in June), the rest of the year. Admission to Teatre-Museu Dalí costs 1000 ptas. Queues are long on summer mornings and for most of the summer there are night sessions from 10 pm to 12.30 am, which cost 1200 ptas.

Other Things to See Combining archaeological finds from Greek, Roman and medieval times with a sizeable collection of art, the **Museu de l'Empordà** can be found at Rambla 2. It opens 11 am to 7 pm Tuesday to Saturday, 10 am to 2 pm Sunday and holidays, from mid-June to mid-September; 11 am to 1.30 pm and 3 to 7 pm Tuesday to Saturday and 11 am to 1.30 pm on Sunday, the rest of the year. Admission costs 300 ptas.

At Rambla 10, the **Museu de Joguets**, Spain's only toy museum, has more than 3500 Catalunya- and Valencia-made toys from the pre-Barbie 19th and early 20th centuries. It opens 10 am to 1 pm and 4 to 7 pm Monday to Saturday (except Tuesday), 11 am to 1.30 pm (and 5 to 7 pm from July to September) on Sunday and holidays, year round except from mid-January to the end of February. Admission costs a rather hefty 750 ptas.

euro currency converter 1000 ptas = €6.01

You can also visit the 18th-century **Castell de Sant Ferran**, on a low hill 1km north-west of the centre.

Places to Eat Carrer de la Jonquera, just down the steps east of the Teatre-Museu Dalí, is lined with cheap restaurants, among them *Restaurant España* (No 20), *Restaurant Versalles* (No 18) and *Restaurant Costa Brava* (No 10), offering basic three-course *menús* from 1150 ptas. *Restaurant La Paella*, two short blocks east on Carrer de Tins, does one for 1250 ptas. They are not great culinary experiences, but are quick and easy.

Restaurant Viarnés (☎ *972 50 07 91, Pujada del Castell 23*) offers traditional local cooking, with the emphasis on seafood. Mains cost from 1500 ptas to 2500 ptas. The nearby *Antaviana* (☎ *972 51 03 77, Carrer de Llers 5)* is another of the Mediterranean cooking crowd. There's a set lunch *menú* costing 1200 ptas.

Getting There & Away Barcelona Bus (☎ 972 50 50 29) runs to Girona (500 ptas, 50 minutes) seven times per day, and on to Barcelona six times per day (1750 ptas, 2¼ hours).

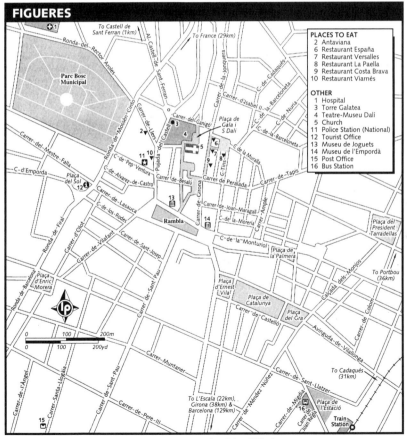

FIGUERES

PLACES TO EAT
2 Antaviana
6 Restaurant España
7 Restaurant Versalles
8 Restaurant La Paella
9 Restaurant Costa Brava
10 Restaurant Viarnés

OTHER
1 Hospital
3 Torre Galatea
4 Teatre-Museu Dalí
5 Church
11 Police Station (National)
12 Tourist Office
13 Museu de Joguets
14 Museu de l'Empordà
15 Post Office
16 Bus Station

euro currency converter €1 = 166 ptas

Figueres is on the railway between Barcelona, Girona and Portbou on the French border, and there are regular connections to Girona (330 ptas to 380 ptas, 30 to 40 minutes) and Barcelona (1125 ptas to 1290 ptas, 2¼ hours).

Costa Brava

The rugged Costa Brava stretches from Blanes (about 60km north-east of Barcelona) to the French border. Although parts of it are truly awful holiday resorts jam-packed with the cheap-charter crowd in search of sand, sun and drinks (Lloret de Mar is a prime example of what to avoid), there are some equally spectacular locations.

If you're driving, it is quite possible to choose a spot anywhere along the coast for a day trip. Those relying on public transport may find it a bit of a stretch and should plan on staying over at least one night. In the peak months of July and August, finding lodgings can be difficult.

Tossa de Mar Marc Chagall called it Blue Paradise. A small white village backing onto a curved bay that ends in a headland protected by medieval walls and towers, Tossa is the first truly pleasant stop on the road north along the Costa Brava. In summer, boats with glass bottoms will take you to some enchanting little coves and beaches to the south and north of the main beach, Platja Gran.

The bus station is just off Plaça de les Nacions sense Estat (Stateless Nations Plaza). Almost next door, at Avinguda del Pelegrí 25, is the tourist office (☎ 972 34 01 08).

On Carrer de Tarull, beside the church in the old town, *Restaurant Marina* (☎ 972 34 07 57) at No 6 offers a fairly good *menú* for 1400 ptas and also does some economical specials such as chicken, chips, salad and beer for 500 ptas. *Es Molí* (☎ 972 34 14 14) at No 5, farther up the same street, serves up classier local cooking, including good prawns and *fideuá* (similar to paella but with vermicelli noodles as the base), and has a tranquil, shady garden patio. There are *menús* for 2700 ptas and a gourmet version for 4815 ptas.

SARFA (☎ 972 34 09 03) runs to/from Barcelona's Estació del Nord up to 10 times daily (1079 ptas, 1¼ hours). In summer you could get a *rodalies/cercanías* train to Blanes (see the Getting Around chapter) and pick up a boat for Tossa. Crucetours (☎ 972 37 26 92), Viajes Marítimos (☎ 608 93 64 76) and Dolfi-Jet (☎ 972 37 19 39) run boats.

Palafrugell & Around One of the most spectacular coastlines on the Costa Brava is that around Palafrugell and there are several low-key beach resorts that truly warrant some effort. A little way inland, Palafrugell is the local transport hub. From there you can fan out to **Calella de Palafrugell**, **Llafranc**, **Tamariu**, **Aigua Blava** and **Fornells de Mar**.

SARFA (☎ 972 30 06 23) runs a bus service from Barcelona's Estació del Nord (1635 ptas, two hours) to Palafrugell up to nine times daily (a few more in summer). Or you can go to Girona first and switch buses there.

In summer, half-hourly buses link Palafrugell to Calella and Llafranc. Only three or four buses daily run to Tamariu.

For the remaining beaches, you need to get to Begur first. Three of the Barcelona–Palafrugell services continue on to Begur.

Fornells de Mar & Aigua Blava A Bus Platges (beach bus) service runs from Plaça de Forgas in Begur to Fornells and Aigua Blava from late June to mid-September.

L'Escala & Empúries L'Escala is a pleasant medium-sized resort on the southern shore of the Golf de Roses. It's close to the ancient town of Empúries (Ampurias in Castilian).

Empúries, founded around 600 BC, was probably the first, and certainly one of the most important, Greek colonies in Iberia. The colony came to be called Emporion (literally, market). In 218 BC, Roman legions set foot on the peninsula here to cut off Hannibal's supply lines during the Second Punic War. By the early first century AD, the Roman and Greek settlements had merged. Emporiae, as the place was then known, was abandoned in the late 3rd century after raids by Germanic tribes. Later, an early Christian basilica and cemetery stood on the site of the Greek town. Then, after over a millennium of use, the whole place disappeared altogether, to be rediscovered by archaeologists at the turn of the 20th century.

Many of the ancient stones now laid bare don't rise more than knee high. You need a little imagination – and perhaps the aid of a taped commentary (300 ptas from the ticket office) – to make the most of this site.

The site opens 10 am to 8 pm from June to September. There's a pedestrian entrance from the seafront promenade in front of the ruins – just follow the coast from L'Escala to reach it. It opens 10 am to 6 pm the rest of the year and the only way in is the vehicle approach from the Figueres road, about 1km from central L'Escala. Admission costs 400 ptas.

L'Escala is famous for its *anchoas* (anchovies) and good fresh local fish, both of which are likely to crop up on menus. The seafront restaurants are mostly expensive but, if your wallet is fat enough, try *Els Pescadors* (☎ *972 77 07 28, Port d'En Perris 5*), on the next bay west from La Platja (five minutes' walk), which does superb baked and grilled seafood, *suquet* (seafood stew) and rice dishes. You will pay from 3000 ptas to 4000 ptas per head unless you opt for the *menú* at 2200 ptas. *L'Olla* and *Volanti*, also on Port d'En Perris, do pizzas for around 700 ptas to 950 ptas.

SARFA has one bus from Barcelona (via Palafrugell) on weekdays (1½ hours), rising to three on Sunday. Five daily run to Figueres (50 minutes) and two to Girona (one hour).

Cadaqués The northern end of the Costa Brava is more barren and, for some tastes, more startling than the coast farther south. The sprawling white village of Cadaqués is one of the highlights of the entire coast. Salvador Dalí spent a lot of time here and in nearby Port Lligat, attracting a stream of celebs to the place.

The pretty town centre is well worth a stroll, and you'll also find a couple of art museums cashing in on the Dalí theme. Twenty minutes' walk from Cadaqués is the **Casa Museu Dalí** in Port Lligat. Visits must be booked (☎ 972 25 80 63) and you are allowed a grand total of about 30 minutes inside as you are guided through. It opens 10.30 am to 9 pm mid-June to mid-September, and 10.30 am to 6 pm Tuesday to Sunday, the rest of the year except mid-January to mid-March (when it closes). Admission costs 1300 ptas (students and seniors 800 ptas).

Restaurant Es Racó (☎ *972 15 94 80, Carrer del Dr Callis 3*) does a fine *parrillada de pescado* (mixed seafood grill) for 2200 ptas per person. Its balcony, overlooking the western half of the beach, catches some breeze.

La Sirena (☎ *972 25 89 74*), in a quiet little patio off Carrer del Call, is a romantic little eating hideaway. The blue-on-white decor is fine and transports you to the classic dreamed-of Mediterranean setting. It closes on Thursday out of high summer.

SARFA (☎ 972 25 87 13) has buses to/from Barcelona (2205 ptas, 2¼ hours) two to five times daily.

WEST OF BARCELONA
Montserrat

Montserrat (Serrated Mountain), 50km north-west of Barcelona, is a 1236m-high mountain of truly weird rock pillars, shaped by wind, rain and frost from a conglomeration of limestone, pebbles and sand that once lay under the sea. With the historic Benedictine Monestir de Montserrat, one of Catalunya's most important shrines, soaring at 725m on its side, it makes a great outing from Barcelona.

The most dramatic approach is by the cable car that swings high across the Llobregat valley from Montserrat-Aeri station, served by regular trains from Barcelona.

From the mountain, on a clear day, you can see as far as the Pyrenees, Barcelona's Tibidabo and even, if you're lucky, Mallorca. It can be a lot colder up on Montserrat than in Barcelona.

EXCURSIONS

Orientation & Information The cable car from Montserrat-Aeri arrives on the mountain just below the monastery. Just above the cable-car station is an information office (☎ 93 877 77 77), open daily from 10 am to 6 pm, with a good free leaflet-map on the mountain and monastery. Past here, a minor road doubles back up to the left to the lower station of the Funicular de Sant Joan. The main road curves round and up to the right, passing the blocks of *Cel.les* (where it is possible to stay overnight), to enter Plaça de Santa Maria at the centre of the monastery complex.

Monestir de Montserrat The monastery was founded in 1025 to commemorate an apparition of the Virgin on the mountain. Wrecked by Napoleon's troops in 1811, then abandoned as a result of anticlerical legislation in the 1830s, it was rebuilt from 1858 onwards. Today, a community of about 80 monks lives here. Pilgrims come from far and wide to venerate the monastery's Black Virgin (La Moreneta), a 12th-century Romanesque wooden sculpture of Mary with the infant Jesus. La Moreneta has been Catalunya's official patron since 1881.

The two-part **Museu de Montserrat** on Plaça de Santa Maria has an excellent collection, ranging from an Egyptian mummy and Gothic altarpieces to art by El Greco, Monet, Degas and Picasso. It opens 9.30 am to 6 pm daily. Admission costs 600 ptas (students 400 ptas).

From Plaça de Santa Maria you enter the courtyard of the 16th-century **basilica**, the monastery's church. The basilica's facade, with its carvings of Christ and the 12 Apostles, dates from 1900, despite its 16th-century plateresque style. Opening times, when you can file past the image of the Black Virgin high above the basilica's main altar, vary according to season. The church opens 9 am to 8 pm (from 8 am on Sunday and holidays), July to September; but tends to close earlier the rest of the year. Follow the signs to the Cambril de la Mare de Déu, to the right of the main basilica entrance.

The **Montserrat Boys' Choir**, or Escolania, reckoned to be Europe's oldest music school, sings in the basilica at 1 and 7 pm Monday to Saturday and 1 pm only on Sunday, except in July. The church fills up quickly so try to arrive early. It is a rare treat as the choir does not often perform outside Montserrat – five concerts per year and a world tour every two years.

On your way out have a look in the room across the courtyard from the basilica entrance, filled with gifts and thank-you messages to the Montserrat Virgin from people who give her the credit for all manner of happy events. The souvenirs range from plaster casts to wedding dresses.

If you want to see where the holy image of the Virgin was discovered, take the Santa Cova funicular down from the main area.

The Mountain You can explore the mountain above the monastery on a web of paths leading to some of the peaks and to 13 empty and rather dilapidated hermitages. The **Funicular de Sant Joan** (580/925 ptas one-way/return) will carry you up the first 250m from the monastery. If you prefer to walk, the road past the funicular's bottom station will lead you up and round to its top station in about one hour (3km).

From the Sant Joan top station, it's a 20-minute stroll (signposted) to the **Sant Joan hermitage**, with fine westward views. More exciting is the one-hour walk north-west, along a path marked with occasional blobs of yellow paint, to Montserrat's highest peak, **Sant Jeroni**, from where there's an awesome sheer drop on the northern side. The walk takes you across the upper part of the mountain, with a close-up experience of some of the weird rock pillars. Many have names: on your way to Sant Jeroni look over to the right for La Prenyada (the pregnant woman), La Mòmia (the mummy), L'Elefant (the elephant), the phallic Cavall Bernat, and El Cap de Mort (the death's head).

Getting There & Away There's a daily bus with the Julià company (☎ 93 490 40 00) to the monastery from Estació d'Autobusos de Sants in Barcelona at 9 am (plus 8 am in July and August) for a return fare of 1400 ptas. It returns at 5 pm.

The alternative is a trip by train and cable car. FGC trains run from Plaça d'Espanya station in Barcelona to Montserrat-Aeri up to 18 times daily. Get the R5 train. Return tickets for 1905 ptas include the cable car between Montserrat-Aeri station and the monastery. The cable car goes about every 15 minutes from 9.25 am to 1.45 pm and 3 to 6.45 pm, Monday to Saturday. The whole trip takes a little over an hour. The price for the cable car alone is 625/950 ptas (one-way/return).

FGC offers various all-in-one tickets. Return-trip tickets for 2800 ptas include the train, cable car to/from Montserrat-Aeri, two metro rides and unlimited use of the funiculars. For 4100 ptas you can have all this, plus museum entrance and a modest dinner at the self-service restaurant.

Probably the most straightforward route by car from Barcelona is by Avinguda Diagonal, Via Augusta, the Túnel de Vallvidrera and the A-18. Turn onto the BP-1213,

just past Terrassa, and follow it 18km north-west to the C-1411. Then head a couple of kilometres south on this road to Monistrol de Montserrat, from where a road snakes about 7km up the mountain to the monastery.

Penedès Wine Country

Some of Spain's best wines come from the area centred on the towns of Sant Sadurní d'Anoia and Vilafranca del Penedès. Sant Sadurní d'Anoia, a half-hour train ride west of Barcelona, is the capital of *cava*, Spanish 'Champagne'. Vilafranca del Penedès, 12km down the track, is the heart of the Penedès DO, which produces noteworthy light still whites. A number of wineries open their doors to visitors and there'll often be a free glass included in the tour, and plenty more for sale. It's a little ad hoc and often you need to call ahead to arrange a visit.

Simply touring around the area in the hope of bumping into wineries is unlikely to yield results. See the Vilafranca del Penedès

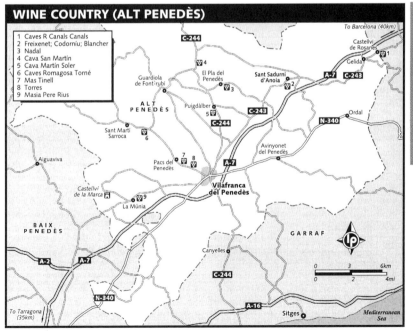

euro currency converter €1 = 166 ptas

section later for tips on where to gather information before embarking on a wine excursion.

Sant Sadurní d'Anoia A hundred or so wineries around Sant Sadurní produce 140 million bottles of cava per year – something like 85% of the national output. Cava is made by the same method as French Champagne and is gaining ground in international markets. Catalan vintners claim that cava

exports rose 30% in 1997! If you happen to be in town in October, you may catch the Mostra de Caves i Gastronomia, a cava- and food-tasting fest that has been held annually since 1997 – this is an opportunity to taste the products of a lot of competing wineries.

Vilafranca del Penedès Vilafranca is larger than Sant Sadurní and much more interesting. The tourist office (☎ 93 892 03 58) on Plaça de la Vila opens 9 am to 1 pm

What's in a Label?

If your bottle is labelled DO *(denominación de origen)*, you can be sure of reasonable quality. DO refers to those areas that have maintained a consistently high quality of wine over a long period. In Catalunya there are nine DO wine areas. Only some wines from Spain's premier wine-growing region, La Rioja, go one better – DOC, or *denominación de origen calificada*. These labels are indicative only. Some fine wines have no such tags.

Other categories of wine, in descending order, are: *denominación de origen provisional* (DOp), *vino de la tierra*, *vino comarcal* and *vino de mesa* (ordinary table wine).

Vino joven is wine made for immediate drinking while *vino de crianza* has to have been stored for certain minimum periods. *Reserva* requires storage of at least three years for reds and two years for whites and rosés. *Gran reserva* is a title permitted for particularly good vintages. These wines must have spent at least two calendar years in storage and three in the bottle. They're mostly reds.

In Catalunya, the nine DO wines come from points all over the region but the bulk are from the Penedès area, which pumps out almost two million hectolitres per year. The other eight DO wine-growing areas, spread as far apart as the Empordà area around Figueres in the north and the Terra Alta zone around Gandesa in the south-west, together have an output of about half that produced in Penedès.

The Catalan regional government decided in 1998 to introduce a new, more generic label, VCPRD (*vinos de calidad producidos en una región determinada* – quality wines produced in a defined region). The idea was to introduce more flexibility to compete with imports. The present DO rules make the mixing of grape varieties from various zones difficult.

As always, there is more to all this than meets the eye. Some of the bigger winemakers were in favour of the change, but opponents were vociferous, claiming that smaller operators would be squashed in an avalanche of generic mediocrity. The Catalan wine industry has been on the boil for some time with court cases and polemics over dodgy competitive practices, shoddy cava production by big name producers and so on. The VCPRD idea was also challenged in the courts which, apparently unmoved by cries that Catalunya's drinking product would suffer, decided the labelling could go ahead.

Those in favour of the new system say the ruling will not affect quality but rather give Catalan winemakers the kind of room to manoeuvre that Australian and Californian competitors have. The system had still not been implemented at the time of writing.

For on-line information about Catalan wines and cava, visit www.interceller.com (Catalan and Castilian only). From here, there are plenty of links to related subjects and individual wineries.

and 4 to 7 pm, Tuesday to Friday, 10 am to 1 pm on Saturday (it also opens 5 to 8 pm on Saturday and 10 am to 1 pm on Sunday in summer). This is a good place to look for information on wineries. Tourist office staff can direct you to several places aside from the big boys so you can see how wine and cava are made and get a glass or two at the end. They also sell a booklet called *L'Alt Penedès* (800 ptas), which lists most of the area's wineries open to the public.

A good place to get a glass or two on the area's wines is the Celler Cooperatiu Vilafranca del Penedès (☎ 93 817 10 35), Carrer del Bisbe Morgades 18–24. It's about a five-minute walk from the tourist office.

One block north of the tourist office, the mainly Gothic **Basilica de Santa Maria** faces the combined **Museu de Vilafranca** and **Museu del Vi** (wine museum) across Plaça de Jaume I.

For further information on wineries and wines in the area, you could approach Penedès Denominació d'Origen (☎ 93 890 48 11, fax 93 890 47 54), Plaça de l' Agora. Located near the A-7 motorway on the way to Tarragona, this is an association of all DO wineries in the region.

Visiting Wineries To do a tour of the area you will need your own transport. As already hinted, you should not expect to wander into any old winery you pass. Many open their doors to the public, if at all, only at limited times during the weekend. The more enthusiastic ones will show you around the place, give you an idea of how wines and/or cava are made and finish off with a glass or two. Since cava is the area's single biggest product, it stands to reason that many of the wineries that open to the public specialise in bubbly rather than in still wines. The following list is by no means exhaustive but should get you started:

Blancher
(☎ 93 818 32 86) Plaça del Pont Romà 5, Sant Sadurní d'Anoia. Just off the town's main road, La Rambla de la Generalitat, this rather huge place has been going since 1955. There are hourly tours from 10.30 am to 1.30 pm at the

weekend. Visits will lead you around the plant and there is also a small museum. During the week you need to call ahead. If you want to picnic on the grounds, they like you to buy a bottle of their cava.

Cava Martín Soler
(☎ 93 898 82 20) Located in an attractive farmhouse surrounded by vineyards, at Puigdàlber, 8km north of Vilafranca. This winery only makes various kinds of cava. It opens for visits 9 am to 1 pm and 2.30 to 7 pm Monday to Friday, and 10 am to 2 pm weekends and holidays.

Cava San Martín
(☎ 93 898 82 74) Just off the C-244, about 10km north of Vilafranca, this small, friendly outfit produces several varieties of wine, including whites, reds and rosés. It is most proud of its bubbly, though. It's best to call ahead.

Caves R Canals Canals
(☎ 93 775 54 46) In Castellví de Rosanes, just off exit 25 from the A-7 south from Barcelona, this cellar opens for visits on Saturday and Sunday morning. You have to call ahead.

Caves Romagosa Torné
(☎ 93 899 13 53) This winery at Finca La Serra is on the road to Sant Martí Sarroca. Again, although it produces other wines, cava is the star. It opens 9 am to 1 pm and 4 to 8 pm Monday to Saturday, 10 am to 2 pm on Sunday and holidays. By the way, if you get here, try to move on to the charming little town of Sant Martí Sarroca.

Codorníu
(☎ 93 818 32 32) Bottled for the first time in 1872, it remains one of the best wineries around. The Codorníu headquarters, a modernist building at the entry to Sant Sadurní town by road from Barcelona, opens for free visits 9 am to 5 pm, Monday to Friday, and 9 am to 1 pm Saturday and Sunday. Codorníu's Web site is at www.codorniu.es.

Freixenet
(☎ 93 891 70 00) This is the best-known cava company (although not everyone agrees its bubbly is the best), based next to the train station in Sant Sadurní d'Anoia at Carrer de Joan Sala 2. It is one of about 20 wineries in Sant Sadurní itself that open, at times, to visitors, although many require you to book ahead. Free tours are given at 9, 10 and 11.30 am and 3 and 5 pm, Monday to Thursday (also Friday mornings, Saturday and Sunday in December). Freixenet's Web site is at www.freixenet.es.

Mas Tinell
(☎ 93 817 05 86) Here is a good drop that ended up on the table for the Infanta Cristina's wedding. Mas Tinell also does some still wines and

technically opens to visitors 9 am to noon and 3 to 6 pm, Monday to Saturday, although they prefer you to call ahead.

Masia Pere Rius

(☎ 93 891 82 74) This cute little farmhouse lies just outside La Múnia on the B-212 about 5km south-west of Vilafranca. Here they show how cava is made and will invite you to taste some of the wines as well as the bubbly. It opens 10 am to 8 pm Monday to Saturday, 10 am to 3 pm Sunday and holidays.

Nadal

(☎ 93 898 80 11) Nadal is just outside the hamlet of El Pla del Penedès. It has been producing cava since 1943. The centrepiece of the place is a fine *masia* (or Catalan country farmhouse), where you can join organised visits in order to become acquainted with the whole process of producing the sparkling wine, including vine-growing and harvesting. A tasting will round off the visit. You can join in at 10 and 11 am, noon and 4, 5 and 6 pm on weekdays; 10.30 am to 12.30 pm on Saturday.

Torres

(☎ 93 817 74 87) Three kilometres north-west of the town centre of Vilafranca on the BP-2121 road near Pacs del Penedès, this is the area's premier winery. The Torres family tradition dates from the 17th century, but the family company, in its present form, was founded in 1870. It revolutionised Spanish winemaking back in the 1960s by introducing new temperature-controlled stainless-steel technology and French grape varieties that helped produce much lighter wines than the traditional heavy Spanish plonk. One of the biggest names in the wine world, the Torres enterprise also has wineries in California and Chile. It produces an enormous array of red and white wines of all qualities, using many grape varieties, including: Chardonnay, Sauvignon Blanc, Merlot, Cabernet Sauvignon, Pinot Noir and more locally specific ones such as Parellada, Garnacha and Tempranillo. Torres opens for visits 9 am to 6 pm Monday to Saturday; and 9 am to 1 pm Sunday and holidays.

Getting There & Away Up to three rodalies trains an hour run from Barcelona Sants to Sant Sadurní (335 ptas, 40 minutes) and Vilafranca (410 ptas, 50 minutes). By car, take the A-2, then the A-7 and then follow the exit signs.

Conca de Barberà

This hilly, green back-country district comes as a refreshing surprise in the otherwise drab

---

An Old Oak Tree

When, back in 1498, Javier Codorníu bought the land that he would turn into the first vineyards of Sant Sadurní d'Anoia, the single greatest feature of his purchase was a hundred-year-old oak tree.

In the following centuries a good number of the surrounding country's business deals were solemnly sworn in the shade of the grand old tree. They say that in those days a witnessed handshake was as cast iron a guarantee as anyone could expect.

By the time the first *cava* was bottled in 1872, the tree had become the symbol of the Raventós i Blanc family that ran the winery, and also of the Can Codorníu farm. For Manuel Raventós, the grandson of the original producer of the farm's cava, protecting the ancient oak has taken priority even over the business of winemaking. After around 600 years, the grand old oak tree of Can Codorníu is not only in good health, it's even growing!

---

flatlands of south-western Catalunya. Vineyards and woods succeed one another across rolling green hills, studded with occasional medieval villages and monasteries.

Monestir de Poblet The walls of this abbey devoted to Santa Maria, as well as being a defensive measure, also symbolised the monks' isolation from the vanities of the outside world. A gate gives access to a long, uneven square, the Plaça Major, flanked by several dependencies including the small Romanesque **Capella de Santa Caterina**. The nearby Porta Daurada is so called because its bronze panels were overlaid with gold to suitably impress the visiting Emperor Felipe II in 1564.

Once inside the **Porta Reial** (royal gate), flanked by hefty octagonal towers, you will be led to the grand cloister, of Romanesque origins but largely Gothic in style. From there you enter the church to witness the sculptural glory in alabaster that is the *retablo* (altarpiece) and Panteón de los Reyes (Kings Pantheon). The raised alabaster coffins contain

EXCURSIONS

such greats as Jaume I (the conqueror of Mallorca and Valencia) and Pere III.

The monastery opens 10 am to 12.30 pm and 3 to 6 pm (to 5.30 pm in winter). Admission costs 500 ptas (students 300 ptas). One-hour guided tours (in Catalan and/or Spanish) start every 15 to 30 minutes.

If you have time, you should explore the surrounding area, particularly the walled town of **Montblanc**, 8km away.

Regular trains from Barcelona to Tarragona via Reus (Ca4 Regional line) stop at Montblanc and L'Espluga de Francolí – the monastery is a 40-minute walk from the latter.

SOUTH OF BARCELONA
Sitges
postcode 08870 • pop 17,600

Sitges attracts everyone from jet-setters to young travellers, honeymooners to weekending families, Barcelona night owls to an international gay crowd – anyone after a good time. The beach is long and sandy, the nightlife thumps until breakfast and there are lots of groovy boutiques if you need to spruce up your wardrobe. In winter Sitges can be dead but it wakes up with vengeance for *carnaval*, when the gay crowd puts on an outrageous show.

Sitges has been fashionable in one way or another since the 1890s, when it became an avant-garde, art-world hang-out. It has been one of Spain's most anticonventional, anything-goes resorts since the 1960s.

Orientation The main landmark is the Església de Sant Bartomeu i Santa Tecla atop a small rocky elevation that separates the 2km-long main beach to the south-west from the smaller, quieter Platja de Sant Sebastià to the north-east. The old part of town climbs gently inland from the church area, with the train station some 500m back, at the top of Avinguda d'Artur Carbonell.

Information The tourist office (☎ 93 894 42 51, fax 93 894 43 05), Carrer de Sínia Morera 1, opens 9 am to 9 pm daily in July and August. It opens 9 am to 2 pm and 4 to 6.30 pm Monday to Friday, 10 am to 1 pm

Saturday, the rest of the year. To book accommodation in advance you can also call (from within Spain) ☎ 902 10 34 28. The office's Web site is at www.sitgestur.com (in Spanish only at time of writing; English and French language sites are under construction).

Museums The **Museu Cau Ferrat** on Carrer de Fonollar was built in the 1890s as a house-cum-studio by Santiago Rusiñol – a co-founder of Els Quatre Gats in Barcelona, and the man who attracted the art world to Sitges.

Next door is the **Museu Maricel del Mar**, with art and artistry from the Middle Ages to the 20th century. The museum is part of the Palau Maricel, a stylistic fantasy built around 1910 by Miquel Utrillo. The **Museu Romàntic** at Carrer de Sant Gaudenci 1 recreates the lifestyle of a 19th-century Catalan land-owning family and contains a collection of several hundred antique dolls.

All three of the museums open 10 am to 1.30 pm and 3 to 6.30 pm Tuesday to Friday, 10 am to 7 pm on Saturday and 10 am to 3 pm on Sunday. Admission to each costs 500 ptas, or 900 ptas for all three.

Beaches The main beach is divided by a series of breakwaters into sections with different names. A pedestrian promenade runs its whole length. Sitges also has two nudist beaches – one exclusively gay – about 20 minutes' walk beyond the Hotel Terramar at the far end of the main beach.

Places to Eat You'll be lucky to find a *menú* for less than 1200 ptas. The self-service *Los Vikingos* (☎ 93 894 96 87, Carrer del Marques de Montroig 7–9) in the thick of the action, does tolerable pasta, pizza and seafood starting at 850 ptas.

Carrer de Sant Pau has a string of good restaurants including the Basque *Eguzki* (☎ 93 811 03 20) at No 3, which has good tapas and a mixed menu of seafood and meat mains from 1000 ptas to 1800 ptas. *Restaurant Miami* (☎ 93 894 02 06) at No 11 has a decent four-course *menú* costing 1875 ptas. It closes on Tuesday.

euro currency converter €1 = 166 ptas

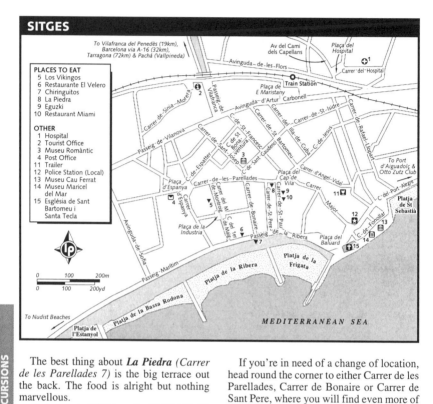

SITGES

PLACES TO EAT
5 Los Vikingos
6 Restaurante El Velero
7 Chiringuitos
8 La Piedra
9 Eguzki
10 Restaurant Miami

OTHER
1 Hospital
2 Tourist Office
3 Museu Romàntic
4 Post Office
11 Trailer
12 Police Station (Local)
13 Museu Cau Ferrat
14 Museu Maricel
   del Mar
15 Església de Sant
   Bartomeu i
   Santa Tecla

The best thing about *La Piedra (Carrer de les Parellades 7)* is the big terrace out the back. The food is alright but nothing marvellous.

Restaurante El Velero (☎ 93 894 20 51, Passeig de la Ribera 38) is a fairly classy fish and seafood joint with most mains costing 1500 ptas or more. It closes on Sunday evening and Wednesday. For real seaside dining you could munch away on expensive tapas at the two *chiringuitos* on Passeig de la Ribera.

Entertainment Much of Sitges' nightlife happens on one short pedestrian strip packed with humanity right through the night in summer: Carrer del 1er de Maig, Plaça de la Industria and Carrer del Marques de Montroig – all in a short line off the seafront Passeig de la Ribera. Carrer del 1er de Maig – or Calle del Pecado (Sin Street) – vibrates to the volume of 10 or so disco-bars all trying to outdo each other in decibels.

If you're in need of a change of location, head round the corner to either Carrer de les Parellades, Carrer de Bonaire or Carrer de Sant Pere, where you will find even more of the same.

Carrer de Sant Bonaventura has a string of gay bars, mostly behind closed doors. *Trailer (Carrer d'Àngel Vidal 36)* is a very popular gay disco.

Some distance from the centre of town are some of the big discos, such as *Pachá (☎ 93 894 22 98)*, in Vallpineda, and the local branch of Barcelona's *Otto Zutz Club* in Port d'Aiguadolç where you will also find other bars along the waterfront.

Getting There & Away From about 6 am to 10 pm, four rodalies trains per hour run from Barcelona Sants to Sitges (335 ptas, 30 minutes). The best road from Barcelona to Sitges is the A-16 tollway. You can call taxis on either ☎ 93 894 35 94 or ☎ 93 894 13 29.

Tarragona
postcode 43080 • pop 112,795
Tarragona was first occupied by the Romans, who called it Tarraco, in 218 BC. In 27 BC Emperor Augustus made it the capital of his new Tarraconensis province – most of what is now Spain – and lived here till 25 BC while directing campaigns in Cantabria and Asturias. It would not have been long afterwards that Tarragona's most famous son, Pontius Pilate, was supposedly born here. Tarragona was abandoned when the Muslims arrived in 714 AD, but reborn as the seat of a Christian archbishopric in 1089. Today it's a mainly modern city, but its rich Roman remains and fine medieval cathedral make it an absorbing place.

Orientation The main street is Rambla Nova, which runs roughly north-west from a cliff top overlooking the Mediterranean. A couple of blocks to the east, and parallel, is Rambla Vella, which marks the beginning of the old town and which follows the line of the Via Augusta, the Roman road from Rome to Cádiz.

The train station is 500m south-west of Rambla Nova, near the seafront, and the bus station is about 2km inland, on Plaça Imperial de Tàrraco.

Information The main tourist office (☎ 977 24 50 64), Carrer Major 39, opens 10 am to 2 pm and 4.30 to 7 pm Monday to Friday, 10 am to 2 pm at weekends and holidays (and extra hours from July to September).

Catedral Tarragona's cathedral is a treasure house. Built between 1171 and 1331 on the site of the Roman city's temple, it combines Romanesque and Gothic features, as typified by the main facade on Plaça de la Seu. The entrance is by the cloister on the north-western side of the building.

The cloister has Gothic vaulting and Romanesque carved capitals. Rooms off the cloister house the Museu Diocesà, with an extensive collection extending from Roman hairpins to some lovely 12th- to 14th-century polychrome woodcarvings of a breast-feeding Virgin.

The interior of the cathedral, over 100m long, is Romanesque at the north-eastern end and Gothic at the south-western end.

The cathedral opens 10 am to 7 pm daily (except Sunday and holidays), July to mid-October; 10 am to 1 pm and 4 to 7 pm April to June and mid-October to mid-November; 10 am to 2 pm the rest of the year. The 300 ptas charge includes a detailed booklet.

Museu d'Història de Tarragona This museum comprises four separate Roman sites and the 14th-century noble mansion, which now serves as the **Museu Casa Castellarnau**, Carrer dels Cavallers 14.

Start with the **Pretori i Circ Romans** on Plaça del Rei, which includes part of the vaults of the Roman circus where chariot races were held. The circus, 300m long, stretched from here to beyond Plaça de la Font. Close to the beach is the well-preserved **Amfiteatre Romà**, where gladiators battled each other, or wild animals, to the death. In its arena are the remains of 6th- and 12th-century churches built to commemorate the martyrdom of the Christian bishop Fructuosus and two deacons, whom they say were burnt alive here in 259.

By Carrer de Lleida are remains of the **Fòrum Romà**, dominated by several imposing columns. The north-western half of this site was occupied by a judicial basilica (where legal disputes were settled), from which the rest of the forum stretched downhill to the south-west. Linked to the site by a footbridge is another excavated area with a stretch of a Roman street. This forum was the hub of public life for the Roman town but was less important, and much smaller, than the provincial forum, the navel of all Tarraconensis province.

The **Passeig Arqueològic** is a peaceful walk around part of the perimeter of the old town between two lines of city walls; the inner ones are mainly Roman while the outer ones were put up by the British in the War of the Spanish Succession.

All these places open 9 or 10 am to 9 pm Tuesday to Saturday, 9 am to 3 pm on Sunday, June to September; 10 am to 1.30 pm and 4 to 6.30 pm Tuesday to Saturday, 10 am

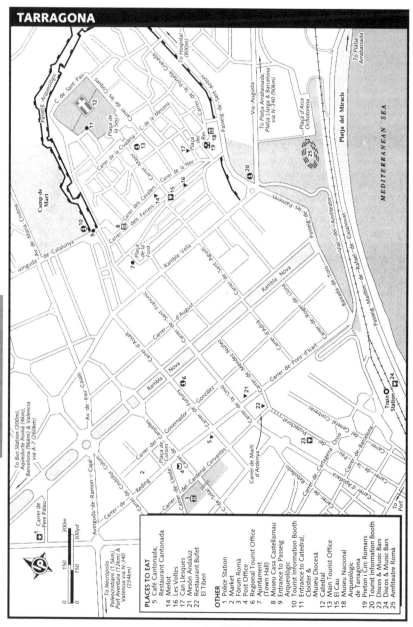

TARRAGONA

PLACES TO EAT
5 Cafè Cantonada;
  Restaurant Cantonada
14 Merlot
16 Les Voltes
17 Can Llesques
21 Mesón Andaluz
22 Restaurant Bufet
  El Tiberi

OTHER
1 Police Station
2 Market
3 Forum Romà
4 Post Office
6 Regional Tourist Office
7 Ajuntament
  (Town Hall)
8 Museu Casa Castellarnau
9 Entrance to Passeig
  Arqueològic
10 Tourist Information Booth
11 Entrance to Catedral,
  Cloister &
  Museu Diocesà
12 Catedral
13 Main Tourist Office
15 El Cau
18 Museu Nacional
  Arqueologic
  de Tarragona
19 Pretori i Circ Romans
20 Tourist Information Booth
23 Discos & Music Bars
24 Discos & Music Bars
25 Amfiteatre Romà

to 2 pm on Sunday and holidays, the rest of the year. Admission to each costs 300 ptas.

Museu Nacional Arqueològic de Tarragona This carefully presented museum on Plaça del Rei gives further insight into Roman Tarraco, although most explanatory material is in Catalan or Castilian. Exhibits include part of the Roman city walls, frescoes, sculpture and pottery. A highlight is the large, almost complete *Mosaic de Peixos de la Pineda* showing fish and sea creatures. In the section on everyday arts you can admire ancient fertility aids including an outsized stone penis, symbol of the god Priapus. The museum opens 10 am to 8 pm Tuesday to Saturday in summer, and 10 am to 1.30 pm and 4 to 7 pm on those days during the rest of the year. It opens from 10 am to 2 pm on Sunday and holidays throughout the year; admission costs 400 ptas and entitles you to enter the museum at the **Necròpolis Paleocristians**. This large Christian cemetery of late Roman and Visigothic times is on Passeig de la Independència on the western edge of town and boasts some surprisingly elaborate tombs. Unfortunately only its small museum was open at the time of writing.

Beaches The town beach, **Platja del Miracle**, is reasonably clean but can get terribly crowded. **Platja Arrabassada**, 1km northeast across the headland, is longer, and **Platja Llarga**, beginning 2km farther out, stretches for about 3km. Bus Nos 1 and 9 from the Balcó stop on Via Augusta go to both (110 ptas). You can get the same buses along Rambla Vella and Rambla Nova.

Places to Eat For Catalan food, head for the stylish *Restaurant Bufet El Tiberi (Carrer de Martí d'Ardenya 5)*, which offers an all-you-can-eat buffet for about 1450 ptas per person. It closes on Sunday night and Monday.

Nearby *Mesón Andaluz (Carrer de Pons d'Icart 3)* is a backstreet local favourite with a good three-course *menú* that costs 1500 ptas. *Café Cantonada (Carrer de Fortuny 23)* has reasonable tapas; next door,

Restaurant Cantonada has pizzas and pasta starting at around 850 ptas.

If cheese is your thing, try a platter *(taula de formatges)* at *Can Llesques* (☎ 977 22 29 06, Carrer de Natzaret 6), a pleasant spot looking onto Plaça del Rei. They do a lot of other dishes too.

Perhaps you'd like to eat under the vaults of the former Roman circus? *Les Voltes* (☎ 977 23 06 51, Carrer de Trinquet Vell 12) has set out its dining area on a couple of different levels. The food itself is a little overpriced for what you are served, but the *menú del día* is not bad at 1500 ptas.

One of Tarragona's seriously classy addresses is the understated *Merlot* (☎ 977 22 06 52, Carrer dels Cavallers 6). All sorts of inventive dishes, starting with Catalan classics as a base, are served in this refreshing place. The heavy exposed stone walls are lightened by paintings and other decoration. You'll probably part company with about 4000 ptas. It closes on Sunday and Monday lunchtime.

Entertainment A cool hangout in a Roman circus vault is *El Cau (Carrer de Trinquet Vell)*. Otherwise the main concentration of nightlife is along the waterfront behind the train station, and in some of the streets in front of it, such as along Carrer de la Pau del Protectorat.

Getting There & Away Up to 40 regional and long-distance trains per day run to/from Barcelona Passeig de Gràcia via Sants. The cheapest fare costs 660 ptas and the journey takes one to 1½ hours. Only three of them stop at Sitges (one hour from Tarragona). There are buses too but the train is easier.

Port Aventura

Port Aventura (☎ 902 20 22 20), 7km west of Tarragona, is Spain's biggest and best funfair-adventure park. If you have money to spare (admission costs 4600 ptas for adults and 3400 ptas for children aged from five to 12), it makes an amusing day out, especially if you have anklebiters in tow. In 1998 Universal Pictures Studios bought up the park and have begun filling it with Americanisms that may or may not appeal. Woody Woodpecker is the new mascot of a park that is billed as a 'world of fun for all ages'. Rocky & Bullwinkle, that famous Catalan pair, have also been catapulted to star status. Sarcasm aside, the park has plenty of spine-tingling rides and other attractions. The big new addition is a virtual submarine created at the staggering cost of 4.5 million pesetas.

The funfair opens from 10 am to 8 pm (to 10 pm at the weekend, to midnight from mid-June to mid-September) from Easter to the end of October. Night tickets, valid from 7 pm, cost 3400 ptas.

Trains run to Port Aventura's own station, about 1km walk from the site, several times a day from Tarragona and Barcelona (1305 ptas return). By road, take exit 35 from the A-7, or the N-340 from Tarragona. Parking costs 600 ptas.

Language

Barcelona is a bilingual city, with both the local Catalan and Spanish (more accurately Castilian – *castellano*) spoken by just about everyone. Indeed, for every Catalan intent on speaking the local tongue there seems to be another who'll favour Castilian. It *is* true that the signs and menus you read will more often than not be in Catalan.

Foreigners will encounter no ill-feeling for muddling through in Castilian – that in itself is appreciated. If you go the whole hog and try your hand at Catalan, you should earn extra brownie points. It's worth the effort to try at least one, as English is not as widely spoken as many travellers seem to expect.

Castilian Spanish

Spanish nouns are marked for gender (either masculine or feminine) and adjectives will vary according to the gender of the noun they modify. Where necessary, both forms are given for the words and phrases below – the masculine generally ends in 'o', the feminine in 'a'.

Pronunciation
Vowels

Unlike English, each of the vowels has a uniform pronunciation which doesn't vary. For example, the letter 'a' has one pronunciation rather than the numerous ones we find in English, such as in 'cake', 'care', 'cat', 'cart' and 'call'. Many words have a written acute accent. This accent (as in *días*) indicates a stressed syllable; it doesn't change the sound of the vowel. Vowels are pronounced clearly even if they are in unstressed positions or at the end of a word.

a	somewhere between the 'a' in 'cat' and the 'a' in 'cart'
e	as in 'met'
i	somewhere between the 'i' in 'marine' and the 'i' in 'flip'
o	similar to the 'o' in 'hot'
u	as in 'put'

Consonants

Most consonants are pronounced the same as their English counterparts. The pronunciation of others varies according to which vowel follows. The Spanish alphabet also contains the letter ñ, which isn't found in the English alphabet. Until recently, the clusters **ch** and **ll** were also officially separate consonants, and you're likely to encounter many situations (eg, in lists and dictionaries) in which they are still treated that way.

b	soft, as the 'v' in 'van'; also (less commonly) as in 'book' when word-initial or when preceded by a nasal such as **m** or **n**
c	as the 'th' in 'thin'
ch	as in 'choose'
d	sometimes not pronounced at all
g	as in 'go' when initial or before **a**, **o** or **u**; elsewhere much softer. Before **e** or **i** it's a harsh, breathy sound, a bit like 'ch' in Scottish *loch*
h	always silent
j	a harsh, guttural sound similar to the 'ch' in Scottish *loch*
ll	similar to the 'y' in 'yellow'
ñ	a nasal sound like the 'ni' in 'onion' or the 'ny' in 'canyon'
q	always followed by a silent **u** and either **e** (as in *que*) or **i** (as in *aquí*); the combined sound of 'qu' is like the 'k' in 'kick'
r	a rolled 'r' sound; longer and stronger when initial or doubled
s	often not pronounced, especially at the end of a word; thus *pescados* (fish) is pronounced 'peh-cow' in Andalucía
v	same as **b**
x	as the 'x' in 'taxi' when between two vowels; as the 's' in 'say' before a consonant
z	as the 'th' in 'thin'

Greetings & Civilities

Hello.	*¡Hola!*
Goodbye.	*¡Adiós!*
Yes.	*Sí.*
No.	*No.*
Please.	*Por favor.*
Thank you.	*Gracias.*
You're welcome.	*De nada.*
Excuse me.	*Perdón/Perdone.*
Sorry/Excuse me.	*Lo siento/Discúlpeme.*

Useful Phrases

Do you speak English?	*¿Habla inglés?*
Does anyone speak English?	*¿Hay alguien que hable inglés?*
I understand.	*Entiendo.*
I don't understand.	*No entiendo.*
Just a minute.	*Un momento.*
Could you write it down, please?	*¿Puede escribirlo, por favor?*
How much is it?	*¿Cuánto cuesta/vale?*

Getting Around

What time does the ... leave/arrive?	*¿A qué hora sale/ llega el ...?*
boat	*barco*
bus (city)	*autobús/bus*
bus (intercity)	*autocar*
train	*tren*
metro/ underground	*metro*

next	*próximo*
first	*primer*
last	*último*

I'd like a ... ticket.	*Quisiera un billete ...*
one-way	*sencillo*
return	*de ida y vuelta*
1st class	*de primera clase*
2nd class	*de segunda clase*

Where is the bus stop?	*¿Dónde está la parada de autobús?*
I want to go to ...	*Quiero ir a ...*
Can you show me (on the map)?	*¿Me puede indicar (en el mapa)?*
Go straight ahead.	*Siga/Vaya todo derecho.*

Turn left.	*Gire a la izquierda.*
Turn right.	*Gire a la derecha.*
near	*cerca*
far	*lejos*

Around Town

I'm looking for ...	*Estoy buscando ...*
a bank	*un banco*
the city centre	*el centro de la ciudad*
the embassy	*la embajada*
my hotel	*mi hotel*
the market	*el mercado*
the police	*la policía*
the post office	*los correos*
public toilets	*los aseos públicos*
a telephone	*un teléfono*
the tourist office	*la oficina de turismo*

the beach	*la playa*
the bridge	*el puente*
the castle	*el castillo*
the cathedral	*la catedral*
the church	*la iglesia*
the hospital	*el hospital*
the lake	*el lago*
the main square	*la plaza mayor*
the mosque	*la mezquita*
the old city	*la ciudad antigua*
the palace	*el palacio*
the ruins	*las ruinas*
the sea	*el mar*
the square	*la plaza*
the tower	*el torre*

Accommodation

Where is a cheap hotel?	*¿Dónde hay un hotel barato?*
What's the address?	*¿Cuál es la dirección?*
Could you write it down, please?	*¿Puede escribirlo, por favor?*
Do you have any rooms available?	*¿Tiene habitaciones libres?*

I'd like ...	*Quisiera ...*
a bed	*una cama*
a single room	*una habitación individual*

a double room	una habitación doble
a room with a bathroom	una habitación con baño
to share a dorm	compartir un dormitorio

How much is it ...?	¿Cuánto cuesta ...?
per night	por noche
per person	por persona

| May I see it? | ¿Puedo verla? |
| Where is the bathroom? | ¿Dónde está el baño? |

Food
breakfast	desayuno
lunch	almuerzo/comida
dinner	cena

I'd like the set menu.	Quisiera el menú del día.
Is service included?	¿El servicio está incluido?
I'm a vegetarian.	Soy vegetariano/ vegetariana.

Time & Dates
What time is it?	¿Qué hora es?
today	hoy
tomorrow	mañana
yesterday	ayer
in the morning	de la mañana
in the afternoon	de la tarde
in the evening	de la noche

Monday	lunes
Tuesday	martes
Wednesday	miércoles
Thursday	jueves
Friday	viernes
Saturday	sábado
Sunday	domingo

January	enero
February	febrero
March	marzo
April	abril
May	mayo
June	junio

Emergencies – Spanish

Help!	¡Socorro!/¡Auxilio!
Call a doctor!	¡Llame a un doctor!
Call the police!	¡Llame a la policía!
Where are the toilets?	¿Dónde están los servicios?
Go away!	¡Váyase!
I'm lost.	Estoy perdido/a.

July	julio
August	agosto
September	setiembre/septiembre
October	octubre
November	noviembre
December	diciembre

Health
I'm ...	Soy ...
diabetic	diabético/a
epileptic	epiléptico/a
asthmatic	asmático/a

I'm allergic to ...	Soy alérgico/a ...
antibiotics	los antibióticos
penicillin	la penicilina

antiseptic	antiséptico
aspirin	aspirina
condoms	preservativos/ condones
contraceptive	anticonceptivo
diarrhoea	diarrea
medicine	medicamento
nausea	náusea
sunblock cream	crema protectora contra el sol
tampons	tampones

Numbers
0	cero
1	uno, una
2	dos
3	tres
4	cuatro
5	cinco
6	seis
7	siete
8	ocho
9	nueve

10	*diez*
11	*once*
12	*doce*
13	*trece*
14	*catorce*
15	*quince*
16	*dieciséis*
17	*diecisiete*
18	*dieciocho*
19	*diecinueve*
20	*veinte*
21	*veintiuno*
22	*veintidós*
23	*veintitrés*
30	*treinta*
31	*treinta y uno*
40	*cuarenta*
50	*cincuenta*
60	*sesenta*
70	*setenta*
80	*ochenta*
90	*noventa*
100	*cien/ciento*
1000	*mil*

one million   *un millón*

Catalan

Pronunciation
Catalan sounds are not hard for an English-speaker to pronounce. You should note, however, that vowels will vary according to whether they occur in stressed or unstressed syllables.

Vowels
a	when stressed, as in 'father'; when unstressed, as in 'about'
e	when stressed, as in 'pet'; when unstressed, as in 'open'
i	as in 'machine'
o	when stressed, as in 'pot'; when unstressed, as in 'do'
u	as the 'u' in 'humid'

Consonants
b	pronounced 'p' at the end of a word
c	hard before **a**, **o** and **u**; soft before **e** and **i**
ç	as the 's' in 'base'
d	pronounced 't' at the end of a word
g	hard before **a**, **o** and **u**; as the 's' in measure before **e** and **i**
h	always silent
j	as the 's' in 'pleasure'
r	a strongly rolled 'r' when at the beginning of a word; as in 'red' when in the middle of a word; often silent at the end of a word
rr	a strongly rolled 'r'
s	as in 'so' at the beginning of a word; as 'z' in the middle of a word
v	as a 'b' in Barcelona; pronounced 'v' in some other areas
x	mostly as in English; sometimes 'sh'

Other letters are approximately as in English. There are a few odd combinations:

l.l	repeat the 'l'
tx	like 'ch'
qu	like 'k'

Greetings & Civilities
Hello.	*Hola!*
Goodbye.	*Adéu!*
Yes.	*Sí.*
No.	*No.*
Please.	*Sisplau/Si us plau.*
Thank you (very much).	*(Moltes) gràcies.*
You're welcome.	*De res.*
Excuse me.	*Perdoni.*
May I?/Do you mind?	*Puc?/Em permet?*
Sorry/Forgive me.	*Ho sento/Perdoni.*
What's your name?	*Com et dius?* (inf) *Com es diu?* (pol)
My name is ...	*Em dic ...*
Where are you from?	*D'on ets?*

Language Difficulties
Do you speak English?	*Parla anglès?*
Could you speak in Castilian please?	*Pot parlar castellà sisplau?*
I understand.	*Ho entenc.*
I don't understand.	*No ho entenc.*

Could you repeat that?	*Pot repetir-ho?*
Could you please write that down?	*Pot escriure-ho, sisplau?*
How do you say ... in Catalan?	*Com es diu ... en català?*

Getting Around

What time does the ... leave?	*A quina hora surt ...?*
flight	*vol*
train	*tren*
bus	*autobús*

I'd like a ... ticket.	*Voldria un bitllet ...*
one-way	*d'anada*
return	*d'anar i tornar*

Where is (the) ...?	*On és ...?*
bus station	*l'estació d'autobusos*
city centre	*el centre de la ciutat*
train station	*l'estació de tren*
tourist office	*l'oficina de turisme*
subway station	*la parada de metro*

How do I get to ...?	*Com puc arribar a ...?*
I want to go to ...	*Vull anar a ...*
Please tell me when we get to ...?	*Pot avisar-me quan arribem a ...?*

baggage claim	*recollida d'equipatges*
departures	*sortides*
exchange	*canvi*
platform	*andana*

Around Town

I'm looking for ...	*Estic buscant ...*
a bank	*un banc*
the city centre	*el centre de la ciutat*
the police	*la policia*
the post office	*correus*
a public toilet	*els lavabos públics*
a restaurant	*un restaurant*
the telephone centre	*la central telefònica*
the tourist office	*l'oficina de turisme*

What time does it open/close?	*A quina hora obren/tanquen?*

I want to change ...	*Voldria canviar ...*
some money	*diners*
travellers cheques	*txecs de viatge*

Accommodation

Is there a campsite/ hotel near here?	*Hi ha algun càmping/ hotel a prop d'aquí?*
Do you have any rooms available?	*Hi ha habitacions lliures?*

I'd like ...	*Voldria ...*
a single room	*una habitació individual*
a double room	*una habitació doble*
to share a dorm	*compartir un dormitori*

I want a room with a ...	*Vull una habitació amb ...*
bathroom	*cambra de bany*
double bed	*llit de matrimoni*
shower	*dutxa*

How much is it per night/person?	*Quant val per nit/persona?*
Does it include breakfast?	*Inclou l'esmorzar?*
Are there any cheaper rooms?	*Hi ha habitacions més barates?*
I'm going to stay for (one week).	*Em quedaré (una setmana).*
I'm leaving now.	*Me'n vaig ara.*

Food

breakfast	*esmorzar*
lunch	*dinar*
dinner	*sopar*
dessert	*postres*
a drink	*una beguda*
Bon appétit/Cheers!	*Salut/Bon profit!*

May I see the menu please?	*Puc veure el menú, sisplau?*
I'd like the set lunch, please.	*Voldria el menú del dia, sisplau.*
The bill, please.	*El compte, sisplau.*

War of Words

Catalan belongs to the group of Western European languages that grew out of Latin (Romance languages), including Italian, French, Castilian and Portuguese. By the 12th century, it was a clearly established language with its own nascent literature.

A Rocky History

The survival or predominance of a language is often closely linked to political and social events dating back centuries, and Catalan's history has certainly been a rocky one.

The language was most closely related to langue d'oc, the southern French derivative of Latin that long reigned supreme as the principal tongue in Gallic lands. The langue d'oc's most conspicuous survivor is the now little-used Provençal.

Until the disaster of the Battle of Muret in 1213 (see History in Facts about Barcelona), Catalan territory extended well across southern France, taking in Roussillon and reaching into Provence. Catalan was spoken, or at least understood, throughout these territories and in what is now Catalunya and Andorra.

In the following couple of hundred years, while the losses of French territory were being compensated by their Mediterranean empire building, the Catalans spread their language south into Valencia, west into Aragón and east to the Balearic Islands (Islas Baleares). The language also reached Sicily and Naples, and the Sardinian town of Alghero is still a Catalan-speaking outpost today.

Dialects

Like most languages, Catalan has its dialects. The main distinction is between western and eastern varieties – the former used in Andorra, western and far southern Catalunya and the Catalan-speaking parts of Aragón and Valencia, the latter in the rest of the Catalan world. Linguistic experts further subdivide these into 12 sub-dialects!

Optimists count about 10 million speakers of Catalan today throughout Spain and in parts of France, but the reality is a little different. Many Valencianos actually prefer Castilian to Catalan and find the whole pan-Catalan phenomenon emanating from nationalist quarters in Barcelona to be profoundly irritating. Indeed, beyond Catalunya, inland northern Valencia and Andorra, you're as likely to hear Castilian spoken as Catalan.

In and around Barcelona itself, much of the population's origins lie in other parts of Spain and, although the second generation has grown up learning Catalan, Castilian still tends to be their first tongue. In Sardinia and France, Italian and French respectively have all but submerged Catalan.

Revival

From 1714 on, the use of Catalan was repeatedly banned. Franco was the last of Spain's rulers to clamp down on it.

Renewed interest in the language first came from intellectual circles with the Renaixença at the end of the 19th century; in rural areas at least, its use had never really waned. Franco loosened the reins a little from the 1960s on, but all education in Catalan schools remained exclusively in Castilian until after the dictator's demise in 1975.

Since Jordi Pujol's nationalist Convergència i Unió (CiU) coalition took control of the Generalitat in 1980, it has waged a campaign to 'normalise' its usage. The Generalitat reckons that 93% of the population in Catalunya understand Catalan and 68% speak it. In Valencia, about half the population speak it, as do 67% in the Balearic Islands.

The big problem is that not nearly as many can write it – the true test of linguistic capacity. Even in Catalunya it's estimated that only 39% write Catalan satisfactorily.

If you find yourself watching chat programmes on local TV you'll occasionally strike comperes speaking Catalan and their interlocutors answering in Castilian.

War of Words

Catalan Today

So tenacious has the CiU's campaign been that in Catalunya today it is virtually impossible to get a public service job without fluency in Catalan. It's not so easy in the private sector either. And just as Franco had all signs in Catalan replaced, Castilian road signs, publicity and the like are now harder and harder to find, although both languages have equal legal status.

Pujol stirred the pot still more in 1998 with his *Llei de Política Lingüística* (Linguistic Policy Law). Socialists and conservatives in and outside Catalunya cried out that Pujol was attempting to impose Catalan monolingualism.

While it doesn't seem unreasonable that public servants, teachers and the like should be able to speak Catalan, it virtually excludes university lecturers, teachers and other professionals from other parts of Spain from working in Catalunya. Castilians see this as a clear case of discrimination and it hardly seems positive for education in the region. In early 2000, the rector of a university in Tarragona found himself in court after having penalised two teachers for distributing exams in Castilian. The prosecution maintained that any action prejudicial to students' (or anyone else's) right to be examined or dealt with in Castilian was unconstitutional.

Some aspects of Pujol's 1998 law have an almost Quixotic touch. The Second 'Additional Disposition' refers to the Generalitat's 'duty' to 'ensure the promotion, use and protection of the Catalan language and generalise and extend knowledge and use of it' in all Catalan territories (ie, all those listed here). One might well wonder what historical justification there could be for bolstering the use of Catalan in Alghero, when it was virtually enforced on locals in the first place, an act of imperialism no less flagrant than any of those of which the Castilians might be accused!

Some Popular Catalan Dishes

allioli – garlic sauce

amanida Catalana – Catalan salad; almost any mix of lettuce, olives, tomatoes, hard-boiled eggs, onion, chicory, celery, green pepper and garlic, with fish, ham or sausage, and mayonnaise or an oil-and-vinegar dressing

arròs a la cassola or *arròs a la Catalana* Catalan paella, cooked in an earthenware pot, without saffron

arròs negre – rice cooked in cuttlefish ink and quite black. It sounds awful but is very good

bacallà a la llauna – salted cod baked in tomato, garlic, parsley, paprika and wine

botifarra amb mongetes – pork sausage with fried white beans

calçots amb romesco – calçots are a type of long onion, delicious as a starter with romesco sauce. Catalans sometimes get together for a *calçotada*, the local version of a BBQ.

cargols – snails, almost a religion in parts of Catalunya; often stewed with *conill* (rabbit) and chilli

coca – a dense, flat pastry, especially popular during Sant Joan (St John) celebrations, when it's decorated with candied peel or pine nuts

crema Catalana – a crème caramel with a burnt toffee sauce

ensaimada mallorquina – a sweet Mallorcan pastry

escalivada – red peppers and aubergines (sometimes onions and tomatoes too), grilled, cooled, peeled, sliced and served with an olive oil, salt and garlic dressing

escudella – a meat, sausage and vegetable stew, the liquid of which is mixed with noodles or rice and served as a soup, followed by the rest served as a main course known as *carn d'olla*. It's generally available in winter only

espinacas a la Catalana – spinach with raisins and pine kernels

esqueixada – salad of shredded *bacallà* (salted cod) with tomato, red pepper, onion, white beans, olives, olive oil and vinegar

fideuá – similar to paella but using vermicelli noodles as the base, it is usually served with tomato and meat/sausage or fish

fricandó – a pork and vegetable stew

fuet – a thin, dried pork sausage, native to Catalunya

mandonguilles amb sipia – meatballs with cuttlefish, a subtly flavoured land–sea combination

mel i mató – honey and fresh cream cheese – simple but delicious

mongetes seques i botifarra – haricot beans with thick pork sausage *music* – a serving of dried fruits and nuts, sometimes mixed with ice cream or a sweetish cream cheese and served with a glass of sweet muscatel wine

pa amb tomàquet (i pernil) – crusty bread rubbed with ripe tomatoes, garlic and olive oil, often topped with cured ham

paella – remember, paella is Valencian in origin – if you only have it once, try to have it in Valencia

pollastre amb escamerlans – chicken with shrimps, another amphibious event

sarsuela (zarzuela) – mixed seafood cooked in *sofregit* with seasonings – it's a Barcelona invention

sobrassada – a spreadable red sausage; a speciality in Mallorca

suquet de peix – fish, potato and tomato soup

tortilla de botifarra – sausage omelette

Here are more words to help you with Catalan-only menus – their Castilian equivalents are given in brackets:

ametller (almendra)	almond
anyell (cordero)	lamb (see *xai*)
bacallà (bacalao)	salted cod
bou (buey)	beef
caldereta	a seafood stew
carxofe (alcachofa)	artichoke
castanya (castaña)	chestnut
ceba (cebolla)	onion
costella (chuleta)	cutlet
cranc (cangrejo/ centello)	crab
entrepà (bocadillo)	bread roll with filling
farcit (relleno)	stuffed
formatge (queso)	cheese
fregit (frito)	fried
gelat (helado)	ice cream
llagosta (langosta)	lobster
llenties (lentejas)	lentils
llet (leche)	milk
llonganissa (longaniza)	pork sausage
oli (aceite)	oil
ostra	oyster
ous (huevos)	eggs
pastís (pastel)	cake/pie
pebre (pimienta)	pepper
peix (pescado)	fish
pernil de la comarca	country-cured ham

pop (pulpo)	octopus
rap (rape)	monkfish
suquet	stew (like a French bouillabaisse)
torrada (tostada)	open toasted sandwich
truita	omelette/tortilla, trout
trucha	trout
xai	lamb

Drinks

tiger nut drink	*orxata*
fruit juice	*suc*
mineral water (plain, no gas)	*aigua mineral (sense gas)*
tap water	*aigua de l'aixeta*
soft drinks	*refrescs*

coffee ...	*cafè ...*
with liquer	*carajillo (cigaló* in northern Catalunya)
with a little milk	*tallat*
with milk	*amb llet*

black coffee	*cafè sol*
long black	*doble*
iced coffee	*cafè gelat*
decaffeinated coffee	*cafè descafeinat*
tea	*te*

Catalunya is famous for its *cava*, the region's 'champagne'.

a beer	*una cervesa*
a champagne	*un cava*
a rum	*un rom*
a whisky	*un whisky*
muscatel	*moscatell*
ratafia (liquer)	*ratafia*

a glass of ... wine	*un vi ...*
red	*negre*
rosé	*rosat*
sparkling	*d'agulla*
white	*blanc*

Shopping

Where can I buy ...?	*On puc comprar ...?*
I'd like to buy ...	*Voldria comprar ...*
How much is this?	*Quant val això?*

Where is the	*On és la/el ... més*
nearest ...?	*propera/proper?*
bookshop	*llibreria*
camera shop	*botiga de fotos*
department store	*gran magatzem*
greengrocer	*botiga de verdures*
	(or *fruiteria*)
launderette	*bugaderia*
market	*mercat*
newsagency	*quiosc*
pharmacy	*farmàcia*
supermarket	*supermercat*
travel agency	*agència de viatges*

condoms	*preservatius/condons*
deodorant	*desodorant*
envelope	*sobre*
magazines	*revistes*
map	*mapa*
newspapers	*diaris*
pen (ballpoint)	*bolígraf*
postcards	*postals*
razor blades	*fulles d'afaitar*
sanitary napkins	*compreses*
shampoo	*xampú*
shaving cream	*crema d'afaitar*
soap	*sabó*
stamp	*segell*
sunblock cream	*crema solar*
tampons	*tampons*
tissues	*mocadors de paper*
toilet paper	*paper higiènic*
toothpaste	*pasta de dents*

Time & Dates

One thing to remember when asking about times in Catalan: minutes past the hour (eg, quarter past, twenty-five past) are referred to as being before the next hour. Thus 'half past two' becomes *dos quarts de tres* (two quarters to three) and 'twenty past nine' becomes *un quart i cinc de deu* (one quarter and five minutes to ten). This is repeated in minutes to the hour, where 'ten to five' becomes *tres quarts i cinc de cinc* (three quarters and five minutes to five).

What time is it?	*Quina hora és?*
It's one o'clock.	*És la una.*
It's two o'clock.	*Són les dues.*
It's quarter past six.	*És un quart de set.*

Monday	*dilluns*
Tuesday	*dimarts*
Wednesday	*dimecres*
Thursday	*dijous*
Friday	*divendres*
Saturday	*dissabte*
Sunday	*diumenge*

January	*gener*
February	*febrer*
March	*març*
April	*abril*
May	*maig*
June	*juny*
July	*juliol*
August	*agost*
September	*setembre*
October	*octubre*
November	*novembre*
December	*desembre*

Numbers

0	*zero*
1	*un, una*
2	*dos, dues*
3	*tres*
4	*quatre*
5	*cinc*
6	*sis*
7	*set*
8	*vuit*
9	*nou*
10	*deu*
11	*onze*
12	*dotze*
13	*tretze*
14	*catorze*
15	*quinze*
16	*setze*
17	*disset*
18	*divuit*
19	*dinou*
20	*vint*
30	*trenta*
40	*quaranta*
50	*cinquanta*
60	*seixanta*
70	*setanta*
80	*vuitanta*
90	*noranta*
100	*cent*
1000	*mil*

Glossary

Items listed below are in Catalan/Castilian (Spanish) where they start with the same letter. Where the two terms start with different letters, they have their own entry – identified as Catalan (C) or Spanish (S). Identified in the same way are words given in only one or the other language, either because that term is predominantly used by all, or because the word is the same in both languages. In a few other cases, the Spanish alone is given as the only distinction from the Catalan is the addition of accents.

abierto – (S) open
aigua/agua – water
ajuntament/ayuntamiento – city or town hall
alberg de joventut/albergue juvenil – youth hostel; not to be confused with *hostal*
alcalde – (C & S) mayor
allioli – (C) sauce of garlic and olive oil, occasionally with egg yolk
altar major/mayor – high altar
amanides – (C) salads
anyell – (C) lamb
apartat de correus/apartado de correos – post office box
arribada – (C) arrival
arròs/arroz – rice
artesonado – (S) *Mudéjar* wooden ceiling with interlaced beams leaving a pattern of spaces for decoration
autonomía – (S) autonomous community or region: Spain's 50 *provincias* are grouped into 17 of these, one of which is Catalunya
autopista – (C & S) tollway
autovía – (S) toll-free dual carriageway

bakalao – (S) ear-splitting Spanish techno music (not to be confused with *bacalao*, salted cod)
Barcelonin – (C) inhabitant/native of Barcelona
barri/barrio – district, quarter of Barcelona
BCN – an abbreviation for Barcelona

biblioteca – (C & S) library
bikini – (C) toasted ham and cheese sandwich
bocadillo – (S) filled roll
bodega – (S) literally, a cellar (especially a wine cellar); also means a winery, or a traditional wine bar likely to serve wine from the barrel
botiga – (S) shop
bústia/buzón – postbox

caixer automàtic/cajero automático – automatic teller machine (ATM)
call – (C) Jewish quarter in medieval Barcelona (and other Catalan towns)
canvi/cambio – in general, change; also currency exchange
canya/caña – a small beer in a glass
cap de setmana – (C) weekend
capella major/capilla mayor – chapel containing the high altar of a church
capella/capilla – chapel
capgròs – (C) huge-headed figure seen in traditional Catalan festivals
carn/carne – meat
Carnestoltes/Carnaval – carnival; the period of fancy-dress parades and merry-making ending on the Tuesday 47 days before Easter Sunday
carrer/calle – street
carretera – (C & S) highway
carta – (C & S) menu
casa de pagès/casa rural – a village or country house or farmstead with rooms to let
castellers – (C) human castle builders
catedral – (C & S) cathedral
cava – Catalan version of champagne
celler – (C) see *bodega*
cena – (S) dinner
cercanías – (S) local trains serving Barcelona's airport, suburbs and some outlying towns
cerdo – (S) pork
cerrado – (S) closed
cerveseria/cervezería – beer bar
chiringuito – (S) covered beach bar

churros con chocolate – (S) deep-fried pastry with hot chocolate

claustre/claustro – cloister

comarca – (C & S) district, a grouping of municipalities

comedor – (S) dining room, sit-down restaurant

comida – (S) lunch, food

comissaria/comisaría – police station

compte/cuenta – bill (check)

comte/conde – count

consigna – (C & S) left-luggage office or lockers

copes/copas – drinks (literally, glasses); *anar de copes/ir de copas* is to go out for a few drinks

cor/coro – choir (part of a church, usually in the middle)

cordero – (S) lamb

correfoc – (C) fire-running, a part of many Catalan *festes* where people run about the streets chased by fire-breathing dragons and the like

Correus i Telègrafs/Correos y Telégrafos – post office

costa – (C & S) coast

desayuno – (S) breakfast

dinar – (C) lunch

duro – (C & S) hard; also a common name for a 5 ptas coin

ensalada – (S) salad

entera – (S) whole

entrada – (C & S) entrance

entremeses – (S) hors d'oeuvres

entrepans – (C) filled rolls

església – (C) church

esmorzar – (C) breakfast

estació d'autobusos/estación de autobuses – bus station

estancs/estancos – tobacconist shops that also sell stamps

ferrocarril – (C & S) railway

festa/fiesta – festival, public holiday or party

FGC – (C) Ferrocarrils de la Generalitat de Catalunya; local trains operating alongside the metro in Barcelona

fin de semana – (S) weekend

fira/feria – (trade) fair

flamenc/flamenco – means flamingo and Flemish as well as flamenco music and dance

futbolín – (S) table football

garum – (Latin) a spicy, vitamin-rich sauce made from fish entrails found throughout the former Roman Empire, including Barcelona

gegant – (C) a huge figure, usually representing kings, queens and other historical figures, often seen parading around at *festes*

gelats – (C) ice cream

gitano – (C & S) the Roma people, formerly called Gypsies

granissat/granizado – iced fruit crush

havaneres – (C) nostalgic songs and sea shanties

helados – (S) ice cream

horchata – (S) tiger-nut drink

hostal – (C & S) commercial establishment providing accommodation in the one-to three-star category; not to be confused with *alberg de joventut/albergue juvenil*

huevos – (S) eggs

iglesia – (S) church

infusión de hierbas – (S) herbal tea

IVA – *impost sobre el valor afegit/impuesto sobre el valor añadido*, or value-added tax (VAT)

llegada – (S) arrival

llet/leche – milk

llibreria or **llibreteria/librería** – bookshop

llista de correus/lista de correos – poste restante

llitera/litera – couchette or sleeping carriage

mariscs/mariscos – seafood

marisquería – (S) seafood eatery

marxa/marcha – action, life, 'the scene'

masia – (C) Catalan country farmhouse

media – (S) half

menjador – (C) dining room, sit-down restaurant

menú – (S) short form of menú del día

menú del día – (S) fixed-price meal available at lunchtime, sometimes in the evening too

mercat/mercado – market

mesón – (S) literally 'big table', a modest eatery

Modernisme – (C) modernism; the architectural and artistic style, influenced by Art Nouveau and sometimes known as Catalan modernism, whose leading practitioner was Antoni Gaudí

Modernista – (C & S) an exponent of Modernisme

moll/muelle – wharf or pier

Mudéjar – (S) a Muslim living under Christian rule in medieval Spain; also refers to their decorative style of architecture

museu/museo – museum

obert – (C) open

oca – (S) goose

oficina de turisme/turismo – tourist office

orxata – (C) tiger-nut drink

ous – (C) eggs

parrillada de pescado – (S) mixed seafood grill

peix/pescados – fish

penya/peña – a club, usually of flamenco or football fans

pica pica – (C) snacks/snacking

picada – (C) sauce of ground almonds, garlic, parsley, pine nuts and breadcrumbs

pinxos/pinchos – Basque for *tapes/tapas*

piscina – (C & S) swimming pool

plaça de braus/plaza de toros – bullring

plat combinat/plato combinado – literally 'combined plate', a large serving of meat/seafood/omelette with trimmings

platja/playa – beach

poble/pueblo – village

pollastre/pollo – chicken

pont/puente – bridge; also means the extra day or two off that many people take when a holiday falls close to a weekend

porc – (C) pork

porta/puerta – gate or door

porto/puerto – port

potable – (S) fit to drink

provincia – (C & S) province; Spain is divided into 50 of them

ración – (S) a larger portion of a *tapa* dish

REAJ – (S) Red Española de Albergues Juveniles, the Spanish HI youth hostel network

Realisme – artistic movement in mid-19th-century Catalunya in which artists sought to reflect in painting what they saw in real life

Reconquista – the Christian reconquest of the Iberian Peninsula from the Muslims (8th to 15th centuries)

refrescs/refrescos – soft drinks

refugi/refugio – shelter or refuge, especially a mountain refuge with basic accommodation for walkers

Renaixença – Renaissance period during the second half of the 19th century. There was a revival in all things Catalan and the Catalan language was readopted by the middle and upper classes

RENFE – (S) Red Nacional de los Ferrocarriles Españoles, the national rail network

retaula/retablo – retable, or altarpiece

riu/río – river

rodalies – (C) see *cercanías*

romesco – (C) sauce of almonds, tomato olive oil, garlic and vinegar

samfaina – (C) sauce of fried onion, tomato and garlic with red pepper and aubergine or courgette

sandwich mixto – (S) toasted ham and cheese sandwich

sardana – (C) traditional Catalan folk dance

serra/sierra – mountain range

Setmana Santa/Semana Santa – Holy Week, the week leading up to Easter Sunday

SIDA – (C & S) AIDS

sidrería – (S) cider bar

sofregit – (C) sauce of fried onion, tomato and garlic

sopa – soup

sopar – (C) dinner

sortida/salida – exit or departure

tancat – (C) closed

tapes/tapas – bar snacks traditionally served on a saucer or lid (*tapa*)

taquilla – (C & S) ticket window
targeta de crèdit/tarjeta de crédito –
credit card
tarjeta telefónica – (S) phonecard
tascas – (S) snack bars
tavernes/tabernas – taverns
ternera – (S) beef
terrassa/terraza – terrace; often means a
cafe or bar's outdoor tables
tienda – (S) shop
torrada – (C) open toasted sandwich
tostada – (S) buttered toast
turisme/turismo – means both tourism
and saloon car; *el turismo* can also mean the
tourist office

turrón – (S) nougat

urbanització/urbanización – suburban
housing development

v.o. – *versión original*, a foreign-language
film subtitled in Spanish
vall/valle – valley
vedella – (C) beef
venta de localidades – (S) ticket office
verdures/verduras – vegetables
vi/vino – wine

xurros amb xocolata – (C) deep-fried
pastry with hot chocolate

INDIAN SUBCONTINENT Bangladesh • Bengali phrasebook • Bhutan • Delhi • Goa • Healthy Travel Asia & India • Hindi & Urdu phrasebook • India • Indian Himalaya • Karakoram Highway • Kerala • Mumbai (Bombay) • Nepal • Nepali phrasebook • Pakistan • Rajasthan • Read This First: Asia & India • South India • Sri Lanka • Sri Lanka phrasebook • Tibet • Tibetan phrasebook • Trekking in the Indian Himalaya • Trekking in the Karakoram & Hindukush • Trekking in the Nepal Himalaya
Travel Literature: The Age of Kali: Indian Travels and Encounters • Hello Goodnight: A Life of Goa • In Rajasthan • A Season in Heaven: True Tales from the Road to Kathmandu • Shopping for Buddhas • A Short Walk in the Hindu Kush • Slowly Down the Ganges

ISLANDS OF THE INDIAN OCEAN Madagascar & Comoros • Maldives • Mauritius, Réunion & Seychelles

MIDDLE EAST & CENTRAL ASIA Bahrain, Kuwait & Qatar • Central Asia • Central Asia phrasebook • Dubai • Farsi (Persian) phrasebook • Hebrew phrasebook • Iran • Israel & the Palestinian Territories • Istanbul • Istanbul City Map • Istanbul to Cairo on a shoestring • Jerusalem • Jerusalem City Map • Jordan • Lebanon • Middle East • Oman & the United Arab Emirates • Syria • Turkey • Turkish phrasebook • World Food Turkey • Yemen
Travel Literature: Black on Black: Iran Revisited • The Gates of Damascus • Kingdom of the Film Stars: Journey into Jordan

NORTH AMERICA Alaska • Boston • Boston City Map • California & Nevada • California Condensed • Canada • Chicago • Chicago City Map • Deep South • Florida • Great Lakes • Hawaii • Hiking in Alaska • Hiking in the USA • Las Vegas • Los Angeles • Los Angeles City Map • Miami • Miami City Map • New England • New Orleans • New York City • New York City City Map • New York City Condensed • New York, New Jersey & Pennsylvania • Oahu • Out to Eat – San Francisco • Pacific Northwest • Rocky Mountains • San Francisco • San Francisco City Map • Seattle • Southwest • Texas • USA • USA phrasebook • Vancouver • Virginia & the Capital Region • Washington, DC • Washington, DC City Map • World Food Deep South, USA
Travel Literature: Caught Inside: A Surfer's Year on the California Coast • Drive Thru America

NORTH-EAST ASIA Beijing • Beijing City Map • Cantonese phrasebook • China • Hiking in Japan • Hong Kong • Hong Kong City Map • Hong Kong Condensed • Hong Kong, Macau & Guangzhou • Japan • Japanese phrasebook • Korea • Korean phrasebook • Kyoto • Mandarin phrasebook • Mongolia • Mongolian phrasebook • Seoul • Shanghai • South-West China • Taiwan • Tokyo
Travel Literature: In Xanadu: A Quest • Lost Japan

SOUTH AMERICA Argentina, Uruguay & Paraguay • Bolivia • Brazil • Brazilian phrasebook • Buenos Aires • Chile & Easter Island • Colombia • Ecuador & the Galapagos Islands • Healthy Travel Central & South America • Latin American Spanish phrasebook • Peru • Quechua phrasebook • Read This First: Central & South America • Rio de Janeiro • Rio de Janeiro City Map • South America on a shoestring • Trekking in the Patagonian Andes • Venezuela
Travel Literature: Full Circle: A South American Journey

SOUTH-EAST ASIA Bali & Lombok • Bangkok • Bangkok City Map • Burmese phrasebook • Cambodia • Hanoi • Healthy Travel Asia & India • Hill Tribes phrasebook • Ho Chi Minh City • Indonesia • Indonesian phrasebook • Indonesia's Eastern Islands • Java • Lao phrasebook • Laos • Malay phrasebook • Malaysia, Singapore & Brunei • Myanmar (Burma) • Philippines • Pilipino (Tagalog) phrasebook • Read This First: Asia & India • Singapore • Singapore City Map • South-East Asia on a shoestring • South-East Asia phrasebook • Thailand • Thailand's Islands & Beaches • Thailand, Vietnam, Laos & Cambodia Road Atlas • Thai phrasebook • Vietnam • Vietnamese phrasebook • World Food Thailand • World Food Vietnam

ALSO AVAILABLE: Antarctica • The Arctic • The Blue Man: Tales of Travel, Love and Coffee • Brief Encounters: Stories of Love, Sex & Travel • Chasing Rickshaws • The Last Grain Race • Lonely Planet Unpacked • Not the Only Planet: Science Fiction Travel Stories • On the Edge: Extreme Travel • Sacred India • Travel with Children • Travel Photography: A Guide to Taking Better Pictures

LONELY PLANET

Guides by Region

Lonely Planet is known worldwide for publishing practical, reliable and no-nonsense travel information in our guides and on our Web site. The Lonely Planet list covers just about every accessible part of the world. Currently there are 16 series: Travel guides, Shoestring guides, Condensed guides, Phrasebooks, Read This First, Healthy Travel, Walking guides, Cycling guides, Watching Wildlife guides, Pisces Diving & Snorkeling guides, City Maps, Road Atlases, Out to Eat, World Food, Journeys travel literature and Pictorials.

AFRICA Africa on a shoestring • Cairo • Cairo City Map • Cape Town • Cape Town City Map • East Africa • Egypt • Egyptian Arabic phrasebook • Ethiopia, Eritrea & Djibouti • Ethiopian (Amharic) phrasebook • The Gambia & Senegal • Healthy Travel Africa • Kenya • Malawi • Morocco • Moroccan Arabic phrasebook • Mozambique • Read This First: Africa • South Africa, Lesotho & Swaziland • Southern Africa • Southern Africa Road Atlas • Swahili phrasebook • Tanzania, Zanzibar & Pemba • Trekking in East Africa • Tunisia • Watching Wildlife East Africa • Watching Wildlife Southern Africa • West Africa • World Food Morocco • Zimbabwe, Botswana & Namibia
Travel Literature: Mali Blues: Traveling to an African Beat • The Rainbird: A Central African Journey • Songs to an African Sunset: A Zimbabwean Story

AUSTRALIA & THE PACIFIC Auckland • Australia • Australian phrasebook • Australia Road Atlas • Cycling Australia • Cycling New Zealand • Fiji • Fijian phrasebook • Healthy Travel Australia, NZ and the Pacific • Islands of Australia's Great Barrier Reef • Melbourne • Melbourne City Map • Micronesia • New Caledonia • New South Wales • New Zealand • Northern Territory • Outback Australia • Out to Eat – Melbourne • Out to Eat – Sydney • Papua New Guinea • Pidgin phrasebook • Queensland • Rarotonga & the Cook Islands • Samoa • Solomon Islands • South Australia • South Pacific • South Pacific phrasebook • Sydney • Sydney City Map • Sydney Condensed • Tahiti & French Polynesia • Tasmania • Tonga • Tramping in New Zealand • Vanuatu • Victoria • Walking in Australia • Watching Wildlife Australia • Western Australia
Travel Literature: Islands in the Clouds: Travels in the Highlands of New Guinea • Kiwi Tracks: A New Zealand Journey • Sean & David's Long Drive

CENTRAL AMERICA & THE CARIBBEAN Bahamas, Turks & Caicos • Baja California • Bermuda • Central America on a shoestring • Costa Rica • Costa Rica Spanish phrasebook • Cuba • Dominican Republic & Haiti • Eastern Caribbean • Guatemala • Guatemala, Belize & Yucatán: La Ruta Maya • Healthy Travel Central & South America • Jamaica • Mexico • Mexico City • Panama • Puerto Rico • Read This First: Central & South America • World Food Mexico • Yucatán
Travel Literature: Green Dreams: Travels in Central America

EUROPE Amsterdam • Amsterdam City Map • Amsterdam Condensed • Andalucía • Austria • Baltic States phrasebook • Barcelona • Barcelona City Map • Berlin • Berlin City Map • Britain • British phrasebook • Brussels, Bruges & Antwerp • Brussels City Map • Budapest • Budapest City Map • Canary Islands • Central Europe • Central Europe phrasebook • Corfu & the Ionians • Corsica • Crete • Crete Condensed • Croatia • Cycling Britain • Cycling France • Cyprus • Czech & Slovak Republics • Denmark • Dublin • Dublin City Map • Eastern Europe • Eastern Europe phrasebook • Edinburgh • Estonia, Latvia & Lithuania • Europe on a shoestring • Europe phrasebook • Finland • Florence • France • Frankfurt Condensed • French phrasebook • Georgia, Armenia & Azerbaijan • Germany • German phrasebook • Greece • Greek Islands • Greek phrasebook • Hungary • Iceland, Greenland & the Faroe Islands • Ireland • Italian phrasebook • Italy • Krakow • Lisbon • The Loire • London • London City Map • London Condensed • Madrid • Malta • Mediterranean Europe • Mediterranean Europe phrasebook • Moscow • Mozambique • Munich • Netherlands • Norway • Out to Eat – London • Out to Eat – Paris • Paris • Paris City Map • Paris Condensed • Poland • Portugal • Portuguese phrasebook • Prague • Prague City Map • Provence & the Côte d'Azur • Read This First: Europe • Romania & Moldova • Rome • Rome City Map • Russia, Ukraine & Belarus • Russian phrasebook • Scandinavian & Baltic Europe • Scandinavian phrasebook • Scotland • Sicily • Slovenia • South-West France • Spain • Spanish phrasebook • St Petersburg • St Petersburg City Map • Sweden • Switzerland • Tuscany • Ukrainian phrasebook • Venice • Vienna • Walking in Britain • Walking in France • Walking in Ireland • Walking in Italy • Walking in Spain • Walking in Switzerland • Western Europe • World Food France • World Food Ireland • World Food Italy • World Food Spain
Travel Literature: Love and War in the Apennines • The Olive Grove: Travels in Greece • On the Shores of the Mediterranean • Round Ireland in Low Gear • A Small Place in Italy • After Yugoslavia

LONELY PLANET

You already know that Lonely Planet publishes more than this one guidebook, but you might not be aware of the other products we have on this region. Here is a selection of titles that you may want to check out as well:

Andalucía
ISBN 1 86450 191 X
US$17.99 • UK£10.99

Barcelona city map
ISBN 1 86450 174 X
US$5.99 • UK£3.99

Canary Islands
ISBN 1 86450 310 6
US$15.99 • UK£9.99

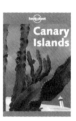

Europe on a shoestring
ISBN 1 86450 150 2
US$24.99 • UK£14.99

Madrid
ISBN 1 86450 123 5
US$14.99 • UK£8.99

Mediterranean Europe
ISBN 1 86450 154 5
US$27.99 • UK£15.99

Read This First: Europe
ISBN 1 86450 136 7
US$14.99 • UK£8.99

Spain
ISBN 1 86450 192 8
US$24.99 • UK£14.99

Spanish phrasebook
ISBN 0 86442 475 2
US$5.95 • UK£3.99

Walking in Spain
ISBN 0 86442 543 0
US$17.95 • UK£11.99

Western Europe
ISBN 1 86450 163 4
US$27.99 • UK£15.99

World Food Spain
ISBN 1 86450 025 5
US$12.95 • UK£7.99

Available wherever books are sold.

ON THE ROAD

Travel Guides explore cities, regions and countries, and supply information on transport, restaurants and accommodation, covering all budgets. They come with reliable, easy-to-use maps, practical advice, cultural and historical facts and a rundown on attractions both on and off the beaten track. There are over 200 titles in this classic series, covering nearly every country in the world.

 Lonely Planet Upgrades extend the shelf life of existing travel guides by detailing any changes that may affect travel in a region since a book has been published. Upgrades can be downloaded for free from **www.lonelyplanet.com/upgrades**

For travellers with more time than money, **Shoestring** guides offer dependable, first-hand information with hundreds of detailed maps, plus insider tips for stretching money as far as possible. Covering entire continents in most cases, the six-volume shoestring guides are known around the world as 'backpackers bibles'.

For the discerning short-term visitor, **Condensed** guides highlight the best a destination has to offer in a full-colour, pocket-sized format designed for quick access. They include everything from top sights and walking tours to opinionated reviews of where to eat, stay, shop and have fun.

CitySync lets travellers use their Palm™ or Visor™ hand-held computers to guide them through a city with handy tips on transport, history, cultural life, major sights, and shopping and entertainment options. It can also quickly search and sort hundreds of reviews of hotels, restaurants and attractions, and pinpoint their location on scrollable street maps. CitySync can be downloaded from **www.citysync.com**

MAPS & ATLASES

Lonely Planet's **City Maps** feature downtown and metropolitan maps, as well as transit routes and walking tours. The maps come complete with an index of streets, a listing of sights and a plastic coat for extra durability.

Road Atlases are an essential navigation tool for serious travellers. Cross-referenced with the guidebooks, they also feature distance and climate charts and a complete site index.

LONELY PLANET

ESSENTIALS

Read This First books help new travellers to hit the road with confidence. These invaluable predeparture guides give step-by-step advice on preparing for a trip, budgeting, arranging a visa, planning an itinerary and staying safe while still getting off the beaten track.

Healthy Travel pocket guides offer a regional rundown on disease hot spots and practical advice on predeparture health measures, staying well on the road and what to do in emergencies. The guides come with a user-friendly design and helpful diagrams and tables.

Lonely Planet's **Phrasebooks** cover the essential words and phrases travellers need when they're strangers in a strange land. They come in a pocket-sized format with colour tabs for quick reference, extensive vocabulary lists, easy-to-follow pronunciation keys and two-way dictionaries.

Miffed by blurry photos of the Taj Mahal? Tired of the classic 'top of the head cut off' shot? **Travel Photography: A Guide to Taking Better Pictures** will help you turn ordinary holiday snaps into striking images and give you the know-how to capture every scene, from frenetic festivals to peaceful beach sunrises.

Lonely Planet's **Travel Journal** is a lightweight but sturdy travel diary for jotting down all those on-the-road observations and significant travel moments. It comes with a handy time-zone wheel, world maps and useful travel information.

Lonely Planet's eKno is an all-in-one communication service developed especially for travellers. It offers low-cost international calls and free email and voicemail so that you can keep in touch while on the road. Check it out on **www.ekno.lonelyplanet.com**

FOOD & RESTAURANT GUIDES

Lonely Planet's **Out to Eat** guides recommend the brightest and best places to eat and drink in top international cities. These gourmet companions are arranged by neighbourhood, packed with dependable maps, garnished with scene-setting photos and served with quirky features.

For people who live to eat, drink and travel, **World Food** guides explore the culinary culture of each country. Entertaining and adventurous, each guide is packed with detail on staples and specialities, regional cuisine and local markets, as well as sumptuous recipes, comprehensive culinary dictionaries and lavish photos good enough to eat.

LONELY PLANET

OUTDOOR GUIDES

For those who believe the best way to see the world is on foot, Lonely Planet's **Walking Guides** detail everything from family strolls to difficult treks, with 'when to go and how to do it' advice supplemented by reliable maps and essential travel information.

Cycling Guides map a destination's best bike tours, long and short, in day-by-day detail. They contain all the information a cyclist needs, including advice on bike maintenance, places to eat and stay, innovative maps with detailed cues to the rides, and elevation charts.

The **Watching Wildlife** series is perfect for travellers who want authoritative information but don't want to tote a heavy field guide. Packed with advice on where, when and how to view a region's wildlife, each title features photos of over 300 species and contains engaging comments on the local flora and fauna.

With underwater colour photos throughout, **Pisces Books** explore the world's best diving and snorkelling areas. Each book contains listings of diving services and dive resorts, detailed information on depth, visibility and difficulty of dives, and a roundup of the marine life you're likely to see through your mask.

OFF THE ROAD

Journeys, the travel literature series written by renowned travel authors, capture the spirit of a place or illuminate a culture with a journalist's attention to detail and a novelist's flair for words. These are tales to soak up while you're actually on the road or dip into as an at-home armchair indulgence.

The new range of lavishly illustrated **Pictorial** books is just the ticket for both travellers and dreamers. Off-beat tales and vivid photographs bring the adventure of travel to your doorstep long before the journey begins and long after it is over.

Lonely Planet **Videos** encourage the same independent, tough-minded approach as the guidebooks. Currently airing throughout the world, this award-winning series features innovative footage and an original soundtrack.

Yes, we know, work is tough, so do a little bit of deskside dreaming with the spiral-bound Lonely Planet **Diary**, the tearaway page-a-day **Day-to-Day Calendar** or a Lonely Planet **Wall Calendar**, filled with great photos from around the world.

TRAVELLERS NETWORK

Lonely Planet Online. Lonely Planet's award-winning Web site has insider information on hundreds of destinations, from Amsterdam to Zimbabwe, complete with interactive maps and relevant links. The site also offers the latest travel news, recent reports from travellers on the road, guidebook upgrades, a travel links site, an online book-buying option and a lively traveller's bulletin board. It can be viewed at **www.lonelyplanet.com** or AOL keyword: lp.

Planet Talk is a quarterly print newsletter, full of gossip, advice, anecdotes and author articles. It provides an antidote to the being-at-home blues and lets you plan and dream for the next trip. Contact the nearest Lonely Planet office for your free copy.

Comet, the free Lonely Planet newsletter, comes via email once a month. It's loaded with travel news, advice, dispatches from authors, travel competitions and letters from readers. To subscribe, click on the Comet subscription link on the front page of the Web site.

Index

Text

Bold indicates maps.

Bold indicates maps.

Places to Stay

Places to Eat

Boxed Text

The sprawling village of Cadaqués, a highlight of the Costa Brava, still draws a crowd of celebrities.

Dalí's surrealist bedroom

Teatre-Museu Dalí, Figueres

Girona's colourful houses

Teatre-Museu Dalí – designed to surprise

The medieval Jewish quarter of Girona

BETHUNE CARMICHAEL

Fortified Monestir de Poblet.

VERONICA GARBUTT

Take a day-trip to Sitges – Spain's most unconventional resort.

ANDERS BLOMQVIST

The fine medieval cathedral, built between 1171 and 1331, dominates Tarragona's skyline.

BETHUNE CARMICHAEL

Monestir de Montserrat, perched high on the 'serrated mountain'

DAMIEN SIMONIS

Street art in historic Tarragona

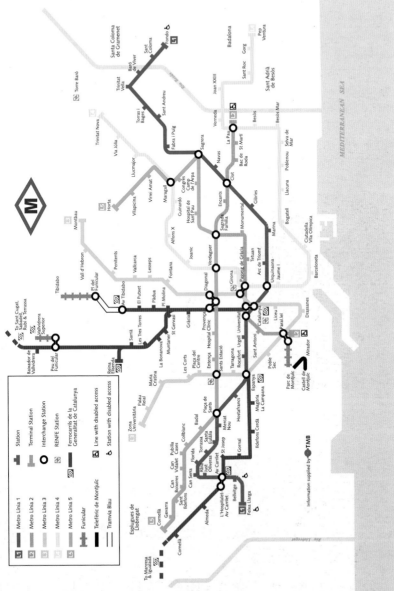

MAP 1

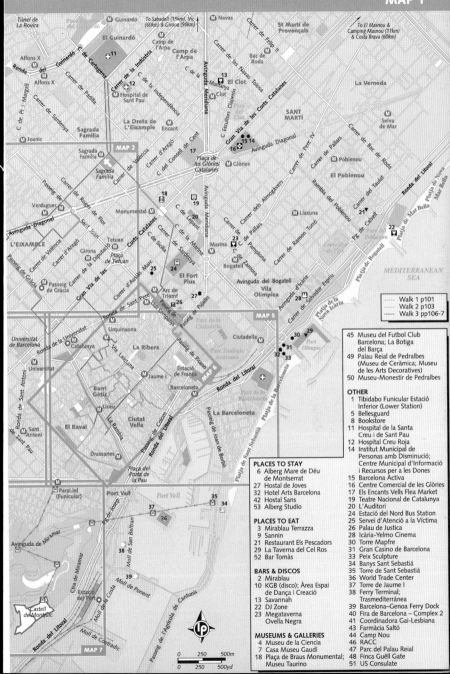

MAP 1

Túnel de La Rovira
Guinardó
To Sabadell (15km), Vic (60km) & Girona (90km)
Navas
St Martí de Provençals
To El Masnou & Camping Masnou (11km) & Costa Brava (60km)

El Guinardó
Camp de l'Arpa
Camp de l'Arpa
Bac de Roda
La Verneda

Alfons X
Alfons X
Ronda del Guinardó
C. de Cartagena
Carrer de la Indústria
C de la
El Clot
Clot
SANT MARTÍ
Selva de Mar

Joanic
Hospital de Sant Pau
La Dreta de L'Eixample
Encant
Gran Via de les Corts Catalanes

Sagrada Família
MAP 2
Plaça de les Glòries Catalanes
Glòries
El Poblenou
Poblenou

Sagrada Família
Carrer d'Aragó
Avinguda Diagonal
Rambla del Poblenou

Verdaguer
Carrer de Roger de Flor
Sant Joan
Carrer dels Almogàvers
Llacuna
Platja de Nova Mar Bella

L'EIXAMPLE
Monumental
Avinguda Meridiana
Carrer de Pallars
Carrer de Ramon Turró
Platja de Mar Bella

Tetuan
Girona
Plaça de Tetuan
Marina
Carrer de Pamplona
Pg. de Calvell

Passeig de Gràcia
Gran Via de les
El Fort Pius
Bogatell
Zamora
Avinguda del Bogatell
Vila Olímpica

Arc de Triomf
Avinguda d'Icària
Platja de la Nova Icària
MEDITERRANEAN SEA

Urquinaona
Parc de la Ciutadella
Ciutadella
MAP 5
Port Olímpic

Universitat de Barcelona
Catalunya
La Ribera
Parc Zoològic Acuarama

Universitat
Jaume I
Estació de França
Barceloneta
Ronda del Litoral

Barri Gòtic
Liceu
Ciutat Vella
La Barceloneta

Sant Antoni
El Raval
La Rambla

Drassanes
Plaça del Portal de la Pau

Paral.lel (Funicular)
Port Vell
Port Vell

Castell del Montjuïc
Estació del Port
Moll de Ponent
Moll de Contradic
Ronda del Litoral
MAP 7

Walk legend
— Walk 1 p101
— Walk 2 p103
— Walk 3 pp106-7

45 Museu del Futbol Club Barcelona; La Botiga del Barça
49 Palau Reial de Pedralbes (Museu de Ceràmica; Museu de les Arts Decoratives)
50 Museu-Monestir de Pedralbes

OTHER
1 Tibidabo Funicular Estació Inferior (Lower Station)
5 Bellesguard
8 Bookstore
11 Hospital de la Santa Creu i de Sant Pau
12 Hospital Creu Roja
14 Institut Municipal de Personas amb Disminució; Centre Municipal d'Informació i Recursos per a les Dones
15 Barcelona Activa
16 Centre Comercial de les Glòries
17 Els Encants Vells Flea Market
19 Teatre Nacional de Catalunya
20 L'Auditori
24 Estació del Nord Bus Station
25 Servei d'Atenció a la Víctima
26 Palau de Justícia
28 Icària-Yelmo Cinema
30 Torre Mapfre
31 Gran Casino de Barcelona
33 Peix Sculpture
34 Banys Sant Sebastià
35 Torre de Sant Sebastià
36 World Trade Center
37 Torre de Jaume I
38 Ferry Terminal; Trasmediterránea
39 Barcelona–Genoa Ferry Dock
40 Fira de Barcelona – Complex 2
41 Coordinadora Gai-Lesbiana
43 Farmàcia Saltó
44 Camp Nou
46 RACC
47 Parc del Palau Reial
48 Finca Güell Gate
51 US Consulate

PLACES TO STAY
6 Alberg Mare de Déu de Montserrat
27 Hostal de Joves
32 Hotel Arts Barcelona
42 Hostal Sans
53 Alberg Studio

PLACES TO EAT
3 Mirablau Terrazza
9 Sannin
21 Restaurant Els Pescadors
29 La Taverna del Cel Ros
52 Bar Tomàs

BARS & DISCOS
2 Mirablau
10 KGB (disco); Àrea Espai de Dança i Creació
13 Savannah
22 DJ Zone
23 Megataverna Ovella Negra

MUSEUMS & GALLERIES
4 Museu de la Ciencia
7 Casa Museu Gaudí
18 Plaça de Braus Monumental; Museu Taurino

0 250 500m
0 250 500yd
LP

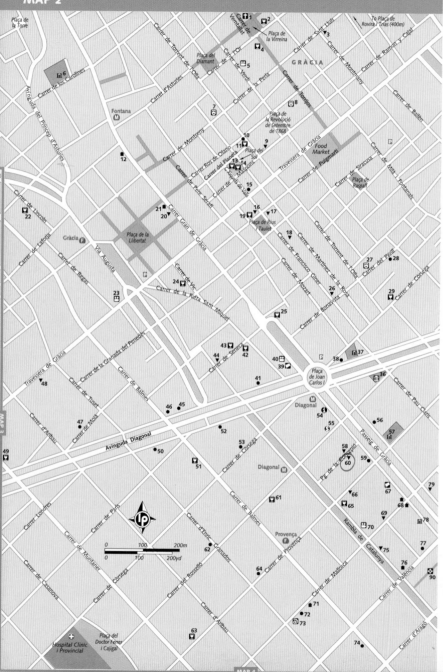

MAP 2

Plaça de la Torre

Carrer de Verntallat 1
2
3 To Plaça de Rovira i Trias (400m)
Plaça de la Virreina
Carrer de Torrent de l'Olla
Plaça del Diamant
Carrer de l'Or
4
Carrer de Sant Lluís
Carrer de Verdi 5
GRÀCIA
6
Avinguda del Príncep d'Astúries
Carrer de los Carolines
Carrer d'Astúries
Carrer de les Perles
Carrer de Montmany
Carrer de Ramón y Cajal
Carrer de Ballén
Carrer de Torrijos
Fontana
7
8
Plaça de la Revolució de Setembre de 1868
Food Market
Carrer de Puigmartí
Carrer de Siracusa
Plaça de Raspall
Carrer de Mulà i Fontanals

Carrer de Montseny
10
11 9
Plaça del Sol
Travessera de Gràcia
Carrer Ros de Olano
Carrer del Planeta
13 14
Carrer del Progrés
Carrer de Pere Serafí
12
15
Carrer de la Vall

21 20
Carrer Gran de Gràcia
16 17
19
Plaça de Rius i Taulet
18
Carrer de Francesc Giner
Carrer de Torrent de l'Olla
Carrer del Perill
22
Carrer de Lincoln
Plaça de la Llibertat
Carrer de Vic
Carrer de Martínez de la Rosa
27
28
Gràcia
Via Augusta
24
Carrer de la Riera Sant Miquel
Carrer de Mozart
26
29
Carrer de Còrsega
Carrer de Lafonja
Carrer de Regàs
23
25
Carrer de Bonavista

Travessera de Gràcia
Carrer de la Granada del Penedès
43 42
44
Carrer de Sèneca
40
39
38 37
36
Carrer de Pau Claris
48
Carrer de Tuset
Carrer de Balmes
41
Plaça de Joan Carlos I
Diagonal
54
55
56
57
Passeig de Gràcia
49
Carrer d'Arïbau
Carrer de Mora
47
46 45
52
50
51
Avinguda Diagonal
53
Carrer de Còrsega
Diagonal
58
60
59
Pg. de la Concepció
66
65
67
79
78
Carrer de París
Carrer d'Enric Granados
61
Provença
64
Carrer de Balmes
Carrer de Provença
69
70
68
77
75
76
90
Carrer de Londres
62
Carrer del Rosselló
Carrer de Mallorca
71
72 73
Carrer de València
Carrer de Muntaner
Carrer de Casanova
63
Plaça del Doctor Ferrer i Cajigal
Hospital Clínic i Provincial
74
Carrer d'Aragó

0 100 200m
0 100 200yd

MAP 2

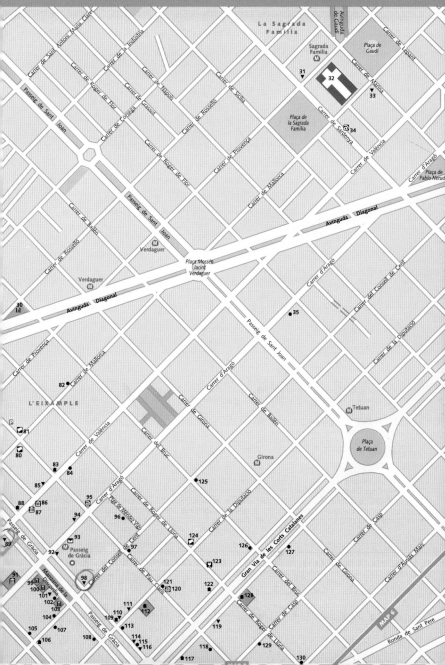

MAP 2

PLACES TO STAY
- 12 Hostal San Medín
- 21 Pensión Norma
- 68 Comtes de Barcelona Hotel; Vasari
- 71 Hotel Balmes
- 76 Hotel Regente
- 83 Hotel Claris
- 88 Hotel Majèstic
- 106 Hostal Neutral
- 109 Hostal Oliva; Adolfo Domínguez
- 112 St Moritz Hotel
- 117 Hotel Gran Via
- 122 Hostal Palacios
- 128 Hotel Ritz

PLACES TO EAT
- 3 Taverna El Glop
- 9 Cal Juanito
- 16 Mario Pizza
- 17 Bar Candanchu
- 18 La Singular
- 20 Botafumeiro
- 26 La Gula
- 31 La Baguetina Catalana
- 33 Celler del Trabucaire (La Casa del Jamón)
- 44 Restaurant Roig Robí
- 48 Pastafiore
- 58 El Japonés
- 60 Tragaluz
- 66 Pastafiore; Pans & Company
- 69 Lizarran
- 75 Bocatta
- 79 Centro Asturiano
- 85 FrescCo
- 89 Cafè Torino
- 92 Restaurant Madrid Barcelona
- 94 L'Hostal de Rita
- 98 Cerveseria Tapa Tapa
- 101 Pans & Company
- 110 Swan
- 111 Thai Gardens
- 114 Ba-Ba-Reeba
- 116 Quasi Queviures (Qu Qu)
- 119 El Café de Internet

BARS & DISCOS
- 2 Café la Virreina
- 4 Café Salambó
- 11 La Ñola
- 13 Café del Sol
- 14 Mirasol
- 19 Bar Chirito de Oro
- 22 Otto Zutz
- 24 Café de la Calle
- 25 Martin's
- 29 Mond Club (Sala Cibeles)
- 42 Member's
- 43 Bahía
- 49 Luz de Gas
- 51 Velvet
- 61 Nick Havanna
- 63 La Fira
- 65 La Bodegueta
- 123 Fuse

MUSEUMS & GALLERIES
- 36 Palau Quadras (Museu de la Música)
- 86 Fundación Francisco Godia
- 87 Museu Egipci
- 91 Fundació Antoni Tàpies

OTHER
- 1 Església de Sant Josep
- 5 Verdi Cinema
- 6 Casa Vicenç
- 7 Teatre Lliure
- 8 Teatreneu
- 10 Wash'N Dry Laundrette
- 15 Acció Llibres Bookshop
- 23 Arkadín Cinema
- 27 Artenbrut
- 28 Poliesportiu Perill (Squash Court)
- 30 Casa de les Punxes (Casa Terrades)
- 32 Sagrada Família; Museu Gaudí
- 34 Inet.center
- 35 Hertz
- 37 Casa Comalat
- 38 Majorica
- 39 German Consulate
- 40 Casablanca Cinema
- 41 Cambra Oficial de Comerç, Indústria i Navegació
- 45 Calvin Klein
- 46 Giorgio Armani
- 47 Institut Français de Barcelona
- 50 Gucci
- 52 Alitalia
- 53 Avis
- 54 Regional Tourist Office (Palau Robert)
- 55 American Express
- 56 Vinçon
- 57 La Pedrera (Casa Milà)
- 59 Librería Francesa
- 62 Galeria Victor Saavedra
- 64 Come In Bookshop
- 67 Canadian Consulate; Happy Books
- 70 Alexis Cinema
- 72 Planet Music
- 73 Cyber Play
- 74 Altaïr Bookshop
- 77 Camper
- 78 Casa Enric Batlló
- 80 Italian Consulate
- 81 Swedish Consulate
- 82 Bd Ediciones de Diseño
- 84 La Casa Elizalde
- 90 Bulevard Rosa; Lufthansa; Centre Català d'Artesania
- 93 Post Office
- 95 Conéctate
- 96 Istituto Italiano di Cultura
- 97 La Tenda
- 99 Casa Batlló
- 100 Casa Amatller; Joyería Bagués
- 102 Regia; Museu del Parfum
- 103 Casa Lleo Morera; Cartier; Loewe
- 104 Antonio Miró
- 105 Xocolateria Valor
- 107 Natura Selection
- 108 Max Mara
- 113 Iberia
- 115 24-hour Pharmacy
- 118 Laie Bookshop
- 120 Café Interlight
- 121 Halcón Viatges
- 124 Belgian Consulate
- 125 TWA
- 126 Pullmantur
- 127 Europcar
- 129 Ca la Dona
- 130 7-eleven

Tragaluz good restaurant
Cafe Torino good coffee & cake.
Cerverseria TapaTapa - good Tapas.
nice setting
corner of street.

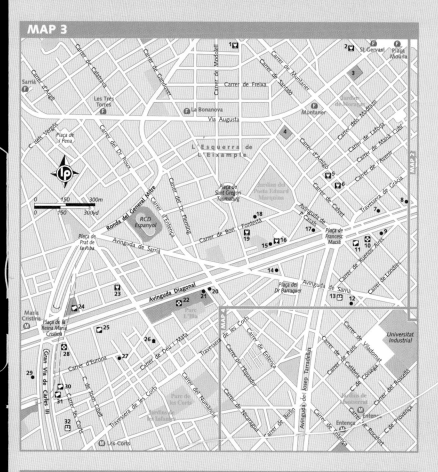

MAP 3

PLACES TO STAY
26 Alberg Pere Tarrès

BARS & DISCOS
1   Cova del Drac
2   La Rosa
5   Universal
6   Mas i Mas
16 The Music Box
19 Fiesta Bori
23 Up & Down

OTHER
3   Institute for North American Studies
4   British Council
7   Zara
8   Loewe
9   Jean Pierre Bua
10 El Corte Inglés
11 UK Consulate; La Boîte
12 Vanguard Rentacar
13 Filmoteca
14 UPS Couriers
15 Giorgio Armani

17 Gianni Versace
18 Ortiga
20 Marks & Spencer
21 FNAC
22 L'Illa del Diagonal
24 Japanese Consulate
25 Netherlands Consulate
27 Ronicar Rentacar
28 El Corte Inglés
29 Bowling Barcelona
30 Australian Consulate
31 Swiss & Irish Consulates
32 Renoir-Les Corts Cinema

MAP 4

PLACES TO STAY
14 Pensión Aribau
29 Hotel Lleó
33 Hotel Mesón
   de Castilla
47 Hostal Sofia

PLACES TO EAT
1 Yamadori
4 Gargantúa i Pantagruel
12 La Flauta
15 Restaurant de l'Escola
   de Restauració
   I Hostalatge
21 La Valenciana
22 Bar Estudiantil
25 Pans & Company
39 Horchateria Sirvent

BARS & DISCOS
5 Zoo Club
6 Arena
7 Arena Clasic
9 Arena VIP
13 Satanassa
16 Este Bar
17 Dietrich
18 Punto BCN
30 Shamrock
35 Metro
37 Paloma

OTHER
2 Xampany
3 24-hour Pharmacy
8 Danish Consulate
10 Alibri Bookshop
11 University Information Office
19 Méliès Cinemes
20 National/Atesa Rentacar
23 Viatgi
24 Julià Tours & Rentacar
26 Llibreria Bosch
27 Casanova
28 Happy Books
31 Castelló
32 CD-Drome
34 Centre de Cultura
   Contemporània de
   Barcelona (CCCB)
36 ECOM
38 La Maison Coloniale
40 Goethe Institut
41 Aerobus Stop from Airport
42 Aerobus Stop to Airport
43 The English Bookshop
44 Punt d'Informació Juvenil
45 Turisme Juvenil de Catalunya;
   Xarxa d'Albergs de Catalunya;
   usit Unlimited
46 Dona i Ocell Sculpture
48 Aerobus Stop
49 Estació d'Autobusos de Sants

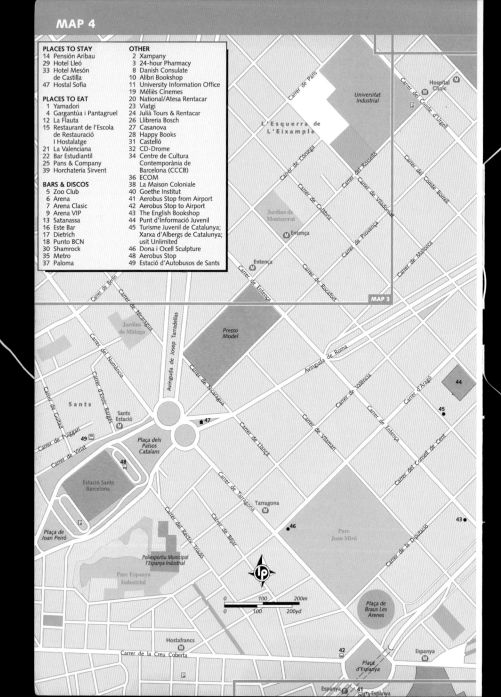

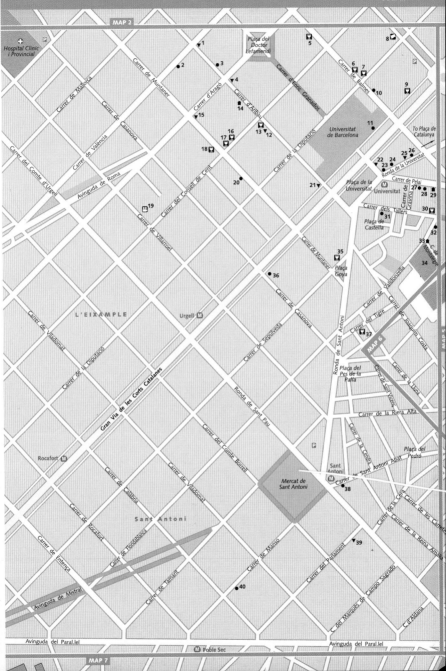

MAP 4

MAP 5

EL CORTE INGLES - DEPT STORE

MAP 2

21

2
3
20
Carrer de Casp
1
Jardins de
la Reina
Victoria
Plaça
d'Urquinaona
M Urquinaona
Carrer de Trafalgar
Passeig de Gràcia
4
5
Ronda de Sant Pere
Carrer d'Ortigosa
Carrer d'En Monec

C. del Rec Comtal
C. del Portal Nou
Carrer de Sant Pere més alt
Plaça de Sant
Agustí Vell
19
18
M
16 17
Carrer de les Mòlas
Urquinaona M
Carrer de Sant Pere més baix
Carrer de Sant Pere Mitjà
Catalunya
Plaça de
Catalunya
Carrer d'en Giralt el Pellisser
Carrer d'Ortigosa
Via Laietana
Avinguda de F. Cambó
6
7
9
8
10
11
Ronda de la Universitat
Carrer d'en Ausiàs
Avinguda del Portal de l'Àngel
Carrer Comtal
Plaça
Antoni
Maura
La Ribera
Carrer de la Princesa
Carrer
13
12
15
Carrer de Bergara
El Triangle
14
Carrer de Pelai
Carrer de
Rosselló
Carrer dels Tallers
Plaça de
Ramon Amadeu
Avinguda de la Catedral
Plaça de
R Berenguer
el Gran
Plaça de
la Seu
C. dels Comtes de Barcelona
Jaume I M
Plaça de
l'Àngel
Carrer de l'Argenteria
Jaume I
Plaça de
Vicenç
Martorell
Rambla de
Canaletes
LA RAMBLA
Carrer de Santa Anna
Carrer de la Canuda
Plaça de la
Vila de
Madrid
Carrer d'En Bot
Carrer de Sant Sever
Carrer del Bisbe Irurita
C. de Sant Sever
Carrer de Jaume I
Via Laietana
Rambla dels Estudis
Ranelleres
Plaça dels
Àngels
Carrer d'Elisabets
Carrer del Pintor Fortuny
Carrer del Carme
Barri
Gòtic
Plaça
del Pi
Plaça de
St Josep Oriol
C. de Sant Honorat
Plaça de
Sant Jaume
Carrer de Ferran
Carrer d'Avinyó
Ciutat
Vella
Jardins
Doctor
Fleming
Carrer de Jerusalem
Plaça de
Gardunya
Carrer del Carme
Carrer de l'Hospital
Rambla de Sant Josep
Plaça de la Boqueria
M
Liceu
Carrer de la Llicona
Plaça de
Sant Miquel
Carrer d'Atzaïr
El Raval
Carrer d'En Robador
Sant Rafael
Rambla del Raval
Carrer de Sant Pau
Plaça de
Sant Agustí
Rambla dels Caputxins
LA RAMBLA
Plaça
Reial
Plaça de
George Orwell
Carrer dels Escudellers
Carrer d'En Cirabassa
Carrer d'En Serra
Carrer del Còdols
Carrer Nou de Sant Francesc
Carrer Ample
Carrer de la Mercè
Passeig d'Isabel
C. de l'Aurora
Carrer de la Riereta
Carrer del Marquès de Barberà
Plaça de
Salvador Seguí
Plaça del
Teatre
Plaça de la Pau
Plaça del
Duc de
Medinaceli
Passeig de Colom
Carrer de les Carretes
Carrer de la Reina Amàlia
Carrer Nou de la Rambla
Carrer de l'Est
Carrer de Sant Pau
Carrer del Parc
La Guàrdia
Rambla de Santa Mònica
Carrer de Josep Anselm Clavé
Ronda del Litoral
Moll de la Fusta
43
Carrer de les Flors
44
42
41
Carrer de Sant Pau
Salitre
Carrer de l'Abat
Carrer de les Tàpies
Carrer de l'Om
Port Vell
Carrer de Sta Madrona
Avinguda de les Drassanes
M
Drassanes
40
Plaça del
Portal
de la Pau
39
Port de
Barcelona
Rambla de Mar
Museum
Marítim
Carrer del Portal Santa
Passeig de Josep
Carrat
38
Moll de les Drassanes
Avinguda del Paral·lel
45
46
Paral·lel
(Funicular)
MAP 7
MAP 4

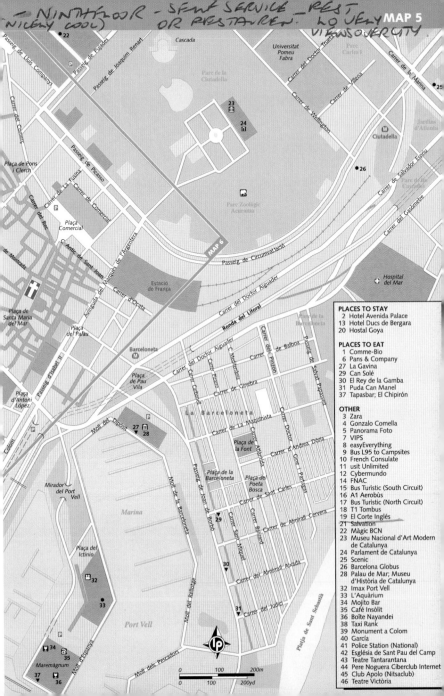

MAP 6 ✱ PLAÇA REIAL NICE SQUARE

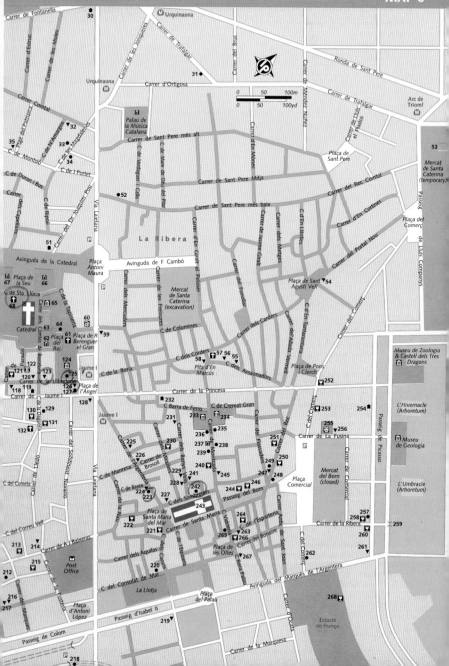

MAP 6

Carrer de Fontanella
30
Carrer d'Estruc
Carrer de les Moles
Urquinaona
Carrer de les Jonqueres
Carrer de Trafalgar
Carrer del Bruc
Ronda de Sant Pere
Urquinaona
Carrer d'Ortigosa
31
Carrer de Méndez Núñez
Carrer de Trafalgar
Arc de Triomf
Carrer Comtal
Carrer d'En Amargós
32
Carrer de les Magdalenes
33
34
Palau de la Música Catalana
Carrer de Sant Pere més alt
Carrer de Verdaguer i Callis
Carrer de Mare de Déu del Pilar
Plaça de Sant Pere
Carrer de Lluis el Piados
53
Mercat de Santa Caterina (temporary)
35
C de Montsió
C de les Magdalenes
C de J Portet
C de Duran i Bas
Carrer
dels Capellans
C de Ripoll
C del Dr Joaquim Pou
52
Carrer de Sant Pere Mitja
Carrer de Sant Pere més baix
Carrer del Rec Comtal
Carrer d'En Cortines
Carrer d'En Monec
Carrer de Jaume Giralt
Carrer dels Mitges
C d'En Llastics
Plaça del Comerç
51
Via Laietana
La Ribera
Carrer d'En Giralt el Pellisser
Carrer d'En Cortines
Carrer del Portal Nou
Passeig de Lluis Companys
Avinguda de la Catedral
Plaça Antoni Maura
Avinguda de F Cambó
67 Plaça de la Seu 66
Plaça de Sant Agusti Vell 54
Carrer dels Mercaders
C de Sta Llúcia
68
Mercat de Santa Caterina (excavation)
65
64
60
Catedral 63
61 Plaça de R Berenguer el Gran
Plaça del Rei
59
Carrer del Fonollar
C del Fonollar
Carrer dels Carders
Carrer del Comerç
Museu de Zoologia & Castell dels Tres Dragons
C de Colomines
C dels Corders
Plaça de Pons i Clerch
L'Hivernacle (Arboretum)
122 121
120
118 119
Carrer de la Llibreteria
123 124
125
126 127
Plaça de l'Àngel
C de la Boria
58
57 56 55
Plta d'En Marcús
C dels Assaonadors
252
Museu de Geologia
130 129
132 131
128
Jaume I
Carrer de la Princesa
Carrer del Comerç
253
254
L'Umbracle (Arboretum)
232
C Barra de Ferro
C de Cremat Gran
231
233
234
251
255
256
Carrer de La Fusina
225
226
230
236
237 238
239
249 250
247 248
Plaça Comercial
Mercat del Born (closed)
C de Manresa
Carrer de Basea
228
229
240 241
245
246
244
257
258
C del Correu Vell
Carrer de Brosoli
227
242
243
Plaça de Santa Maria del Mar
222
223 224
C dels Sombrerers
Passeig del Born
260
261
259
213
214
Carrer de A J Baixeras
215
Post Office
220
221
Carrer de Santa Maria
264
265 266
263
262
Carrer de la Ribera
212
C del Cometa
C del Consolat de Mar
La Llotja
Plaça de les Olles
267
268
216
217
Plaça d'Antoni López
219
Plaça del Palau
Estació de França
218
Passeig d'Isabel II
Passeig de Colom
Carrer de la Marquesa

0 50 100m
0 50 100yd

Taxidermisva - nice - Tapas. r eating.

MAP 6

PLACES TO STAY

13 Pensión Noya
21 Hotel Nouvel
23 Hotel Continental
30 Hostal Fontanella
36 Hostal Lausanne; Zara
39 Hostal Campi
41 Le Meridien
47 Hostal Galerias Maldà;
   Maldà Cinema
49 Hostal-Residencia Rembrandt
51 Hotel Colón
74 Hotel Call
75 Pensión Fernando
77 Albergue Arco
82 Hotel Jardi
88 Hostal Paris
94 Hotel San Agustín
96 Hotel Principal
98 Hotel Joventut
99 Hostal La Terrassa
101 Hotel Peninsular
102 Hotel España; Fonda Espanya
103 Hostal Residencia Opera
104 Hostal Mare Nostrum
109 Pensión Europa
110 Pensión Bienestar
119 Hotel Rey Don Jaime I
127 Hotel Suizo
134 Hostal Levante
145 Pensión Villanueva
146 Pensió Colom 3;
   Disco-Bar Real
148 Hotel Oriente
165 Hotel Cuatro Naciones
167 Youth Hostel Kabul
171 Hotel Roma Reial
179 Casa Huéspedes Mari-Luz
180 Alberg Juvenil Palau
184 Pensión Alamar
190 Hotel Barcelona House
191 Hotel Comercio
197 Hostal Marítima; García
199 Hostal Nilo
203 Hostal El Cantón
232 Pensión Lourdes
254 Hotel Triunfo

PLACES TO EAT

8 Buenas Migas
11 Bar Kasparo
12 Café Zurich
14 Pastafiore
19 Pans & Company
20 Bocatta
22 Self-Naturista
27 Hard Rock Cafe
32 Bocatta
35 Els Quatre Gats
37 The Bagel Shop
40 Champion Supermarket

42 Ra
45 Granja La Pallaresa
48 Croissanterie del Pi
50 Pans & Company
54 Restaurant L'Econòmic
55 Pla de la Garsa
56 Restaurante Bunga Raya
58 Lluna Plena
59 Comme-Bio (La Botiga)
73 Salterio
78 Mesón Jesús
81 Xocolateria La Xicra
85 Irati
89 Juicy Jones
92 El Convent
95 Rita Blue
100 Restaurant Els Tres Bots
106 Café de l'Òpera   *coffee drunk*
107 Les Quatre Barres
108 Sushi-Ya
111 Can Culleretes
113 Pans & Company
118 Bocatta
120 Santa Clara
123 Bon Mercat   *coffee*
126 La Colmena
128 Il Caffè di Roma
135 La Cereria
137 El Gran Café
141 El Taxidermista   *Rest*
142 Les Quinze Nits   *Rest*
149 Restaurante Pollo Rico
150 Kashmir Restaurant Tandoori
153 Salsitas
175 Restaurante Senshe Tawakal
177 La Verónica
181 Slokai
185 Venus Delicatessen
186 Felafel & Kebab Takeaway
187 Wagamama
189 Buen Bocado
192 La Fonda Escudellers
193 Los Caracoles
198 Ristorante Il Mercante di
   Venezia
200 El Paraguayo
201 Margarita Blue
204 Joy
206 Le Tre Venezie
209 Bar Celta
210 Restaurant Pitarra
214 El Salón
216 Sidrería La Socarrena
217 Tasca El Corral
219 Restaurant Set Portes
224 Sagardi
225 Senyor Parellada
226 La Carassa
227 Restaurante Mar de la Ribera
228 L'Ou Com Balla
229 La Flauta Mágica

231 Habana Vieja
241 El Pebre Blau
245 Centre Cultural Euskal Etxea
247 Little Italy
256 Café Kafka
261 Dionisos
263 Gades
267 Cal Pep

BARS & DISCOS

1 Benidorm
2 Granja de Gavà
3 Casa Almirall
5 Café Que Pone Muebles
   Navarro
9 L'Ovella Negra
18 Boadas
71 B.O.2
76 Schilling
83 Bar del Pi
97 Bar Aurora
121 Paradise
130 Bar Pilarica
131 Cafè de l'Acadèmia
139 Bar Malpaso
140 Sidecar
143 Glaciar
144 Barcelona Pipa Club
151 Bar Marsella
152 The Quiet Man
154 London Bar
156 Bar La Concha
160 Bar Pastís
161 Kentucky
162 Moog
168 Jamboree
169 Sala Tarantos
170 Karma
172 Al Limón Negro
173 Bar Reixas
174 Thiossan
176 Shanghai
183 Harlem Jazz Club
188 Zoo
194 Dot
202 Antinous
208 Bar Center Point
211 Bar (Nameless)
213 Parnasse
215 Bar Los de Extremadura
221 La Vinya del Senyor
222 Abaixadors 10
230 El Nus
240 El Xampanyet
244 Miramelindo
246 El Copetín
250 Borneo
251 Gimlet
252 El Foro
253 Luz de Luna
258 Magic